Broken Promises?

Broken Promises?

The Argentine Crisis and Argentine Democracy

Edited by
Edward Epstein and David Pion-Berlin

LEXINGTON BOOKS

A Division of
ROWMAN & LITTLEFIELD PUBLISHERS, INC.
Lanham • Boulder • New York • Toronto • Oxford

LEXINGTON BOOKS

A division of Rowman & Littlefield Publishers, Inc.
A wholly owned subsidiary of The Rowman & Littlefield Publishing Group, Inc.
4501 Forbes Boulevard, Suite 200
Lanham, MD 20706

PO Box 317
Oxford
OX2 9RU, UK

Copyright © 2006 by Lexington Books

British Library Cataloguing in Publication Information Available

Library of Congress Cataloging-in-Publication Data

Broken promises? : the Argentine crisis and Argentine democracy / edited by Edward
Epstein and David Pion-Berlin.
    p. cm.
Includes bibliographical references and index.
ISBN-13: 978-0-7391-0928-1 (cloth : alk. paper)
ISBN-10: 0-7391-0928-6 (cloth : alk. paper)
 1. Financial crises—Argentina. 2. Argentina—Economic conditions—1983- 3.
Argentina—Economic policy. 4. Argentina—Politics and government—1983-2002. I.
Epstein, Edward. II. Pion-Berlin, David.

HC175.B745 2006
330.982—dc22
                                                                2005036683

Printed in the United States of America

⊖™ The paper used in this publication meets the minimum requirements of American
National Standard for Information Sciences—Permanence of Paper for Printed Library
Materials, ANSI/NISO Z39.48–1992.

To all those who have suffered during the recent Argentine crisis.

Contents

Part I

Introduction

1

The Crisis of 2001 and Argentine Democracy

Edward Epstein and David Pion-Berlin

The crisis that exploded at the end of 2001 is examined here primarily in terms of its effects on the current Argentine democracy. The question of "broken promises" pointed to in this volume's title is meant to focus attention on the notable decline in public confidence in fundamental democratic institutions. Such a fall in trust levels became increasingly apparent to observers by the time of the October legislative elections that year with the sharp increase in the number of blank and spoiled ballots cast by those who voted. Following the collapse of the De la Rúa government that December, many citizens came to repudiate the entire body of politicians, loudly repeating in frequent street demonstrations what became the virtual mantra of the angry crowds that began to fill the new political vacuum: "Let's get rid of them all, without a single exception" ("Que se vayan todos, que no quede ni uno solo" in Spanish).

This crisis is scarcely the first that Argentines have experienced in terms of the maladroit functioning of democracy in their country. President Fernando de la Rúa was forced to step down only halfway through his term on December 20, 2001, amid street violence. A return to something close to institutional normality would occur only after a further two years of rather embarrassing political improvisation. Similar chaotic conditions had led President Raúl Alfonsín to resign six months early, in mid-1989. Looked at dispassionately, their cases represent the abject failure of two of the four chief executives chosen by the populace via

3

elections in the democracy of the last twenty-plus years,[1] certainly a rather inauspicious record. But the current democratic regime established in 1983 was not unique with its difficulties; it had been preceded by earlier democracies, all with their own particular crises. Successful military coups in 1976, 1966, 1955, and 1930 had each resulted in dictatorships replacing democracies, where each of such earlier democratic attempts had exhibited signs of significantly eroded political legitimacy by the time of its overthrow. Such crises go back all the way in Argentine politics to that country's first established democracy.

Given the overuse of certain terms in common speech, this analysis of democratic crisis in Argentina would be more clear if that concept were provided with some reasonable definition. The notion of "crisis" to be used here refers to the effects of sharply worsening perceptions held by the citizenry as a whole (or by some strategic subgroups) of then prevailing political conditions under the existing democracy. Such a negative appraisal may refer to a particular administration or—what would be far more serious—might pertain to the functioning of key political institutions under any likely government administration. While a crisis may be resolved within the boundaries of existing political practices, the more serious a crisis, the more likely it will produce a marked departure from normalcy, even including the substitution of questionable democratic institutions. In our view, such a sense of political crisis would continue for at least as long as the events described still looked to be in flux; that is, where they did not appear to conform to any widely known pattern of political behavior. The crisis would be over only when a new pattern emerged that became widely known and accepted. In the extreme case, the resolution of the crisis might lead to a new non-democratic type of politics.

In any account of the problems of Argentine democracy, the responses of the citizenry to how its politicians and political institutions perform are judged to be of special importance. Without their broad support, any democratic regime is likely to be especially vulnerable to challenges from critical interest groups like the military or big business whose commitment to popular government has not always been very strong. In recent years, what some have labeled a "crisis of representation" has affected how citizens saw particular presidents (and most political leaders) and what was seen by many as their woefully inadequate efforts to address important issues. On matters like economic recession and unemployment, mass poverty and the exclusion of many from a decent life, and the management of public funds and dubious government contracts, politicians were often judged seriously indifferent to popular concerns. The increasingly negative appraisal of politicians spilled over to those institutions where they dominated like the established political parties, the Congress, and the executive branch. Even members of ostensibly less political bodies like the courts and the police were seen as equally corrupt and self-serving.

What follows in this introductory chapter falls into two parts: (1) a discussion of the causes and most immediate consequences of the recent Argentine crisis, followed by (2) an appraisal of the efforts first of President Eduardo Duhalde and more recently of President Néstor Kirchner to rebuild support for Argentina's democratic institutions that was severely undermined by the crisis. We will take each of these topics in turn.

Characteristics of the Recent Crisis

The spontaneous popular protest that began on the evening of December 19, 2001, leading to President De la Rúa's resignation the next day was a product of accumulated feelings of frustration and anger that had been building up for some time among parts of the citizenry. His imposition of a State of Siege that first night during his televised address to the nation was the final straw for many who had come to perceive the members of the government as insensitive, uncaring, and self-serving.[2] The heavy-handed official repression that subsequently produced the death of at least twenty-five protestors contributed a further sense of moral outrage to this highly negative evaluation of the government. What had produced such feelings? What had set in motion this train of events that not only undermined the De la Rúa administration, but seriously eroded the legitimacy of the existing democratic regime in which the former had operated? We will address the causes and most immediate consequences of the recent crisis in a roughly chronological order.

De la Rúa of the Radical Party and Carlos "Chacho" Alvarez of FREPASO (Frente País Solidario, or Front for a Country in Solidarity) had made up the successful Alliance ticket for president and vice president in the 1999 national elections. Their victory against their Peronist Party rivals principally reflected dissatisfaction with the outgoing Menem administration over economic issues like the lack of jobs and low salaries, with crime and corruption, as well as with government policies toward education, retirees, and health care.[3] Despite widespread criticism during the campaign of the neo-liberal economic model that Menem had introduced after returning the Peronists to power a decade earlier (even, to some extent, by their defeated candidate for the presidency, Eduardo Duhalde), the Alliance government made no serious effort to adjust official policies to take into account popular discontent. Moreover, the initial economic recession that had begun in late 1998 before the elections would worsen under the new government.

The democracy in which that election took place had been dominated by the two traditional Argentine national parties, the Peronists and the Radicals, where the latter were now joined within the Alliance by FREPASO, a new political force made up of those Peronists who had refused to accept their party's ideological shift to the right under Menem, in coalition with various small reformist parties on the left.[4] The existence of two large parties or voting blocs in a presidential election allowed voters the choice of either confirming the incumbent party in power (as in 1995) or of rejecting it, turning to the opposition (as in 1989 and, of course, 1999).[5]

While such possible alternation might seem quite normal for liberal democracies elsewhere, it was something new for Argentina. In the democracies that had existed in the country through 1976, one party had always been dominant in all fair national elections—first the Radicals in the 1916–1930 period and then the Peronists, between 1946 and 1955 and again during the 1973–1976 interval. The party with what seemed an inevitable majority of the vote in free elections was allowed to run things. Vigorous opposition to the dominant "national movement" of the time was typically considered a sign of disloyalty to the nation and to the party leadership that claimed the right to decide national policy. Conventional liberal democracy with possible party alternation in power emerged in Argentina only with the 1983 democratic regime.[6]

The shift from such a majoritarian to a more liberal democracy represented a significant change in citizen attitudes. Now citizens could believe that a future election offered the possibility for change, not only of the ruling party, but even of policies judged as failing to meet popular needs. Given such altered expectations about change achieved through the ballot box and the increasingly serious nature of economic conditions, the electorate's decision to replace the Peronists with the Alliance in 1999 should have produced some corresponding shifts in key government policy. What produced the crisis of representation referred to earlier was the inability of any of the dominant parties to successfully address what were seen as the major issues,[7] given a context where the principal Argentine political leaders saw no real possibility of altering economic policy in any way challenging the dictates of prevailing international orthodoxy. Despite promises made during the 1999 campaign, the new government elected proved no more responsive to citizen wishes than its Peronist opponents had been after retaining power in 1995.

Even in the years of significant economic expansion during the first half of the 1990s, the Argentine economy had depended on major new foreign borrowing to sustain itself. The public foreign debt, which had been 60 billion dollars in 1989 near the beginning of Menem's first government, amounted to some 99 billion dollars around the time of his re-election in 1995, and eventually totaled about 145 billion dollars by 1999, when the Alliance came to power. If Argentina's ability to service this debt (calculated in terms of the interest owed as a percent of export earnings) had improved from a critically high 43% in 1989 to a more manageable 28% in 1995, by 1999 the burden returned to close to earlier high levels at 41%.[8] By the last year, the country, in effect, was doing little more than simply recycling its large debt, borrowing new funds so as to maintain currency on its old obligations. What was seen as critical in order to maintain the entry of new funds were attractively high interest rates and continued approval by the International Monetary Fund (IMF) of the country's overall economic policy position.

The weak link in such neo-liberal policies was the 1991 Convertibility Plan that set the exchange value of the Argentine peso at one to one with the U.S.

dollar as a means of bringing the country's previous critical inflation problem under control.[9] By most accounts, the peso became seriously overvalued by the late 1990s, a situation that undermined the country's ability to export and, in so doing, diminished the hard currency export earnings needed to service the foreign debt. While a consensus eventually formed that some way out of the rigid terms of convertibility needed to be found so that the peso could be devalued to a more realistic level, government officials were afraid that any sudden abandonment of convertibility might cripple all those who had borrowed in dollars as well as lead to a return to high inflation. The continuation of the policies promoting Argentina as an open economy attractive to foreign lenders meant that the government promoting these had only limited control over important aspects of the national economy. Although faced with popular dissatisfaction with the results of economic policies that pleased the international banks whose cooperation was deemed essential, the Alliance government lacked the political will to risk any challenge to the status quo.

Table 1.1 provides percentage figures on annual GDP growth, on open urban unemployment, and on poverty in the Greater Buenos Aires area plus a national reading, if only for the very end of the 1991–2002 series when such statistics for other urban areas first became available. As is apparent, the table contrasts the 1991–1998 period of relative prosperity (but including the negative effects of the Mexican devaluation in 1995) with the 1999–2002 years of continuing economic recession in Argentina. What is surprising is the increase in job-related problems that took place while the economy was growing, a change that seemed linked to Menem's neo-liberal policies.[10] The percentage of those living below the officially calculated poverty line based on minimal expenditure varied with the level of joblessness. As would be expected, more unemployment meant more poverty. As a consequence of the economic depression that emerged by 2002, poverty reached levels never previously recorded in modern Argentina. Paralleling the Buenos Aires figures, the worst situation for urban poverty nationally was the 57.5% registered in the October 2002 government survey. To get a more complete account of job insecurity in Argentina, one ought to add the 27.5% classified as underemployed to those with no jobs at all. These figures suggest that those with little or no such economic concerns were only a small minority of the population, a shocking situation for what had been the richest country in Latin America just prior to the recent economic decline.

The apparent inability of the De la Rúa government to do anything about the declining economy had the effect of causing many citizens to question the competence of the new president and of his administration. As of a Gallup poll of October 2000, the president's personal approval rating, which had registered 70% when he first took office, was now at 32%, down from 37% the month before. By June 2001, it had fallen much further, to only 15%.[11] Figures on the administration

Table 1.1. Economic Precipitants of 2001 Crisis*

	% GDP Growth (Yearly Change)	% Urban Unemployment	% Urban Poverty	
a. Years of Relative Prosperity				
			Greater Buenos Aires	Nation
1991	10.6	6.5	25.1	n.a.
1992	9.6	7.0	18.6	n.a.
1993	5.7	9.6	17.3	n.a.
1994	5.8	11.4	17.6	n.a.
1995	−2.8	17.3	23.5	n.a.
1996	5.5	17.2	27.3	n.a.
1997	8.1	14.9	26.2	n.a.
1998	3.9	12.8	25.1	n.a.
b. Years of Recession				
1999	−3.4	14.2	26.9	n.a.
2000	−0.8	15.1	29.3	n.a.
2001	−4.4	17.4	34.1	38.3
2002	−10.9	19.7	52.2	55.3

Sources: GDP from Dirección Nacional de Cuentas Nacionales, Instituto Nacional de Estadística y Censos (INDEC), Argentine Government; urban unemployment and poverty both from Encuesta Permanente de Hogares, INDEC.
* Unemployment and poverty figures are averages of May and October surveys except for June rather than May in 1991 for unemployment and April rather than May in 1996 for poverty in Greater Buenos Aires area; the national urban poverty figure in 2001 is only that of October that year. Poverty figures are by person rather than by household.
n.a.= none available.

as a whole also fell rapidly, to even lower levels. In August 2000, a Graciela Römer poll reported only 37% of the population satisfied with the government, down from 58% that April. By November 2000, Gallup reported that those seeing the government as doing a good job were now only 11%, down from 14% in October.[12] Importantly for a government that pledged itself to repair the damage associated with its predecessor's policies, by August 2000, 43% of those sampled saw no difference between the policies of the Alliance and those of Menem's administration. Some 58% now complained about unemployment, 48% about crime, 47% about the new labor reform law passed at the insistence of the IMF, and 28% about education and health care. Ironically, one of the most positive aspects of the De la Rúa government suggested by that survey was the perceived transparency and honesty in the use of public funds.[13]

The irony, of course, relates to the accusations that soon surfaced less than a month after that poll was taken of the bribes supposedly paid by key officials of the "clean" De la Rúa administration to induce a number of senators to switch their vote on the government's labor bill. De la Rúa's perceived lack of being forthcoming about the scandal not only tarnished his image, but soon led to the resignation of Vice President Alvarez in protest, and the collapse of the Alliance as a viable political arrangement. When the court involved eventually dropped charges against all the senators accused of being implicated, faith in the justice system plummeted from what had already been not very high levels. A Gallup poll administered in December 2000 suggested that only 18% of the Argentine population then still confided in the courts, the lowest level since the new democracy started in 1983. Moreover, if 30% of the people polled thought that the Argentine administration of justice had deteriorated during the year 2000, 54% saw it as simply no worse than before.[14]

Public confidence in key political institutions over time is an important measure of popular support for a country's democracy, allowing an evaluation not just during the administration controlled by one party, but permitting a comparison with what occurs during the government of the rival party, as in a two-party-dominant political system like Argentina's. Data exist to suggest that such confidence declined throughout most of the Menem years when the Peronists had a majority. According to various Graciela Römer polls taken while Menem was president, those expressing either some or much confidence in all Argentine political parties dropped from an already rather low 24% in 1993 to only 10% in 1999, while those similarly confiding in the Congress declined from 31% to an almost equally poor 13% in the same period.[15] Although low, the figures for 1999 (and for 1995, another presidential election year when conditions might have changed with a new administration) represented modest improvements from the year immediately previous. Data from the Latinobarómetro surveys for 1996 and 2001, that is, from early in Menem's second term and from the last year of De la Rúa's Alliance government, reported a similar fall in the percentage of those expressing some or much confidence in the Argentine Congress.[16] Although the information available here on public confidence in key political institutions is somewhat sketchy for the time compared, what was taking place seemed to go beyond just the loss of trust in one administration or the party then in control to what seems of more serious concern for Argentine democracy, a general loss of trust in how the institutions themselves might function regardless of which party had power.

A similar pattern is revealed in terms of the more complete series of poll results concerning the level of overall satisfaction with the functioning of Argentine democracy, made available from Latinobarómetro from 1995 onward. Here those reporting themselves somewhat or very satisfied with their democracy fell from 51% in the 1995 presidential election year to 34% in the next year as support for Menem deteriorated with the recession (that began in the second quarter of 1995 after the elections) producing rising unemployment and poverty in early 1996. Subsequently, satisfaction rose to 42% in 1997 and 49% in 1998, possibly due in part to rising expectations about a possible Alliance government. Finally, one sees a dramatic collapse of such voter satisfaction from the still solid 46% registered in the single poll taken in late 1999/early 2000 as De la Rúa first took office, with the figure falling sharply to 20% in 2001 as confidence in the president continued its earlier decline, and then to only 8% in 2002 under a Duhalde government appointed to serve out the rest of De la Rúa's term by the Peronist-controlled Congress selected in 2001.[17]

The unusual circumstances of the October 2001 legislative elections that preceded by only a few months De la Rúa's ouster and the full explosion of the crisis suggest that what has been described about declining public satisfaction with Argentina's democracy was indicative of something unusual happening. It was far more than just the electorate's sequential swing from one party to another, as might constitute a normal pattern in a fully consolidated liberal democracy. What the press would describe as the "voto bronca" (literally, the vote of those annoyed or irritated) protest vote that took place then suggested that many Argentines were now largely fed up with the entire political system, regardless of party.

Table 1.2. Voting in Elections for Chamber of Deputies, 1991–2001 (%)

	Positive Vote	Abstention	Blank Vote	Spoiled/Null Vote
2001	57.37	24.54	8.11	9.98
1999*	79.07	17.77	2.33	0.83
1997	72.51	21.53	4.65	1.31
1995*	75.65	17.71	5.97	0.67
1993	75.43	19.46	4.06	1.05
1991	74.34	19.86	5.03	0.77

Sources: 1991–1997, Dirección Nacional Electoral, Ministerio del Interior; 1999–2001, Yann Basset, "Abstención y voto negativo," in Isidro Cheresky and Jean-Michel Blanquer (eds.), *De la illusion reformista al descontento ciudadano* (Rosario: Homo Sapiens, 2003), 60.
* Presidential election years when positive vote normally rises.

As can be seen in Table 1.2, the positive vote made up of people voting for any candidate fell sharply in 2001 after having risen two years earlier when the Alliance was the favorite for the presidency (with elections for both offices held simultaneously). While electoral abstention rose to a modern high despite supposed compulsory voting in Argentina, what was particularly surprising was the increase in blank and especially in spoiled/null ballots cast. Where casting a blank ballot could be attributed to apathy or lack of enthusiasm for all of the candidates running by those afraid of violating the legal requirement to vote, a spoiled vote is a considerably more negative act, suggesting a high degree of political alienation from the democratic system itself.

As one well-known observer, Juan Carlos Portantiero, stated in a press interview about the 2001 elections,

> The people [did] not feel represented by anyone. . . . The major loser in the elections [was] the government. The Alliance lost half of its vote from the last election but, curiously, it was not the Peronists who attracted these, but the so-called "protest vote." The Peronists also saw their percentage of the vote fall in relation to 1999. . . . [They] maintained their historical average, that oscillates around 30%, but were not capable as the opposition to become an attractive alternative for the electorate.[18]

Another prominent commentator, Rosendo Fraga, the head of the Centro de Estudios Nueva Mayoría think tank, suggested that the negative vote was strongest in the large urban centers of the country and among the better educated and more affluent. Referring to a poll the Centro carried out in the Federal Capital of Buenos Aires and in Santa Fe, two areas with the highest negative voting in the election, he reports that 37% of respondents there attributed such voting to "the lack of credibility of the political system," 30% saw it as "a protest vote," and 23% linked it to "the lack of credible candidates."[19] A Graciela Römer poll on the same topic reported that 70% of the population was dissatisfied with the country's political institutions, although 90% still thought that democracy was the best system. As Römer's stated,

> The perception of disenchantment with politics is less a cynical posture toward the democratic system as such. It has more to do with the perceived banal treatment of the [existing] social contract, and the extent to which a strong suspicion exists that the concern of the political leadership is restricted to defending its own privileges rather than finding solutions for the problems of the citizenry.[20]

If the high negative voting in the October 2001 elections was a kind of warning for both the De la Rúa government and the other politicians as well, it was one that was largely ignored. With the events of December 19–20, 2001, the crisis emerged into view with full intensity.[21]

Without going into detail here on matters described elsewhere in this volume, events like the acceleration of road blockages by "piquetero" protestors, the development of neighborhood assemblies in Buenos Aires and in other urban areas, and the spread of barter clubs for those with a reduced cash income can all be seen as responses to the political crisis and its economic ramifications. A portion of the population that previously had felt alienated from the political system now engaged in forms of direct collective action both to be politically heard and simply to economically survive.

The crisis beginning in late 2001 had been very hard on most Argentines. Such economic deprivation would worsen through much of 2002.

The De la Rúa government, including its controversial Minister of Economics Domingo Cavallo, was forced out, but the badly shaken Argentine democracy somehow managed to survive its most severe challenge since being established in 1983.

The second section of this chapter examines the efforts first of the transitional Duhalde administration and then the government formed after the 2003 presidential elections by Néstor Kirchner to deal with the disaster inflicted on the population and to take political initiatives to rebuild linkages with Argentina's citizens. Only the reestablishment of significant popular confidence in the nation's political institutions could strengthen that democracy.

Exiting the Crisis: Duhalde, Kirchner, and Public Opinion

The remarkable set of events following December 2001 demonstrated an effort by a largely discredited Argentine political class to get through the crisis without inviting a military reaction. At least in this regard they succeeded. De la Rúa's resignation on December 20, 2001, touched off an unprecedented chain of succession. By the end of the month, the presidency would change hands four times, before finally resting in the hands of former Peronist governor and 1999 presidential candidate Eduardo Duhalde. If there ever was a vacuum of power at the apex of the political system, it was during the last twelve days of December 2001. But that vacuum was filled by Argentine lawmakers who, meeting in joint session and operating within legal guidelines, determined how the nation's top post would be filled. Throughout it all, the military remained garrisoned. Commenting on De la Rúa's demise that triggered these unprecedented events, former army commander Martín Balza said, "This was the first time a government [an Argentine government] is ousted without military intervention, without a tank in the streets."[22]

Rhetorically, Duhalde seemed to hit most of the right notes, striking a balance between national defiance and humility. He announced the abandonment of the convertibility scheme and an impending devaluation, and he vowed to maintain the moratorium on debt repayment. Soon thereafter, he spoke of the need to end the destructive alliance of "political power and financial might" that had sold the nation out to foreign creditors and international financial institutions at the expense of internal production and consumption.[23] He even created a new Ministry of Production. But while offering solutions, he also admitted that he and his party had been "part of the problem, just like all the others who have governed this country, civilian and military."[24] In March of 2002, in a speech before Congress, he said that there was still a "formidable crisis of representation" as the public continued to vent its furious anger against the entire political class.[25]

Indeed, Duhalde himself was not spared the public's wrath. A "cacerolazo" protest (demonstration of people banging on pots and pans) erupted three weeks into his term over the administration's refusal to fully lift the freeze on cash withdrawals from bank accounts. Throughout 2002, Duhalde was the victim of a number of such demonstrations, many of which demanded either his resignation or, at the very least, a call for early elections. When two piquetero protesters were killed by the police during an anti-government demonstration, Duhalde felt compelled to move the elections scheduled for September 2003 forward to April.

Even if the economy had cooperated more with Duhalde—which for the most part it did not—it was unlikely that the president could have capitalized politically. He had entered office with a serious handicap: he had been selected, not elected, as president. He lacked electoral legitimacy and was essentially a caretaker, whose mission it was to avert any further catastrophes and hopefully deliver a modicum of political, social, and economic stability to his successor, whoever that might be. As shown in Figure 1.1 on page 21, Duhalde's public approval ratings seldom moved above single digits, and it was only just prior to his departure on May 26, 2003, that he earned a respectable rating of 59.5%—an indicator of either public recognition of his service or, more likely, relief that he had successfully handed over the presidency to his elected successor, Néstor Kirchner.

Néstor Kirchner was elected president with just 22% of first-round votes. Though polls indicate he would have defeated Carlos Menem handily in a second round, Menem denied him the opportunity by pulling out of the race. Thus Kirchner came into office with a handicap. He did not have a solid electoral mandate, even if as polls suggested he was undoubtedly popular with the voters. Part of his appeal was the image he cultivated of himself as the anti-Menem candidate. His track record gave his appeal credence. This former governor of the southern province of Santa Cruz had been a Peronist militant in his youth and by the 1970s was increasingly left-leaning. He forged an internal movement, the "Corriente Peronista," within the Peronist Party that took issue with Menem's human rights policies and that finally broke with Menem after the the latter announced his quest for a third consecutive term as president. Kirchner had also been a fairly effective governor. When he won that post in 1991, the public account deficit was 1.2 billion pesos and the province was stagnating economically. When he exited office twelve years later, Kirchner could boast that he left behind a province with a fiscal surplus, good economic growth, and one of the nation's lowest levels of poverty, unemployment, and social unrest. But counter to Menem, he turned the province's economy around by rejecting neo-liberal austerity programs in favor of neo-Keynesian expansion of consumption and investment spending.

Could a former governor from a remote, sparsely populated region of Argentina now govern the entire nation effectively? Could he bring Argentina out of its crisis by governing effectively? How would Kirchner deal with an angry public that had only too recently expressed its revulsion at the entire political class? He pursued several strategies. He took aim at key institutions that had become closely associated with the former president and with cronyism, corruption, and lack of respect for human rights. In one stunning blow, he purged the military high command of nearly half its officers who had been part of the "Dirty War" of the 1970s, or who might have interfered with human rights inquiries were these to re-open. First in line to go was General Ricardo Brinzoni, the often irksome army leader whose private dealings and public pronouncements at times appeared to challenge civilian control. To choose his replacement, Kirchner had to reach down some twenty places on the Army's seniority list until he found General Roberto Bendini, someone he knew and trusted.[26] The new retirees walked away without a fight. Active duty officers have remained subordinate and out of the political limelight ever since then.

Kirchner then announced his support for the Congressional annulment of the Alfonsín era "End Point" and "Due Obedience" laws that had put an end to human rights trials for military offenders. Although the Congress would proceed to eliminate those laws, the constitutionality of that legislation would have to be settled by the Supreme Court (this occurred only in June 2005).[27] Here Kirchner confronted yet another legacy of the Menem period: a court that had been stacked with obsequious judges who had rendered verdicts in exchange for payoffs and favors and who, to all intents and purposes, had then comprised an automatic majority for the former president and his positions and interests.[28] They would undoubtedly prove troublesome for this new, more progressive president, especially on issues having to do with human rights, corruption, and the economy. The Supreme Court thus represented another political target for Kirchner because it had become, in the eyes of the Argentine public, an institution associated with the worst cronyism of the past. The president would push his congressional allies to launch impeachment proceedings against several judges, including the former chief justice of the court. They did, and by the end of 2004, the president's goal of ridding the High Court of Menem's judges had been achieved.[29]

Kirchner also launched a campaign to clean up Argentina's notoriously corrupt, repressive, and ineffective police forces. The Buenos Aires provincial police had long been presumed to be engaged in abusive and criminal activities including torture, use of excessive deadly force, theft rings, prostitution, and kid-nappings for ransom. It was suspected that in exchange for impunity, police routinely funneled their ill-gotten gains to the bank accounts of various Peronist politicians. Within weeks of assuming office, President Kirchner relieved fifty-two federal police commissioners of their duties and in November of 2003 ordered a "complete cleansing" of the Buenos Aires provincial police as part of a "no impunity" campaign.[30] After the kidnap and murder of a middle-class student in March 2004 triggered massive protests, the federal government passed a series of laws enacting stiffer punishment for criminals, and Kirchner resumed his purge of the Buenos Aires police force while at the same time increasing the number of officers on the beat. By the end of 2004, crime was reported to be down 11.2% in Buenos Aires, while kidnappings, homicides, and robberies fell 46%, 28.5%, and 10.4%, respectively.[31]

Of course, economic recovery would be central to any effort by Kirchner to move Argentina beyond the crisis phase and restore the public's confidence in the government. The president's policies in Santa Cruz were a clue to what was to come. Kirchner would insist on a program of domestic economic expansion and job stimulation that would not be sacrificed before the interests of foreign creditors. Argentina, he argued, would not sign any debt repayment scheme that was inconsistent with a policy of immediate and sustained economic production and popular consumption. In a speech before Congress, he stated, "We will not pay debt at the cost of hunger and the exclusion of millions of Argentines, generating more poverty and increasing social conflict so that the country returns to exploitation."[32]

Kirchner staked out a tough, nationalistic negotiating position with foreign creditors. He sensed quite correctly that the IMF had been placed on the defensive, having been chastised at home and abroad first for its unwavering, uncritical support for Menem's Convertibility Plan and then for its abandonment of Argentina as the nation plunged into its greatest economic crisis as a result of that very plan. In August 2003, the IMF Managing Director Horst Köhler took the unusual step of admitting that the Fund had made mistakes in handling Argentina. Köhler was feeling pressure from G-7 members including the United States who were pushing the Fund to show greater flexibility with a country whose staggering debt was causing anxiety for Western banks and bondholders. Sensing that Argentina's bargaining position with the Fund had improved, the president was not about to merely submit to the usual IMF package of harsh austerity measures. On the contrary, he rejected utility rate hikes as the Fund had wanted, and when a 2.9-billion-dollar debt fell due in September 2003, he refused to dip into Central Bank reserves to make the payment as the Fund had urged. Argentina went into technical default on that payment, but twenty-four hours later the Fund relented and signed a new, more favorable deal with Argentina to refinance the three-year, 21-billion-dollar debt owed to multilateral lending institutions.[33] Argentina sealed the agreement without conceding to the Fund anything that would have undermined its expansionary programs at home.

From that moment on, the government would continue to drive a tough bargain with creditors, vowing never to restructure its debt on terms that would compromise its growth plans.[34] Argentina let its foreign bondholders know that the best offer they were likely to get was about thirty cents back on each dollar in face value, a write-off of 70% of that portion of the nation's debt. Bondholders were understandably upset with a deal that would result in losses for them about twice that of previous debt settlements (like those of Russia and Ecuador).[35] They held out for more, but Argentina would not budge. In a nearly three-year game of "chicken," the bondholders blinked first, and on March 3, 2005, 76% of them agreed to Argentina's terms of repayment.[36] Most of the Argentine default was now resolved.

To what extent do these moves represent an end to the crisis and a renewed ability to govern the nation? Objectively, one can look to see whether economic indicators point to a recovery. Subjectively, we can look toward public opinion polls that sample how Argentines perceive the situation. Here we will want to know the extent to which citizens have faith in presidential leadership, in the government as a whole, and in political institutions, especially parties.

Table 1.3. Economic Indicators for Argentina, 1996–2004

Indicators[1]	1996	2001	2002	2003	2004[a]
GDP growth rate	5.5	-4.4	-10.9	8.7	8.8
Inflation rates	.1	-1.5	41.0	3.7	9.1[b]
Gross Domestic Investment (% GDP)	19.6	15.6	10.8	14.2	19.1
Unemployment[2]	17.2	17.4	19.7	15.0	12.5
Real Wage growth			-21.2 (IV)	9.2 (IV)	14.2 (II)
Poverty[3]	27.3	34.1	52.2	51.7	44.3[c]

Sources: 1996–2003 data from Economic Commission for Latin America and the Caribbean (ECLAC), *Economic Survey of Latin America and Caribbean, 2003-04*, 132–34. Data on poverty are for Greater Buenos Aires, and found at the Instituto Nacional de Estadistica y Censos (INDEC) website under "Evolución de la indigencia, la pobreza, y la desocupación en el GBA desde 1988 en adelante," <http://www.indec.mecon.ar/>; 2004 inflation figure from Bloomberg.com, <http://quote.bloomberg.com/apps/news?pid=10000086& sid=aWHmpAoMtLVI&refer=news_index>.
[1] GDP, inflation figures are annual variations; those for real wage growth are quarterly.
[2] Unemployed as a percentage of economically active population.
[3] Percentage of population at or below poverty line.
[a] Figures for GDP and unemployment are preliminary.
[b] Latest inflation figure represents the change in the consumer price index from March 2004 to March 2005.
[c] Figure for poverty rate is first quarter of 2004.

Recent economic trends appear in Table 1.3. As can be seen there, the nation has recorded two impressive years of growth in its gross domestic product in 2003–2004, after having experienced drastic economic contraction in the 2001–2002 period. These rates compare favorably with the peak performance years during the first Menem administration. The most recent report of the Economics Ministry states there have been nine consecutive quarters of growth since the recovery began in early 2002—the first time that has been achieved since 1997.[37] According to the Economic Commission on Latin America, all sectors have contributed to the recovery, including agriculture, manufacturing, construction, and wholesale and retail commerce. The government reports especially strong growth in labor-intensive areas such as textiles, metal manufacturing, and construction.

Inflation has fallen to single digits, though not as low as that recorded during the mid-1990s.[38] With economic growth on the rebound, prices stabilizing, and demand increasing, investors—both domestic and foreign—are slowly beginning to return to Argentina, thus contributing to the increase in gross domestic investment. The latest gross domestic investment figure (Table 1.3) comes from Economics Minister, Roberto Lavagna, and, if accurate, competes favorably with the best years of the 1990s. Anecdotally, China has announced plans to invest 20 billion dollars in Argentina over the next decade, and South Korean, German, and Brazilian firms are beginning to return.[39]

Obviously, then, a snapshot of the Argentine economy over the last two years indicates that the worst is now probably over. But it is also obviously too soon to tell for just how long the current upturn will continue. Economists are not sure how firm a footing this recovery has. Some say that there is an underlying fragility to the economy, that much of the ground that was lost has been regained mainly by re-using idle capacity and taking advantage of unusually high international prices for export commodities like those of soybeans and wheat. What will happen when installed capacity is fully utilized and export prices return to more normal levels? Will there be an abundance of new capital investments—especially from abroad—to expand the nation's productive potential?[40] How will the government compensate for an inevitable fall in the prices for Argentine primary goods and the resulting declining trade surplus? Argentina does not have a sufficient store of available domestic savings and capital; it is a country that is greatly dependent on the outside. The government's bet is that Argentines who have held their money abroad will begin to repatriate it and that new foreign investors will continue to see Argentina as an attractive market, especially after the nation's deal with foreign bondholders and the IMF. But it is simply too soon to tell whether such forecasts are reasonable.

In terms of poverty, although it is true that the numbers have declined since 2002, the current figures are still sobering. More than four in ten Argentines still live at or below the poverty line. Consider that in 1994, under an administration that paid little attention to alleviating poverty, as few as 16% of Argentines were poor. Today, there are still vast sectors of a former middle class that were forced into poverty and are struggling to keep afloat. Finally, while real wages have risen in the last two years, earnings for salaried workers are still 20% lower than they were in 1998. Even more disturbingly, the Fundación de Investigaciones Económicas Latinoamericanas (FIEL) reports that overall income levels are now where they were thirty years ago.[41]

In sum, while there are encouraging signs of improvement, Argentina has a long way to go before it can declare complete recovery. Argentines can still recall better days, when unemployment rates were in single digits, and when a substantial majority of citizens were not poor. And it is those recollections that will be used by the public to make comparisons with today's circumstances, and to hold politicians accountable. If economically Argentina could be said to be in a post-crisis situation, it could also be said that the nation has not yet rediscovered the kind of development levels it once enjoyed.

Presented below is another set of indicators that are perceptual in nature but have implications for Argentina's economic future. Transparency International is an international nongovernmental organization dedicated to exposing and combating corruption. Annually, it releases a composite index that ranks countries according to the degree to which corruption is perceived to exist among public officials and politicians. The index reflects the views of important risk analysts, as well as key corporate and bank-related institutions (for example, Political and Economic Risk Consultants, the World Bank, EBRD, Merchant International Group, Economic Intelligence Unit) on how common corruption is in a given country, and what obstacles it poses for doing business there. For that reason, the index provides the degree of confidence of prospective investors weighing the pros and cons of doing business in Argentina.

Table 1.4. Argentine Corruption: International Comparisons, 2000–2004

Year	Argentina's Rank	Number of Countries Ranked	% of Countries with Less Corruption than Argentina	Argentina's Score (10 best, 0 worst)
2000	52	90	57	3.5
2001	57	91	62	3.5
2002	70	102	68	2.8
2003	92	133	69	2.5
2004	108	145	74	2.5

Source: Transparency International, Corruption Perceptions Indices, 2000–2004, <http://www.transparency.org/>.

Table 1.4 reveals that, with respect to other countries, Argentina's image has deteriorated progressively from the pre-crisis to the post-crisis period. While, for example, 57% of all ranked countries were rated "cleaner" than Argentina in 2000, by 2004 that number had swelled to 74%. In absolute terms as well, the situation has declined, with Argentina's corruption score moving backward from 3.5 to 2.5. In South America, only Paraguay, Bolivia, and Venezuela were rated as worse. In all fairness, it must be said that President Kirchner's recent efforts to reduce corruption would not necessarily be captured in this index. The index relies on a three-year rolling average to produce scores, which means that perceptual changes will likely emerge only over a longer time period. Nonetheless, current perceptions do matter, and foreign businesses that view this disturbing data may take a "wait and see" attitude before venturing into Argentina.

We next turn to the political dimension of Argentina's recovery attempt under Kirchner. As suggested at the beginning of this chapter, how citizens view the performance of those in power is critical to the stability of a democracy. When it comes to assessing democratic strengths and weaknesses, answers are found in citizens' perceptions. Consequently, public opinion poll data is presented below that distinguishes between personal, governmental, and institutional levels of analysis. The public's view of President Kirchner as an individual leader may be quite different from its views on the administration, political parties, or, for that matter, the democracy as a whole. Certainly if the president's performance is thought to be strong, that could improve the image held of the institutions of government. But it is also clear that the public does discriminate between its faith in the nation's leader and its faith in its political institutions.

A citizenry that has withstood such economic suffering would, understandably, yearn for a president who could step in, take charge, and lead their nation out of its worst crisis. Expectations ran high that Kirchner would be that individual, and so far the public has given him unusually high marks for his performance, as shown in Figure 1.1 on page 21.

Kirchner enjoyed an impressive spike in his popularity early on when it soared to nearly 90% in August 2003. The public wanted a president who would stand up to special interests, foreign creditors, and human rights violators, and Kirchner appeared to be that individual. It was unlikely that he (or any president, for that matter) could maintain those levels. As the initial enthusiasm subsided, the president's public image declined somewhat as well. Nonetheless, and despite the peaks and valleys, the president has maintained an impressive average approval rating of about 77% during his first two years in office.

By way of comparison, former President Carlos Menem's approval ratings soared to 80% by his third month in office, but then fell to 48% by his seventh month in office, and to 22% a year and a half into his first term. Menem never regained the popularity that he enjoyed early on. It is particularly interesting to note that in 1994, when his economic Convertibility Plan was in full gear and had already produced dramatic results (high growth, very low inflation), Menem's approval ratings hovered around only 40%, considerably lower than Kirchner's current marks. By 1996, Menem's approval had plummeted to 19%. According to a Gallup poll at that time, Argentines gave his administration credit for low inflation and currency stability, but expressed great displeasure over its indifference about and failure to stem the rising tide of unemployment, which affected 17.1% of the work force that April.[42] Kirchner, by contrast, has attacked unemployment head on with reasonably good results so far.

Are Argentines placing too much stock in their president and his abilities to transform their nation? Perhaps. But it would also be unwise to suggest that this is all a display of irrational exuberance. The president could not have achieved let alone sustained this positive image had he not delivered programmatically, and undoubtedly his personal approval rating is tied to his policies on human rights, the courts, police, crime and the military, and especially the economic recovery detailed above.

The second set of data reflects public opinion about the national government. Undoubtedly, many people associate governmental efficacy with presidential efficacy. For that reason, the figures on governmental approval parallel the president's. Nevertheless, one notes that approval levels are consistently lower for the government than for the president and averaged 58% during the same time period. That indicates that the public is unwilling to give all those in the cabinet and administration the same high marks they reserve for the president alone. Presidential popularity does not translate fully into governmental popularity.

In another survey, the Universidad Torcuato Di Tella assessed public confidence in the government on a monthly basis, from November 2001 to November 2004. It used a composite scale that measured public views of government overall and specifically adherence to special vs. general interests, efficiency in administering public funds, honesty vs. corruption, and problem-solving abilities. This study also records a huge increase in public confidence in government during the first two months of Kirchner's term, followed by an uneven decline up until November 2004. Despite that decline, confidence levels remain well above those scored throughout the Duhalde presidency. The public rated the Kirchner government's problem-solving capacity the highest, and its honesty and efficiency somewhat lower.[43]

Other data refer to political parties. Once known for its stable two-party system of Peronists and Radicals, Argentina is still reeling from the harmful effects of the crisis. The Radical Party is recovering from its worst defeat in history, in 2003; the Peronists are badly divided; and third parties have yet to make their mark. In any democracy, parties are the key institutions charged with aggregating and articulating public preferences and concerns. Thus, public sentiment about parties is critical, because it reveals whether or not a society believes its interests are being adequately represented.

Table 1.5. Argentine Support for Political Parties, 2003–2004

Year	Argentina		Latin America		Argentina's Rank in Latin America
	Some	None	Some	None	
2003	44	56	42	58	9th (of 17)
2004	39	61	45	55	12th (of 18)

Source: Latinobarómetro, "Informe resumen, 2003," 44–45; "Informe resumen 2004," 29–30.

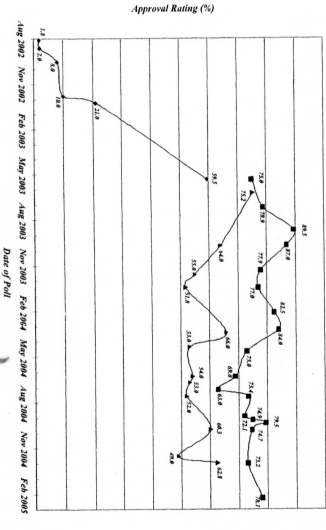

Figure 1.1 Argentine Public Approval Ratings: President vs. Government

Approval Rating (%)

Date of Poll

Source: Data assembled from polling results of various agencies, as reported in Centro para la Nueva Mayoría, Sondeos de Opinión Pública, www.nuevamayoria.com/ES/

Unfortunately, we have only limited data on this issue. On page 20 are the results of a poll conducted by Latinobarómetro in 2003 and 2004. A national sample of Argentines was asked if the election were held now what party or parties, if any, they would vote for. What the results clearly demonstrate in Table 1.5 is that a majority of Argentines preferred no party to any party at all, and that the non-party majority has increased over the last year. Argentina is now in the bottom two-thirds of Latin American nations insofar as its attachment to parties is concerned. After two years of economic recovery, the public remains skeptical of political parties, even as it continues to produce substantial support for Néstor Kirchner, the president and national leader.

President Kirchner understood from the outset that there was a crisis of confidence in Argentine political parties, including his own. In an interview shortly before assuming office, he acknowledged that the Argentine public associated parties with the narrow particularist interests of its leaders and not as forces for change nor as vehicles for genuine representation.[44] Parties change slowly, and if Kirchner was to recover the public trust that had been lost in political institutions, it was clear to him that he would have to move quickly and to the beat of his own drum, not waiting for Peronist Party stalwarts to catch up. Thus Kirchner began as a kind of anti-party president, reasoning that he had little to gain from working solely within the confines of his own party—one which was perceived by the public to be part of the problem, not the solution. He was determined to stake out his own positions on issues—irrespective of how unpopular they may have been with Peronist leaders.

This tendency to act on his own is reflected in the president's relations with the Peronist-dominated Congress. After the 2003 legislative elections, Peronists solidified their hold on both chambers, commanding 130 out of 257 seats in the Chamber of Deputies, and 41 of 72 seats in the Senate. Before the elections, the Peronist Party had held 116 and 40 seats, respectively. That meant that the party enjoyed not only a majority but a quorum as well, meaning they did not need the participation of other parties to pass legislation. This would seem to be an opportune time for Kirchner to work closely with the Congress to promote his legislative agenda. Yet, in his first year of office, he resorted to decree authority, not congressionally mandated laws, with great frequency. He used executive Decrees of Necessity and Urgency some 67 times, surpassing the record of 64 such decrees for one year previously held by Menem.

Clearly, the president has had an uneasy relation with many members of his own party. Promoting controversial policies and brandishing a brusque, confrontational style, he has managed to alienate if not infuriate many key members of his own party. Party members have walked out on him during congressional addresses, have rejected him as party head, and have criticized his foreign policy. He, in turn, has selectively supported non-Peronists—including Radicals—in various provincial gubernatorial and legislative election races.[45] Yet despite these problems, what he has done makes political sense. As the anti-party president, he has managed to strike resonant populist chords with a citizenry that is tired of party politics as usual and has been looking for real change.

By the same token, no one is seriously predicting total divorce between Kirchner and the party any time soon. Although, after lengthy negotiations, he finally did break with the Duhalde faction in Buenos Aires province, the president has preferred to keep one foot inside the party confines and the other outside, trying "to generate a new space which goes beyond the Peronist Party."[46] His notion of a so-called "transverse alliance" is one that seeks to govern less from a single-party base and more from that of a coalition, bringing in progressive voices even if they are non-Peronists.[47] In fact, in October 2004, Kirchner created a political organization called the Coordinating Body for a New National Project (Mesa Coordinadora para un Nuevo Proyecto Nacional) incorporating piquetero organizations, selected trade unionists, human rights groups, and leftists outside the party. In reaching beyond elite political figures to bring on board some from the ranks of the unemployed and others normally excluded from conventional politics, the president understood that some mechanism had to be created institutionally to channel the discontented, or else risk a public once again drawn to the refrain it had abandoned amid the 2003 election campaign, "que se vayan todos."

Despite Kirchner's dislike (shared by many citizens) for the entrenched Peronist leadership, the president is likely to continue to work with the powers that be within his own party. In this marriage of convenience, they need the president and he needs them. For example, Peronist governors—indeed, all governors—depend overwhelmingly on the federal government for tax revenue sharing and benefit at election time from federally funded public works projects. Revenue-sharing formulas will have to be renegotiated with Kirchner, and public works expenditures come largely at the discretion of the president. Likewise, the president understands that the upcoming 2005 mid-term congressional elections will be a kind of referendum on his leadership so far. The president would like pro-Kirchner candidates to run and to win, but he needs the support of provincial (largely gubernatorial) Peronist Party bosses who have the power to help draw up official ballot lists of party candidates in this closed-list, electoral system.[48]

What does this all amount to? Has Argentina overcome its crisis? Are political leaders governing effectively? The short answer is that the worst of the crisis is over for now, and that Argentina appears to be in some kind of post-crisis phase of development. What is not yet apparent is how durable, let alone irreversible, this post-crisis phase is or whether the nation can put itself on a trajectory toward a more stable and prosperous equilibrium. On the one hand, the economy seems to be back on track, the military remains garrisoned, violent street protests have subsided, and crime has declined. The public has by and large given the president and, to a lesser extent, his administration high marks for performance. On the other hand, the staying power of the economy has yet to be fully tested. Many foreign investors will undoubtedly remain wary, waiting to see whether the economy can continue to rebound and whether levels of corruption begin to decline significantly. Meanwhile, the public remains skeptical about the political parties and other political institutions (including Congress and the courts). If the president's personal popularity does not translate into substantial gains in public respect for governing institutions, then the Argentine democracy itself is the loser. Without a substantial and growing base of support for the nation's political institutions, combined with a sustainable economic recovery, Argentina will not be able to declare that the 2001 political crisis is fully over.

Notes

1. Five, if Menem, who was re-elected in 1995, is counted twice.

2. For one analysis of the events of December 19–20, 2001, see Federico Schuster, German Pérez, Sebastián Pereyra, et al., *La trama de la crisis: Modos y formas de protesta social a partir de los acontecimientos de Diciembre de 2001* (Buenos Aires: Informe de Coyuntura 3, Instituto de Investigaciones Gino Germani, Universidad de Buenos Aires, 2002).

3. In an April 1999 Mora y Araujo & Asociados poll (described in their *Analisis sociopolítico de la coyuntura argentina*, 1999, 20), 85% of those polled selected the lack of jobs as Argentina's principal problem. Other issues also seen as important were delinquency and insecurity (selected by 30%), low salaries (26%), corruption (25%), education (25%), retirees (18%), and health care (16%).

4. Marcos Novaro and Vicente Palermo, *Los caminos de la centroizquierda: Dilemas y desafíos del Frepaso y de la Alianza* (Buenos Aires: Losada, 1998); Julio Godio, *La alianza* (Buenos Aires: Grijalbo, 1998).

5. The initial presidential election of the current democracy, that of 1983 won by the Radical Party, might be seen as a rejection of the Peronists who had formed the last democratic government during the previous, very brief 1973–1976 democratic regime.

6. Juan Carlos Portantiero, "La transición entre la confrontación y el acuerdo," in *Ensayos sobre la transición democrática en la Argentina*, ed. José Nun and Juan Carlos Portantiero (Buenos Aires: Puntosur, 1987), 281–82; Carlos Waisman, "Argentina," in *Democracy in Developing Countries: Latin America*, ed. Larry Diamond, Juan Linz, and Seymour Martin Lipset (Boulder, Colo.: Lynne Rienner, 1989), 86.

7. For discussions of the decay of the traditional Argentine political parties, see Inés Pousadela, "Los partidos políticos han muerto: ¡Larga vida a los partidos!" and Edgardo Mocca, "Los partidos políticos: Entre el derrumbe y la oportunidad," both in *¿Qué cambió en la política argentina?*, ed. Isidoro Cheresky and Jean-Michel Blanquer (Rosario: Homo Sapiens, 2004).

8. United Nations, Economic Commission for Latin America and the Caribbean, *Economic Survey of Latin America and the Caribbean*, various years.

9. Jorge Schvarzer, *Convertibilidad y deuda externa* (Buenos Aires: Libros del Rojas, EUDEBA, 2002); Eduardo Basualdo, *Sistema político y modelo de acumulación en la Argentina* (Buenos Aires: Universidad Nacional de Quilmes, 2001).

10. Among others, here see Luis Beccaria, *Empleo e integración social* (Buenos Aires: Fondo de Cultura Económica, 2001).

11. *Latin American Southern Cone Report*, November 14, 2000; June 26, 2001.

12. *Latin American Southern Cone Report*, September 5, 2000; November 14, 2000.

13. *Latin American Southern Cone Report*, September 5, 2000.

14. *Noticiero de Norte a Sur*, February 2001, <www.denorteasur.com/asp/articulo.asp ?numero=234&id=309>.

15. Data provided courtesy of Graciela Römer, Buenos Aires, 1999.

16. The figures were 25% satisfaction in 1996, dropping to 17% in 2001. Argentine data from Latinobarómetro 1996 and 2001 surveys, <www.latino barometro.com>.

17. Argentine data from Latinobarómetro surveys from 1995 through 2002, <www.latinobarometro.com>.

18. "La gente no se siente representada," *La Nación Line*, October 18, 2001. For similar comments about the greater ability of the Peronists to retain their traditional vote despite the growing cynicism of many about all politicians, see Juan Carlos Torre, "Los húerfanos de la política de partidos: Sobre los alcances y la naturaleza de la crisis de representación partidaria," *Desarrollo Económico* 42 (January–March 2003): 647–65.

19. Rosendo Fraga, "El significado del voto en blanco y nulo," October 16, 2001, <www.observatorioelectoral.org/informes/analisis/?country=argentina.file=0110161>.

20. "El 70% está insatisfecho con las instituciones políticas," *La Nación Line*, October 28, 2001.

21. Rumors circulated of efforts by Peronists close to Carlos Rukauf, governor of Buenos Aires Province, to organize crowds of looters to help destabilize the De la Rúa government. Former President Raúl Alfonsín, a rival of De la Rúa in the Radical Party, may also have played some role in seeking the president's ouster. See Miguel Bonasso, *El palacio y la calle: Crónicas de insurgentes y conspiradores* (Buenos Aires: Planeta, 2002), 149–52.

22. *Agence France Presse*, January 12, 2002, lexis-nexis <http://web.lexis-nexis.com/universe/>.

23. "Argentine Leader Seeks Broad Powers in Economic Crisis," *New York Times*, January 5, 2002, A3.

24. "Peronist for the Present," *New York Times*, January 3, 2002, lexis-nexis <http://web.lexis-nexis.com/universe/>.

25. *Latin American Southern Cone Report*, March 5, 2002 RS-02-02: 1.

26. "Quiet Exit of Argentine Top Brass Says Much," *Los Angeles Times*, June 14, 2003, A3.

27. *La Nación Line*, June 15, 2005. This Supreme Court decision created the possibility for reopening court cases interrupted in 1986 of those officers then accused of human rights violations. Some of these officers are still serving in the Argentine military.

28. "Argentine Leader Calls for Impeachment of Supreme Court," *New York Times*, June 6, 2003, lexis-nexis <http://web.lexis-nexis.com/universe/>.

29. "New Supreme Court Judge Appointed," *Latin News Daily*, December 22, 2004, lexis-nexis <http://web.lexis-nexis.com/universe/>.

30. "Argentine Moves Against Police Corruption," *New York Times*, November 17, 2003, lexis-nexis <http://web.lexis-nexis.com/universe/>.

31. "Crime Falls," *Latin News Daily,* January 11, 2005, lexis-nexis <http://web.lexis-nexis.com/universe/>.

32. *Dr. D. Néstor Carlos Kirchner, Mensaje Presidencial a la Honorable Asamblea Legislativa, March 1, 2004* (Buenos Aires: Secretaría Parlamentaría, Dirección Publicaciones, 2004), 7.

33. "IMF Deal a Close Victory," *Inter Press Service*, September 11, 2003, lexis-nexis <http://web.lexis-nexis.com/universe/>.

34. The government has insisted on lower fiscal surplus targets, on balancing targets with domestic growth rates, on keeping a cap on utility rates, and on continuing to tax exports to generate government revenues.

35. "Many View Argentina's Comeback with Skepticism," *Washington Post*, March 4, 2005, lexis-nexis <http://web.lexis-nexis.com/universe/>.

36. "Con una adhesión al canje del 76%, la Argentina dejó atrás el default," *La Nación Line*, March 4, 2005.

37. Ministerio de Economía, República Argentina, *Economic Indicators*, March 2005 <http//www.mecon.gov.ar>.

38. With higher world energy prices, Argentine inflation in 2005 seems likely to rise to at least 11–12% (see "Economía ahora acepta que la inflación podría llegar al 11%," *Clarín Internet*, April 12, 2005).

39. "Economic Rally for Argentines Defies Forecasts," *New York Times*, December 26, 2004, lexis-nexis <http://web.lexis-nexis.com/universe/>.

40. "Becoming a Serious Country," *The Economist* 371, no. 8378 (June 5, 2004): 3.

41. "Sliding Downwards?" *Latin American Regional Report: Southern Cone*, January 21, 2005, RBS-04-02: 14.

42. Menem's ratings reported in *BBC Summary of World Broadcasts*, February 16, 1990; *Latin American Weekly Report*, April 19, 1990, and March 7, 1991; *United Press International*, August 3, 1994, August 23, 1996; *Latin Finance*, September 1998, all lexis-nexis <http://web.lexis-nexis.com/universe/>.

43. Universidad Tocuato Di Tella, Escuela de Gobierno, "Indice de Confianza en el Gobierno," pp. 1–3, <http://www.utdt.edu/departamentos/gobierno/icg.htm>.

44. Néstor Kirchner and Torcuato Di Tella, *Después del derrumbe: Teoría y práctica política en la Argentina que viene* (Buenos Aires: Galerna, 2003), 125.

45. "Kirchner Courts Opposition," August 24, 2004, lexis-nexis <http://web.lexis-nexis.com/universe/>.

46. Néstor Kirchner and Torcuato Di Tella, *Después del derrumbe*, 130.

47. To some extent, this strategy follows from the president's own experiences in Santa Cruz, where he created a multi-party electoral front, Frente para la Vitoria Santacrucena, and then, after winning the governorship, brought members of the opposition into his cabinet. On his recent efforts to create a broader base of support, see "Kirchner Gets a Backup Party," *Latin American Weekly Report*, October 19, 2004, lexis-nexis <http://web.lexis-nexis.com/universe/>.

48. Mark Jones, et al., "Amateur Legislators—Professional Politicians: The Consequences of Party-Centered Electoral Rules in a Federal System," *American Journal of Political Science* 46 (July 2002): 656–69.

Part II

Causes of the Crisis

2

The Democratic Process in Argentina*

José Nun

> When we shift from what is best for prosperity to what is worst, the
> consensus would probably be that when there is a stronger incentive to
> take than to make—more gain from predation than from production and
> mutually advantageous activities—societies fall to the bottom.
>
> —Mancur Olson[1]

1

Certainly few observers would object to describing the recent Argentine situation in terms of the "disintegration of civil order, a breakdown of social discipline, the weakness of leaders, and the alienation of citizens." The only problem is that this picture was actually one sketched in the mid-1970s for Europe, North America, and Japan in an important report on democratic governability that the Trilateral Commission entrusted to three well-known specialists.[2] Is this account then only a tranquilizing memory meant to provide us consolation so we don't despair because of the poverty that Argentina is experiencing at this moment?

Not precisely. Because what above all is important to consider is the reasoning on which a description such as this is based. And this involves providing an interpretation of the supposedly negative consequences that these same factors had, factors that authors like Raymond Aron or Daniel Bell twenty years earlier had considered the true pillars supporting the capitalist democracies of the West.

One was the mixed economy (seen by many as the most important economic innovation of the twentieth century); another, the Welfare State ("a type of capitalism moderated by an injection of socialism," in the words of T. H. Marshall); and the third, sustained and growing prosperity.

According to Huntington and his colleagues in the Trilateral Commission Report, all these contributed so much activism to the democracy of the 1960s that things departed from their normal pattern, unleashing the governability crisis of the 1970s. In accord with this highly conservative reading, the people—stimulated by criticism presented in the mass media and by the emergence of new social movements—developed exaggerated expectations, raised ever greater demands, and ended up losing confidence in institutions and challenging the existing bases of authority at all levels. In a word, a series of unacceptable *excesses* supposedly occurred that destabilized the political system. What were these "excesses" (a term that plays a key role in the Report)? An excessive reduction of inequalities and an excessive increase in political participation that ended up producing an "excess of democracy" (*sic*) that became an excessive burden on governments;[3] and from this, recurrent fiscal crises and the inflation that would become the "economic illness of democracies."[4]

As can be seen, the description that I transcribed at the beginning of this chapter alluded to a particular state of things that was basically attributed to the excess of those from below, favored by policies of full employment, by progressive income redistribution, and by the great amount of growth that characterized the "thirty glorious years" of the postwar period. This diagnosis would herald the policies that right-wing governments like those of Thatcher and Reagan would implement a little later, with the explicit purpose of defusing the "democratic bomb," re-imposing order, broadening and strengthening the position of the large economic conglomerates, and disciplining a work force that was seen as having acquired too much power. The struggle against inflation from then on displaced the fight against unemployment as the principal macroeconomic concern, and both the mixed economy and the Welfare State were put on trial with all blame directed at them.

The Argentine case illustrates an evolution that has little or nothing in common with what was described above for the developed countries—really its exact opposite—that for some time produced results immensely more disastrous than what happened in such places. There is a critical aspect of the Argentine evolution that was not envisioned in the analysis to which I have referred (despite the key role that it had in the outbreak of the depression of the 1930s in the industrialized capitalist countries). I speak of the severe governability crisis that can be caused by the excesses of those *at the top,* not those below. Stated differently, what happens to representative democracy when it is defined simply as a system of possible equilibrium in which the popular majority is subjected without any concern to the interests and designs of economic and politically dominant minorities? When far from having an "excess of democracy," there is an "excess of concentrated, exclusionary rent-seeking capitalism"? If all the representative democracies we know are at their heart elected oligarchies, what happens when one of these oligarchies seeks to perpetuate itself through all the means in its power and becomes increasingly disconnected from its base, contributing to the marginalization and impoverishment of a great part of the population?

To be fair, while it is clear that the informants used by the Trilateral Commission did not either then or now pay any attention to this type of excess, at least they were convinced that "a social structure in which wealth and education are found concentrated in the hands of a few cannot lead to democracy."[5] In truth, they were only repeating one of the major premises on which the analysis of every theorist of procedural democracy from Schumpeter onward was founded and that unfortunately their Latin American disciples of the last two decades were determined to ignore with a determination worthy of a better cause.[6]

Here lies one of the most important keys for decoding a part of what I elsewhere called the "Argentine enigma."[7] According to the theoretical and ideological modernization paradigm disseminated since the 1950s, countries in effect pass through three major historical stages: first, that of economic development; almost simultaneously, the stage of social development; and finally—once these prerequisites are present—that of political development understood as the installation of a constitutional regime of representative democracy. In the postwar years, Argentina enjoyed appreciable levels of economic and social development; nevertheless, its political outcome was Peronist populism and not representative democracy (as happened, let us say, in Uruguay or in Chile). This is the anomaly that Germani and others tried to explain and with which I will not concern myself here except to say that it provided the historical basis for the construction of a very imbalanced type of citizenship where the social dimension clearly predominated over the civil and the political.

What I am now interested in noting is the extent to which a half century later this enigma has inverted its terms. As the roles indicate, Argentina is now a representative democracy while at the same time the country is notably underdeveloped economically and socially (in terms of the collapse of its currency, of salaries, industries, equality, social protection, nutrition, growth of its production, etc.).

In brief, previously, modernization did not bring us democracy. Today, democracy seems far from bringing us modernization. The thesis I want to defend is that this result is due to the characteristics and particular effects of the social aspects of the type of capital accumulation that began to take form from the mid-1970s and reached its height in the 1990s. It is worth clarifying that reference to social aspects of accumulation is not simply to speak of the economic system, but of the always particular institutions, rules, and public and private practices through which this system is set up, of the operational modes that characterize it, of the type of actors who shape it, and of the relations established between the economic and the political regime of government.[8]

2

In his posthumous work already cited, Mancur Olson resorts to what he prudently calls a "metaphor" to shed light on certain central mechanisms related to the logic of economic power. Through historical examples, he distinguishes the behavior of those he calls "roving bandits" from that of "stationary bandits." The interests of the first are very restricted, consisting basically in taking possession of all that they find in their path so that, like Attila, it is of no concern to them whether the grass grows again since they have no intention of staying. The second, on the other hand, are concerned to leave their victims enough to allow them to continue producing so that they can continue to be exploited; it is even probable that they provide their victims with certain public goods like education, health, security, etc., to increase their productivity and, in this way, the surplus that they expropriate. Going even further, their participation in society can become so integral a part of it that "their own self interest brings them to act as if they were totally benevolent."[9]

My citation of Olson is as intentional as is his metaphor. I believe that it helps us to understand an important aspect of what has happened in Argentina since the current cycle of finance capital hegemony was initiated. That beginning can be set in the mid-1970s first with the measures introduced by Economics Minister Rodrigo (what became known as the "Rodrigazo") and later, in a context of intense political repression, the program of his successor Martínez de Hoz that opened the economy and totally liberalized financial movements. Going beyond their origins, the advantage of focusing on these key events is to establish from the beginning that the initiation of this cycle was a deliberate result of measures adopted by governments that had policy alternatives available to them. The result of this first alliance between the non-benevolent "stationary bandits" who controlled the economic levers of the military dictatorship and the "roving bandits" who arrived mounted on their petrodollars to obtain enormous speculative profits (in addition to—among other things—the unproductive use that was made of available funds) was an unprecedented crisis: a large fall in production per capita, a phenomenally regressive redistribution of income, an annual three-digit inflation rate that no other country put up with for as long a period, and an oppressive foreign debt that would be the basis for the operations of the so-called "financial establishment" (or *patria financiera*).

This was the situation when the government of Raúl Alfonsín sought to inaugurate a political regime of representative democracy (or rather, as he himself was very late in understanding, the transition to a regime with such characteristics). Note that, like roving bandits, speculative financial capital is essentially short term in its operation, moving on with great rapidity in the face of any sign of risk. This is what happened here after the disaster of the Falklands War and the Mexican default of 1982. In a context in which interest rates in the central countries were rising as well, such groups perceived that Argentina was also technically in a virtual cessation of payments. They did not immediately notice the increasing contradiction between the verbal attacks that Alfonsín publicly made against special interests and the actual practices that relied increasingly on a dialogue behind closed doors between Radical Party officials and the leaders of those interests and of the multilateral financial organizations.[10]

It is not surprising then that in the middle of growing economic deterioration (like the failure of the Austral Plan, the flight of bank deposits, the lack of credit) and political problems (defeat in the legislative and gubernatorial elections of 1987) the government ended up by openly seeking to appeal to both domestic and foreign speculators with the so-called Spring Plan. How? By guaranteeing them that there would be no devaluation and by investing in the austral currency, they would receive an interest rate of 10% per month at a time when the interest rate in the United States was 10% annually.[11] How did they finance this extraordinary transfer of resources? Essentially by the "inflationary tax" that increasingly weighed more on workers and all other citizens with fixed incomes.

The problem is that mobile capitalists soon began to smell the risk of a highly unstable situation, complicated by the unexpected political rise of the then still feared Menemist populism. The Alfonsín government sought to restrain them with the promise of a loan that the World Bank would give Argentina, although it became known some time later that in reality it would not be immediately accessible.[12] Finally, in February 1989 there was a run on the banks, after a large-scale hemorrhaging of Central Bank reserves failed to prevent a devaluation. Inflation became unstoppable, and between May and June surpassed 100% monthly. The storm blew Alfonsín away (he was responsible for much but not all of the winds that produced it), and he had to turn over the presidency six months before the end of his term.

My objective here of course is not to produce a chronicle or even less a detailed examination of what occurred in the last two decades, but simply to point out the plausibility of the thesis I earlier suggested. But before continuing, it is suitable to clear up several possible misunderstandings.

The first is that the Olson metaphor that I defend is obviously not applicable to the entirety of capitalist groups that have operated and still operate in Argentina. The reader should not confuse a part (which I see as very important) of history with all of history. Stated differently, big businessmen and especially economic groups may or may not behave as if they were either roving or stationary bandits, according to circumstances. My argument is that in Argentina particularly favorable conditions were created for the majority of them to do so, with the added point that the logic of roving bandits prevailed; over the years both the area for and the traditionally benevolent behavior of stationary bandits were visibly reduced. This happened in a situation of predicted frequent conflicts between these bandits that strengthened the "protective" role of the real Mafias enmeshed in the state bureaucracy.

The second clarification (precisely because I allude to styles of behavior) is that mobile capital has not been nor is it necessarily foreign while stationary capital has not been nor is it necessarily domestic in origin. In essence, one of the principal themes of Alfonsín's 1983 campaign was that he pledged himself to unravel what were the real characteristics of the foreign debt his government inherited, distinguishing between legitimate and illegitimate creditors, since a good part of the latter consisted of Argentine citizens who had sent capital abroad only to later bring it back disguised as fake loans.[13] This is a topic that like so many others would remain an unfulfilled promise, something that would offend people increasingly in the next few years.

If, on the other hand, not all capitalists operating in the country should be treated as stationary bandits, there were many very important groups who were accustomed to act as if they were, never questioning the propriety of such behavior. Considerable evidence of this is found, ranging from the one-sided contracts with the state (signed by what came to be called the *patria contratista* or "contract-enriched elite" with its basic corruption) to large-scale tax evasion and acts of fraud meant to swindle the Treasury found in a good number of the supposed "industrial promotion" schemes introduced, from that moment on.

3

With the presidency of Carlos Menem, the excesses of those at the top would grow in a manner as spectacular as it was scandalous. If the Alfonsín government courted the large groups of businessmen, anticipating what they would do and negotiating to swap advantages it would give them in exchange for their support, the Menem government from the beginning simply turned management of the economy over to one of these groups. At the same time, it took advantage of the crisis to obtain from Congress a delegation of legislative powers to the chief executive of a scope and depth that no Argentine constitutional government had ever previously enjoyed.

First using omnibus legislation like the Economic Emergency and State Reform Laws and later through a body of tax measures, the government gained exclusive say in many policy areas: over the privatization of a long list of public companies, as well as the concessions of almost all public services; the possibility to authorize foreign indebtedness to cover all this; the level and characteristics of trade tariffs; the creation or suppression of public subsidies; sole control of the application of the value-added tax; decisions over the de-regulation or re-regulation of markets; etc.[14] As someone who later would be one of the top ideologues of Menemism explained early on, the government sought to reconstruct the power of the state "from its roots up," to implement what "conceptually can precisely be called a 'conservative revolution.'"[15]

Use was newly made of an exorbitant rate of interest to attract investment and the country again began to move toward hyperinflation. While the price of the dollar shot up, a fresh economic team sought to control it using a procedure unlikely to generate much public confidence. At the end of 1989, the Bonex Plan confiscated all fixed-term bank deposits, substituting for them bonds maturing in ten years that initially reduced the value of the original deposits by 70%. The rate of the dollar fell, but at the cost of a strong recession and rapidly rising inflation. A little later, Domingo Cavallo was made economics minister and, at the beginning of 1991 in a context where the exchange rate was obviously overvalued, launched the Convertibility Plan, setting a one-to-one parity between the peso and the dollar. The Plan would achieve two things: it would end inflation and definitively consolidate the cycle of finance capital hegemony.

It is true that in the next three years the Argentine economy grew at an exceptionally high rate. But as would be better appreciated later, a series of circumstantial factors that would not be repeated were involved here, ones that did not affect the increases in productivity that various sectors experienced.[16] In the first instance, the international liquidity of mobile capitalists was at an all-time high, and many also turned their eyes to Argentina, in addition to other places, attracted by an absolute absence of restriction on capital movement, very favorable interest rates, the support given the country by the international credit organizations, a series of fiscal incentives, and the free exchange rate guarantee provided by the Convertibility Plan. In the second place, this flow was greatly strengthened by the least controlled and most rapid privatization program with the lowest business risk in memory, that famous "sale of the crown jewels" that liquidated and denationalized the greater part of all public enterprise.[17] A third element that also turned out to be momentary was the expansion of tax collection obtained through an increasingly regressive tax system, one that came to depend on ever higher indirect taxes like the VAT while exempting the financial earnings and dividends of the owners of corporate business.

In any case, the lack of a genuine program for development and especially of positive industrial policies (with a very few exceptions favorable to big business like the special situation protecting the automobile industry based on the virtual reserve of the domestic market to a handful of assembly plants) led to the expansionary phase ending in the 1995 recession, influenced to a great extent by the withdrawal of mobile capital frightened by the Mexican crisis of the previous year. The picture once again changed favorably in the 1996–1998 period, up until the second half of that last year when the country entered a process of growing depression. (This was the moment selected by the International Monetary Fund to invite Menem to speak before its General Assembly, a privilege shared until then only by the presidents of the United States.)

In the new social regime for financial accumulation that began to emerge in the 1970s, movements of short-term capital were seen as constituting the autonomous factor accounting for the fluctuations of production and employment.[18] One of the most visible effects of this dynamic has been the historically never before experienced frequency and intensity of the waves of recession experienced by the country: 1975–1976, 1978, 1981–1982, 1989–1990, 1995, 1999–2002. Under the conditions described here, the weakness and vulnerability of the autonomous sources for generating foreign exchange demonstrated by the facts of the present case suggested that a program like the Convertibility Plan could be maintained only at the price of continuous foreign borrowing (which strongly increased from 1993) and by an extraordinary increase in under- and unemployment that soon reached their highest levels in the country's history. In reality, these are two factors that are intertwined. Ever since the introduction of the Brady Plan, the conflict-filled alliance between mobile and stationary capital always made servicing the debt the principal focus of economic policy, so as to avoid setting off an alarm in the computers of mobile capitalists.[19]

4

People say that Milton Friedman never accepted an official position, so as to avoid having his orthodox neo-liberalism tarnished by the obligations that political activity always requires. His Argentine followers have lacked the same concern; on the contrary, they have sought to exaggerate the impact of such official commitments so as to avoid the responsibility falling to them for the present disaster. For example, it is true that the Convertibility Plan was locally generated and that the IMF never welcomed it. But this does not change the fact that they gave it widespread support and made Argentina the model case for the advantages and effectiveness of the so-called "Washington Consensus." In effect, the neo-liberal canon was one of the greatest ideological supports of the particular "conservative revolution" headed by Menem; as late as 1998, then IMF head Michel Camdessus did not hesitate to call him the "best President" that the country had had "in the last fifty years."

According to this canon, the motor for growth is investment in fixed capital that, in turn, requires low interest rates. At the same time, this is possible only in a context of stable prices and high levels of saving. Consequently, inflation is seen as the principal enemy of growth. To fight it, one must among other things shrink the size of the state and have a balanced budget, a flexible labor market to avoid any inflationary pressure from salaries, and a free trade policy to promote competition. This is, it is said, exactly the path followed by the United States under Clinton. What evidence is there to confirm this? That country's rapid growth in the 1950s and 1960s when inflation was low; its poor results since, when inflation rose and savings declined; and the bonanza of the 1990s when stable prices returned, the fiscal deficit disappeared, savings increased, and the government drastically reduced its role.

As often happens, the logic of this type of reasoning is impeccable when one accepts its premises. And these are premises that have little basis in fact, as has been reasonably demonstrated.[20] The error is to have attributed a causal link to two processes that simply coexisted at the same time. The decline of United States inflation occurred *prior* to the policies I mentioned above. Not only did such growth not result from those policies, but they seriously limited it, failing to resolve the problem of inequality, and bringing the country to the edge of recession. What happened then? As with the steam engine and the electric motor, major technological changes always take time to mature. It is only recently, since the end of the 1980s, that the informatics revolution began to really bear fruit, generating unexpected and spectacular increases in productivity. It was these increases that made profits (but not prices) increase. It is to these that that monetary stability was due, not to deregulation and a balanced budget. Moreover, the push for and a good part of the funds that initially financed that revolution came from the government. Remember, for example, the enormous defense expenditure that Reagan (whom Galbraith called "a great Keynesian" for this) implemented.

One can outline an alternative model quite distinct from that of neo-liberal propaganda, much more firmly based in historical evidence, and having the explicit goal of equitable development. In this model, the motor for growth is technological innovation, not investment itself. To a considerable degree such innovation is a non-accidental product of a specific context. What is needed are public and private policies actively promoting research and development, big government investment in infrastructure, the continual expansion of education and training, etc. The priority is not a fiscally balanced budget, but balanced social growth. But this is not obtained simply by saying it. The model requires that demand expand to the maximum, not in any old way, but through the increase of salaries encouraged by both state and trade union action. As Lester Thurow showed, higher salaries lead to higher productivity and not, as was believed, the reverse.[21] As to the rest, everything indicates that the most meaningful sign for markets is the extent of expected future demand and not the level of interest rates.

5

From the perspective of the reading adopted here, the non-application in a case like Argentina of principles like those mentioned (that, for example, had already functioned successfully in their particular way in Southeast Asia) but rather of those of the "Wall Street model" (or the "Washington Consensus") supported among other things opening the gates of the country increasingly to roving capitalists and inducing the rapid concentration and centralization of stationary capitalism. The latter combined rising financial values with production-based rents in oligopolistic markets that produced many more external than domestically oriented chains of multipliers. The consequences that followed are today irrefutable.

To cite Schvarzer, "In the 1949–1974 period, industry multiplied its value-added more than three times, becoming the motor of the economy and the principal source of employment and wealth in the country." In contrast, official figures properly recalculated "suggest that industry did not grow in terms of its productive contribution over the last quarter of the century."[22] The tremendous resulting deindustrialization process was not compensated for by other mechanisms creating wealth that benefited the entirety of society. According to different criteria used in measurement, product per capita increased between 48% and 67% over the twenty-five years of the "closed economy" (1949–1974); in the following quarter of a century dominated by neo-liberal policies, such growth was practically nil. And the country passed from traditionally occupying first place in Latin America in income per capita to today being behind Uruguay, Chile, Brazil, Mexico, and Venezuela.[23]

This absolutely should not be read as an unrestricted elegy for the "closed economy," but as a critique of the unusual *excesses of those at the top* who are at the center of the supposed "conservative revolution" from which Argentina is suffering. As the average measure that it is, the lack of growth per capita hides the brutal shift of income toward the richest *who have turned out to be the winners in every phase of the economic cycle*. Official data from November 2001 for the Federal Capital and Greater Buenos Aires indicate that the difference between the 20% with the most resources (who have 53% of the income) and the 20% with the least resources grew from 7.8 times in 1974 to 14.6 times in 2001; if one takes only the first and the last decile, there is evidence that the difference expanded from 12 to 28 times. (Given the propensity of the rich to under-declare their income and of the poor to over-declare theirs, in reality it is probable that these gaps are much greater. One should remember that the figures refer to annual income and not to accumulated wealth.)

This increase in inequality that places Argentina among the fifteen countries with the worst income distribution in the world has been accompanied by three other phenomena of similar gravity. One is unemployment: in 1993 at the height of the Convertibility Plan, open unemployment for the first time in the last half century reached 10%, doubling after the Tequila crisis and today affecting approximately one-third of a work force where the overwhelming majority lacks any form of social protection. To this one can add similar figures for under-employment, with between 40% and 50% of the workers not officially registered (including many employed in large companies or in the public sector). A second phenomenon is the decline of real income from 1984 (barely interrupted in 1991–1992) so that the worker earnings ended up falling to levels analogous to those of a half century earlier. In the third place, as of 2002, over half the population was below a poverty line that barely exceeds the minimum needed for mere subsistence (and this in a country that produces food sufficient for a population ten times larger than the present one). To this one can add that six out of ten of the new poor created in the last decade have come from the formerly powerful Argentine middle class.

These elements are sufficient to indicate the looting that has occurred in Argentina and why it is not arbitrary to use a metaphor like Olson's to try to understand it, at least in part. The cycle of finance capital hegemony clearly has also been that of the excess in the participation of large-scale capital in public affairs to its exclusive benefit. I now intend to explore some of the general effects that this has had on the governing political regime.

6

If it is clear that banditry does not recognize frontiers, it is also true that one of the principal obligations of governments is to protect their citizens from it and to stop it from prospering. As Manent emphasizes, the function of guarding and protection is always inherent in the legitimate exercise of sovereignty.[24] This was not the case in Argentina, especially in the past decade. Moreover, in order to carry off its own type of "conservative revolution," it was not sufficient for Menemism to obtain the extraordinary delegation of legislative powers to which I have already referred, nor to resort incessantly to "decrees of urgent necessity" and the partial or total veto of laws that did not please it. It also needed to increase to the maximum its independence from the courts so that the type of extreme decisional power it exercised was never subject to judicial control. It obtained this in two ways that shook the bases of a state of law that earlier had been seriously weakened by the End Point and Due Obedience Laws and that later would be further undermined by the amnesty granted those responsible for military state terrorism.

On the one hand, it increased the size of the Supreme Court from five to nine members, assuring itself of an "automatic majority" that ratified even the least defensible of its measures. (Here I add information that transcends the merely anecdotal. The only explicit justification given for the increase was that the Court would be able to divide into two specialized chambers so as to operate with greater efficiency. In its first decision, the Court decided *not* to divide itself into separate chambers.) On the other hand, the government managed to completely revise the jurisdiction of the federal courts—that is, the specifications dealing with the cases they could resolve, loading the courts with judges who were politically loyal. Added to the administration's control of Congress, both circumstances not only achieved the de facto destruction of the division of powers, but also resulted in a regrettable fall in the suitability of critical sectors of the judiciary.

To this were added phenomena like the sinecures, the purely capricious nominations and promotions in certain courts, and a general under-financing gravely affecting both judicial action and credibility, resulting in the loss of prestige of judges who surely did not deserve it. (In this sense, it is perhaps useful to warn that systems like the courts are indivisible: it follows that when one part is corrupted—especially if this affects the head—people lose faith in the whole where the use of any specific resource is unclear.)

At the same time, a similar erosion of the directive centers of the judiciary guaranteed the impunity of numerous public officials and of political, business, and union leaders, people who gave in to the climate of the moment, colluded with both mobile and stationary capitalists, and amassed enormous fortunes to facilitate their activities regardless of whether these were legal or not. This is to say that the low "opportunity cost" of corruption acquired such magnitude from then on that a trade unionist (today a senator) could say without blushing or suffering any negative consequences, "If we stopped stealing for two years, the country would be saved." The situation was widely denounced by the healthier parts of the press and, not by accident, the reply of the accused (including the president of the Republic) was always the same: let the courts decide."[25]

Under these conditions, and despite the efforts that were made, it was not possible to create a highly able, well-paid, and ethically irreproachable public bureaucracy that as in other countries could guarantee the continuity, transparency, and efficiency of state action. Conspiring against this was the atmosphere of corruption, the clientelist favors, the constant changes in top personnel, and the inadequate and often capricious budgetary allocations. This is to say that this important space in the state for the design, implementation, and evaluation of public policies and for the defense of the collective interest failed to function even moderately well. Three examples that illustrate this with great clarity are the sterile accumulation and very meager results of social programs, the general failure (if not the direct complicity) of those agencies charged with supervising and regulating the performance of the companies that were privatized, and the overwhelming incompetence of fiscal controls at all levels.[26]

The other side (and often the cause) of these considerable limitations of the state bureaucracy was the persistent partisan take-over of places meant for professional career officials. This tendency began during the government of Alfonsín (who, furthermore, broke a long-time Radical Party tradition by occupying both the party presidency and the presidency of the Republic) and culminated under Menem, with both men reducing party autonomy to a minimum. Here one could compare the Justicialista Party of the 1990s to the Mexican PRI, given their organization "from the top down, from cabinet offices down to every local territorial unit" and their partial or total financing with public funds at a time when "money replaced voluntary enthusiasm as a strategic resource in internal struggles."[27]

Such struggles no doubt existed but were rarely a sign of any real democratic party vitality. With both the Radicals and the Peronists, these consisted in confrontations, negotiations, and agreements among party chiefs, be they on the eve of elections, in the constant disputes for funds between governors and the central administration, or at the level of legislative debates and deals. There was no authentic citizen participation, not even when the center-left FREPASO coalition entered the scene, an entity that depended essentially on the continuous presence of its leaders in the mass media and not on any more or less coherent organizational force to grow beyond its initial bases.

There is little doubt that the crisis of representation has become a quite habitual phenomenon in various contemporary societies, with factors varying from the fragmentation and disintegration of social classes to the image of politics portrayed on television—not to mention the enormous weight acquired by large corporations in this globalized world—all being strongly influential. It is also certain that in representative democracy by definition there ought always to exist some distance between those governing and those governed. Such a distance varies between two extremes: where there is none, we encounter direct democracy; where it is total, tyranny. In between, the amount of such separation that is tolerable is indeterminable a priori, depending on history, cultural traditions, competing ideologies, organizational forms, etc. What I am trying to say, therefore, is that under the conditions I have described for Argentina, the distance became so big that from the mid-1990s it ended up leading to the virtual breakdown of any representation. Going just a little bit further, this breakdown is the more visible aspect of a much greater problem that the failure of the De la Rúa government worsened. I allude to a true vacuum in public life, what Hegel called the loss of an objective sense of morality or *Sittlichkeit*. We could refer thus not to the Kantian individual subjectivity of what one ought to do, but to collective morality, to the language expressed daily in the institutions and concrete practices of a society that provides a sense of existence to those who inhabit it.[28] In this regard, when institutions no longer fulfill the purposes for which they were created and people lose confidence in the politicians, businessmen, trade unionists, or police, one enters an alienated world lacking any sense.[29]

Again, let empirical evidence suffice.[30] For the large majority of Argentines interviewed at the beginning of the crisis in late 2001/early 2002, politics had become synonymous with terms for corruption and privilege, where some 75% of the sample showed no interest in getting involved in it (PNUD). Three of every four neither identified with the Argentine democratic system nor believed that the rest of the citizenry confided in it (IBOPE). Fewer than 5% had a positive view of legislators (0.9%), the Judiciary (0.8%), judges (1.8%), Congress (4.9%), governors (1.8%), or of the relationship of political parties (2.2%) or the state (4.8%) with society (IBOPE). Some 70% thought that citizen opinion counted for nothing and a majority stated that large-scale national and foreign capital has more power than the government (PNUD). It is worth noting that only some 25% of those interviewed in early 2002 in a PNUD poll stated that politicians were those principally responsible for the crisis the country was experiencing, while some 72% attributed the situation to "the entire leadership class"; that is, to "the politicians, bankers, trade unionists, businessmen, judges, etc." To all this one can add that the repudiation of the privatized public services had risen to an unheard-of 88% (PNUD).

The data presented here have an important corollary. While some 76% of the respondents in June 1995 considered that "democracy is preferable to any other form of government," around 40% in both October 2001 and February 2002 no longer believed that. It is no surprise that such a figure exhibited a clear positive correlation with the economic and social level of those interviewed (PNUD). Still further, between four and five of every ten people interviewed in October admitted that they would tolerate "an authoritarian government if problems of safety and economics were in some way resolved" (PNUD). In addition, it is revealing that the proportion of those offering the opinion that a democracy can function without political parties increased almost 50% between October 2001 and February 2002, rising from 28% to 41% (PNUD).

Of course, an organic crisis of such depth always produces multiple reactions. One of these—noticed and characterized by the same Hegel two hundred years ago—consists precisely in an even more intense retreat to the crude individualism of the "save yourself whoever can" sort, which increases the bandit-like behavior I mentioned before. A second response is flight: the potential and actual flow of emigrants today reaches levels without precedent during periods of constitutional government. A third case is the increase in phenomena varying from seeking refuge in religious communities, in the "culture of narcissism," or in esoteric practices, to addiction and criminality, especially among the young.

At the other extreme, in addition to the strengthening of existent social movements, new and original attitudes of solidarity of various forms and impact emerged among diverse sectors of society: the National Front for the Struggle against Poverty (that in December 2001 managed to collect over three million votes in its call for a minimum income for the unemployed), the "piquetero" movements of the unemployed, the barter clubs, the popular assemblies, the "cacerolazo" street protests of people banging on pots and pans, etc. The obvious question is why this popular reaction against the looting took so long and why these mobilizations were only relatively marginal in effect.[31]

To answer this would require studies that are still not available. I imagine at any rate that the answer among other things has to be seen first in the expectations that the fall of the dictatorship awoke, and afterwards by the defeat of hyper-inflation, as well as the saturation of ideological space by neo-liberalism that it alone provided the only possible answers, together with the way in which the political parties and trade unions (with a few exceptions) ended up taking over the channels for expressing citizen views and the disillusion that followed from the unfulfilled promises of the leaders in whom many believed. Whatever its form, the threshold for popular protest is usually high in representative regimes. Here in early 2002, this was finally close to being breached by the desperation of the marginalized (and their need to make themselves heard), as well as by the indignation of those sectors of the middle class that, on the one hand, saw their savings once again confiscated and, on the other, slowly began to construct new spaces for equality and solidarity.

In any case, it is pertinent to my argument to point out that the increasing foci of resistance that broke out in those months would add three major demands to the predictable calls for work, safety, justice, or education: (1) that the looting of the country should cease, (2) that ties be cut with the International Monetary Fund (seen as the source responsible for and the guarantor of the economic policies adopted in the 1990s), and (3) that all the politicians should go ("Que se vayan todos").

7

At the level of the social attributes needed for capital accumulation, I said that the neo-liberal canon was the principal ideological support for what happened in Argentina, refracted through the prism of the plunder that I described. To this one should add that a doctrine of negative liberty has prevailed at the level of the political regime in power where liberty is simply the absence of any government interference. The combination of that canon and this doctrine served here to clear the way for the bandits and to justify the excesses of those at the top.[32] We shall rapidly see why.

The neo-classical/neo-liberal schema rests on three known bases. One is the strict separation of the economy from politics since it is presumed that the first is endowed with its own self-sufficient logic. Another that necessarily derives from the first is the idea that economic agents operate guided purely by criteria of instrumental rationality. The third is that the problem of income distribution is not central, as Adam Smith or David Ricardo believed, but should be resolved by laissez-faire, where, in the meantime, nothing should interfere with any action affecting the market. (As Von Hayek stated in the 1940s, "The demand for a just income distribution is a relic of the past based on the primary emotions and fomented by prophets and moralists.") Therefore, from such a perspective, the role assigned to the state is minimal and subsidiary, and the task of the present is to put an end to the importance this topic had over the last two hundred years.

In respect to the doctrine of negative liberty, one reinforces it by pursuing another path to the same goal. If liberty, on the one hand, is merely synonymous with the absence of foreign obstacles to individual action, among other things, it is obvious that market deregulation, the relaxation of restrictions, the primacy of private initiative, and the like prevail as necessary principles. But what above all tends to follow from this perspective is that once liberal democracy is established, all citizens are free by definition since it is thought that liberty is something that can exist independently of its actual use.[33] Note that, in this view, anyone is free to study, to circulate, to associate, etc.; if one fails to do this for lack of the means, that does not affect one's condition as a free person, simply his capacity to make use of the liberty that it is presumed he enjoys in all areas.

Whether one wishes to acknowledge it or not, the conclusion reached is exactly what neo-liberalism has always claimed in its struggle against the Welfare State: that is, that government has the obligation to limit itself to guaranteeing the liberty of its citizens, not to assuring its exercise. To the contrary, every time that it attempts to achieve the latter, it would be violating its mission since it ends up interfering with the liberty of economic actors and of markets that are the only way to obtain an optimal allocation of available resources.

Thus a logical circle plagued with fallacies is here completed, one which was no less effective from an ideological perspective, to the extent that it was taken for granted by the principal Argentine parties in one way or another. Above all, this ignores that any commitment to liberty also implies a commitment to the social preconditions that make it possible. If these are not present, if that "basic equality of conditions" of which Tocqueville spoke does not exist, if a person does not possess even a minimum amount of dignity and is dominated by fears as elementary as whether he can survive, he is deprived of any moral autonomy and his presumed liberty is just a fantasy. As Leon Blum maintained years ago, "Any society that wishes to assure men of liberty ought to begin by guaranteeing their basic existence."[34]

At the same time, all historical evidence indicates that it is incorrect to postulate a sharp separation between economics and politics, as if markets, for example, could function beyond the institutions and norms that structure them, or that property rights did not imply a right to exclude others that requires enforcement by public authorities. It has been clear for some time that one can have a state without capitalism, but not capitalism without a state. From here, one sees that so-called deregulation is, in reality, the name always given to re-regulation favoring new interests, as the Argentine case abundantly demonstrates.[35]

But, specially, there is no valid proof that collective economic welfare can be generated merely through laissez-faire. First, as ul-Haq once made clear, because all models of production contain determined distributive goals and not others. And second, without sustained action by the state, the famous "spillover effect" is nothing more than a neo-liberal propagandistic slogan.[36] Above all, because wherever mobile capitalists dominate and governments do not protect their people, the degree of benevolence of stationary capitalists is reduced almost to the point of disappearance and their behavior is increasingly similar to that of the first group. The culmination of this process is not only tax avoidance or capital flight, but the movement of their businesses to other countries, or, often, their sale to mobile capitalists who mortgage them, gut their resources, and divide them up. All this, without mentioning the repeated practices of back-to-back loans that permit them to obtain extraordinary profits as, for example, with the indiscriminate conversion of bank debts in dollars into pesos decreed in early 2002 by the government amid a devaluation process that had gotten out of control.

The consequences are now fully visible, and they make the similarity of Argentine representative democracy to those habitually cited as paradigms (the developed Western capitalist nations) ever more remote. There is little reason to wonder about this. I have explained elsewhere what I called "the singular Latin American paradox of our days": that is, "while in the First World both the old and the new democracies were consolidated in the context of a marked decline in inequality, poverty, and polarization, here the opposite is happening, and the current democratization processes are accompanied by a critical increase in the three phenomena."[37]

But there is something that singles out and makes the Argentine situation worse. First, together with Uruguay and later with Costa Rica, Argentina was the capitalist country with the highest level of social integration in Latin America. If in other places the concern was and remains how to incorporate those who were largely excluded from full rights, the Argentine drama focuses on the increasing marginalization of those who had been so incorporated many years earlier. In terms of the dimensions of citizenship classically defined by T. H. Marshall, we witness the profound and extended process of partial or full deprivation of citizenship occurring within the crisis of institutions and public liberties to which I alluded. The question that is raised is to establish at what point a representative democracy loses its right to the name, given the low percentage of full citizens it houses.

8

How will this story end? I do not know. I am only sure that for it to end well, it will be necessary, among other things, to liquidate the banditry; to strengthen (and in many cases to change) institutions; to reconstruct the social safety net and public life, with all that this implies in normative terms and in terms of organization; to implement positive policies for production and employment; to redistribute income and wealth progressively; to expand citizenship rights; to reform both politics and the public bureaucracy at national and provincial levels; and to decisively put an end to the excesses of those at the top.

I stress that the experience of successful liberal democracy demonstrates that its consolidation has depended on a state-promoted and guaranteed social accord reconciling capitalism's desire for profit with the prosperity and welfare of the majority of citizens. When this commitment is weakened (or fully disappears), those democracies are weakened (or fully disappear).

Is there any indication that Argentina is moving toward such an accord? One might possibly think so, given the unprecedented drama both of the situation the country recently has gone through and of certain official declarations, plus the quite auspicious fact that even under such circumstances, some 80% of the population still believes that it is possible to improve the quality of politics and the politicians (PNUD).

However, a weak government like Duhalde's increasingly would give in to the pressure of those domestically and abroad responsible for the catastrophe, allowing the media spokesmen of the neo-liberal position, after a brief silence, to enthusiastically return to their special advocacy. Symbolic of what I am describing is the appeal for the resumption of guaranteed legality (or "seguridad jurídica") raised like a banner by the same people who profited as many times as they could from the erosion of laws and contracts and from the many forms of corruption that became common.

It is worth providing a couple of examples. The petroleum companies (which thanks to the legislation passed by Menem are no longer nationally owned and are obliged to return to the country only some 30% of the income they obtain through exporting a non-renewable resource like the one they exploit) have eluded with impunity the measures that required them to keep local prices at international levels (and not higher). As Zaiat notes, "With the deregulation of the sector during the 1990s, the petroleum companies made an extraordinary profit of 4.5 billion dollars by not complying with the law. That legal anomaly was paid for by the consumers."[38] In their turn, in connivance with the appropriate authorities and in a country experiencing deflation, the privatized public utilities arranged to index their prices by U.S. inflation (*sic*), violating explicit dispositions of the Convertibility Law. Thanks to this, they obtained 9 billion dollars in additional profits in the 1991–2000 period. In neither of these cases did mobile and stationary capitalists or their local and foreign partners raise their voices to denounce the lack of legal order that such maneuvers implied; they were also silent when the De la Rúa government suddenly decreed the reduction of the salaries of public employees and the pensions of retirees. On the other hand, they rend their garments when some judge today orders bankers to testify who not long ago were presumed to have organized the flight of billions of dollars from Argentina, or when proposals to revise the unfair contracts of privatized companies arise.

Another important symbolic act is the conduct of the International Monetary Fund that not only called for the reinstatement of legal guarantees, but demanded major adjustments and cuts of public spending during a recession that had gone on for over four years and finally became a true depression. What country of the so-called First World would follow such a path under those conditions? But its actions suggest that the Fund considers one of its principal missions is to protect mobile capitalists and not to assume the responsibility it should to compensate the Argentine people for the economic policies it so decidedly influenced and supported in the 1990s. Here its major preoccupation is that Argentina pay its foreign debt, not helping it at all to recover the money (about the same or possibly more than the amount of that debt) that our stationary capitalists illegally sent abroad.[39]

All this is obscured by a moralist rhetoric that has been spreading throughout the world with the force it once had only in small towns: "Argentina lived beyond its means and it is now just that it pay for its excesses." What is notable is that this argument is used to protect the interests of those who committed such excesses, because it is doubtful that even the most callous of international bureaucrats would dare to say that well over fifteen million poor people have been living here beyond their means. But it is not only that. If we exclude the bandit-like behavior to which I have referred, it is not at all certain that Argentina has "lived beyond its means": it had a primary surplus (that is, before adding in the payment of interest) in its budget for various years, despite being heavily burdened by phenomena like the costs of the privatization of its social security system, the elimination of employer contributions to pensions, or businesses' non-payment of taxes. It is probable that there would be no need for any economic adjustment if, for example, the retirement system could be restructured, employer contributions reincorporated, and payments on the debt suspended for a couple of years (especially taking into account that creditors—whether legitimate or not—were conscious of the risks they assumed when they decided to buy Argentine bonds to obtain the high interest they offered).[40]

To the extent that the Argentine government accepts such pressures and tries to comply with the obligations these would impose, it is obvious that any social agreement as discussed earlier would be impossible, due to the continuation of the social regime governing capital accumulation that brought us to where we are. Worse still, social inequality would worsen, discontent and protests would increase, and almost any alternative including an open return to authoritarian repressive practices like what the country has experienced so many times in different forms might be imagined.

Most elementary prudence would suggest that it is time to decidedly change direction. But the facts (and entrenched interests) are deeply rooted, and I do not believe that this will occur simply because those someone called the "owners of the country" suddenly decide to become altruistic gentlemen. Consequently, it would not be difficult to predict that a probably long period of high social conflict has begun. One can observe that this period would be shortened and resolved more or less peacefully and productively only if both the majority of Argentines and the rest of the world understand the true nature of what has happened and if they be conscious of the way in which the excesses of those at the top have impeded and continue to impede representative democracy from extending durable roots in Argentina and operating as it should.[41]

Notes

* Translated by Edward Epstein. This chapter was written in March 2002 while Duhalde was president and prior to the Kirchner government.

1. Mancur Olson, *Poder y prosperidad* (Buenos Aires, Siglo XXI, 2001), 1.

2. See Michel Crozier, Samuel Huntington, and Joji Watanuki, *The Crisis of Democracy* (New York: New York University Press, 1975), 2.

3. See especially Crozier, Huntington, and Watanuki, *The Crisis*, from 64 and 113–14.

4. This corresponds to the report's conclusion in Crozier, Huntington, and Watanuki, *The Crisis*, 164.

5. *The Crisis*, 5.

6. For a full discussion of this topic, see my book *Democracia: ¿Gobierno del pueblo o gobierno de los politicos?* (México, D.F.: Fondo de Cultura Económica, 2000). (Translator's note: This is now available in English as *Democracy, Government of the People or Government of the Politicians?* [Lanham, Md., Rowman & Littlefield, 2003]). According to Robert Dahl, for example, all the requisites for democracy can be condensed into the requirement for a firm principle of equality. As he cites Schumpeter, "If a physicist observes that the same mechanism functions in different ways in distinct epochs and places, he concludes that its functioning depends on conditions outside itself. We can only come to the same conclusion in regard to the democratic system."

7. See my article "El enigma argentino," in *Punto de Vista* 71 (December 2001): 1–5.

8. For further elaboration one can refer to José Nun and Juan Carlos Portantiero, *Ensayos sobre la transición democrática en la Argentina* (Buenos Aires, Puntosur, 1987) and to my article "Populismo, representación y menemismo," in *Sociedad* 5 (October 1994): 91–122.

9. Olson, *Poder y prosperidad*, 31. It is known, for example, that in places controlled by the Mafia the population is protected from being robbed by others, while the Mafia in reality is defending its own interests.

10. According to an account never denied, several weeks before announcing the Austral Plan in June 1985, then Economics Minister Juan V. Sourrouille brought a draft to Washington to use in explaining the project to, and obtaining approval for it from, International Monetary Fund authorities (Joaquín Morales Solá, *Asalto a la illusión* [Buenos Aires: Planeta, 1990], 256). As cited by another observer, "the day before the Austral Plan, Alfonsín received the Captains of Industry at Olivos" (Horacio Verbitsky, *La educación presidencial* [Buenos Aires: Puntosur, 1990], 114). See also Pierre Ostiguy, *Los capitanes de la industria* (Buenos Aires: Legasa, 1990).

11. As Morales Solá (*Asalto*, 46) points out, "Those who might have speculated in the financial market between November 1988 and January 1989 obtained a 30% dollar profit—a yield in three months that would require over three years in a fixed term account in any capital of the developed world."

12. On this topic, see Walter Graziano, *Las siete plagas de la economía argentina* (Buenos Aires: Norma, 2001), chap. 1.

13. To appreciate this question in all its magnitude, it is estimated that over two-thirds of today's total public foreign debt derives from the 48-billion-dollar debt encumbered by the last military dictatorship, adding the interest involved. See Jorge Gaggero, *FMI/Argentina: El major alumno en la picota* (Buenos Aires: April 2002, unpublished monograph).

14. See Vicente Palermo and Marcos Novaro, *Política y poder en el gobierno de Menem* (Buenos Aires: Norma, 1996), 256ff.

15. Jorge Castro, in *El Cronista*, September 24, 1989. For a useful review of this and other similar works, see Fabián Bosoer and Santiago Leiras, "Los fundamentos filosófico-políticos del decisionismo presidencial en la Argentina, 1989–1999," in *Argentina entre dos siglos*, ed. Julio Pinto (Buenos Aires: EUDEBA, 2001), 41–90. Castro considered Menem a kind of Argentine Cavour who produced changes in the country similar to those implemented by the Party of the Moderates in the Italian Risorgimento. He even compares the situation produced in Argentina by Menem's policies with the effective displacement of the old order that took place in Italy and with the development of the Italian north (that led the Versailles Peace Treaty to convey the status of Great Power upon Italy), causing one to seriously question the particular sense Castro wants to give to the notion of "conservative revolution."

16. On the technological changes that had already begun to be felt since the military dictatorship in selected areas (especially in agriculture and in certain segments of industry), see my "Vaivenes de un régimen social de acumulación en decadencia," in Nun and Portantiero, *Ensayos*, 83–116. For an updated view of this whole topic, I recommend Bernardo Kosacoff and Adrián Ramos, *Liberalización, estabilidad y desarrollo: El caso argentino* (Brasilia: FUNCEB, 2002).

17. "Telephones, electricity, water, and some transport services passed from being

public to private monopolies; their rates, set in long-term contracts, rose according to inflation in the United States even while prices in Argentina were falling. And interest rates continued high. Banks lent dollars for 25% despite that, in theory, risk was low." I took this valid if constrained account from the conservative publication *The Economist*, March 2, 2002, where it sought to explain the Argentine collapse. For a more extensive and rigorous analysis of this crucial topic, see the various *Documentos de Trabajo* produced since 1996 by the Economics and Technology Sector of the Project on Privatization and Regulation in the Argentine Economy, FLACSO/SECYT/CONICET, Buenos Aires.

18. See the paper "Los ciclos económicos en la Argentina: Del modelo primario exportador al sistema de hegemonía financiera," delivered by Aldo Ferrer at the Academía Nacional de Ciencias Económicas, 1995).

19. "The goals mentioned concerning economic activity and employment were subordinated to the recycling of foreign funds needed to supplement domestic resources destined for debt service," Ferrer, "Los ciclos," 9. Concerning conflicts between economic elites, particularly since the 1995 crisis, see especially Eduardo Basualdo, *Concentración y centralización del capital en la Argentina durante la década del noventa* (Buenos Aires, Universidad Nacional de Quilmes, 2000).

20. For an excellent analysis of the topic, see Barry Bluestone and Bennett Harrison, *Growing Prosperity* (Boston: Houghton Mifflin, 2000). It is significant that an economist as prominent as Robert Heilbroner did not hesitate to risk his reputation (in his own words) to argue that this book is as important as Keynes's *General Theory*.

21. Lester Thurow, "Wages and the Service Sector," in *Restoring Broadly Shared Prosperity*, ed. Ray Marshall (Austin: University of Texas Press, 1997).

22. Jorge Schvarzer, "Economía argentina: Situación y perspectives," *La Gaceta de Económicas* (June 24, 2001): 6.

23. See *La Nación*, March 17, 2002, 10, based on official data.

24. Pierre Manent, *Cours familier de philosophie politique* (Paris: Fayard, 2001).

25. See, for example, Horacio Verbitsky, *Robo para la corona: Los frutos prohibidos del árbol de la corrupción* (Buenos Aires: Planeta, 1996).

26. A comparative statistic: while tax collection surpassed 30% of GDP in Brazil, in Argentina it barely reached 21%.

27. Marcos Novaro, "El presidencialismo argentino entre la reelección y la alternancia," in *Políticas e instituciones de las nuevas democracies latinoamericanas*, ed. Isidoro Cheresky and Inés Pousadela (Buenos Aires: Paidós, 2001), 84. The argument this author uses seems curious in claiming that "the difficulties resulting from the Menemist model are not due to a supposed 'party weakness,' as maintained in some analyses, but to the high level of State involvement: *such a role supposes high transaction costs in the formation of any policy consensus, sees party structures as highly dependent on public resources, and places institutions at risk by eliminating any difference between party and State*," Novaro, 85–86 (italics added).

28. I develop these questions in *La rebellión del coro* (Buenos Aires: Nueva Visión, 1989) and, more recently, in José Burucúa, et al., "Variaciones sobre un tema de Hegel," in *La ética del compromiso* (Buenos Aires: Altamira/Fundación OSDE, 2002).

29. "Argentina is a very debilitated State on the edge of anomie, passing through a risky situation that gets worse because we have weak institutions and a society that is disintegrating, prone to fall into misfortune," from a statement by Justice Minister Jorge Vanossi, in *La Nación*, March 17, 2002, 11.

30. The data are unpublished and come from two different sources: on the one hand, national surveys carried out by PNUD in October 2001 and February 2002 for its "Informe sobre la democracia en Argentina" (hereafter PNUD); on the other, the national survey carried out by IBOPE OPSM in February 2002 for its "Monitor de tendencies económicas y sociales" (hereafter IBOPE).

31. In February 2002, only 20% of those interviewed said that they had attended a neighborhood public meeting or a protest march in the last two months (PNUD). It is clear that this refers to national data and does not reflect the full intensity of protests recorded in the principal urban centers, especially in the Federal Capital and Greater Buenos Aires. Another undeniable indicator of the existent discontent is the fact that in the October 2001 legislative elections, 40% of the citizens either did not vote or else cast a blank or spoiled ballot.

32. I would emphasize that it was that way here; in other places with a long republican tradition, consolidated institutions, etc., the effects were less devastating.

33. This is the position held by theorists as important as Isaiah Berlin and John Rawls. For a very convincing refutation, see Gerald Cohen, "A Lack of Money Is a Lack of Liberty" (mimeo).

34. On this see my *Democracia*, 100–103. To also escape from any possible populist-demagogic type objection: the lack of freedom does not necessarily imply a lack of resistance, as slave revolts long ago proved. And naturally every person has the ultimate liberty of letting himself die. But this is not of what I am speaking, but of the full enjoyment of constitutional rights on which representative democracy is founded.

35. See Daniel Azpiazu, Graciela Gutman, and Adolfo Vispo, *La desregulación de los mercados* (Buenos Aires: Norma, 1999).

36. As I have indicated elsewhere, it is of note that neo-liberal propaganda demagogically changed into *spillover*, which in its original version was no more than the *trickle-down effect* quite reasonably attributed to sustained economic growth.

37. Nun, *Democracia*, 127.

38. Alfredo Zaiat, "Chasman y Chirolita," Cash supplement from *Página 12*, March 17, 2002, from whom I took both examples.

39. According to official sources, Argentine bank deposits abroad have varied between 85% and 120% of the amount of total national public debt, and it is estimated that close to 90% of these deposits result from tax evasion (Gaggero, *FMI/Argentina*).

40. It is appropriate to clarify that adjustments of the type demanded would not be necessary if other adjustments permitted the country to be set on a genuine and self-sustained path of equitable development.

41. Some bad historical memories are not easy to forget, even if the epochs and circumstances are different. As Rita Thalmann writes in *La République de Weimar* (Paris: P.U.F., 1986), 122, "The occidental democracy that the Weimar republicans sought to promote required the integration of ever broader social strata through their increasing participation in the benefits of the system. . . . In short, there could be no democracy in Germany without a profound reform of society's structures." I hope that this and other similar examples can still serve as a form of warning.

3

Police, Politics, and Society in the Province of Buenos Aires*

Marcelo Fabián Sain

1. The Avellaneda Incident and the Extreme Politicization of the Police

During a march by "piquetero" protestors on the Federal Capital on Wednesday, June 26, 2002, two such activists, Darío Santillán and Maximiliano Kosteki, were murdered in Avellaneda, the locality in the southern part of Greater Buenos Aires bordering the capital. Inspector Alfredo Fanchiotti and others from the Buenos Aires Provincial Police were held responsible. During that day an extremely violent police repression of such assembled groups of the unemployed took place by special infantry and security forces of the provincial police, as well as units from the Naval Prefecture under the control of the federal government then headed by Argentine President Eduardo Duhalde, the de facto leader of the Peronist Party in the province.

Some time before, Felipe Solá, the Peronist governor of Buenos Aires Province who succeeded Carlos Ruckauf when he resigned, had announced his intention to seek the Peronist Party nomination for governor in the elections to take place in April 2003. His proposal was strongly opposed by the principal pro-Duhalde leaders who controlled the powerful local Peronist political machine. They were opposed not only because Solá was unaffiliated with their faction, but because his decision to seek re-election had been made without any effort at nego-

51

tiating with them for their support, something without which it would be difficult for Solá to win. Having governed the province with no regular consultation of the Duhalde forces, he furthermore had pointed out on more than one occasion that the province was in disarray, something he linked to various earlier administrations. Duhalde himself had governed the province between 1991 and 1999, to be replaced by Ruckauf until the latter resigned in January 2002 to become foreign minister in Duhalde's presidency.

For its part, the Buenos Aires Peronism, which had set up a broad-based socio-political clientelist network of conservative populist hue, was competing with piquetero groups representing parts of the unemployed. These groups had sprung up in Buenos Aires Province challenging the Peronist clientelist structures for the representation of the unemployed poor in the metropolitan area. Between 1999 and 2001, such groups had obtained an important organizational presence and a high degree of social mobilization expressing their sectoral demands.[1] Such success had intensified their confrontation with Buenos Aires Peronism.

The tragic events of Avellaneda took place in special circumstances. During the days before the piquetero mobilization, there were numerous statements by officials of the national government linked to the Duhalde Peronists advocating the use of force by the police to restrain the announced piquetero demonstration. The head of the Cabinet, the Duhalde loyalist Alfredo Atanasof, suggested that the relation between the government and the piquetero groups constituted a "kind of war."

What is certain is that the events that cost the lives of Santillán and Kosteki include the open struggle between Buenos Aires Peronism and the piquetero groups as well as the need of the former to politically weaken and discipline the insolent Governor Solá. Because of these factors, the police action occurring that June 26 was not intended to control, limit, or demobilize the piquetero protest, but rather to provoke an open confrontation between the police and the mobilized poor such as what took place. The head of the operation was Inspector Alfredo Luis Fanchiotti, an officer who over the previous twenty years had carried out duties in police stations in the southern zone of Greater Buenos Aires. In that position he had developed strong political ties with Duhaldista leaders, especially with Oscar Rodríguez, who some years before had been Mayor of San Vicente and from January 2002 was assistant secretary for domestic intelligence in the national Secretariat of State Intelligence (Secretaría de Inteligencia de Estado, or SIDE). Fanchiotti had participated in police operations at the behest of Rodríguez, pressuring and threatening opposition journalists of the area and, more recently, the piquetero leaders who would later organize the demonstration of June 26, 2002. What is clear from the judicial record are the frequent calls on that day between Franchiotti's cell phone and different SIDE offices, which can be reasonably explained only if Franchiotti's activity was being monitored from the SIDE. Furthermore, the police operation was conducted using a non-police radio frequency to hinder the taping of such communications by the central switchboard at Department Police Headquarters in Lomas de Zamora, itself under the command of Inspector Osvaldo Vega, an officer also closely linked with the Duhalde forces in the area and with Rodríguez.[2] In addition to Franchiotti, First Sergeant Carlos Néstor Leiva and Officer Héctor Mario De la Fuente directly participated in the murder of Santillán, as was recorded on films and accounts by reporters present at the scene. Franchiotti was arrested several days later, but the others implicated were fugitives for over a year. For them to have been able to remain at large it was evident that they received protection from those responsible for their apprehension, in particular from Inspector Claudio Smith, then in charge of Departmental Headquarters, an officer with the closest links to the Duhalde political group.[3]

These close ties between certain sectors of the Buenos Aires Provincial Police and Duhalde-controlled Peronism serve as an example of the high degree of politicization of those parts of the police and of their political manipulation as a way of reconciling internal party differences.

We are not dealing here with really novel behavior. In December 2001, during the social disturbances that led to the resignation of then President Fernando de la Rúa, the encouragement of certain Duhaldista local leaders, mayors, and provincial office holders in the looting of businesses and markets and in the acts of violence carried out in Greater Buenos Aires and the Federal Capital that precipitated his fall was notorious. The evident police passivity there in the face of such facts was guaranteed and even ordered by the appropriate political officials, according to certain judicial accounts. At that moment, the Buenos Aires provincial government was in the hands of Duhalde loyalist Ruckauf.[4]

This set of deeds is the work of a police structure integrated into the political system that had been taking form over recent decades under the influence of Buenos Aires Peronism. What are the most notable features of this system of security in the province of Buenos Aires? We will get to them.

2. The Historic Structure of the Buenos Aires Provincial Police

The system of public safety in Argentina, of which the police makes up one particular aspect, is structured on the basis of a body of traditional parameters that result from a long historic process.[5] In that context, the Argentine police as an institution was basically shaped as a body at the service of successive national governments more than of local communities, using it as a concept of safety based on the obligation to protect the state rather than on citizen rights and liberties. It acquired a strongly state-centered cast. Similarly, under earlier authoritarian regimes, military governments assumed rigid control over the police, later using them as a key instrument for the repressive domestic order run by the armed forces. All this laid the groundwork for a sweeping militarization of police organization and activities. It also resulted in the institutionalization of strongly illegal secret practices and attitudes in police work[6] that were never checked on or altered by the various civilian administrations that followed with the return to democracy.

Thus the police agencies of our country, far from being established as civil and citizen-oriented police, were created as guardians of the established political order and as militarized state-oriented police more sensitive to the views and interests of successive governments and their various top leaders than to the dictates of law. They were riddled by illegal and widely found secret practices accepted within the institution itself.

As a result of this historical process, a traditional model for the organization and activities of public safety was set up in our country; its most important characteristics emphasized lack of political control of public and police safety matters and independent police control of public security and of the police system itself.[7]

In the province of Buenos Aires these tendencies acquired particular form and notable impact, especially in the 1990s.

For the duration of the military dictatorship (1976–1983), the Buenos Aires Provincial Police was a key part of the state terrorist apparatus controlled by the First Army Corps, which had jurisdiction in that province. From a headquarters run at the time by then Col. Ramón Camps there operated eight "secret detention camps," in which the systematic torture and murder of thousands of persons who had "disappeared" took place.[8] In this context, "operative groups" of police that had actively participated in the repression designed and introduced by the armed forces—particularly by the army—were setting up a model for "crime fighting" based on the direct or indirect "control" of illicit activities by diverse criminal organizations or groups. The model referred to linked together a variety of forms of official complicity, concealment, protection, prosecution, and repression of certain outlawed activities and of specific criminal groups. At the same time, it led to the creation of a sweeping system of police self-financing based on money generated by criminal activity tolerated, controlled, or directly organized by the most involved police sectors.[9]

Moreover, the main institutional parameters that had structured the organizational and functional bases of the Buenos Aires Provincial Police since the end of the nineteenth century were in this way renewed and expanded.

In effect, the provincial police was built historically on the basis of an organic-functional structure marked, on the one hand, by the police command's exclusive jurisdiction over and control of all crime prevention and criminal investigation. On the other hand, this implied a centralized police leadership exercised by an army-like "general staff," with a closed, ultra-hierarchical, and highly military structure. Furthermore, it was based on a personnel pattern characterized by a career structure for the police with recruitment, benefits, and promotions of an essentially military character.

Similarly, those parameters also presumed a set of institutionally reinforcing police practices, that is, practices run by and oriented toward the self-preservation of the police establishment, rather than focusing on efficiency in crime prevention or in the identification of those responsible. Such a self-serving orientation has been based on a type of policing oriented toward illegal and extra-institutional forms of control aimed at controlling all types of non-criminal behavior considered by the police agency as harmful to a certain notion of self-defined "public order." This police action relies on the prevalence of dissuasive and preventive practices practices based on the direct use of force and "heavy handed" criteria.

Thus, the result of these tendencies has been the creation of a police system that is inefficient not only at the time of recording, preventing, and warding off new aspects of crime as they appear, but also in constructing the referred-to model of regulatory policing of crime.[10]

Police inefficiency is a response to the profoundly dated nature of Buenos Aires police doctrine as well as the outmoded organizational and functional arrangements that affect the development of crime prevention and suppression. With a few exceptions, the police bear a series of institutional defects that are the source of that inefficiency, including (i) the inadequate way in which direction, coordination, and control of the policing system are carried out by its top leaders; (ii) the high concentration of personnel and resources at the top of the organizational structure; (iii) the significant fragmentation and compartmentalization of police functions between the principal branches of the police and among the different units that make them up; (iv) the lack of a system set up for the recording, classification, constantly updated analysis of the provincial crime situation; (v) the notorious absence of a doctrine and specialized structures for the production of intelligence on serious crime prevention; (vi) the lack of a unified base of information on the different types of crime occurring in the province and those committing them; (vii) the anachronistic structure of police personnel weighted toward having a significant part committed to carrying out non-police tasks like the custody and movement of those arrested, administrative duties, or escorting court officials, politicians, legislators, and others; (viii) the high number of police units, sections, or stations of an administrative nature absorbing an enormous quantity of human resources in doing non-police activity; (ix) the lack of community policing oriented to the prevention and elimination of lesser crimes, minor social conflicts, unrest, and marginal localized public disorder; (x) the lack of specialized units for criminal investigation of major organized crime; (xi) the absence of a police career resting on professional criteria and based on the training and performance of police personnel; (xii) the existence of police careers built on the basis of a single professional grouping, without distinguishing between the tasks of crime prevention and criminal investigation; (xiii) the predominance of criteria of subordination and hierarchy as a means of better institutional control to the detriment of proper police behavior; and (xiv) the absence of criteria and structures for ongoing specialized police skill-building and training given the priority for creating a generalist police type.

Likewise, under the influence of these dated practices, a context has been constructed likely to produce behavior and forms of organization and functions far removed from legality and the maintenance of a system for the direct and indirect regulation of certain criminal activities by part of some members or groups in the Buenos Aires police. Within the control of the provincial police one certainly sees created and legitimized a body of widely found institutional practices that take for granted arbitrary and illegal forms of professional behavior. Conspicuous among these practices are "the poor treatment, torture, the refusal to provide protection, blackmail and extortion, corruption, arbitrary arrests, falsification of evidence, the collection of money for police protection, as well as participation in criminal activities and the cover-up of such complicity."[11] Traditionally, the crime control exercised by certain sectors of the police has supposed protection of and participation in activities like prostitution, secret gambling, and lesser illicit acts. Nevertheless, in recent years such involvement has expanded to a whole range of serious criminal activities such as the trafficking and sale of drugs, the dismantling of stolen cars, robberies carried out by hijackers, and kidnapping—activities found among the form of organized crime previously mentioned that, as indicated, has greatly expanded in scope due to police control and sponsorship.[12]

Consequently, the different civilian provincial governments succeeding each other after the restoration of democracy in 1983 not only failed to redress this perverse pattern of police behavior, but during their respective administrations allowed such practices to be consolidated and expanded.[13] During all these years, Buenos Aires political institutions were characterized by recurrent political lack of control in matters of public safety whereby provincial political leaders and particularly successive government authorities delegated to the police a monopoly over the administration of public security in the province. That is to say that an institutional sphere exclusively controlled and run by the police was set up on the basis of criteria, orientations, and instructions defined and applied autonomously without any firm involvement by the provincial government. Added to the systematic absence of comprehensive policies on matters of public safety and the government's indifference and/or lack of experience in what to do about the different problems that presented themselves in that regard, such a tendency permitted the police apparatus to acquire broad margins of institutional autonomy in respect to the organs of government.

This situation acquired particular characteristics in the administration of Eduardo Duhalde. As someone who maintained smooth relations with highly representative heads of the Buenos Aires Provincial Police of that time, from his assumption as governor in 1991, he tried to make up for the lack of government police policy by formulating a program on provincial safety. Taken as a whole, this program reinforced and deepened the parameters of function and organization that had been developed by the police since the 1970s. In effect, Duhalde established an explicit and consensual tie with the Buenos Aires Police that basically consisted in granting that institution a great quantity of material and financial resources, a broad degree of freedom of maneuver in its activities, and the promise of governmental non-interference in the institutional activities and practices developed by the most active sectors of the police. All this produced a security situation that would not be responsive to even strong social demands. That is, the political powers allowed the police establishment to run its own affairs and organize itself on the basis of a "heavy hand" model, as well as the old arrangement of illegal financing from police participation in an extended network of criminal activities basically relying on secret gambling, prostitution, narcotics trafficking, and specialized robbery. In return, the political powers expected the police to develop an effective effort in preserving acceptable levels of citizen security and quiescence in relation to problems or crimes of a lesser nature. This arrangement consisted then in a strategy of a "fight against common crime" based on the direct control (via police participation) and indirect control (via police protection) of major crime that involved both less important criminal groups and major crime syndicates that produced enormous sums of "dirty money" as a consequence.[14]

Contrary to official expectations, this arrangement resulted in a situation with no institutional control over the Buenos Aires Police. The police not only became totally inefficient in the prevention and solution of crimes but permitted such acts to increase behind the institutional defense of "criminal regulation," never adequately taking into account the body of burgeoning social and political changes.

During those years, the crime rate in the province of Buenos Aires grew noticeably as the number of police officers fired but exonerated as a result of the commission of abuses and crimes while carrying out their duties increased at the same time. Between December 1991 and April 1997, 3,805 officers were terminated—that is, 8% of the force—of whom 3,418 were legally charged and/or tried for the commission of various offenses. Among this last group, 60% were tried for robbery, abuse of authority, and/or the falsification of public evidence, while the remaining 40% included homicide, light and serious injuries, torture, criminal fraud, and the illegal sale of drugs.[15] Similarly, the participation by members of the Buenos Aires Police in the bombing of the headquarters of the Argentine Jewish Community or AMIA carried out in July 1994, and particularly the torture and murder of newspaper reporter José Luis Cabezas in January 1997, with other notorious criminal acts were definitively a clear expression of the state of institutional decomposition present in the police force. These cases provide evidence of the collapse of the security system in the province of Buenos Aires and the powerful need to implement in-depth institutional changes, not just to reverse the corruption and functional incompetence of the Buenos Aires Police, but also to begin a sweeping process of internal rehabilitation.

All this made Duhalde himself decree the civilian takeover of the Buenos Aires Police and the naming of Luis Lugones (a Peronist leader also serving as a provincial deputy) as the new police head, following the defeat that Buenos Aires Peronism suffered in the national legislative elections of October 1997. Such civilian intervention occurred between the months of December 1997 and March 1998. All this presumed the beginning of a process of general reorganization of the provincial security system in the context of which a series of meaningful changes in the Buenos Aires police structure would take place. But, on the whole, it was all cut short in little time without political/institutional support and without long-term continuity.[16]

Those formal changes were included in Law 12,154 on Public Security and particularly in Law 12,155 on the Organization of the Police of Buenos Aires

Province, passed and promulgated in August 1998.[17] Law 12,154 set up a system of provincial public security, instituting mechanisms for community participation in security matters. Law 12,155 created three new police bodies that were different from an organizational/functional point of view, namely the Departmental Security Police, the Investigatory Police with Judicial Duties, and the Highway Safety Police. These three were defined as "civilian institutions of an armed, hierarchical, and professional character."

Law 12,155 gave the Departmental Security Police the basic responsibility for crime prevention and the maintenance of public safety. This police body was established with "functional, administrative and financial autonomy" along the lines of the eighteen judicial departments existing in Buenos Aires Province, but with overall coordinating reserved for the General Directorate of Operative Coordination. Similarly, a General Directorate for the Evaluation of Information for the Prevention of Crime was created for such matters and provided with "a technical structure specialized in carrying out police intelligence activities leading to crime prevention."

In turn, the Investigatory Police with Judicial Duties was established with the basic task of getting involved in criminal investigation at the request and under the orders of the appropriate judicial authority, but ruling out any possibility that the police undertake any investigation prejudicial to administrative authority. Among its specific duties it was entrusted with that of "organizing and maintaining the capacity and services necessary to carry out investigations of complex crimes and drug trafficking" and maintaining "up-to-date data bases and information systems necessary for the completion of its mission." Here it was structured following the lines of the eighteen Departmental Investigatory Branches and furthermore was linked to the General Directorate for Complex Investigations and Narco-Crime as well as to the General Directorate for a Scientific Police. The Investigatory Police was in charge of the realization of "all technical and scientific studies that might be required for a court trial" and with developing "scientific methods leading to the uncovering of all aspects of a crime." The Police for Highway Safety was given as its basic function the task of protecting public safety pertaining to the transit and transport of people.

Finally, although not considered a basic component of the provincial police system, the Service for the Custody and Transport of Prisoners was created to take charge of watching over and protecting those detained for the presumed commission of crimes, both during their stay in police buildings and jails and during their eventual removal as ordered by the appropriate legal authority.

Similarly, the Ministry of Justice and Safety was created in August 1998 with the goal, pertaining to security, of organizing and managing provincial police groups and the activity of private security firms; to coordinate the relations of the police and the community; to investigate, plan, and implement acts of police intelligence conducive to the prevention of crime; and planning, coordinating across different jurisdictions, and carrying out actions for the struggle against narco-trafficking in the area of its competence, among other responsibilities.

In this way, civil government remained in charge—at least formally—of the institutional and operative behavior of the different police bodies created in the referred-to process of institutional reform.

The reorganization carried into effect was based definitively on the identification of different essential functions within the police system (that is, criminal investigation, preventive security, highway safety, and the custody and movement of those arrested), and the analogous creation of different police bodies in charge of each of these functions, organizationally structured in different forms in accord with its functional responsibility and with its respective operative leadership body. One was thus dealing with a process of functional differentiation, organizational disaggregation, and decentralization of its operational command. Similarly, in accord with a new model of management and governing public safety, this system would not be run by a police leader, but by someone named by the executive branch in a new ministry in charge of the entire system of provincial safety.

The collapse of security and the Buenos Aires Police that led to efforts at reorganization made evident the need to base them on new legal and institutional pillars. However, the institutional reform then implemented in the Province of Buenos Aires only partially satisfied this need. In effect, this reform resulted in insufficient results.

In light of the crisis in which the system was immersed, the initial changes introduced had some consequences (at least at the formal level), but not enough to produce an effective, complete restructuring of the system. Such limitations were particularly so in reference to all aspects of the institutional practices habitually carried out by the system's principal civil and police officials, given their style and mode of behavior. Among the accomplishments, one ought to mention the establishment of new legal and institutional bases for the system of public security and the Provincial Police, particularly the establishment of new institutional rules for coordinating ties between the police and the government, the justice system, and the community.

However, the important modifications introduced on the normative level did not have a similar effect on the institutional, organizational, and functional situation of the security system and the Provincial Police. From then on, the notorious delays found in the programming and implementation of basic structural measures in key areas of the system resulted in the advances sought never becoming more than mere legal changes, not changes in actual practices.

During the process of institutional reform brought about from the end of 1997, there was no resistance nor destabilizing action by the police who opposed the changes that took place, or consequently, by those who had been removed from the force. We are not dealing with a minor issue, given that between December 1997 and June 1998, 1,200 officers had been dismissed and hundreds of court cases were begun against those suspected of having committed illegal acts in the course of their duties.

At the end of June 1998, after the exoneration and dismissal of 309 inspectors and assistant inspectors indicted and/or legally tried, one saw the first important reaction from the police. Some of those officers assembled in front of the Ministry of Justice and Safety, then headed by the lawyer León Arslanián, in an act of protest. None of this had an effect on the course of the reform process, but it was observed that several leaders of Buenos Aires Peronism were present at the protest, notably Senator Horacio Román, Chairman of the Security Committee of the provincial upper house and well-known critic of the police reorganization process under way.[18] Such a presence not only indicated the visible differences existing between Minister Arslanián and key legislators of the party in power on police reform, but also made manifest the historic ties between provincial party leaders and the Buenos Aires Police. In effect, the police exonerations resulting in those months, and especially the purge of June, provoked the reaction of numerous Peronist mayors from Greater Buenos Aires who were advocates for the retention in their posts of the inspectors who had been replaced or expelled from the force. An extensive system of payoffs had been created between those mayors and the police where the first guaranteed certain police protection to the second in return for contributions by the latter from funds coming from illegal gambling, prostitution, and even narcotics trafficking, auto robberies, and other serious crimes, as Minister Arslanián himself recognized later. On that occasion he stated, "I had to fend off pressures coming from mayors that took place when we hit their collection system, but that did not make us give up."[19] By May that year, it was already apparent that the police reform had not been able to eradicate the "illegal collections" that partially supplied the Buenos Aires Police with resources coming from "clandestine gambling and prostitution," in his words.[20]

One should say that the main reaction to the reform process did not come from the police but from the political scene, principally from the provincial leaders and legislators of the governing party, those who tried hard to see to it that reform did not touch the mayoralties and did not block the system of illegal funds collected from criminal sources kicked back by the Buenos Aires Police that fed the coffers of Buenos Aires local politics.

The evident continuation of this situation indicated that if for Governor Duhalde police reform was a political/electoral necessity, by reason of the same need, he could not dispense with the political/party structure largely built on the relation between the provincial government and the municipal governments run by Peronists, nor with the traditional lines of legal and illegal finance that had supplied resources to that structure in recent years. In sum, such factors seemed to mark the limits of the institutional reforms under way.

At the end of 1999, with the assumption of Ruckauf as governor of the province of Buenos Aires, a sweeping process of police counter-reform was begun, tending to re-create the central parameters of the traditional system of organization of the Buenos Aires Police.

The lack of ordinances for key aspects of Laws 12,154 and 12,155; the limited work undertaken in programming and implementing a new system of preventive police security and criminal investigation; the tenuous efforts in retraining of police personnel in preventive duties and averting criminal matters; lack of any police education on the protection of human rights; the delays in creating forums for community participation on safety matters; the lack of coordination and absence of a province-wide comprehensive strategy in the fight against narco-trafficking and against the illegal acts of organized crime syndicates; and the noticeable delay in the creation and putting into effect of a provincial system of police information and intelligence meant for crime prevention all eroded the limited changes implemented during the reform tried by then Minister Arslanián and supported the referred-to counter-reform.[21]

The creation in the same month of the Superintendency for the General Coordination of the Buenos Aires Provincial Police[22] constituted a critical moment in this process of counter-reform. That body was normatively defined as a permanent working organ given the function of police coordination and the implementation of strategies, policies, and instructions issued by the minister in all matters pertinent to the provincial police. For this, the superintendent was given the basic functions of strategic coordination and the control of policies formulated and ordered by the minister, the verification of their implementation, the detection of and information on observed problems and breakdowns, and the formulation to the minister of suggestions for modifying the distribution of police personnel and the coordination of the development of the distinct police sectors. It dealt in principle with general coordination, leaving in the hands of the minister the running of the system as a whole. However, in practice, the office functioned as a unified police leadership, genuinely autonomous from political power.

A series of factors produced the effective revision of the police system instituted by Law 12,155, placing real control in the hands of the superintendent. These include the continuous informal delegation of leadership prerogatives by successive ministers to the superintendent; the organizational structuring of the superintendency like a military "general staff" that brought together an excessive number of general directorates controlling the operational leadership of the different police sectors (thereby rivaling the leadership of the old Buenos Aires Police); the organizational and functional reunification under a single top command of the different police bodies created in that law; and the notable continuation of a militaristic police subculture that considers the superintendent as the "Police Commander" or the one who creates his own resolutions and service orders as the "superior," to the detriment of the figure of the minister. The superintendent saw himself strengthened by the reoccurring incapacity of the political parts of the Safety Ministry to formulate criminal and security policies within which the institutional life of the police bodies should have developed.

All this allowed the creation within the ministry of a marked functional and organizational differentiation and compartmentalization between the police superintendency and the rest of the ministry, especially the subsecretariats, casting the superintendent's office as a truly autonomous area within the Safety Ministry. This definitively eroded the comprehensive leadership prerogatives over the security and police system that the minister legally possessed and reinforced the traditional image of institutional autonomy that the police agency historically used to link itself with political power in Buenos Aires Province.

In this respect, an exceptional institutional situation was created that continues to the present, one that was never changed by present Governor Solá. As was mentioned, during the reform process a functionally decentralized and organizationally varied police system was instituted along the lines of different police functions, with the different police bodies prepared under ministerial leadership. Meanwhile, during the counter-reform, they sought to reunify the police system with the dilution of the organizational and functional distinctions legally set up and the creation of a unified police command. The result of these contradictory processes has produced a hybrid configuration characterized by a political system partially decentralized and partially reunified, with two contradictory institutional logics coexisting.

Moreover, the absence of institutional directives on the organization and functioning of the Buenos Aires Police System, the de-emphasis of the crime problem as an organizational and functional center of the system, the noticeable lack of a picture of the provincial crime situation, and the constant changing within shortened intervals of ministerial and police authorities (each of whom had different, even opposing, concepts and perspectives from the other)—all these hindered the institutionalization of a police system in tune with the social changes occurring and particularly with the increase in and more complex nature of crime in Buenos Aires Province. Thus the organization and daily functioning of the different branches of the provincial police sectors were generally decided and structured in an autonomous, dissimilar, partial, and sectoral form in accord with not always clear and at times even contradictory directives, mandates, and criteria formulated as much by the centralized general directorates as by the separate departmental commands in a framework characterized by a general lack of logistical and operational planning and by a growing deprofessionalization. The result of this has been the creation of a police system that, far from producing considerable levels of political collective self-interest, constitutes a polyarchy of areas, dependencies, and hierarchies, each compartmentalized, uncoordinated, and independent of the others.

At present, the Buenos Aires police system, which accounts for 45,960 individuals, making up the largest armed force in the country, includes a series of deficiencies in its functioning and organization. Its most important general feature is its profound organizational, functional, and doctrinal out-of-date nature in facing the increase in and more complex nature of crime occurring in recent years in the province. Furthermore, this situation has generated a context favorable to the institutional perpetuation of practices and forms of organization and functions far removed from legality, favorable to the maintenance of a system of direct and indirect control of certain criminal activities by individual members or component groups of the police system itself.

3. The New Crime Problem in Buenos Aires Province

In recent years in Buenos Aires Province, violence and crime have significantly increased. Between 1990 and 2003, the figure for criminality has experienced an increase close to 100%, a situation also accompanied by a rise in criminal violence. In 2002, a total of 347,566 criminal acts took place, including among others 1,964 homicides—over half of all those reported for the entire country—720 sexual assaults, 134,654 non-violent robberies, 10,832 robberies resulting in injury or death, 79,735 thefts, and 2,309 kidnappings. Except in the case of such rapes, in 2001 the crimes reported were notably fewer than in 2002. In 2001, 300,470 criminal acts were committed, including 1,632 homicides, 848 sexual assaults, 108,281 non-violent robberies, 10,070 robberies resulting in injury or death, 61,591 thefts, and 1,300 kidnappings.[23] Furthermore, in 2003, a total of 360,482 crimes were reported, a notable increase from the previous year.[24]

For its part, during the last two years in the Greater Buenos Aires area (where over 75% of all criminal acts committed in the province took place), the percentage of those becoming victims of some crime has been equally high, as has the violence of the crimes. In 2002, 42.2% of the population were victims of some crime. In the year 2000, 39.3% were, while the figure for 2001 was 39%. In 2002, 35.9% of the population were victimized by a crime against property, while 12.3% experienced a violent robbery. In 1998, the figure for such violent robberies was 11.1%, rising to 14.5% in 1999, but dropping to 12.3% in 2000 and 11.6% in 2001, before rising again in 2002.[25]

Greater Buenos Aires itself contains certain poor neighborhoods where the absence of state control has led to incidents of violence by broad-based criminal networks.[26] There certain forms of common crime including the distribution, sale, and consumption of drugs within and outside these genuine "ghettos" have become the basis of an alternative form of life for many of the youth of such impoverished areas. As Javier Auyero has appropriately pointed out, "The 'drug invasion' together with the lack of jobs is the dominant concern of the slums of the Federal Capital and Greater Buenos Aires." He adds, "The dissemination of drugs and alcohol feeds a cycle of distrust and interpersonal violence; although its origins and purposes are unclear, this cycle permeates the entire atmosphere of slum life and affects its basic routines."[27] Within these areas as well as in adjacent neighborhoods is concentrated the largest number of violent and criminal acts, especially the greatest number of murders.

Now then, in this context, it is not only common delinquency that has increased, but also crime run by criminal organizations that can count on broad logistical and operative resources and whose illegal activities likely generate a high level of economic output.

The trafficking and retail commercialization of illegal drugs—especially cocaine and marijuana—make up the most important and most profitable illegal activity for these criminal groups. In the most recent years, such trafficking, distribution, and local consumption has notably increased.[28] Buenos Aires Province is not a producer of such drugs, nor do the main international routes for the trafficking of the drugs produced in the region toward the principal international markets pass through its territory. The marijuana and cocaine trafficked, stored, and distributed in its cities are produced in neighboring countries—respectively, Paraguay and Bolivia—and are introduced into the province on its northern and northeastern frontiers by groups of local and foreign drug traffickers who, if not part of a cartel, have become increasingly more concentrated.[29] After crossing numerous provincial jurisdictions, the drugs finally arrive in Buenos Aires, where they are distributed in the retail market in a decentralized fashion. According to official Argentine and international estimates, the 1990s saw a notable increase in the traffic and local consumption of drugs, an increase of between 10% and 30%, although other estimates suggest that in the last fifteen years the general consumption of prohibited drugs has quintupled.[30]

For its part, the illegal trafficking and sale of arms does not constitute a highly profitable criminal activity, but its relevance relates to the fact that these provide the source of arms for a great part of criminal violence. According to official information provided by the Ministry of Safety of Buenos Aires Province, the significant growth of criminal violence is accompanied by an increase in the trafficking, possession, and illegal use of arms for a criminal purpose in that province. According to the Center of Police Operations and the Subsecretariat for Planning and Logistics of that ministry, in 2000, of the 380,069 criminal acts reported in the province, 12,882, or 3.38%, were committed with firearms. In 2001, of the 308,878 criminal acts reported, 15,631, or 5.06%, were committed with firearms, while in 2002, of the 361,718 crimes, 18,920, or 5.23%, were so committed.[31] This is to say that between 2000 and 2002, the total number of crimes reported diminished slightly, while the percentage of those committed with firearms increased by almost 50%. In 2002, the provincial police seized 10,647 firearms in various operations, with 73.4% of these occurring in the jurisdiction of Greater Buenos Aires, where the highest figures on violent crime are found. In that year, the number of arms seized increased 11%; for the 2000–2002 interval, the increase was 39.3%. Of the arms seized in 2002, 86% were handguns, the weapons most often used for the violent crimes found in the metropolitan Buenos Aires area.[32]

The robbing and stripping down of cars for the sale of illegal auto parts constitutes one of the fastest growing, most complex, and most profitable criminal activities taking place in Buenos Aires Province. This crime problem furthermore brings with it the highest levels of violence, particularly on the occasion of car robberies, now one of the principal occasions for homicides. Moreover, it implies an intricate relation between the different groups that participate in the affair; that is, those in charge of the robbing of the vehicle, those who manage the shops where the stolen cars are stripped down and the parts sold, the "recovery business" for robbed cars, and the police system. The bulk of the shops are located in Greater Buenos Aires and the sale of the auto parts includes the City of Buenos Aires. In Buenos Aires Province, the other side of the criminal process occurs with the "recuperation" of the robbed cars, an activity carried out by numerous legal or illegal enterprises managed by ex–police chiefs, based on information and favors exchanged with different chiefs still active on the force.

According to official sources, in Buenos Aires Province alone in the year 2000, there were 58,510 auto robberies. In 2001, such acts increased slightly, reaching 58,974 cases, while in 2002 there was a minor decrease, to 58,326 cases recorded.[33] According to the car dealers and insurance companies, in metropolitan Buenos Aires in 2002, car robberies increased 34.6% from the previous year. In the first quarter of 2003, this type of robbery increased 8.2% from all of 2002 and 48.7% in comparison with the first quarter of 2001.[34]

Furthermore, car robbery implies an important and increasing degree of criminal violence. In 2002 in Buenos Aires Province, over 40% of homicides taking place in the province were committed during the robbery of a car, while in the same time eight of ten Buenos Aires police killings occurred in the same circumstances.[35] In the first two months of 2003, the robbery of cars from their owners using firearms slightly exceeded those committed while the cars were parked on the street, 50.5% to 49.5%. During earlier years, those proportions were different. In 2001 armed robberies of cars was 39.3% of the total robberies committed, while in 2002, the figure hit 46.9%.[36]

Another aspect of organized crime that has begun to develop during recent years, especially in Greater Buenos Aires and in the rest of the province, is that of robberies labeled as assaults carried out by hijackers, with the robbery of merchandise in transit set up by relatively complex bands in charge of the robbery itself, the storage, and the retail distribution to businesses that will sell it. In Buenos Aires Province in the year 2000, 1,864 cases of such hijacking were registered, in 2001 the figure declined to 1,491 cases, but in 2002 it rose again, to 2,357 cases.[37]

Finally, a new type of crime that has shown a considerable development principally in Buenos Aires Province has been kidnapping. In 2002, there were 146 kidnappings in Buenos Aires Province, of which 50 were kidnappings with ransom demands and 96 were cases of so-called "express kidnappings" where the victims were deprived of their freedom for a few hours for lesser amounts of money.[38] In the first semester of 2003, 207 cases of kidnapping were reported.[39] For the most part, the kidnappings with ransom demands taking place in the province seem to have occurred with apparent police support, as a form of neutralizing certain political efforts to introduce changes in the police or to pressure government authorities to obtain benefits.[40]

Now then, in Buenos Aires Province, the range of criminal undertakings mentioned provides an account of police participation in the makeup and protection of the involved gangs, as well as in the development of criminal activities uncovered there. The significant territorial deployment of these undertakings and of the groups that have implemented them, the ease with which certain places that serve as operational and logistical bases for their development are maintained, the degree of internal structure that the different groups and subgroups in charge of the development have obtained for the different functions of the criminal organizations, and the great operational, logistical, and intelligence development managed by such gangs have all been possible thanks to police protection and complicity or due to the direct intervention of certain groups within the police active in the criminal business carried out by the gangs.[41] To be sure, however, some of the most developed and best organized of these criminal groups have begun to gain autonomy from police management or control, relating to the police in ways that combine different degrees of complicity, competition, and/or open confrontation.[42]

4. The Failed State and Future Challenges

In regard to this new set of tendencies, Buenos Aires Province constitutes a kind of failed state; that is, a state with marked deficiencies in the elaboration of appropriate knowledge and a diagnosis of the new problems dealing with security and in the structuring of an institutional system of public security that is up to date and efficient in its theoretical base, its organization, and its functioning. Such deficiencies have resulted in the province's weakened ability to exercise a monopoly of force in confronting groups and individuals who challenge its position.

This failed state combines certain very visible features: (i) the systematic absence of governmental determination to broach as a basic question the crime problem and matters of public security; (ii) the continuing governmental delegation of the administration of public security to the police, permitting high levels of police autonomy and self-regulation; (iii) the lack of a registry and of an ongoing official picture of the crime problem, of its spread, deployment, and evolution, and of any resulting police monopoly of such possible awareness; (iv) the systematic lack of government recognition of the true institutional state of the Buenos Aires police system in the implementation of its preventive and investigative duties and the non-existence of a government bureaucracy specializing in those matters; (v) the consistent lack of strategies of reform and modernization of the public safety system, especially that of the police, and the ensuing maintenance of the present dated institutional scheme, all within a markedly conservative framework; (vi) government connivance with pockets of police corruption and with recurrent police practices of crime control; and (vii) the politicization of certain police sectors and their consequent manipulation by some of the party leaders in reference to the illegal financing of local political activity and the informal control of the use of force to resolve political disputes.

In short, it is in these characteristic aspects—the lack of political control of security and police self-government—that one finds the Buenos Aires failure to check, to weaken, and even to root out the new forms of criminal violence, especially those derived directly from the lack of experience by the state in the efficient exercise of its police power in the face of the illicit; that is, those criminal ways tolerated, assisted, or directly brought into being by certain sectors of the police themselves.

From the end of the 1990s, the successive failures of initiatives trying to reform and modernize the Buenos Aires police system have been due not to police resistance, but rather to the inconsistency and lack of experience of provincial government authorities in establishing the institutional conditions and policies necessary to develop and sustain a program of actions of that sort. The supposed need to maintain existing conditions so as to be able to deal with any possible police challenges or revolt has been only a pretext for inaction.

Certainly, those police sectors resistant to any kind of institutional transformation do truly maintain a certain capacity for mafioso responses to any initiative likely to introduce changes curtailing the police monopoly over the administration of public security and, consequently, that would mean the weakening of the network of crime manipulation and illegal financing run by those sectors. Such a response could vary from that of "sit down strikes" and strict "working to rule" to "liberation zones" for the behavior of gangs and criminal groups with no police presence, and the direct or indirect continuation of strongly visible criminal acts, kidnappings, and violent homicides. Police resistance of this type would tend to discredit the political authorities, making them appear to the public as incapable of controlling and administering public security.

However, broad police sectors disposed to institutional modernization also exist. It would be these that would act and even neutralize the behavior of the conservative groups. Such action would require that political power be persistent in outlining and developing a strategy of change and offer the modernizing ranks the support and means necessary to confront and internally direct the reform of traditional police practices and orientations, as well as the necessary institutional purge.

In this context, the continuation of the present system of public and police security does not provide an adequate institutional framework to efficiently face the challenges imposed by a scenario in which, for diverse reasons, crime is increasing and becoming ever more complex. Moreover, the unscrupulous way in which the Buenos Aires political class has dealt with the crime problem makes it likely that such matters will continue to be exploited in handling factional differences or election rivalries. This would suggest that, more than being a political-cultural imperative, police modernization constitutes a necessary institutional requisite for democratic consolidation.

Notes

* Translated by Edward Epstein.

1. Maristella Svampa and Sebastián Pereyra, *Entre la ruta y el barrio: La experiencia de las organizaciones piqueteras* (Buenos Aires: Biblos, 2003), chap. II.

2. Horacio Verbitsky, "La tentación de la violencia" and "La marca," *Página 12*, Buenos Aires, July 28 and August 4, 2002, respectively.

3. Gerardo Young, "¿Quién protege al policía prófugo que les tiró a los piqueteros?" *Clarín*, Buenos Aires, June 22, 2003.

4. For these matters, see Miguel Bonasso, *El palacio y la calle: Crónicas de insurgentes y conspiradores* (Buenos Aires: Planeta, 2002); Jorge Camarasa, *Días de furia* (Buenos Aires: Ed. Sudamericana, 2002); and Guillermo Arisó and Gabriel Jácobo, *El golpe SA: La guerra de intereses que estalló en el 2001 y dejó al país en ruinas* (Buenos Aires: Norma, 2002).

5. See Julio Maier, "Breve historia institucional de la policía argentina," and Julio Maier, Martín Abregú, and Sofía Tiscornia, "El papel de la policía en la Argentina y su situación actual," both in *Justicia en la calle: Ensayos sobre la policía en América Latina*, ed. Peter Waldmann (Medellín: Biblioteca Jurídica Diké, 1996); Martin Edwin Andersen, *La policía: Pasado, presente, y propuestas para el futuro* (Buenos Aires: Ed. Sudamericana, 2001); Máximo Sozzo, "Usos de la violencia y construcción de la actividad policial en la Argentina," in *Violencias, delitos y justicias en la Argentina*, ed. Sandra Gayol and Gabriel Kessler (Buenos Aires: Manantial, 2002).

6. See Martin Edwin Anderson, *La policía*, and Alejandra Vallespin, *La policía que supimos conseguir* (Buenos Aires: Planeta, 2002).

7. In this regard, I continue the interpretative and analytical framework that I developed more amply in Marcelo Fabián Sain, *Seguridad, democracia, y reforma del sistema policial en la Argentina* (Buenos Aires: Fondo de Cultura Económica, 2002), chaps. 2 and 3. Also see Daniel Miguez and Alejandro Isla, "Conclusiones: El estado y la violencia urbana. Problemas de legitimidad y legalidad," in *Heridas urbanas: Violencia delictiva y transformaciones sociales en los noventa*, ed. Alejandro Isla and Daniel Miguez (Buenos Aires: Editorial de las Ciencias and FLACSO-Argentina, 2003), 7.

8. See CONADEP (Comisión Nacional sobre la Desaparición de Personas, or National Commission on the Disappeared), *Nunca más: Informe de la Comisión Nacional sobre la Desaparición de Personas* (Buenos Aires: EUDEBA, 1984).

9. Carlos Dutil and Ricardo Ragendorfer, *La Bonaerense: Historia criminal de la policía de la Provincia de Buenos Aires* (Buenos Aires: Planeta, 1997).

10. Martín Latorraca, Hugo Montero, and Carlos Rodríguez, "Policía y corrupción policial," in *Le Monde Diplomatique*, Buenos Aires, May 2003.

11. Ruth Stanley, "Violencia policial en el Gran Buenos Aires: ¿Necesita el neoliberalismo una policía brava?" in *Violencia y regulación de conflictos en América Latina*, ed. Klaus Bodemer, Sabine Kurtenbach, and Klaus Meschkat (Buenos Aires: Nueva Visíon/ADLAF/HBS, 2001), 239.

12. Dutil and Ragendorfer, *La Bonaerense*; Latorraca, Montero, and Rodríguez, "Policía y corrupción policial."

13. These measures were promoted by Radical Alejandro Armendáriz and by Peronist Antonio Cafiero (1987–1991). The administration of Peronist Eduardo Duhalde came next (1991–1995), with his re-election in 1995 to a second term as head of the

provincial executive branch, a term that ended on December 10, 1999. Immediately after, Carlos Ruckauf became governor (1999–2002), serving until January 2002, when he stepped down, leaving the office in the hands of the vice-governor, Felipe Solá (2002–2003). In September 2003, Solá was elected governor for an additional four-year term.

14. Dutil and Ragendorfer, *La Bonaerense.*

15. *Clarín*, Buenos Aires, April 20, 1997, second section.

16. I have amply discussed this process in Sain, *Seguridad, democracia, y reforma*, chap. 3.

17. Published in *Boletín Oficial de la Provincia de Buenos Aires*, La Plata, August 11, 1998.

18. See *Pistas*, Buenos Aires, no. 22, July 1998.

19. Cited in Horacio Verbitsky, "La ley del Far West," in *Página 12*, Buenos Aires, December 20, 1998. On the occasion of the purge of the police chiefs taking place in June 1998, Minister Arslanián recognized that such a measure had been decided upon, taking into account the "crime indices by department" and "that for collection," here referring to the illegal system of secretly collected funds coming from the criminal management developed by the police (in *Pistas*, Buenos Aires, no. 22, July 1998).

20. *La Nación*, Buenos Aires, May 9, 1998.

21. Sain, *Seguridad, democracia, y reforma*, chap. 3.

22. In December 2001, the title of this job was modified to General Police Superintendency, but this did not change its functions nor its character as an organization for work and coordination.

23. *Clarín*, Buenos Aires, July 6, 2003.

24. Dirección Nacional de Política Criminal, *Hechos delictuosos registrados en la Provincia de Buenos Aires, 2002* (Buenos Aires: Ministerio de Justicia y Derechos Humanos, 2003).

25. Dirección Nacional de Política Criminal, *Estudio de victimización: Gran Buenos Aires, 2002* (Buenos Aires: Ministerio de Justicia y Drechos Humanos, 2003).

26. Nathalie Puex, "Las formas de la violencia en tiempos de crisis: Una villa miseria del Conurbano Bonaerense," in Isla and Miguez (eds.), *Heridas urbanas.*

27. Javier Auyero, "Introducción: Claves para pensar la marginación," in Loic Wacquant, *Parias urbanos: Marginalidad en la ciudad a comienzo del milenio* (Buenos Aires: Manantial, 2001), 17.

28. United Nations Office of Drug Control and Crime Prevention, *World Drug Report, 2000* (Oxford: Oxford University Press, 2000), chap. 1, parts 1.2 and 1.3.

29. See Observatoire Géopolitique des Drogues, *The World Geopolitics of Drugs, 1998/1999* (Paris: Observatoire Géopolitique des Drogues, 2000), chap. V.

30. Rolando Barbano, "Los narcos en el espejo," in *Viva* supplement, *Clarín*, Buenos Aires, June 29, 2003.

31. Ministerio de Seguridad de la Provincia de Buenos Aires, *Delitos cometidos con armas de fuego: Informe preliminar* (La Plata: Ministerio de Seguridad, 2003).

32. *La Nación*, Buenos Aires, June 15, 2003.

33. Ministerio de Seguridad de la Provincia de Buenos Aires, *Estadística delictual* (La Plata: Centro de Operaciones Policiales, Sección Estadísticas, 2000, 2001, 2002).

34. *La Nación*, Buenos Aires, June 22, 2003.

35. *Página 12*, Buenos Aires, July 6, 2003.

36. *La Nación*, Buenos Aires, June 22, 2003.

37. Ministerio de Seguridad de la Provincia de Buenos Aires, *Estadística delictual.*

38. Subsecretaría de Planificación y Logística, *Información sobre secuestros en el ámbito de la provincia de Buenos Aires* (La Plata: Ministerio de Seguridad de la Provincia de Buenos Aires, 2003).

39. *La Nación*, Buenos Aires, December 14, 2003.

40. Marcelo Fabián Sain, "Hay omisión, complicidad o participación," Interview, *Página 12*, Buenos Aires, July 6, 2003; Gonzalo Sánchez, "Asuntos internos, negocios sucios," in *Noticias*, Buenos Aires, July 5, 2003.

41. Marcelo Fabián Sain, "Modernizar la policía ataca la ineficiencia y la corrupción," in *Debate*, Buenos Aires, no. 17, July 4, 2003.

42. Rolando Barbano, "Los narcos en el espejo."

4

The Costs of the Convertibility Plan: The Economic and Social Effects of Financial Hegemony*

Jorge Schvarzer

The crisis that Argentina experienced—one of the deepest and most extended in its history—is the consequence of the strategy implemented in the 1990s known as the Convertibility Plan. Launched at the beginning of 1991, that program tried to limit inflation by modifying the national economic structure; instead, it ended in the economic collapse whose consequences are still being felt. Comprehension of this crisis requires that the logic of that program be understood. Such understanding, in turn, will illuminate the critical evolution of economic activity and the form in which social phenomena like marginalization and poverty were shaped. Their magnitude and duration have surprised even Argentines themselves.

Convertibility in Perspective

The application of the Convertibility Plan did not occur in a vacuum, but in the context of a strong and prolonged deterioration of the Argentine economy. From mid-1975, the country entered into a spiral of elevated inflation and relative stagnation that clearly contrasted with the extensive prior period known for its application of import substitution industrialization. Aggregate statistics clearly show the difference between one period and the other. Average inflation in the

1960–1974 period was on the order of 25% annually, a high amount but one to which economic actors had accustomed themselves, however, so that such a rate did not prevent results in the productive sphere and in income distribution from being reasonable (at least in relative terms and compared to what occurred later). On the other hand, between 1975 and 1991, when the Convertibility Plan was launched, average inflation rose to 350% annually, with the added fact that in none of the intervening years was that variable ever below 100%. A similar contrast is observed with the evolution of Gross Domestic Product, or GDP. This grew at an average rate of 4% in the 1960–1974 period (fifteen years that included only one year of strong recession); in contrast, there was no real growth in the fifteen years following, when the annual figures for GDP never at any time surpassed the previous high reached in 1974. Parallel with such overall stagnation and the absolute fall in per capita product, income distribution began to show a clearly regressive tendency, if obscured by the changes in economic policy in the interim.

The accumulation of an enormous debt in foreign currency between 1976 and 1981, moreover, generated a foreign crisis in that last year. It is important to point out that this crisis broke out prior to the spread of the "debt crisis" that exploded with Mexico's public debt moratorium in the final months of 1982. What was critical is that the external adjustment strategy that had to be applied from the beginning of the debt crisis made Argentina, like the rest of the Latin American countries, experience a "lost decade," as the Economic Commission for Latin America appropriately labeled the 1980s. In consequence, one can state that from the so-called "Rodrigazo" (introduced in June 1975), the Argentine economy changed direction; it was no accident that such a new orientation was consolidated and amplified with the economic policy implemented under the military dictatorship that seized power in the March 1976 coup d'état.[1]

At the end of the 1980s, Argentina again suffered an inflationary explosion, when prices increased forty times in value in a few months (February to July 1989). That economic crisis, a true social scourge, coming in the midst of the general election campaign, decisively contributed to the resignation of the outgoing president (Raúl Alfonsín) and the early assumption of the President-elect (Carlos Menem), the executive who would be responsible for the Convertibility Plan; that leader's stay in office for ten and a half years thanks to re-election after six years assured the continued application of the plan.[2]

The first two years of the Menem government did not resolve any of the grave problems that the Argentine economy was experiencing. Inflation was reduced from the highest levels reached but was not contained; more so, there was a new leap of prices in January 1990. During all this, the recession begun in 1988 worsened, bringing a very deep fall in GDP at the end of the decade, while certain changes in the system were accentuated: the continual arrears in the value of the dollar, the decline in salaries (in respect to the 1980s average), and the contraction in the demand for labor (something that would be strongly felt over the course of the next decade).

In such a context, the Convertibility Plan can be seen as a type of shock program that apparently sought to end inflation and produce a new direction for the Argentine economy. Its initial successes, as much in respect to price stabilization as in the mentioned cyclical recovery of economic activity, contributed to give it a halo of success that did not always correspond with reality.

The Strategy of Convertibility

Convertibility was based on two basic measures linked to each other, plus a series of connected policies that tended to consolidate the goals sought. The first was to establish a fixed exchange rate with the dollar (with one peso worth one dollar, which greatly facilitated the constant reference to one or the other currency, treating them as if they were equivalents) that the government guaranteed, assuring that supply or demand continued in dollars at that price. This guarantee was linked to the second measure, which in essence was a monetary rule: the government promised to not issue new pesos except to buy foreign exchange (when the stock of reserves increased) and to absorb local currency when people wanted to buy dollars (lowering the stock); it was assumed that, at the initial moment, the stock of foreign exchange was equal to the quantity of domestic currency in circulation, so that that stock would always be equal to the pesos circulating in the country.

Fixed exchange rate policies were fading throughout the world owing to the difficulty of sustaining that variable in the face of the enormous movement of liquid capital between countries. Nevertheless, it was supposed that the close tie of the exchange rate with monetary policy created a different situation in the Argentine case. The guarantee was maintained despite the fact that the level of the exchange rate established for convertibility resulted in a very high parity for the Argentine peso. In effect, the dollar exchange rate was set at a value that was exactly half of that seen in the country over the past three decades.[3] Furthermore, convertibility produced a rarely seen unification of the exchange rate, given that historically there had been different rates for different economic activities; consequently, the new exchange rate strategy led to a revaluation of the peso that was greater for some areas (industry and financial transactions in general) than others (agriculture saw the least relative total revaluation). These results had a clear impact on foreign trade levels because it stimulated imports while discouraging certain exports that failed to adjust to the new situation; it also affected services, especially those related to foreign tourism, one of the sectors most favored by the specific magnitude of peso revaluation for those who traveled.

The effects of the peso revaluation were reinforced in the area of imports by the rigid strategy of unilateral tariff reduction carried out under the generic concept of producing "foreign opening."[4] This reduction was accompanied by the elimination of other non-tariff barriers such as the requirement to "buy nationally made goods" and the suspension of numerous sanitary norms and anti-dumping provisions. Thus stimuli for imports were mounting while local production previously protected was affected.

While all this was happening, the monetary restriction produced new barriers to real economic activity. The norm impeded financing a potential budget deficit with emission, so that the Treasury had to assume debt when its accounts didn't balance, a phenomenon that occurred during almost the entire convertibility period. Furthermore, it kept the Central Bank from assuming its function as a "lender of last resort," as occurs throughout the world in banking crises; this restriction did not seem important in the moments of economic expansion, but it played a decisive role in the crises of 1995 and 2001. Finally, monetary restriction kept the money supply from keeping up with the evolution of activity, unless the stock of reserves increased at that same rate; consequently, a long period of scarce money and elevated interest rates tended to limit the possibility of the economy growing. This phenomenon has a minimum presence in the first years (1991–1994), because in that stage the economy was emerging from an intense recession, but it operated as a major restriction during the entire period following. The official strategy to resolve that difficulty that it had itself created was to encourage the use of the dollar in the local market, a process that alleviated that restriction, but at the cost of less possibility of regulating the monetary supply and the financial system by the official body charged with that task.

The political energy in the sale of public enterprises during the first years of the Menem government contributed to providing resources to the government and allowed the reduction of its operative deficit, facilitating the consolidation of convertibility. By 1994, that strategy was exhausted, coinciding with the first great crisis of the model. The next step of the government was to privatize the social security system, creating by law a capitalization system for the contributions of salary earners that would be managed by financial enterprises especially charged with that purpose; the Treasury gave up receiving the contributions of current workers, while it maintained its commitment to support existing retirees, plus those who would retire in intervening years until the private system was fully functional (a period estimated as several decades). This original privatization produced a deficit in public accounts close to 10% of national Treasury total income due to the difference between income and expenditures of state retirement funds. According to actuarial figures, the deficit would be resolved only in the long term. Defenders of the proposal claimed that it solved the public sector's "inter temporal" deficit because it eliminated one of the largest expenditures required for future decades; critics pointed out the perverse effect of the deficit that the law created that obliged the state to reduce other expenditures or go into debt (as actually happened) to pay for its activities.

The privatization of the largest businesses in the country, specifically public enterprises and services, was undertaken by firms run by foreign capital. As these businesses served the domestic market, the purchasers took advantage of the special protection given such concessions, capturing an appreciable rent due to their position; however, those activities did not generate the foreign currency indispensable for their new owners themselves to be able to send these profits abroad. Furthermore, once in charge of operations, the purchasers reduced their use of local suppliers so as to benefit their associates and providers abroad; this is to say that their entry into the country contributed to the growth of the supply of concessionaire services while it generated negative effects for local businesses providing parts and capital goods. The increased demand for imported goods widened the deficit in the commercial balance, due to the measures for opening the economy mentioned, while the sending of profits to the home office created considerable pressure on the demand for foreign exchange in the external balance. In sum, one can state that every measure adopted to deal with any of the restrictions existing in the Argentine economy produced new problems, especially in the external sector, owing to the strategy adopted.

One last decisive aspect of the period was the formal creation of MERCOSUR, the Southern Common Market, which had taken its first steps in the 1980s and which presented good possibilities for the expansion of the economies of the regional trade bloc. The agreement to move toward a common external tariff helped moderate the pretensions of the Argentine government in seeking to reduce the level of customs protection to the maximum possible. MERCOSUR permitted the signing of a special agreement for the automobile industry that generated the only positive policy implemented by Argentina in that decade in the manufacturing sector. Its effects ought to be taken into account to contrast them with what took place in sectors where there was no such policy. In conclusion, MERCOSUR had various positive effects on the Argentine economy although it was never a full common market as had been planned in the previous decade; the dynamism of the trade between Argentina and Brazil in the 1990s suggests the possibilities that are created with appropriate policies.

The Effects of Convertibility: The Evolution of Net Production

Convertibility tended to deeply modify the local productive structure. Its application in general promoted the expansion of primary activities such as agriculture in the Pampas region (also favored in the 1994–1997 years by a cycle of rising international prices that lifted producers' income), the extraction of petroleum (the privatized former state company allowed the over-development of reserves), mining (concentrated in several big projects), and fishing (where an excessive catch total was recorded, putting some species at risk of extinction). At the same time, there was an increase in the supply of certain public services that were behind in relation to demand, among which telephones specially figured; from their privatization, those services showed a certain boom until they saturated the effective demand under existing conditions.

On the other hand, the majority of manufacturing industry was negatively affected, with the exception of the foods sector (favored by the local low price supply of raw materials); some basic industries (already strengthened thanks to industrial promotion programs of the 1970s and 1980s) that were in condition to compete abroad, such as steel, aluminum, and petrochemicals; and the automobile industry (although the expansion in vehicle assembly did not reflect a parallel increase in activities such as the manufacture of auto parts since the assembly plants were allowed to acquire a huge amount of ingredients and parts abroad). The branches most affected were textiles and clothing, machinery, the manufacture of durable goods, furniture, and electronics, overwhelmed by massive low-priced imports from the rest of the world.

These changes produced widespread negative effects, as much in foreign trade (in generating a structural deficit in the commercial balance) as in total employment (since the contraction of sectors of manufacturing that were very high in employment coincided with the expansion of primary goods sectors that had a low labor content and were incapable of reversing that tendency).

These results are difficult to assess in accounts of production due to a series of methodological problems.[5] Even so, one can say that during the decade of convertibility there first was a rapid recovery in activity after the intense fall registered from the end of 1988 to the beginning of 1991; that boom ended in mid-1994, slowly shifting to a recessionary cycle, given the "Tequila crisis" originating in Mexico that lasted a couple of years. There was a new recovery in 1997 and 1998, although it is probable that the figures for real growth are likely to be again exaggerated by the statistical series, and the recovery surely was brief; a new recession began toward the end of the latter year and continued until it became a formidable depression in the second semester of 2001.[6] Before the collapse of the model, GDP had fallen 20% from the high point reached in 1998.

One can say that the evolution of production in the ten years of the duration of the model included two stages of boom and two recessions; the latter lasted half of the period and the second one ended in a definitive depression. Half of the time of the formal boom corresponded to a process of reactivation (the recovery of earlier productive levels thanks to foreign credit, corroborated in the negative total of the commercial balance). If one takes as a variable per capita production, itself more representative of the capacity of the system to satisfy its inhabitants' demands, the totals for 1999 (at the end of the Menem government) were already below the levels for 1980.[7]

As with per capita production, there was a modification in income distribution in favor of the strata with the greatest resources and of the foreign capital that entered during privatization. Under "zero sum game" conditions, the improvement in the income of one stratum implies a relative and absolute deterioration in the income of the poor. In other words, the changes in income distribution would not have had an effect so negative in absolute terms if the per capita product had increased in the interim.

The Effects of Convertibility: Evolution of the External Sector

In 1990 Argentina exported goods worth 12.5 billion dollars and imported around 4.3 billion; the commercial balance that year generated an unheard-of surplus of 8 billion dollars. Imports were not normal, given the restrictions in place as well as the effects of the recession, but their amount reflected the demand produced by the Argentine economy in the 1980s. Very soon after, the foreign economic "opening" and convertibility modified that state of affairs. From April 1991 with the launching of the plan, the country began to import at a rate of a billion dollars per month; these purchases totaled 12 billion dollars in 1992, reversing the earlier positive total in the commercial balance, given that exports remained stable. Imports continued increasing and from then on, the balance was permanently and structurally negative due to its links to domestic activity. The commercial deficit got worse because of the deficit in the balance of services and earnings derived from foreign investment, where this gap could be covered only by new indebtedness.

The evolution of exports provided a certain respite. At the beginning, there was no reaction in the local supply of goods, but toward 1994 one notes a rapid increase in exports, helped by the greater production of raw materials and stimulated by the rise in agricultural prices in the international market (especially soybeans). To this can be added an increase in sales to Brazil, which revalued its national currency with the Real Plan and made the goods of different Argentine sectors more salable. The area that benefited most was automobiles, thanks to the programs for trade compensation signed to integrate the activities of the assembly plants on both sides of the frontier. Foreign sales doubled between 1993 and 1997, with 60% of this increase explained by raw material sales (agricultural, fish, petroleum, and hides), and 30% more by the sales to Brazil, half of which derived from automobiles.[8] The overwhelming presence of these products in the increase of foreign sales allows any explanation based on an effective increase in productivity or competitiveness in the global economy to be discounted; the great advance was in raw materials with minimal processing, with almost no effect on employment or other productive linkages. The only exception was in a protected, very special sector of manufacturing, automobiles.

The positive effect was very brief, since exports again stagnated from 1998. They failed to regain momentum for various reasons. One reason was because a new fall in international prices counteracted the greater supply in tons of certain basic goods like soybeans; another was because the Brazilian devaluation and the subsequent contraction of the domestic market of that neighboring country undercut Argentine supply. But imports continued their rise, so that the commercial balance was negative in the whole period except in 1995 (when foreign purchases fell owing to the economic crisis of that year) and in 2001 (for the same reason).

The balance in services was also negative owing to the revaluation of the peso. The effect of foreign travel was notable, given that relative prices made it more economical to take trips abroad than in one's own country. The strongly negative results in tourist services can be added to equally negative ones in other key sectors like freight, insurance, etc. At the time the total was compensated for by the massive entry of foreign capital that came with privatization or with the purchases of domestic companies (plus a body of speculative capital that sought short-term profits). That movement produced a contradictory effect: at the moment it entered, it allowed the deficit in the balance of payments to be dealt with, but it produced the normal wave of foreign exchange remittance as profit, which increased over time.

The sum of these effects produced a structural deficit in the current account.[9] To manage this, the country needed the massive, continuous entry of new foreign capital to permit the repatriation of foreign exchange implied by the negative accounts in the mercantile balance, services, and profits. Such income came as new investment or as loans, but in both cases it generated an additional demand for future remittances abroad in the form of interest or dividends; it thus aggravated from year to year the same problem that it sought to resolve.

The only possible solution to this dilemma was the generation of a positive result in the commercial balance, or in some sectors of the services balance, that would make it possible to meet this demand for foreign exchange. The increase in exports, however, ceased from 1998 when certain external stimuli mentioned above disappeared. The Brazilian devaluation reduced that country's purchases while it increased the competitiveness of its exports to Argentina; the fall in the international price of soybeans and other raw materials affected the profitability of producers and discouraged their plan to expand local supply; the international overvaluation of the dollar diminished local competitiveness, since the peso was tied to that currency.

The reduction of imports, in turn, was accomplished only through recession. That effectively took place from 1998, but it was difficult for such a (harmful) means to generate enough, given the magnitude of demand created by convertibility. It is certain that tariff (such as the application of anti-dumping provisions) or semi-tariff mechanisms (using technical or food-related norms to limit the entry of certain goods)—even applying a "buy national" strategy (suspended by official policy)—would have been able to reduce foreign purchases. But the rigid decision of the government to maintain economic "opening" to the extreme, something that Argentine and international financial leaders considered essential, resulted in those means being rejected until it was too late.

The services balance offered the same difficulties in finding an equilibrium point. The disappearance of an Argentine flag merchant marine (as a consequence of official policy) was a barrier to gaining cargoes to be shipped abroad, all won by foreign companies. The elimination of subsidy provisions for domestic insurance companies made it difficult to obtain part of those operations for local capital. The tourist flow imposed a demand for foreign currency that could not be alleviated except by restrictions that would be unacceptable to society and, moreover, might be taken as a sign of economic policy weakness, producing a "run" on the dollar. On the other hand, the consumption of imported goods and the trips abroad were some of the factors that reinforced convertibility's positive image among the middle-sector groups in the population that ignored the wider cost of those activities.

Consequently, the fate of convertibility remained fundamentally based on the massive entry of foreign capital, either though new credits or through the purchase of domestic assets.[10]

The Effects of Convertibility on the Budget

Public revenue had fallen notably in 1990 due to the recession and its consequences for taxes. In 1991 income began to recover until it returned to "normal" levels in 1993. While this was happening, the Treasury enjoyed the advantage of receiving money from privatization, as expenditure remained low thanks to state-sector salaried workers losing ground in terms of income after economic adjustment.[11] In the interim, the government took advantage of the large expansion of public income to eliminate a series of minor taxes considered "distorsionary." In 1994, it made a major decision: to "privatize" the pension system that, in essence, implied a large transfer of the contributions in that area to private businesses created for that purpose. These could take possession of and use resources intended for future payments to their presumed beneficiaries.

The private pension system implied the shift of some 4 billion pesos annually from public reserves to the private financial sector, an intense outflow from the operations of the national Treasury. It was clear that that transfer did not decrease actual pension costs; that expenditure was large (relative to the scale of Treasury operations) due to the broad number of retirees in the country as explained by the age pyramid, although the average amount paid to each was limited (less than that paid out in the 1980s). It is evident that these expenditures were destined to continue growing during the decades of transition, as new candidates became old enough for retirement. This is to say that the shift to privatization brought about an involuntary collapse of fiscal equilibrium, due not to the increase of expenditure but to the fall in public income.

The subsequent evolution of public accounts did not show significant variations after 1994. There was a fall in income during the first recession with an increase in the deficit, and improvement in the brief boom cycle of 1997–1998. The imbalance imposed on public accounts forced the state to take on debt, a task that took place through new obligations assumed in dollars and not in pesos; such a strategy had as its real cause the need to cover the gap in the balance of payments analyzed above.

Until 1997, the entry of international financial capital was fairly fluid, except for some problems during the Tequila crisis. But thereafter difficulties began. The Asian crisis (1997) marked a tendency for the exhaustion of the supply of funds for emerging markets that continued with the Russian and Brazilian crises. The best evidence of this new foreign scene was the increase in the premium paid for new credit linked to "country risk." It is obvious that the rise in rates led to higher future interest payments. These, in turn, would have to be financed with new credits that increased the nominal amount of debt. The increase in total public expenditure (see Table 4.1) reflected a clearly financial phenomenon.

Table 4.1. Evolution of the National Budget, 1993–2000
(in Billions of Dollars–Equivalent Pesos)

	1993	1994	1995	1996	1997	1998	1999	2000
Current Income	38.25	37.74	36.61	33.58	39.50	40.40	40.00	40.40
Current Expenditure	29.89	32.00	32.13	31.57	35.20	34.75	36.40	35.10
Primary Surplus	8.36	5.74	4.48	2.01	4.30	5.65	3.60	5.30
Interest	2.55	2.92	3.89	4.46	5.50	6.45	8.00	9.50
Final Total	5.81	2.82	0.59	-2.45	-1.20	-0.80	-4.40	-4.20

Source: Based on budgetary data from the Secretaría de Hacienda, Ministerio de Economía.

Interest rose from 2.55 billion pesos/dollars in 1993 to 9.50 billion in 2000, and close to 11 billion in the final year of convertibility (2001). This last sum represented more than a quarter of the total Treasury income compared to 7% eight years before. The 7 billion pesos annually that was added as interest paid between 1993 and 2000 is larger than the 4.20 billion pesos total registered in the last year. In other words, current expenditures of the public sector increased at the rhythm of 3% annually between 1993 and 2000 (equivalent to the increase in social expenditures), but interest climbed 20% annually, eroding the fiscal accounts. There are those who blame the state for "fiscal irresponsibility" for having increased public expenditure to the point where such spending made the balanced budget required for convertibility impossible. Such discourse has various fallacies despite being frequently heard. In the first place, this is so because it takes the year 1990 (with the lowest expenditure in recent decades coinciding with an intense recession) as the base for its analysis and, furthermore, because it ignores both the change of methodology used in the calculus of expenditure and the loss of income derived from the change in the retirement system.[12]

The Effects of Convertibility on the Monetary and Financial System

In the first years of convertibility, one notes strong increases in the demand for pesos and rapid growth in bank system deposits; both reflected the return to a certain normalcy, after the negative impact of hyperinflation and the intense recession. That advance was interrupted toward the end of 1994; the Tequila crisis caused a flight from the peso and a demand for dollars, due to concern that convertibility was on the point of collapse. The flight of deposits reached 18% of the total registered in the system, where it was estimated that the system could not tolerate a loss above 20%. The deterioration was restrained thanks to the credits rapidly granted by international organizations and through an intense and successful manipulation of monetary and financial norms.

The crisis revealed a defect in the new dispositions adopted by the Central Bank. The bank had lost the right to issue currency and was prohibited by law from playing the role of lender of last resort in case of a bank crisis, since to create such liquidity implied breaking the basic rule of convertibility. The expectation that there would be no crisis with the system was incorrect, but the challenges of 1994–1995 were resolved by the intervention of the Bank of the Nation, which assumed the role of lender of last resort clandestinely if efficiently.[13]

After the crisis, the monetary authorities decided to promote the use of the dollar as local money and encouraged bank operations in that currency. As a measure of insurance, the banks were required to maintain reserves abroad in dollars, although it became evident that such reserves would in no way be sufficient in case of a serious crisis (as really occurred at the end of 2001). Under these conditions, the problem of lender of last resort continued to exist without any solution. Toward 1997, people began to imagine a "monetary accord" with the United States where that country would assume such a role, but this was rejected by Washington.[14] The only factor that allowed the system to function was social trust in the monetary mechanisms in place, although this would turn out to be no more than a fantasy.

Thus the monetary and financial system was "dollarized." Dollar deposits in local banks increased without pause during the decade. Their total rose from 20% of the total in 1990 to 41% in 1994, continuing to increase in the next years until it surpassed 60% of the total in 2000; two thirds of the deposits and bank credits were denominated in dollars at the end of convertibility. Funds were loaned to those who bought local goods in pesos who needed to repay them from earnings, also in pesos; this situation created a credit risk that was avoided only as long as convertibility was maintained. Other funds began to be destined in increasing amounts to finance the Treasury, which ended up obligated in dollars to local banks.

This "dollarization" phenomenon was repeated throughout the system in which money circulated. The wide acceptance of the dollar as a substitute for the peso was a fact that could be measured in banking and estimated for the rest of the market. Other measures promoted "dollarization," like the agreements with the majority of the concessionaires for public services who fixed prices in dollars that, surprisingly, were adjusted by changes in the United States price index.

The system was a time bomb. If it exploded, there was no mechanism for recovery. There was no lender of last resort in the financial system, no mechanism for dealing with contracts in dollars (in the case of a potential devaluation), nor were there dollars available to meet demand in case of a loss of confidence in the peso.[15] All depended on a factor as fragile and random as the general faith in stability or, rather, in the ever wider fear of a collapse whose costs were as serious as they were unpredictable.

The Effects of Convertibility on Employment and Income

With the inflationary spiral of the 1980s, real salaries fluctuated, but only within certain parameters since there was little unemployment and the unions had the capacity to impose their demands in the moments of expansion. Despite the prolonged stagnation, unemployment never passed 6% in that period, because business as much as the public sector tended to maintain the existing situation in the hope of a change of conditions. In 1989, the first hyperinflationary jump caused a brutal fall in fixed incomes (salaries and pensions); the second quarter that year marked the first experience with widespread hunger in the country amid elections and with expectations of some solution to the crisis. The subsequent recovery was not enough to allow real incomes to return to their starting point. The buying power of the average salary was at 70% of the 1980s average and remained there from that point on since convertibility stabilized things at that new level.[16]

One notes that the buying power of salaries had fallen (in terms of the market basket of goods and services that measures the cost of living), but some durable goods like TVs and radios had also dropped in price relative to incomes; this suggests that salaried workers found themselves with the possibility of obtaining goods that up until then had been hard to acquire while at the same time they were losing purchasing power in terms of local goods (including items as important as food and transport, for example). This situation made possible a debate over the stated and real evolution of salaries in that entire period that still continues today.[17]

The debate would have been theoretical if, as occurred in other situations, workers began to demand improvements in their income, taking advantage of their social presence and the activity of their unions. But such demands were much milder or more limited than at other times. Key here was the actual pressure of the unemployed that increased its presence throughout the entire 1990s. The concern of businessmen to contain their costs in the face of economic opening was another factor that was reflected in a change of conduct between those sectors exposed to foreign competition, as opposed to providers of local services: the former had to adjust their prices to survive while the latter, with less "market pressure," showed some tendency to accept salary improvements, at least in moments of boom.[18] Official policy contributed to this state of things, as much with its energetic position toward the union movement (when it sought salary hikes) as with administrative means. One of these was to establish a minimum wage well below the level of the previous decade; this measure altered its social meaning, shifting it from being a minimum that protected workers from greater deterioration in their income to being a threshold that definitively authorized greater salary reductions because it was set well below the average levels recognized in the labor market.[19]

The drop in salary was accompanied by notable declines of health and retirement benefits. The obligatory contributions that had existed until then to guarantee the protection of workers were disappearing. The government itself reduced them, citing the utility of lowering labor costs, while businesses illegally employed workers without benefits to avoid the cost, with no fear of reprisals from authorities who ignored such practices. The evasion reduced company expenses at the cost of the progressive deterioration of protection. Conditions thereafter reached unsustainable levels in regard to health care and retirement. The majority of social funds that provided health care for workers were close to or in bankruptcy, while the possibility of receiving a retirement pension was seriously reduced: in 1994, 23% of people over 65 years old had no pension; that figure increased to 35% by 2001. Also, as only 40% of the salaried work force presently contributes for retirement, such inadequacies in the safety net are going to increase in future years as a perverse consequence of the economic model.[20]

Argentine unemployment fluctuated around 4% in the 1970s and 6% in the 1980s; in 1994, during the most successful stage of economic recovery, it jumped to 10%. The next year, with the Tequila crisis, the figure abruptly shot up to 20%, a level that had no relation to the fall of output and that can be explained only by the accumulation of earlier phenomena linked to the breakdown of labor relations. Later in the decade, unemployment tended to return to levels of 14% to 15%, well above the earlier experience of the country. In the period 1994–2001, which covers eight of the somewhat more than ten years of convertibility, unemployment averaged 14%, never once dropping below the 12% threshold. These levels, never previously experienced in modern Argentina, mark a rupture in the labor market in terms of social relations. The magnitude and prolonged nature of unemployment form a new stage in the history of employment in the country.[21]

The causes of unemployment are still the subject of analysis owing to the lack of adequate information. Even so, one can present some limited explanation that if not very precise does contribute to the understanding of the subject. The privatization of public companies contributed to the firing of a large number of workers; such a process led to a reduction of around 200,000 jobs, to which ought to be added the jobs lost in businesses supplying them that ceased operation when the new owners elected to buy their supplies abroad. The contraction of production indicated by the closing of a great number of factories added to the "rationalization" required by the times, producing an additional loss of 300,000 positions. Finally, the relative stagnation of construction, which never returned in the 1990s to the levels reached in 1980, implied the absence of demand for 200,000 jobs versus what was recorded in better periods.

These figures, whose order of magnitude is in itself significant, ought to be adjusted by additional facts like the multiplier effect of unemployment on other domestic activities. Additionally, the principal activities that grew in the period (pampean agriculture, petroleum extraction, fishing, and public services) did not generate new jobs or did not do so in sufficient magnitude to modify the earlier tendencies. There was some increase of employment in personal services (from restaurants to beauty salons) aimed at the middle and upper sectors of society, although such needs could not counteract the negative effects of the mentioned losses.

Unemployment is today a structural phenomenon in Argentina, as much for its magnitude as its causes. Worse yet, the crisis that began toward the end of convertibility was affecting the labor market even more, to the point of creating conditions of extreme vulnerability that will be dealt with below.

The Final Crisis of Convertibility

Convertibility had its first major crisis at the end of 1994. The recession, together with a "run" on the peso, was basically attributed to the Mexican crisis that broke out at that moment and limited the influx of financial resources. Such an explanation does not sufficiently explain why the impact was very strong in Argentina but not so pronounced in other Latin American countries; the different responses to the impact of the Tequila crisis suggest that an important vulnerability had been created in the foreign sector. Such vulnerability would be felt more strongly in another crisis that would become terminal; this began in 1998 and had several original aspects that contributed effects over three difficult years.

The first was the brusque fall in the international prices of agricultural goods produced in the Pampas region, especially soybeans. The earlier rise in the 1994–1998 period stimulated the expansion of those crops and the growth of exports; in reverse, the fall in prices had a strong impact on the profitability of producers. Producers tended to go into debt to maintain their production in conditions of low or no profitability, even beginning to hope for a devaluation that would alter their income.[22] On the other hand, that price fall slowed the growth of these exports (given that larger quantities were exported, but at very low prices), thus contributing to generate a very sharp imbalance in the country's commercial balance.

The second cause of negative effects was the Brazilian devaluation of 1999 in the country that had become Argentina's principal trade partner. The greater competitiveness of Brazilian exports produced a massive inflow of goods produced in that country while local exports fell. The Brazilian recession, furthermore, reduced the demand for various goods, including one as important as automobiles, so that the commercial exchange shrank, with the balance tending to be unfavorable for Argentina.

There were other more limited effects, such as the sharp momentary fall in petroleum prices close to the year 2000 that strongly affected local export figures in that area (that now exceeded 3 billion dollars). Additionally, the rise of interest in the United States had an impact in that it affected the level of international rates.[23] Such an increase meant that Argentina should pay ever larger sums as interest on accumulated debt; such obligations could be compensated for only by new credits at a moment in which international flows were retreating from "emerging markets" owing to the risk experienced in the successive crises that broke out (in East Asia, Russia, and, later, Brazil, that would be finally joined by the one that undid Argentina, and one in Turkey). The continuing rise of the figure measuring "country risk," which defined the cost that the government needed to pay for new credits, exposed Argentina's problems that could be resolved only through a devaluation that would allow it to recover ground on the external front.

Managing the Difficulties of 2001

The Argentine government made a series of efforts to handle the debt payments owed to its creditors. The first was an agreement referred to as the "shield" (or "blindaje") that included a package of credits promised by diverse groups of creditors to deal with the obligations that were coming due in 2001. Such credits were not enough, as well as being tied to various measures that the Argentine government had to adopt. The resignation of Economics Minister José Luis Machinea in March 2001 was the first sign of the crisis. The president named in his place Ricardo López Murphy, an economist who expressed the ideological position that any solution required the reduction of public expenditure; his goal was to generate a greater surplus of pesos to meet the obligations of the debt.[24] His proposal to reduce the university budget, among other cuts, caused such an intense social reaction that the president himself asked for his resignation after only fifteen days in office.[25]

The political crisis was temporarily resolved with the designation of Domingo Cavallo as economics minister, an act that surprised society with the unexpected return of the man who had been the "Father of Convertibility" in the Menem government. One of the first measures of the new minister was to create a subsidy for exports based on a formula that linked the dollar to the euro; he argued that the revaluation the dollar was undergoing in relation to the European currency created competitiveness problems for the export of local goods. Such a "convergence factor" had little effect on real activity, but it was a first sign that Cavallo indirectly recognized that the exchange rate of the Argentine peso was over-valued.[26]

In his next move, Cavallo embarked on new refinancing for the debt that sought to postpone the payments promised for 2001 to 2003, so as not to be affected by the restriction on foreign credit reflected in the continuing rise of Argentina's "country risk." Such a "mega-deal" (or "mega-canje") involved the exchange of bonds coming due in that period for others of longer maturation and at much higher interest rates. The minister was willing to pay any future price that would allow him greater short-term maneuverability, although the form in which this operation was carried out (paying a 150-million-dollar commission to a bank assisting in this task) and its elevated costs caused political protests and a request for a judicial investigation.[27]

The "mega-deal" included asking local banks and the AFJP private pension funds for dollars where they would turn over part of their dollar deposits in exchange for new domestic debt certificates.[28] This indicates that an appreciable part of the foreign debt was, in effect, now held by domestic financial groups.

Such almost desperate measures produced a deterioration in the balance sheets of banks that had an increasing body of debts among their assets, while their reserves were sharply declining. These fell because one part was being used to pay foreign commitments, given the absence of fresh credit, as well as due to the demand for foreign currency from private groups (especially the banks themselves that sought to gain protection from the foreseeable risk). The fall in foreign currency had the repercussion of reducing the amount of money in circulation (given the requirements of convertibility), thus contributing in this way to deepening the process of recession.

The final available solution to pay the capital and interest coming due that greatly exceeded the funds obtained by the means described was to turn to international entities like the IMF that, in sum, lend more for political than for economic reasons. The government did turn to them, but such an option encountered difficulties when the new administration in the United States (which took office in January 2001) began to apply a new policy concerning the general relief of debtor nations meant to save private creditors. The refusal of the International Monetary Fund to give new credits to Argentina, with the consent of (or pressure from) the U.S. Treasury, marked the beginning of the end of convertibility.

The quantity of money fell 30% in the course of 2001, an unheard-of amount that explains the difficulties experienced by the Argentine economy in this period of the agony of the model. To compensate in part for these inconveniences, the government turned to the emission of financial instruments that, although they were not money, fulfilled the role of money. Some were emitted by the national treasury (so-called "Lecops") and sent to the provinces (that in turn used them to pay their bills), and others were emitted by local governments (such as the Patacones issued by Buenos Aires Province) to resolve their cash problems. These emissions began around September 2001 and reflected an odd kind of irony: the government fulfilled its commitment to maintain in circulation an amount of money equal to its foreign currency reserves, while it issued paper that was recognized as "quasi-money" in order to evade the strict restrictions of convertibility.[29]

In October, the IMF announced that it would not lend new funds to the country. From then on, the flight of reserves accentuated the scarcity of money and deepened the recession. The result became inevitable. In order to limit the increasing exit of funds from the financial system (owing to the lack of money in circulation) that now was becoming unbearable, at the end of November 2001 the government decreed a freeze of bank deposits (the so-called "corralito") and the closure of the exchange market. Depositors could not take out their money from banks nor could they exchange pesos for dollars (based on convertibility).

The crisis was on. The exchange rate nominally remained at one to one, but now no one believed in that rate. The blocking of bank operations augured a quick return to the black market should a final decision not be made, and it prevented the removal of pesos (beyond a small sum each week decided by the authorities), but it especially prevented the removal of dollars so that many people began to feel that they had been swindled. The anger of savers exploded, while the sudden move to an almost total scarcity of pesos struck a new blow against society. The lack of available money stopped a great part of economic transactions, especially those realized in cash (from bus or taxi transportation to domestic service, to mention only a few of the more obvious). The most negative effects in this situation fell on the self-employed and the poorest, whose numbers increased with the changes in the employment structure and the long recession. The breakdown in the flow of physical money destroyed the economy's capacity to attract income and pushed those on the margins into even deeper poverty. In hardly three weeks of such an unheard-of experience, the desperate mobilization of the poor seeking food and of the middle class demanding the return of their savings generated a grave social crisis. In one of the first large-scale mobilizations, numerous people died due to police repression; this set the political process under way for its final denouement. The resignation of the minister of economics and, as an almost inevitable consequence, that of the president of the nation himself (who preferred to leave rather than admitting that the economic system had collapsed), marked the height of the crisis.

The political blow that unleashed the economic and social crisis created five presidents in ten days and marked the definitive departure from convertibility. One of the successive presidents during this stage of upheaval declared a default on the debt, a measure that only expressed in words the reality of the situation; another devalued the peso, a largely formal decision that only released tension created by the earlier "non-decision" when the exchange market had been closed in hope of a miracle that did not happen. Later, a new transitional government started out on the difficult road of change and adjustment, amid the longest and deepest recession that Argentina had ever known, a recession that was combined with hunger, political crisis, and social protests.

Notes

* Translated by Edward Epstein.

1. The "Rodrigazo" was the name popularly given to a packet of economic measures applied in June 1975 by Economic Minister Celestino Rodrigo that included an abrupt devaluation of 100%, plus an increase in public service charges of 200%; such decisions made inflation and the final breakdown of the local productive sector more likely. That policy is analyzed in detail in Jorge Schvarzer, *La política económica de Martínez de Hoz* (Buenos Aires: Hyspamerica, 1986), where the entire economic strategy carried out during the military government is dealt with, as are its early consequences.

2. Menem was elected for a six-year term to begin December 12, 1989, but took office early, on July 8 of the same year. He was re-elected in 1995 (after a constitutional change that allowed re-election and shortened the presidential term to four years) and turned over the office on December 12, 1999. His stay in the presidency was the longest known in the country's history (ten and one-half years), one that would have been impossible under the country's former constitution (which permitted only a single six-year term with no immediate re-election), as well as under the one approved in 1994 (which allows one re-election after four years, so that one can serve only eight consecutive years). The phenomenon of his serving so long is explained by his active role in the reform of the constitution, following the earlier version in his first period in office and the present version in his second term. Such a political presence is another element that permitted the economic measures described in the text.

3. This result, as was evident from the beginning of such a strategy (and as was amply debated throughout the period) is statistically corroborated in Benjamin Hopenhayn, Jorge Schvarzer, and Hernán Finkelstein, "El tipo de cambio en perspectiva histórica: Aportes para un debate," *Notas de Coyuntura*, no. 7 (October 2002), CESPA, Buenos Aires.

4. The reduction was unilateral because the government did not take advantage of the opportunity to try to negotiate with other governments for a mutual reduction of tariffs, as other countries customarily have done in similar circumstances. The announced "opening" consequently was one for imports because it facilitated the massive entry of foreign goods, but not one for exports, as a good part of the economic literature supposes when it uses this term, imagining that it will stimulate economic growth via a greater supply of goods for the world market.

5. Such a methodological topic, the same as for the behavior of particular productive sectors, as noted above, is discussed in great detail in Jorge Schvarzer, "La estructura productiva argentina a mediados de la década del noventa: Tendencias visibles y un diagnóstico con interrogantes," *Documento de Trabajo*, no. 1 (July 1997), CREED, Buenos Aires.

6. The exaggeration of the indices for the calculation of the increase of production in 1997 and 1998 is analyzed in Jorge Schvarzer, "Indicadores industriales y diagnósticos de coyuntura en la Argentina: Precauciones de uso y elementos para un balance actualizado," *Documento de Trabajo*, no. 3 (December 1999), CREED, Buenos Aires, as well as in Jorge Schvarzer and Javier Papa, "El indicador sintético de servicios públicos y la marcha de la economía real (1993–2001)," *Notas Técnicas*, no. 1 (April 2002),

CESPA, Buenos Aires. Although the topic forms part of a study in progress seeking to confirm this interpretation, the figures already found suggest that this hypothesis is correct.

7. These data can be seen in greater detail in Jorge Schvarzer and Mariana Rojas Breu, "Algunos ragos básicos de la evolución económica argentina durante las dos últimas décadas vista en el contexto latinoamericano," *Notas Técnicas*, no. 2 (September 2002), CESPA, Buenos Aires.

8. See the analysis in Jorge Schvarzer, "La estructura productiva argentina," and in Schvarzer and Ivan Heyn, "El comportamiento de las exportaciones argentinas en la década del noventa: Un balance de la convertibilidad," *Notas Técnicas*, no. 3 (November 2002), CESPA, Buenos Aires.

9. This topic is carefully analyzed for the 1990s in Mario Damil, "El balance de pagos y la deuda externa bajo la convertibilidad," *Boletín Informativo Techint*, no. 303 (December 2000), Buenos Aires. This analysis not only confirms the tendency toward a structural foreign deficit but adds that the deficit was continually present in private sector transactions so that the public sector had to go into debt, as actually happened, to compensate for this.

10. Carlos Rodríguez, ex–chief advisor to Economics Minister Roque Fernández (1996–1999) (and work colleague of his in the center for economic analysis and interest group known as CEMA) said after the failure of convertibility that "the Argentine financial system is designed for an economy that attracts the entry of 20 billion dollars in capital per year. And here there was 20 billion in capital flight" (comments in *Ambito Financiero*, October 31, 2001). Although not of such magnitude, the flight mentioned occurred at the end of convertibility, as will be discussed later. What is important is the reference to the need for the continual entry of foreign capital for the system to function by one of that program's principal ideologues and administrators.

11. The series on income and on expenditures in the public sector are not directly comparable for the period 1989–1992 owing to the changes in relative prices occurring then that, added to inflation, make it very difficult to convert them into constant pesos. Also, in 1993, the government changed the methodology used to measure and classify expenditures from then on but did not make corrections for earlier years. For this reason it seems curious that there would be a broad debate on the evolution of public spending in that period that totally ignores the effects of such problems of methodological criteria used in measuring that variable. Here I have opted to present a synthesis that indicates the principal tendencies based on reasonable assumptions, avoiding statistical details that would only confuse the text.

12. One of the biggest advocates of this view is Ricardo López Murphy, the economist at FIEL (the Fundación de Investigaciones Económicas Latinoamericanas, a foundation dedicated to economic studies supported by large businesses), first minister of defense, later briefly economics minister under President De la Rúa (in March 2001) and, more recently, a candidate for president in the April 2003 elections.

13. An excellent review of the functioning of the monetary system in that critical period and of the problems that the rules for convertibility created can be seen in Alfredo F. Calcagno, "El régimen de convertibilidad y el systema bancario en la Argentina," *Revista de la Cepal*, no. 61 (April 1997), Santiago de Chile.

14. Although there were numerous "leaks" in the professional media, the negotiations on this matter between officials of the different countries were secret and continued over an extended time period given that they began at least by 1997 and continued to mid-2001 in Cavallo's final period as minister. For the debate in the United States on this

topic, see Mariana Rojas Breu, "El debate en torno a la dolarización: Ideas y propuestas," *Documento de Trabajo*, no. 2 (May 2002), CESPA, Buenos Aires.

15. This last point is important. The law stated that reserves ought to equal the quantity of money in circulation, but the banking system created money (through the phenomenon known as a multiplier), so that the potential demand for dollars would always be greater than the available supply. It is sufficient to suggest that toward the end of convertibility, total reserves of all kinds never hit 30 billion dollars, but deposits in the financial system exceeded 70 billion (in pesos and dollars), and money in circulation amounted to another 15 billion; as a result, achieving a balance was impossible.

16. These data are based on the salary series prepared by FIEL, based on surveys of companies to establish net salary levels (that is, what was actually received including incentive and overtime), corrected for inflation. These data are consistent with other similar statistics.

17. In a general way, one can point out one particular case as an example: the minimum salary was around the equivalent of 100 dollars in the 1980s, when a TV cost 500 dollars retail. From 1991, that salary nominally had risen to 400 dollars (but not in real buying power), while TVs tended to fall in price due to technological change abroad. Consequently, their relative price fell from five minimum salaries to only one (and later on even less), contributing to the confusion of many analysts as to the actual evolution of real salaries.

18. The statistical series on net salaries, although incomplete, allows one to observe that workers in banks and other service sector businesses did better than those inindustry.

19. Measured in pesos of constant purchasing power, the official minimum salary in the 1990s fell to half of that in the previous decade, something that explains the effect noted. On the other hand, such a change allowed retirement and minimum pensions to remain at very low levels (in relation to the minimum wage), levels that officials said could not be increased due to the need for a "balanced budget."

20. The information on those enrolled and contributing to a retirement plan is from ANSSES, the government agency in charge of the system. The number of those over 65 with no benefits comes from a study by SIEMPRO, the official body for the analysis of such statistics. The projection of data on present contributors allows one to suggest that 60% of those over 65 will in the future have no pension, which would thus become the privilege of a few.

21. Unemployment and its consequences in the period are from a formal and statistical point of view dealt with in Jorge Schvarzer and Héctor Palomino, "Entre la informalidad y el desempleo: Una perspectiva de largo plazo sobre el mercado de trabajo en la Argentina," *Encrucijadas*, review of the University of Buenos Aires, no. 4, 1996. The theoretical model analyzing the labor market as a social relationship and its implication for the country is dealt with in Jorge Schvarzer, *Implicación de un modelo económico: La experiencia argentina entre 1975 y 2000* (Buenos Aires: A-Z Editora, 1998).

22. The international price of soybean oil went from an average of 450 dollars per ton between 1988 and 1993 to 600 dollars between 1994 and 1998; it later fell sharply to 300 dollars in 2001, with such a level being a tragedy for local producers. It is not too much to state that the increase of 1994 to 1998 explains the expansion of crops and exports that, in a sense, made life under convertibility possible with the improvement in the commercial balance. This analysis, with data to support it, is found in Jorge Schvarzer, "La fragilidad externa de la economía argentina," in *La Gaceta de Económicas*, Buenos Aires, October 28, 2001.

23. The rediscount rate set by the United States Federal Reserve fell from 7% at the end of the 1980s to 3% in the first four years of convertibility, helping to support this monetary experience; on the other hand, it rose to 5% at the endof 1994, a change that to a good extent created the Tequila crisis. In 2000 it rose to 6%. Its subsequent fall to almost ridiculous levels came too late for convertibility, which was already beginning to collapse. See Jorge Schvarzer, "La fragilidad externa."

24. Naturally, the proposed reduction of expenditure implied the sharpening of the already intense recession, a phenomenon that would permit demand for imports to diminish while salaries were reduced, so as to create a kind of solution for the debt via indirect means that would not be explicitly mentioned in that discourse.

25. López Murphy's decisions have to be seen as due to a diagnosis that seems to ignore that Argentina's problem was its strong foreign imbalance due to the overvalued exchange rate and the accumulation of an enormous debt owed in foreign currency. This situation could not be dealt with by creating a budgetary surplus in pesos since these had to be converted into dollars to pay the service on the debt. Such a proposed solution, however, was considered good by creditors who expected only a gesture rather than a real solution from the Argentine government.

26. According to various defenders of convertibility, the revaluation of the dollar against the euro in that period was a factor that affected exports from Argentina (because the peso was linked to the dollar), although it seems to be stretching credibility to give it such importance. One should add that those analysts rarely mentioned the impacts pointed out in this text whose importance is undeniable.

27. Congressman Mario Cafiero was one of those most involved with these accusations in the Chamber of Deputies; as a result of those efforts, he later wrote a book together with Javier Llorens entitled *La Argentina robada* (Ediciones Macchi, 2002), where the "mega-deal" is explained along with other operations. It is the most detailed account that exists of this matter, although the presentation is not always easy to follow for the interested reader.

28. AFJPs (Administradoras de Fondos de Jubilaciones y Pensiones, or Retirement and Pension Fund Accounts) were created in 1994 as private businesses to manage the resources that salaried workers contributed for their retirement. They rapidly became entities operating with enormous financial resources, a good part of which were destined to finance the public sector (whose deficit originated with the diversion of such funds that previously it had received directly).

29. This topic is analyzed in part in Jorge Schvarzer and Hernán Finkelstein, "Bonos, cuasimonedas y política económica," *Notas de Coyuntura*, no. 8 (January 2003), CESPA, Buenos Aires.

Part III

Citizen Responses

5

The Piquetero Movement in Greater Buenos Aires: Political Protests by the Unemployed Poor During the Crisis*

Edward Epstein

The wave of social protests by so-called "piqueteros" (or picketers) that became commonplace in the Buenos Aires region in recent years represents an innovation of considerable importance in Argentine politics. Rather than consisting of unionized workers engaged in strikes of whatever kind as the name might suggest, those involved represent a successful effort at mobilizing some of those individuals who have rarely been actively involved as an organized force in national politics: the chronically unemployed poor, their families, and local sympathizers of a similar impoverished background. This reference to trade union politics, however, is neither irrelevant nor merely coincidental. Although the traditional labor movement associated with the Peronist-controlled General Confederation of Labor (Confederación General de Trabajo, or CGT) is quite removed from the present discussion about the recent political mobilization of numbers of the jobless in or near the Argentine Capital, the adoption in certain situations of analogous political strategies adopted from a trade union context by piquetero leaders is seen as quite relevant to the understanding of such popular protest in contemporary Argentina.

The type of political action for which the piqueteros are best known is their temporary blockage of strategic roads and bridges in what has been referred to as "cortes de ruta." The most immediate purpose of such an occupation of public space has been to induce government officials to pay serious attention to the economic needs of the participants. What is sought typically is some type of unemployment relief, be it in the form of actual jobs, the provision of a short-term cash subsidy often in return for a community-based labor commitment, or simply bags of food. As open unemployment grew to record levels in Argentina, the piqueteros have demanded inclusion in government relief programs like the various stages of the Jobs Program (or Programa Trabajar) of 1996–2002 or the more inclusive Program for Unemployed Female and Male Heads of Family (Programa Jefas/Jefes de Familia Desocupados, hereafter the Programa Jefas/Jefes), that replaced it from mid-May 2002.

The primary goal of this chapter is to provide a general discussion of the piquetero movement as it has developed in a Greater Buenos Aires traumatized by a profound national economic crisis.[1] While the Capital region was picked for study here because of its centrality to a national decision-making process that the piqueteros have sought to influence, the phenomenon of using road blockages as a political tactic actually began earlier in places in the Argentine interior like Jujuy, Salta, and Neuquén and soon spread to Buenos Aires.[2]

The present essay begins with an overview of the economic crisis itself and the effects of the heightened unemployment in eroding existing social ties like conventional trade union membership or inclusion in a traditional neighborhood-based clientelist network. These are ties that in the past linked particular working-class individuals to the status quo politics typically associated with the Peronist Party. Such information on the changing socio-economic structure that poor Argentines have had to confront is meant to serve as a necessary preface for discussion of the principal question this chapter addresses: how the piqueteros emerged as an influential social movement. Each of the three remaining major sections is organized around one of the triad of analytical categories—"political opportunity structures," "mobilizing structures," and "framing processes"—that dominates the version of social movement theory associated with the work of Doug McAdam, Sidney Tarrow, and Charles Tilly.[3]

The section associated with increased opportunity begins with a discussion of the political changes derived from the economic crisis that allowed emerging piquetero leaders to see what appeared to them as heightened possibilities for the strategic use of political mobilization of some of the now quite numerous poor. Here group leaders have utilized the threat of road blockages as a significant bargaining chip with which to exact concessions from the government. While such "cortes" have been a direct challenge to government authority and were probably illegal under Argentine law, the risk of government repression seemed reduced as long as public support for that government and for most public institutions remained low. As the movement grew in the Buenos Aires area, it dividedpolitically along lines reflecting the differing tactics each group adopted in its relations with a government seen as increasingly politically vulnerable due to its inability to resolve the crisis.

The portion of the chapter dealing with organizational factors for social mobilization deals with the uses made of the places in government relief programs obtained by piquetero leaders for some of their members. Importantly, with the access to such places, these leaders usually gained control over the labor contribution officially required of all program beneficiaries. Some critics have seen such control as constituting the material basis for what they described as a new version of political clientelism. If such a characterization is to be useful, however, it is only in recognizing within such a clientelism the distinctive new emphasis given in the piquetero communities to personal participation and group discussion for individuals who had seen much of their previous social roots weakened by the crisis. The reorganized social communities to which those who became piqueteros were attracted would benefit significantly from any material resources coming from official aid programs. While the small size of the monthly payments paid to recipients would only partially alleviate their individual poverty,[4] a portion of such incoming funds could be pooled with the work contributions due to the group sponsoring the inclusion of these beneficiaries. These shared resources have helped to finance a series of piquetero-organized services like joint food kitchens, nurseries, and even small workshops around which the new social communities of the poor have been constructed.

The section dealing with cultural factors that frame individual perceptions on participation in piquetero mobilizations focuses on how conditions within a piquetero group affect how those involved understand their own involvement. Such conditions have permitted some of the unemployed and their families to restructure their identity from the largely negative social role of being isolated poor individuals with no work to a more positive one of being part of a community where each member contributes to the whole. What is emphasized here is not only the occasional activities on the picket line, but what takes place on a continuing basis in the local poor neighborhoods reorganized by the piqueteros with the emergence of a more participatory style of collective decision-making allowing members to feel more meaningful. If the rhetoric of all piquetero groups shares such a commitment to the centrality of the local community and to greater participation in it, many groups place an additional focus on their linkages to the outside political world through labor union and political party allies. Where this more external orientation exists, it seems related to a rather vertical authority structure in each group where the leadership enjoys considerable autonomy in decision-making. Only those piquetero groups that have resisted such alliances seem also to have adopted a more horizontal style of leadership with a much more actively involved general membership.

A final part of the chapter represents a short update on the current state of the piquetero movement and of recent government responses, reflecting in particular the revival of the economy during 2003 and 2004. The eventual shift in government strategy by a new and still popular president, Néstor Kirchner, imposing limits on popular protest by radical piquetero groups in late 2004, reinforces the notion used here that understands social movements as a type of mass mobilization that takes advantage of particular conditions. Once such a moment of opportunity has passed, movements like the Argentine piqueteros are likely to find a far more difficult political environment in which to operate from that which initially facilitated such social mobilization.

The Economic Crisis

By 2002, the dramatic deterioration of the Argentine economy that had been ongoing since 1998 had produced a social calamity. While a large percentage of Argentina's total population were suffering in differing degree, the focus here is on those who involuntarily became part of the expanding pool of the long-term unemployed poor, since it is from this group that the piqueteros have come.

The most important economic changes in terms of an understanding of the piqueteros relate to those in the labor market. Here one sees a decade-long increase in the percentage of precarious jobs and worsening structural unemployment, problems that seem adjuncts of the market-oriented economic innovations introduced by the Menem government in office from 1989.[5] While open unemployment rose notably during the brief 1995 recession, it got much worse during the far more serious downturn that began in mid-1998 and continued over the next four years.

In 2002, when economic production sharply contracted an alarming 11.1%, Argentines saw a spike in the level of already serious existing poverty.[6] This worsening of poverty was due to the negative effects on real income of the short-term resurgence of inflation caused by the abandonment of exchange rate convertibility at par with the dollar and the resulting big peso devaluation. By May 2002, national unemployment hit an Argentine modern record figure of 21.5% of the work force. By that October, the official statistics would have been worse still if those enrolled in the minimally paid government relief programs with their community work obligations had been included among the unemployed.[7]

As a consequence of this record level of unemployment, the government statistics office INDEC reported that 54.3% of the population of Greater Buenos Aires were living beneath the official poverty line as of October 2002. Furthermore, of that total body of poor people, 24.7% were depicted as suffering from poverty so extreme they could no longer afford adequate food.[8] These are the worst statistics on poverty in the Capital region since relevant income data were first available there. Such dramatically worsening figures help to understand why people in and near Buenos Aires were attracted to the piquetero groups.

The concern here is how these disastrous economic events affected the growing numbers of the poor, especially those who were unemployed with little real prospect of a job under existing conditions. One particular social aspect of the crisis that various observers have noted relates to the sense of personal isolation and social exclusion derived from chronic unemployment and poverty that has affected the identity of many Argentines in a society where one's job typically defines one's identity.[9]

The increased isolation of many poor individuals in the 1990s decade reflects not only their heightened joblessness, but also related factors that affected existing social groups linked to Peronist politics. The overwhelmingly Peronist trade union movement organized around a divided CGT seemed to exhibit little interest in such unemployed workers. Also important was the at least temporary organizational erosion of the Peronist clientelist network in the Buenos Aires region as its local financing contracted with the economic crisis.

Historically, many working-class Argentines had looked to the trade unions of the CGT to provide them with health care and other social benefits, as well as to act as their political voice before the national government. With the decay of traditional Argentine labor from the late 1980s on in terms of its ability to mobilize workers in mass protests, the union movement saw its collective political influence considerably reduced with the now markedly more conservative, business-oriented Peronism of the Menem government.[10] Uncertain as to how to respond to the new conditions, the unions fragmented politically into what became by the mid-1990s three major rival confederations—the officially recognized Peronist CGT, a dissident Peronist CGT, and the non-Peronist left-leaning Argentine Workers Central (Central de Trabajadores Argentinos or CTA), not to mention smaller groups like the Trotskyist Class Combat Movement (Corriente Clasista Combativa, or CCC), which was originally active largely in the interior province of Jujuy but later spread to other areas including Buenos Aires. As long-term unemployment increased in the 1990s, those unable to pay the dues necessary to maintain active membership seemed abandoned by the more traditional unions linked to the CGT.

In the Greater Buenos Aires area (and elsewhere), a number of poor individuals had previously secured a form of dependent political integration via traditional clientelist structures linked to the local Peronist Party.[11] Here they had been strongly encouraged to exchange their personal political support for party leaders in return for inclusion in public poverty relief programs whose benefits party activists controlled.[12] But as the crisis intensified, such clientelist practices were often partially undercut by decreased government finances, especially from provincial and local sources. As one observer notes, food distribution programs for the poor like the "Life Support Plan" (Plan Vida) with its network of largely female political block-workers (the so-called "manzaneras") created in the province of Buenos Aires in the 1990s by then Governor Duhalde and his wife were to deteriorate as provincial governments, including that of Buenos Aires, increasingly ran out of cash.[13] Those needy individuals who had benefited from such a political use of official relief programs were, like former union members, often forced to look elsewhere for help in their economic survival.

The emergence of piquetero communities should be seen as one particular response to the economic crisis and the opportunities for the political mobilization of parts of the poor recognized by those who became the leaders of these new working-class groups. Such opportunities were particularly political in nature, reflecting the weakening social control of the Argentine state and of the major political parties that seriously competed for its key offices. By the late 1990s, the piqueteros were becoming of increasing importance in a political system that eventually would reach a condition not far from collapse.

Opportunity Structures Resulting from the Crisis

So-called "political opportunity structures" are based on the calculation by movement leaders at a specific moment of "the degree to which groups are likely to gain access to power and to manipulate the system."[14] In this calculation, such strategically oriented individuals can be seen as constructing what could be understood as a crude matrix of the possibilities versus the risks involved in such efforts at seeking to influence the political system as these are affected by perceived "changes in institutional rules, political alignments, or alliance[s]."[15] By the end of 2001, Argentine politics had become highly unstable, with existing political alliances breaking down and opportunities for new forces clearly present.

Recent Argentine Presidents Menem, De la Rúa, and Duhalde were each seen at particular moments during his time in office as increasingly vulnerable to political challenges from new groups like the piqueteros. Each president would see the popular approval level of his administration erode with a deterioration of public confidence in how it was thought to be managing the economic crisis. Such a decline in presidential personal image during recent years parallels a falling public confidence in the performance of most public Argentine institutions.[16] By the time of De la Rúa's sudden resignation in December 2001, his support on the Index of Confidence in Government (Indice de Confianza en Gobierno, or ICG) developed at Di Tella University in Buenos Aires was a dismal 0.76 on a scale that varies potentially between a minimum of 0 and a maximum of 5. In the case of the appointed—not elected—Duhalde, someone who had never enjoyed much popular legitimacy as president, his support fell from an already meager 1.36 ICG score in January 2002 when he first took office to an embarrassingly low of 0.32 that September as the economy was near its worst. His score thereafter would never get higher than a still anemic 0.91 in January 2003.[17] The increased political vulnerability resulting from such eroded legitimacy of these different recent Argentine presidents seems due to the negative impact of the poor economy on popular perceptions of their governments.

Prior to the economic collapse, these governments were each caught in a very difficult political situation where any significant economic policy changes were likely to alienate critical sources of emergency loans like the International Monetary Fund, or IMF, on which Argentina had become dependent. This external constraint continued until the IMF itself cut off all funds to the De la Rúa government in October 2001, setting the stage for the implosion of his administration.

Given the external pressure on policy-makers to maintain existing orthodox economic measures, the party shift in control of the presidency from Peronism to the Radical Party/FREPASO Alliance that resulted in 1999 with the election of De la Rúa brought no relief from increasingly unpopular policies.[18] This absence of any significant policy response heightened public cynicism and frustration. By the turn of the millennium, many Argentines saw the traditional political class and the existing democracy as increasingly unrepresentative.[19] New accusations of political corruption aimed at the De la Rúa government, which, ironically, had itself campaigned for greater political transparency after the excesses of the Menem years, reinforced this view of a general disregard of the public by most traditional politicians.[20]

The well publicized increase of the national political protest vote (the so-called "voto bronca") in the October 2001 legislative elections seriously affected the Alliance parties, as well as their Peronist rivals (who fared less badly, regaining control of Congress). With the angry protests by savers unsuccessfully trying to get their largely frozen funds out of a banking system on the edge of collapse, even the middle class was now alienated from a government that its members had heavily supported only two years earlier. The rapidly worsening political scene came to a head with an outbreak of pent-up popular anger on December 19–20, 2001, immediately after President De la Rúa went on national television that first evening to decree the imposition of a State of Siege in response to looting in certain poor neighborhoods. By then, he and his government were widely perceived as simply not caring about popular concerns or the growing desperation of the poor. The political response to the ham-fisted government repression against new protesters that followed was a sense of widespread moral repudiation caused by the well-publicized death of at least twenty-five protesters nationally plus the wounding of hundreds more—and, consequently, the rapid collapse of the government.[21] With the Peronist opposition refusing to join with the Alliance in a government of national unity, the president's resignation on the 20th only halfway through his term seemed the only outcome. Although economic conditions were to deteriorate even further under several successors appointed in turn to serve out the remaining two years by the new Peronist majority in Congress, these men would be more careful about any new resort to such open repression of public protest in areas in or near the Capital where the mass media were likely to be present.

The lessening of visible government repression seems to reflect a shift in official evaluations of what was politically possible in controlling mass protests. The kinds of violent sanctions still imposed against piquetero groups in more isolated places already had become far less common in the Greater Buenos Aires area; instead, government officials began to be more sophisticated in their treatment of these protesters, pursuing a policy of divide and conquer. In official rhetoric, piquetero groups would be subdivided into so-called good protestors and bad ones. Those "moderates" thought to be more open to negotiations might be quietly bought off for the moment with offers of a specified number of places in government relief programs. Those leftist groups seen as less susceptible were typically vilified as "trotsko" extremists.

The decline of the likelihood of repression made political bargaining between officials and piquetero leaders a new reality for as long as the government felt so politically vulnerable.[22] Were this vulnerability to disappear with an eventual economic recovery, however, open government repression would again become more likely.

Table 5.1. Organized Road Blockages (Cortes de Ruta) in Argentina, 1997–2004

Year: Locality:	1997	1998	1999	2000	2001	2002	2003	2004	Total Period
*Buenos Aires	23	9	82	119	452	587	441	430	2,143 (29%)
*Federal Capital	11	9	58	51	170	299	306	358	1,262 (15%)
Jujuy	37	13	1	79	136	414	109	50	839 (13%)
Salta	4	0	2	41	59	212	56	28	402 (6%)
Santa Fe	9	4	13	21	39	129	98	31	344 (5%)
Tucumán	7	0	23	48	55	122	43	39	337 (5%)
Córdoba	22	1	4	11	34	158	32	23	285 (4%)
Neuquén	10	7	10	52	66	42	51	9	247 (4%)
All Argentina:	140	51	252	514	1383	2336	1278	1181	7135(100%)

Source: Adopted from Centro de Estudios Nueva Mayoría, "Sensible incremento de los cortes de rutas durante marzo," <www.nuevamayoría.com/ES/INVESTIGACIONES/socio_laboral/2005>. These data derive from various Federal Police reports, supplemented by newspaper accounts.

* The province of Buenos Aires and the Federal Capital together constitute Greater Buenos Aires.

As a president became perceived as increasingly vulnerable to political pressure with the worsening economy, piquetero leaders became more emboldened in organizing road blockages in the strategic Buenos Aires region. Some leaders no doubt took their cues from the perceived impunity of others as the government by 2001 tacitly came to accept as normal stoppages by the less radical groups and the bargaining that produced an increase in the number of places in relief programs for their piquetero members. The Centro de Estudios Nueva Mayoría in the Argentine Capital has published figures that are reproduced in modified form above in Table 5.1, indicating the overall trend in such piquetero actions by locality, including the two areas making up the Greater Buenos Aires region itself.

In terms of the national total of such occurrences during the 1997–2004 period for which data are available, the particular importance of Buenos Aires Province and of the nearby Federal Capital—together constituting the area of Greater Buenos Aires—stands out (as does that of Jujuy Province in the interior). Such figures indicate the accelerating nature of this form of political protest through 2002, when the number of protests nationally peaked in May when the Programa Jefas/Jefes went into effect.

The piquetero groups that emerged in the Greater Buenos Aires area would have a territorial basis, organizing individuals in different poor neighborhoods where the unemployed live.[23] These areas are largely found outside the Capital in impoverished parts of the province of Buenos Aires like La Matanza to the west or various poor localities to the south.

Departing from a traditional model of labor recruitment based on the incorporation of members through national-level affiliated unions to which they belonged, the CTA (itself limited to only a few such national unions like the Teachers and the State Workers) actively sought to reach out to individuals from various non-unionized parts of society, including retirees, the disabled, women, youth, and especially the large numbers of the newly unemployed.[24]

Less successful in attracting unemployed individuals than autonomous subdivisions of unions formally aligned at the national level with the CGT,[25] the CTA appears to have shifted to a strategy of encouraging the affiliation of existing groups of unemployed individuals already involved in activities like land invasions. Examples of such a linkage with the CTA were Luis D'Elía's Federation of Land, Housing, and Habitat (Federación de Tierra, Vivienda, y Hábitat, hereafter the FTV) and, until at least mid-2002, Jorge Ceballos's Neighborhoods Arisen (Barrios de Pie). Given the loose confederal structure of the CTA, the leadership of the Central would have little direct influence over its piquetero affiliates and their members among the unemployed, except through their leaders.

While some piquetero groups, like those linked to the CCC (especially that part led by Juan Carlos Alderete) and to the Workers Party or Partido Obrero (as with its Workers Pole or Polo Obrero led by Néstor Pitrola), also saw such a more political tie as useful to their agenda, others seem to have consciously avoided any partisan connection for fear of compromising their autonomy of action. This distinction between more externally oriented groups (like the tactically flexible FTV and the Alderete CCC, or the more ideologically defined Polo Obrero) contrasts sharply with other groups organized in more inward-looking social arrangements like those forming the loosely structured Aníbal Verón Coordinating Group (Coordinadora Aníbal Verón).[26] For those groups with a more external orientation, these ties could provide useful political resources from allies who had greater actual experience with national politics. Already nationally involved groups like the CTA labor confederation or the more openly political Partido Obrero, in turn, might see their piquetero affiliates as a means of strengthening their political legitimacy at a time when most trade unions and political parties were seen by much of the public as largely self-serving and corrupt.[27]

Mobilizing Structures for a New Style Clientelism?

"Mobilizing structures" refer to those organizations "both formal and informal, through which people come together and engage in collective action" including that of a contentious nature, during which the structure is made more effective by its leaders' access to "solidarity incentives and sanctioning mechanisms."[28] The leaders of what became the different piquetero groups rapidly saw gaining access for some of their members to nationally funded government relief programs intended for the unemployed poor as something central to their new organizations' survival and possible numerical expansion.

Securing places for needy individuals in such programs would establish a group leader as a necessary facilitator in linking humble citizens to a highly bureaucratic government that otherwise might seem remote and even inexplicable in its dealings with the public. While aid schemes like the nationally run *Programa Trabajar* were in theory open to any citizen who met the basic qualifications, poorer Argentines typically knew better: from their experience with the country's entrenched clientelist practices, they understood that securing a place in such a program probably required the help of someone with the right personal contacts in that bureaucracy.[29]

Critics of supposedly clientelist practices by piquetero leaders saw the members as being manipulated due to such poor individuals' need for the small cash payment provided by continued enrollment in the Programa Jefas/Jefes or the earlier Programa Trabajar. Here those who participated in the potentially dangerous confrontations with the government represented by the organized road blockages were seen as being obliged to do so for fear of being ousted from the work program controlled by group leaders, and thereby losing their monthly income.[30]

While such participation has been, indeed, expected by the piquetero community from its members, this criticism seems much too simplistic in what seems its rather one-sided discussion of what was going on within the community. As Auyero has pointed out in his analysis of traditional Argentine clientelism, the perception of feeling manipulated in such a relationship is connected to the degree one identifies his needs with those of the group.[31] Those trusting in the group and its leadership are likely to see their contributions to that group in more positive terms than those who are poorly integrated. Given the origins and inclusionary seen as new style communities, the identity of the members with the group is likely to have been far more meaningful for many than with conventional clientelist ties.

Table 5.2. Places in Programa Jefas/Jefes Controlled by Piqueteros by Late 2002

Group/Leader	# of Places	Group Political Tie
FTV (L. D'Elía)	36,000	CTA; ex Frente para el Cambio, FREPASO
CCC (J. C. Alderete)	21,000	CCC/Partido Comunista Revolucionario
Polo Obrero (N. Pitrola)	10,000	Partido Obrero
MIJD (R. Castells)	7.300	Ex CCC, with ties to Partido Obrero, MST, and PTS
Coordinadora Aníbal Verón	7,000	Independent
Barrios de Pie (J. Ceballos)	6,000	Patria Libre; ex CTA
MTR (R. Martino)	5,000	Independent
MST Teresa Vive	5,000	MST
MTL (B. Ibarra)	4,000	Partido Comunista
Total Places:	101,300	

Source: Number of places from *La Nación Line*, November 23, 2002; Political ties from Julio Burdman, "Origin y evolución de los 'piqueteros,'" <www.nueva mayoría.com/invest/sociedad/cso180302>, 2002.

Notes: FTV = Federación de Tierra, Vivienda, y Hábitat; CTA = Central de Trabajadores Argentinos; CCC = Corriente Clasista Combativa; MIJD = Movimiento Independiente de Jubilados y Desocupados; PTS = Partido de Trabajadores por el Socialismo; MTR = Movimiento Teresa Rodríguez; MST Teresa Vive = Movimiento Sin Trabajo Teresa Vive; MST = Movimiento Socialista de los Trabajadores; MTL = Movimiento Territorial de Liberación.

While the reciprocal obligations for piquetero members found would qualify such groups as clientelist, the piquetero version seems qualitatively different from earlier forms given its far greater stress on active participation within the community. Such a greater commitment to the group, in turn, probably has made it far more effective in its collective activities.

The piquetero bargaining for places in official aid programs that became increasingly common under the De la Rúa Alliance government seemingly flourished under the Duhalde administration.[32] One newspaper account published in late 2002 indicated the relatively widespread nature of such practices under Duhalde in terms of the number of such positions thought to be allocated to the leaders of particular piquetero groups.

While the number of places then supposedly controlled by the various piquetero groups was considerable, the 100,000-plus people believed to have secured a place in the Programa Jefas/Jefes through the agency of the different piquetero organizations made up only 5% of its total of about two million beneficiaries throughout Argentina at that time; the percentage of piqueteros found among the 800,000 poor then enrolled in this program in Buenos Aires Province, however, was probably higher given the greater level of piquetero activities there than elsewhere.[33] A glance at the number of places controlled by each group suggests the possible utility of having an external ally, be it a labor organization like the CTA or CCC, or even one of the small leftist political party groups. If such alliances may be helpful under certain circumstances, they may not always be an unmixed blessing.

Probably a more important explanation for the distribution of program places than simply having an experienced ally relates to the nature of the ally and its links to the political structure. The groups that were best able to take advantage of the crisis situation were those that were most politically adept at using the bargaining opportunity. If all the piqueteros tend to utilize a Marxist-like rhetoric of some sort, what particularly distinguishes one from the other in terms of their effectiveness relates to the degree of perceived flexibility employed by their leaders in their dealings with the national government. The terms commonly utilized by much of the media that contrast so-called "moderates" or "dialoguistas" with so-called "hard-liners" or "combativos"[34] suggest what it seems was the key distinction. The more tactically flexible groups here were the FTV of D'Elía and—for a time—the CCC of Alderete, groups both located in the La Matanza area that closely coordinated their actions from at least late 2001 until late 2003.[35] Critically, only these two groups were chosen by the Duhalde government from the entire piquetero movement to officially participate in the Consejo Consultivo Nacional, the central body charged with managing the national Programa Jefas/Jefes, along with various non-piquetero organizations.[36] Excluded from any such influential role on this strategic body, the hard-liners making up the National Piquetero Bloc (Bloque Nacional Piquetero) have resented this official favoritism, repeatedly accusing their rivals of having "sold out" to the government.[37]

The division between so-called hard-liners and moderates found in the recent piquetero movement seems remarkably similar to that encountered among rival groups of national trade unions affiliated to the Peronist CGT in the 1960s and again in the 1980s/1990s. With their differences in bargaining tactics and in the degree of autonomy from their members, such union leaders saw their ties to a state that could distribute or withhold important advantages as central to their success as agents for the workers in collective bargaining. In return for negotiated government benefits, the trade union moderates could call off threatened general strikes.[38]

To the extent that the current piqueteros and their various allies have for the moment superseded the more conventional CGT unions as the political representatives of many poorer members of the labor force, they have inherited important parts of the strategic practices derived from historical Peronism. Their moderation versus more hard-line activities seems an all-too-familiar pattern of division that might reflect not only the opportunities presented to more strategically minded leaders by a more vulnerable national government, but various leadership rivalries and alliances within a divided piquetero movement. If the form of mobilization has changed with different structural conditions, the cultural framing legitimating such bargaining activities derives from their previous familiarity to many participants derived from CGT-style trade unionism.

Framing the New-Style Piquetero Communities

"Framing processes" are culturally "learned routines [involving] shared meanings" that make up a "repertoire of contention" or a series of legitimized forms of mobilization for protesting collectively held grievances.[39] Interviews with participants reinforce the idea that the grievances of the piquetero groups focus on the lack of available work and the degradation that long-term unemployment has created for the poor. Piquetero leaders have justified their adoption of the blockade of strategic roads as a strategy for conflict, arguing that it is necessary to force an otherwise unresponsive government to provide poor relief.[40] The ensuing negotiations with such a government can be understood by piquetero members because they are so clearly modeled on the type of bargaining that Argentine trade unions have engaged in historically at the national level, seeking to extract economic benefits from appropriate government officials. Here the piquetero movement is seen as the successor to the unions as the representative of those parts of the working class able to organize themselves collectively under the new economic conditions.

Such a socially constructed understanding of reality continues in terms of a new group identity. Within the piquetero communities, blame for the undesirable status of being poor has been shifted away from those unable to find work; such poor individuals now were deemed merely the unwilling victims of the capitalist system and those who benefit from it. The piqueteros have been told that the government and the traditional political class were the ones who should bear responsibility for the human disaster caused by the explosion of mass unemployment, not the poor who have suffered its costs.[41] Logically, if it was the government that was at fault for the crisis, then it would be the government that was expected to provide badly needed jobs, income, and food.

While the piqueteros have adopted traditional forms of relating to the national government like the type of strategic bargaining already described, what is new for them that was typically absent with the CGT unions is the commitment such groups of the unemployed poor have made toward more participation in their own decision-making.[42] Such a participatory emphasis makes sense given the need for more cohesive communities required for survival in a politically unstable world where piquetero protests and possible government repression are a continuing reality.

What has been stated so far relates to important common beliefs and under-standings that provide important parts of the framing for the recent piquetero mobilization. What follows next attempts to take this cultural analysis a step further, seeking to indicate certain key differences in basic group priorities that may explain the notable divisions that emerged within the piquetero movement found in the Buenos Aires region. Clearly, given the still limited empirical infor-mation about the many piquetero groups under study, the particular elements chosen for emphasis here reflect more than would be usual the subjective personal judgments of the author. The present effort to map the cultural topography dividing the piqueteros emphasizes three elements: (a) the degree of leadership autonomy or what has been described as a more vertical versus a more horizontal linkage with group members;[43] (b) the relative importance of national politics and external political alliances versus group autonomy and internal community soli-darity; and (c) the basic orientation adopted toward the government, or the dis-tinction between moderates and hard-liners. Figure 5.1 below links three different patterns of alternatives chosen from these characteristics with five of the more important piquetero groups found in the Buenos Aires area in 2002–2003 when such activism was at its height.

Figure 5.1. A Possible Cultural Map of the Piqueteros of Greater Buenos Aires (c. 2002)

	TYPE 1	**TYPE 2**	**TYPE 3**
Leadership Orientation:	Personalist Leadership	Personalist Leadership	Rotational Leadership
	/	/	\
Primary Value Orientation:	External Political Alliances	External Political Alliances	Internal Community Solidarity
Bargaining Orientation Toward Government:	/	/	\
	Moderate	Hard-Line	Hard-Line
Examples:	FTV	Polo Obrero	Coordinadora Aníbal Verón
	CCC (Alderete)	MIJD	

Note: The threefold division of the piquetero movement reflects suggestions made by Cross and Montes Cató in their interview with the author July 4, 2002 (see Note 26). For the complete names of groups abbreviated here, see the notes in Table 5.2 above.

The type of group leadership exercised seems critical for understanding how piqueteros interpret the external political world in which their street blockages take place and the type of local community with which they identify. With the important exception of the Coordinadora Aníbal Verón,[44] the groups mentioned as examples in Figure 5.1 appear to have one dominant leader who not only represents the membership in all bargaining with the government, but probably has the power to shape the outcome of key aspects of how the community operates internally.[45] Such a leadership role can be described as vertical in style in the sense that those exercising it are expected to make most of the decisions for the group. After informing the rank and file of their reasons, leaders like D'Elía, Alderete, Pitrola, and Castells can expect to have their decisions almost automatically endorsed by the community without open dissent. If the members of the group are given the opportunity to participate in assemblies, such participation is unlikely to challenge the group leader. The various parts of the Coordinadora, however, appear to operate very differently, having adopted a more horizontal style of leadership where no one can expect to represent the group consistently nor enjoy autonomous power. Leadership is rotated as a matter of principle.[46] Given the absence of any established leadership figure here, group discussion in the parts of the Coordinadora is likely to be far more meaningful than what is understood to take place in most other piquetero groups.

The style of leadership adopted, in turn, has a strong influence in the overall priorities of the group. Those groups with a single dominant leader also seem to have usually followed a policy of seeking to increase their group's political influence by securing external alliances, either with labor bodies like the CTA and CCC or with one or more small leftist parties. Those rejecting such alliances, like the Coordinadora Aníbal Verón affiliates, have argued that the possession of important allies is likely to compromise group interests where they come into direct conflict with those of the ally. What seems ultimately at stake is whether external political alliances or matters of internal community solidarity are to be given priority as the primary group value orientation, should conflicts occur. The maintenance of such ongoing alliances by the FTV, CCC, Polo Obrero, and MIJD, each with its dominant leader, suggests that such external linkages are likely to be a particularly important element in such leadership thinking. Only the Coordinadora clarifies its priorities by avoiding any possibly compromising alliances, again as a matter of basic principle.[47]

The third element here, the bargaining orientation adopted toward the government, seems to reflect some combination of the strategic evaluation of group leaders, those of external allies, and what can be described as core values embedded in group ideology. Those piqueteros on the ideological left making up the Bloque Nacional Piquetero have pursued a more combative strategy than the FTV and CCC. If the hard-line stance of the Bloque Piquetero has distanced their groups from government officials, vulnerable presidential administrations nevertheless were at times forced to concede some places in official poverty programs to these radicals. But the more flexible position of the FTV/CCC seems to have produced better results in a material sense, with these two groups combined accounting for 56% of all piquetero-controlled places in the Programa Jefas/Jefes, according to the information provided above in Table 5.2.

What is suggested is that the cultural makeup of the newly organized poor has important subdivisions in terms of how its participants understand their personal roles as activists and the piquetero groups that provide them with a more meaningful identity through their affiliation. Such differences are important for understanding their participation in the mass mobilizations that forced vulnerable governments to make important concessions to protest groups seemingly outside the traditional political system, but employing a bargaining strategy that found widespread acceptance by both the government and its working class opponents.

Recent Responses to a Changing Environment

By 2003 and early 2004 as the Argentine economy began to emerge from the depths of earlier years, hard-line piquetero protests became even more politicized. Leaders like Pitrola of the Polo Obrero and Castells of the MIJD (now frequently joined by former moderate Alderete of the CCC) continued to confront the government—of Duhalde and, after the 2003 elections, of Néstor Kirchner—with frequent street blockages and demonstrations on behalf of demands for their members. Moderates like D'Elía of the FTV and Ceballos of Barrios de Pie, in turn, ceased most of their participation in "cortes" and would eventually become open political allies of Kirchner,[48] as the lines of cleavage that divided the piquetero movement solidified further. While the new conditions led to an overall decline in total road blockages, the shifting political conditions saw such protests now increasingly focused in the Capital. The figures for 2003 and 2004 in Table 5.1 show the rising importance as a venue of the Federal Capital, home to the government. The Capital was the site of 12.3% and 12.8% of the national total in 2001 and 2002, respectively; by 2003 and 2004, those percentages had doubled to 24.0% and 24.8%, now being second in frequency behind only those for nearby Buenos Aires Province.[49]

In the face of the ever more frequent protests snarling traffic in the center of the Capital and occasional acts of violence by militants, a public opinion once fairly sympathetic to protests by the unemployed began to turn against the piqueteros, no doubt encouraged by more hostile accounts in the press and in the coverage shown on television.[50]

After initial uncertainty as to the most appropriate political response, the Kirchner government finally decided on the seeming compromise of continuing official tolerance of the piqueteros' right to protest but—now for the first time—accompanied by a well-publicized overwhelming police presence at such public demonstrations, a change seen by the hard-liners as actions meant to be intimidating. When one such "tolerated" organized radical protest got out of hand in the Plaza de Mayo just outside the presidential palace (during a state visit by the new head of the International Monetary Fund), the police violently dispersed all protestors, violent and non-violent alike.[51] This greater willingness of the Kirchner administration to use measured repression may mark a decisive moment in the phenomenon of a piquetero movement now seeing its mobilizational capacity erode amid slowly falling poverty levels and a much more hostile public opinion.[52] A contributing factor to the government's new resolve after months of dithering—something seen as critical in the present analysis—is President Kirchner's continuing relatively strong personal popular support when compared to that of his immediate predecessors.[53] His eventual response to the piquetero radicals was that of someone who clearly wants to be perceived by voters as a strong national leader.

Notes

* An earlier version of this chapter appeared in the *Canadian Journal of Latin American and Caribbean Studies* 28, nos. 55–56 (2003). It is reprinted here with permission.

1. The current Argentine crisis ought not to be seen as a situation confined only to that country. Instead, what has occurred in Argentina should be understood as but an extreme case of the combined economic, social, and political problems linked to the acceleration of globalization that have negatively affected most of the countries of Latin America in varying degree in recent years.

2. Javier Auyero, *La protesta: Retratos de la beligerancia popular en la Argentina democrática* (Buenos Aires: "Serie Extramuros," Universidad de Buenos Aires, Libros del Rojas, 2002); Gabriela Delamata, "De los 'estallidos' provinciales a la generalización de las protestas en Argentina: Perspectiva y contexto en la significación de las nuevas protestas" (manuscript, Depto. de Ciencia Política, Universidad Nacional San Martín, 2002); Norma Giarracca, et al., *La protesta social en la Argentina: Transformaciones económicas y crisis social en el interior del país* (Buenos Aires: Alianza, 2001); Germán Lodola, "Social Protests under Industrial Restructuring: Argentina in the Nineties (manuscript, Department of Political Science, University of Pittsburgh, 2002); Maristella Svampa and Sebastián Pereyra, *Entre la ruta y el barrio: La experiencia de las organizaciones piqueteras* (Buenos Aires: Biblos, 2003); Raúl Zibechi, *Genealogía de la revuelta, Argentina: La sociedad en movimiento* (La Plata: Letra Libre, 2003).

3. Doug McAdam, John McCarthy, and Mayer Zald, eds., *Comparative Perspectives on Social Movements: Political Opportunities, Mobilizing Structures, and Cultural Framings* (Cambridge: Cambridge University Press, 1996); Doug McAdam, Sidney Tarrow, and Charles Tilly, "Toward an Integrated Perspective on Social Movements and Revolutions," in *Comparative Politics*, ed. Mark Lichbach and Alan Zuckerman (Cambridge: Cambridge University Press, 1997), 142–73; Sidney Tarrow, *Power in Movement: Social Movements and Contentious Politics* (Cambridge: Cambridge University Press, 1998).

4. Program participants receive the equivalent of 150 pesos per month for themselves

and their families. While never a large amount with which to provide for a family, what was once worth 150 dollars lost a significant part of its buying power as inflation rose during the course of 2002. As a result, piquetero groups in time would include an increase in this amount as part of their revised demands from the government (*La Nación Line*, February 20, 2003).

5. Ernesto Villanueva, ed., *Empleo y globalización: La nueva cuestión social en la Argentina* (Buenos Aires: Universidad Nacional de Quilmes, 1997); Luis Beccaria, *Empleo e integración social* (Buenos Aires: Fondo de Cultura Económica, 2001); Eduardo Basualdo, *Sistema político y modelo de acumulación en la Argentina: Notas sobre el transformismo argentino durante la valorización financiera (1976–2001)* (Buenos Aires: Universidad Nacional de Quilmes, 2001).

6. *La Nación Line*, February 21, 2003.

7. *Clarín Internet*, December 27, 2002.

8. *La Nación Line*, December 28, 2002.

9. Delamata, "De los 'estallidos,'" 5.

10. Edward Epstein, "Explaining Worker Mobilization in Recent Argentina and Chile" (paper presented at international congress of the Latin American Studies Association, Washington, D.C., September 2001).

11. Javier Auyero, "Cultura política, destitución social y clientelismo político en Buenos Aires: Un estudio etnográfico," in *Desde abajo: La transformación de las identidades sociales*, ed. Maristella Svampa (Buenos Aires: Universidad Nacional de General Sarmiento/Biblos, 2000), 181–208; Javier Auyero, *Poor People's Politics: Peronist Survival Networks and the Legacy of Evita* (Durham, N.C.: Duke University Press, 2001); Steven Levitsky, *Transforming Labor-Based Parties in Latin America: Argentine Peronism in Comparative Perspective* (Cambridge: Cambridge University Press, 2003).

12. Auyero, "Cultura política."

13. Delamata, "De los 'estallidos,'" 9.

14. Peter Eisinger, "The Conditions of Protest Behavior in American Cities," *American Political Science Review* 67 (1973): 11–28.

15. McAdam, Tarrow, and Tilly, "Toward an Integrated Perspective," 153.

16. *La Nación Line*, September 2, 2002, based on Catterberg and Associates polls. Information on public confidence in political institutions is found in the annual Latino-barómetro surveys for most Latin American countries including Argentina. Confidence in Argentine political parties fell from an already low 16% in 1996—but near the Latin American regional average—to close to zero in 2002, by far the lowest country figure listed (*The Economist*, August 17, 2002: 29). The approval rating of specific Argentine presidents is found in various Argentine polls. According to those produced by Graciela Römer, the Menem administration ended its second term with some 18% approval, a considerable decline from approval figures near 60% in mid-1993. The approval rating for De la Rúa, which had been slightly over 50% as of February 2001, had plummeted to 13% by September 2001, three months before his December resignation when, presumably, it would have been lower still (*La Nación Line*, September 21, 2001).

17. <www.utdt.edu/departamentos/gobierno/icg>.

18. For such policy perceptions, see Römer opinion data given in *La Nación Line*, January 3, 2003.

19. Cecilia Cross and Juan Montes Cató, "Crisis de representación e identidades colectivas en los sectores populares: Acerca de la experiencia de organizaciones

piqueteras," in *La atmósfera incandesente: Escritos políticos sobre la Argentina movilizada*, ed. Osvaldo Battistini (Buenos Aires: Asociación Trabajo y Sociedad, 2002), 85–100; Delamata, "De los 'estallidos,'" 14–15.

20. María Matilde Ollier, *Las coaliciones políticas en la Argentina: El caso de la Alianza* (Buenos Aires: Fondo de Cultura Económica, 2001).

21. Federico Schuster, German Pérez, Sebastián Pereyra, et al., *La trama de la crisis: Modos y formas de protesta social a partir de los acontecimientos de Diciembre de 2001* (Buenos Aires: Informe de Coyuntura 3, Instituto de Investigaciones Gino Germani, Universidad de Buenos Aires, 2002).

22. The government-inflicted violence in Avellaneda just south of the Capital where two piquetero activists in the Coordinadora Aníbal Verón, Maximiliano Kosteki and Darío Santillán, were murdered in cold blood on June 26, 2002, by the local police during a protest seems a possible exception to this pattern of lessened repression (*La Nación*; *Clarín*; *Página 12*, all June 27, 2002). While never adequately explained, this incident may have been organized by officials in the police seeking to embarrass both Duhalde and his ally, the governor of Buenos Aires Province, in whose jurisdiction it occurred. Whatever its origins, when its nature as an intentional murder became public, it generated a major political crisis for both officials. A direct consequence of this scandal was Duhalde's decision to move forward the presidential elections scheduled for October 2003.

23. Maristella Svampa, interview by author with Universidad Nacional General Sarmiento sociologist, Buenos Aires, July 3, 2002.

24. Claudio Lozano, interview by author with CTA Secretary for Studies, Buenos Aires, June 5, 2001.

25. Juan Montes Cató, interview by author with CEIL-PIETTE political sociologist, Buenos Aires, July 8, 2002.

26. Cross and Montes Cató, "Crisis de representación," 91; Cecilia Cross and Juan Montes Cató, interview by author with political sociologists at CEIL-PIETTE, Buenos Aires, July 4, 2002.

27. Montes Cató, interview, July 8, 2002.

28. McAdam, Tarrow, and Tilly, "Toward an Integrated Perspective," 155.

29. MTSS (Ministerio de Trabajo y Seguridad Social), *Programa Trabajar III: Documento Base* (Buenos Aires: Secretaría de Empleo y Capacitación Laboral, 1998); *La Nación Line*, April 22, 2002; *Clarín Internet*, January 25, 2003.

30. *Clarín Internet*, September 26, 2002.

31. Auyero, "Cultura política," 204–7.

32. Delamata, "De los 'estallidos,'" 16.

33. *La Nación Line*, October 1, 2002. Many other individuals not connected to the piqueteros were enrolled through the local councils set up by the government in different political jurisdictions. Here more traditional party-linked clientelism is likely to have been at work, as there seems to have been little real control by the Duhalde government on how these councils actually work (*La Nación Line*, August 29, 2002).

34. *Clarín Internet*, February 1, 2003; *La Nación Line*, February 14, 2002.

35. Luis D'Elía, the FTV piquetero leader, has emphasized his group's conscious avoidance of violence in their protests. In road blockages, FTV leaders claim to keep one lane open to traffic so as not to needlessly inconvenience drivers while group members publicize their views (interview by author with Luis D'Elía, Buenos Aires, July 8, 2002). His use of language similar to that used by the government in distinguishing between

"good" and "bad" piqueteros contributed to the alienation of those once associated with the FTV from the Barrios de Pie group led by Jorge Ceballos (*Clarín Internet*, July 1, 2002). His announcement of his candidacy for governor of Buenos Aires Province as part of a possible Party of the Argentine Workers, or Partido de los Trabajadores Argentinos, linked to the CTA (*La Nación Line*, March 11, 2003) may well have led to the eventual split between D'Elía and his CCC ally Juan Carlos Alderete that took place by the end of 2003.

36. *La Nación Line*, April 22, 2002. By late 2003, one source estimated that D'Elía's FTV may have controlled some 75,000 places in various government aid programs, including the Programa Jefas/Jefes (*Clarín Internet*, September 12, 2003).

37. *La Nación Line*, April 22, 2002, November 23, 2002. Initial attempts of the various piquetero groups to present a united front toward the De la Rúa government in mid-2001 soon collapsed, given the different tactical positions espoused by the moderates and the hard-liners. For an account sympathetic to the latter by a supporter of the Polo Obrero, see Luis Oviedo, *Una historia del movimiento piquetero: De las primeras coordinadoras a las asambleas nacionales* (Buenos Aires: Rumbos, 2001), 153–60.

38. Edward Epstein, "Labor-State Conflict in the New Argentine Democracy: Parties, Union Factions, and Power Maximizing," in his edited volume, *The New Argentine Democracy* (Westport, Conn.: Praeger, 1992), 124–56; James McGuire, "Distributive Conflict, Party Institutionalism, and Democracy," in his *Peronism Without Perón* (Stanford: Stanford University Press, 1997), 262–86.

39. McAdam, Tarrow, and Tilly, "Toward an Integrated Perspective," 156–57.

40. Cross and Montes Cató, "Crisis de representación," 87–88.

41. Cross and Montes Cató, interview, July 4, 2002.

42. Here see the interview quoted by Cross and Montes Cató in "Crisis de representación," 94.

43. This last point about types of leadership representation reflects the discussion found in Cross and Montes Cató, "Crisis de representación," 91, which distinguishes between vertical versus horizontal tendencies, the importance of group delegation versus deliberation, and the presence of personalism versus leadership rotation.

44. The Coordinadora Aníbal Verón split apart into rival factions in 2003; the issue of continued political autonomy seems important as one of the factors behind such divisions (Svampa, personal communication with author, August 2004).

45. Rosalía Cortés, interview by author with FLACSO sociologist, Buenos Aires, June 25, 2002.

46. MTD Solano (Movimiento de Trabajadores Desocupados de Solano), *Situaciones* 4 (December 2001): 20.

47. MTD (Movimiento de Trabajadores Desocupados en la C.T.D. "Aníbal Verón"), *Trabajo, dignidad y cambio social: Una experiencia de los movimientos de trabajadores desocupados en la Argentina* (May 2002), 21.

48. *La Nación Line*, December 19, 2003.

49. Calculated from annual column data in Table 5.1.

50. *La Nación Line*, December 3, 2003; *Clarín Internet*, December 9, 2003.

51. *La Nación Line*, *Página 12*, September 1, 2004.

52. *La Nación Line*, September 18, 2004.

53. The results from the Di Tella University Index of Confidence in Government suggest that the Kirchner government's new position toward the piquetero hard-liners may be having some positive effect on popular confidence. The ICG score of September 2004

rose slightly, to 2.13 from 2.07 the previous month, after having noticeably declined from 2.49 in July and from higher levels at the beginning of the same year (*La Nación Line*, August 23, September 29, 2004). Obviously, however, the issue of security and public order linked to the piqueteros is not the only issue of importance to different parts of the public.

6

Political Mobilization in Neighborhood Assemblies:
The Cases of Villa Crespo and Palermo*

Maristella Svampa and Damián Corral

The year 2002 was by any reckoning extraordinary in the broadest sense of the word, as Argentina slipped into the gravest political, economic, and social crisis in its entire history. It was a time when the country surprisingly discovered itself to be a deeply mobilized society increasingly divided between those with excessive wealth and those suffering economic desperation, a society fighting to recover its capacity for action through the reconstitution of ties of cooperation and solidarity that had been strongly undermined during the lengthy decade of neoliberalism.

The events of December 2001 opened a new space for the reappearance of activist politics with the involvement of multiple social groups. The slogan "Get rid of them all, so that not one is left!" ("¡Que se vayan todos y que no quede ni uno solo!" in Spanish) that the crowds repeated amid the noise of the pots being banged in the streets revealed the extent of the collapse of support for conventional political representation, as well as its displacement toward new forms of political action. In particular, this seemed a rupture with the limited world of formalistic, self-centered institutional politics subordinated to the established economic and financial interests that so typified the 1990s. In this sense, neighborhood assemblies were the legitimate replacement for this rejected model, expressing a shift toward a politics arising more from within Argentine society itself.

This new scenario gave greater visibility to existing social movements, above all to the piquetero groups of the unemployed poor, some of which began to develop a linkage to other social sectors, especially with the more activist parts of the middle class. At the same time, this opening made possible and promoted the emergence of other self-organized parts of society: neighborhood assemblies, barter clubs, groups of savings-account holders whose money was frozen in the banks, workers' self-managed factories, and counter-cultural collectives.

In the present chapter, we propose to analyze some of the political dimensions of the mobilizations that had their origin during the days of December 19 and 20, 2001, and that had their epicenter in the City of Buenos Aires. In this regard, we first will provide an account of the general phenomenon of neighborhood assemblies, so as to later concentrate on the specific cases of two in the Argentine Capital—those of the Villa Crespo and the Palermo districts—that we studied in 2002. At the end, we will provide a series of overall conclusions concerning the difficulties as well as the legacy of this social movement.

The Assemblies as a Multi-Dimensional Space

> We are in the assembly because we need to find a new form of social organization. If we suggest unified action, the question is whether those who take a more party-oriented approach to politics can function there. We are neither proposing that nor one of opposition [to the parties]. First we have to discuss what we want and how. [We need to discover] what are the things that divide us and those that unite us so as to be able to march together.
>
> —Member of Palermo Assembly

No one can deny that the neighborhood assemblies have constituted one of the most novel expressions of the social mobilizations that developed from December 19 and 20, 2001. Despite its heterogeneity, we believe that the assembly process took form in an environment where specific sociopolitical dimensions were intermixed.

First, the neighborhood assemblies constituted a space for organization and deliberation, itself conceived as breaking with traditional forms of political representation while favoring forms of self-organization linked more closely to society, to those aspiring to more equal relations and tending toward the exercise of direct action.

Second, they expressed the emergence of a new form of action fundamentally challenging the status quo. This was action that broke with the fatalistic discourse and ideology of the 1990s that there could be no alternative to what was happening, thereby returning to individuals their capacity to become genuine actors in public life; certainly, many people became masters of their own destiny both individually and collectively. In the same way, the assemblies brought with them the promise of creating places for solidarity and trust through which social ties, badly undermined after a decade of neo-liberal commercialization, could now be reconstructed.

Third, and amplifying the former point, these new experiences provided a sector of the middle class, especially those from the City of Buenos Aires, with an important place in the political scene. In effect, the neighborhood assemblies arose as a space for the reconstitution of the political identity of the middle class, a move that took as its starting point its present fragmentation and heterogeneity, in contrast with the relative cultural uniformity and greater prospect for social integration that it once had in the past.

In this sense, one should recognize that the neighborhood assemblies provided important spaces for intermixing, encounters, and discussion for different social sectors that had lacked any previous connections. This experience was doubly so, within as well as outside one's own movement. From the point of view of social composition, an important amalgam of the middle class came together, including merchants, employees, and professionals from both public and private sectors, themselves linked to administrative, educational, and health care jobs. But many of those present were now impoverished, and some had a record of high job instability. Also included were unemployed people from different backgrounds, as well as young people of quite radical views. Many of these participants were having their first political experience in these assemblies.

Neighborhood differences were very important, since in some places there was a strong presence of the professional middle class, whose role seems closely associated with the affluent, cosmopolitan nature of the City of Buenos Aires. Finally, as a major corollary, the assemblies emerged as a space for meeting social actors with different economic horizons and life opportunities, showing degrees of social complexity that varied with the neighborhood.

In sum, the assemblies were a complex public space in which these particular aspects were intermingled to varying degrees. Nevertheless, this multidimensional space was from the beginning permeated by different tensions and policy ambivalence whose persistence put at risk their initial dynamics. Today, many people ask about the reasons for the crisis and fragmentation of the assembly movement, as well as about the meaning and direction that a body of such differing elements eventually assumed.

To provide the phenomenon here under analysis with some historical perspective, we provide a schematic chronology presenting many of the most important moments or milestones that characterized the assembly movement when it was at its most active in 2002.

(1) January–February: The stage was set for the creation of the neighborhood assemblies and of the Centenary Park City-Wide Assembly (the so-called "Interbarrial"). At this moment, the use of "cacerolazo" protests with their

This was the period of greatest enthusiasm. Plenary sessions enjoyed the participation of 100 to 150 persons per assembly.

(2) From February or March, different commissions (including ones on health, politics, the press, the unemployed, etc.) began to fully function, something that would favor the discussion process and the recovery of a capacity for taking collective action.

(3) On March 24, the different neighborhood assemblies of the capital and of the metropolitan region made their first appearance at a political event, that repudiating the 1976 military coup, where the presence of long columns of "neighbors" strongly contrasted with the absence of the traditional political parties.

(4) Competition for the leadership of the assembly movement by the different parties of the traditional left, including the Workers Party (or Partido Obrero/PO), the Socialist Workers Movement (or Movimiento Socialista de los Trabaja-dores/MST), and the Communist Party (or Partido Communista/PC) strengthened the tendency toward fragmentation that the movement had exhibited from its beginning, a situation that led to the departure of many "independent," non-party members. The celebration of May Day that year constituted a moment for a change of direction due to the strong pressures created by the left-wing political parties on the local assemblies as well as at the Centenary Park City-Wide Assembly, to guarantee turnout at their own party events.

(5) During May, pressure from "independent" members of the different assemblies produced a major change in the character of the Centenary Park City-Wide Assembly. The slogan shifted from "one person, one vote" to "one assem-bly, one vote." In short, the City-Wide now became an institution representative of the neighborhood groups.

(6) Also in May, a further coordinating body was created at a level above the City-Wide Assembly, commonly referred to as the Colombres group (after the name of the street where it habitually met). This new space for the expression of views was openly partisan, in contrast with the City-Wide Assembly that could not be, at least not explicitly so. Colombres arose as a result of pressure from the left-wing parties (principally the MST and the PO) to create a supreme decision-making body for the entire assembly movement, despite the complaint of other groups and of "independents."

(7) In June, a grave act of police repression occurred at the Pueyrredón Bridge in nearby Avellaneda, culminating in the murder of two piquetero pro-testers, Darío Santillán and Maximiliano Kosteky, both activists in the Unemployed Workers Movement of the Aníbal Verón Coordinating Group. This criminal act was seen as part of a political effort to delegitimize the piquetero movement (that was itself initially blamed for the deaths) and to create the possibility of establishing an openly repressive state. However, the publication of photos showing how the murders occurred ruined that plan, forcing a shift in government policy. Now President Duhalde saw himself obliged to call early

general elections, while having to adopt a more legalistic line in handling the "piquetero question." On the other hand, the murders shook Argentine society and generated massive marches repudiating such violence. Finally, the change of scene brought with it greater visibility for the separate sectors of the piquetero movement, deepening the elective affinity that now was developing between them and parts of the mobilized middle class.

(8) During the month of July, various assemblies occupied different unused buildings that mostly belonged to either the Banco de la Provincia de Buenos Aires or the Banco de Mayo. These occupations lasting some two weeks did not produce any response from the mass media. Nevertheless, the courts with surprising speed initiated legal writs for evicting those involved and gaining forced entrance to some of the occupied buildings.

(9) From the months of September and October, the neighborhood assemblies developed links with "cartoneros" (desperately poor people nightly collecting discarded cardboard boxes and newspaper from garbage piled at street curbs throughout the city). These inter-class relations varied from simply providing aid and cooperation, for example, vaccinations of cartoneros and food prepared in the street in so-called community kitchens (the "ollas populares"), to, in some cases, acts challenging the authorities such as what took place in the buildings first occupied by assembly activists but later kept going by cartoneros themselves actually living on the site.

(10) In respect to joint action, by November the Centenary Park Inter-City decayed both in terms of the number of participating assemblies and in regard to the topics under discussion. The Colombares group was by then experiencing the same fate, given that many individual assembly members from the beginning did not feel represented there. Playing an important role in this situation was the only slight connection between the formal mandates of the neighborhood assembly delegates and the decisions that were made at Colombares. In the context of a crisis of institutions for coordinating joint action, groups began to support the idea of their own autonomous action. Thus some of the most highly mobilized groups like the Cid Campeador Assembly continued meeting to think about the character and matters to be included in their own assembly space.

(11) On the first anniversary of December 19–20, there was no single joint act, but rather two acts, each differing in kind and size. On the morning of December 19, one sector of the assemblies (that most willing to act on its own) carried out "urban picketing" that consisted in the blockage of streets in downtown Buenos Aires near the Stock Exchange and the Central Bank, with the goal of interrupting financial activity. These actions, accompanied by rich and colorful staging and artistic performances, were coordinated by different assemblies, counter-cultural collectives, and student groups. In this case, there would be no speeches, but only a series of direct acts against the political class and the symbols of capitalist power like finance capital. In contrast, a day later, on December 20, there was a large mobilization that would finish up in the Plaza de Mayo, the site of the national government. Flags and handkerchiefs mostly belonging to different

there was a large mobilization that would finish up in the Plaza de Mayo, the site of the national government. Flags and handkerchiefs mostly belonging to different piquetero groups provided color for the demonstration. Characteristically, the assemblies that turned out here did not try to occupy the historic plaza, but remained on side streets from where they followed the well-attended event. A brief communiqué read by two assembly members was inserted among some twenty piquetero speeches.

The Assemblies of Villa Crespo and Palermo: Their Origin, Organizational Evolution, and Type of Participant

The "Gustavo Benedetto"[1] Assembly of Villa Crespo (a traditional middle-class neighborhood) was formed after the events that occurred on December 19 and 20 that ended the presidency of Fernando de la Rúa. On those two days, some 5,000 people gathered at the intersection of Scalabrini Ortiz and Corrientes—streets in the heart of the Villa Crespo neighborhood—with some 300 of them continuing to meet over the next several days. After a short time, the assembly divided into three separate groups, each named after a separate street corner in the Villa Crespo neighborhood: the Corrientes and Juan B. Justo Assembly, the Angel Gallardo and Corrientes Assembly, and the Scalabrini Ortiz and Corrientes Assembly. As the largest of the three assemblies, with some 150 members, this last retained the name of the original group. It was controlled by the left-wing parties.

After the split, this "Gustavo Benedetto" Assembly began to function through different commissions: labor, the press, culture, services, political action, health, and community purchases. Meetings were set for once a week, on Wednesdays at 8 p.m. in the Pugliese Plazoleta located at the corner of Scalabrini Ortiz and Corrientes. At its beginning, the assembly counted in its ranks on ample participation by independent residents, themselves varied in their socio-economic make-up but with greater presence of people from the lower middle class. As the months went on, there was a strong loss of members so that participation became limited to the most combative members of the middle class, who assumed a broad political commitment that went beyond the defense of their own personal economic interests.

After a number of assemblies, discussion of the identity and ideological orientation of the group became more important, touching on the type of political action needed to have an impact on the neighborhood and for ties to other nearby assemblies and organizations. This shift to such local matters was represented both as a tactic for group preservation and as something needed to satisfy the wishes of members from the neighborhood. The proposal for local self-control proposed by some residents contrasted with the form of struggle, confrontation, and ideological perspective that young militants from the Communist Party and members who were themselves more oriented toward political reflection and deliberation.[2]

With the group's seizure of a building, its activities grew in number:[3] members organized a discussion program on films, a workshop on helping in the schools, a talk by leftist economists, recitals, celebrations for Children's Day, and other cultural activities. In this way, activities of local self-management that had been set aside until then because of the greater importance of the more immediate needs of the movement now became invigorated. The availability of their own site brought in new members and attracted old neighbors and militants who had left the assembly, gradually closing the gap between residents and assembly political activists that had acted as a restraint on group action.

The assembly found in Palermo (a comfortable middle-class neighborhood) contrasts with that of Villa Crespo, both in how it was set up and in its organizational capacity. Like Villa Crespo, Palermo began functioning in the first half of January, usually attracting somewhat fewer than 100 people. Some of the early topics for discussion among the members included a diagnosis of the current political situation and what should be done, the question of elections, the economy, and the foreign debt. A majority of the members were "independents" with little direct political party connection, but with some notable presence of young people from the university or political parties. Those participating in the assembly averaged close to 50 years of age, with many of them being professionals. A short time later, they began to get together once a week in a neighborhood bar, where they met until the local Centro de Gestión y Participación, or CGP (Center for Management and Participation), an agency of the Buenos Aires municipal government, gave them a place. By then, the assembly was attracting some 50 people each month, but participation eventually fell to half that by the final month.

At its beginning, the Palermo Assembly showed signs of suffering from organizational weakness in terms of how it ran its commissions. One noted for its activism in the first months was the Health Commission, although it later virtually disintegrated. Neither the Management Control Commission that at first was concerned with the analysis of the law on local communities and the idea of a budget created by direct citizen participation (the "participatory budget") nor the Commission for Community Purchases with an image of concern for charity carried much weight in the full assembly.[4] Dominated by strong personalities, the Commissions for Culture, Politics and Economics, and Organization and Security all found it impossible to assume a pattern of active decision-making during their duration. For its part, the Press Commission was among other things responsible for the production of the assembly's own radio program, which was broadcast weekly on FM Palermo, something that guaranteed it an interesting means to spread news of its activities throughout the neighborhood and the surrounding area.

We want to emphasize that the Villa Crespo Assembly maintained stable ties with the Inter-Assembly Health Commission, possessed channels for easy dialogue with other assemblies in the area, and took an active participation on the

with the Inter-Assembly Health Commission, possessed channels for easy dialogue with other assemblies in the area, and took an active participation on the
Inter-Assembly Commissions for Public Services, the Inter-City Assembly, and
in Food Forums. Contacts were gradually established with the activist National
Piquetero Bloc to the point where a small group of assembly militants became
members of one of the autonomous neighborhood piquetero groups still existing
there today. But contacts farther from the neighborhood were much weaker.
Encouraged by some party activists, there was strong distrust toward the social
organizations, cooperatives, or NGOs that approached the assembly from the
outside, with members suspecting that such groups merely wanted to use such a
linkage to their own advantage. There would, for example, be no lasting ties to
groups like the savings account holders.

The Palermo Assembly, on the other hand, was more open to external groups.
It established contacts at the local CGP with leaders of the well-known NGO
Citizen Power (or Poder Ciudadano), who attended the weekly meetings of the
assembly's Management Control Commission and offered a workshop on participatory budgeting in which the members of the commission participated.
Similarly, the assembly participated in the Palermo area inter-zonal meetings. On
different occasions, some assembly activists took part in marches of the Argentine
Savers Movement. Individuals also made contact with the Alejandro Olmos
Movement involved with the issue of the illegitimacy of the Argentine foreign
debt and with noted constitutional specialists who spoke on the problem of
elections.

Problematic Aspects in the Evolution of the Assemblies

In the heat of debate over various months, the two assemblies under discussion
in general demonstrated different views on external political contacts. Referring
to this matter, we want to utilize the contrasting images of "bridge" and "door"
suggested by Georg Simmel, the thinker par excellence of "social disintegration."[5]
Stated briefly, while the notion of "bridge" contains the idea of connection and
linkage, that of "door," through its recognition of separation as an initial
condition, implies an affirmation of division, bringing with it the idea of
withdrawal, of closure, even if from what was originally an opening. Amid
general social disenchantment, the metaphor of a "bridge" suggests alternatives
emphasizing the need to reconstruct the political system as a more participatory
democracy with the recovery of space for this within the state. In contrast, the use
of the metaphor of "door" suggests a more radical critique of the political system
of representation and the need to create new forms of sociability, social networks,
and organizations of solidarity outside of and distant from established institutional
structures. Associated with the latter view, one also finds positions calling for the
complete replacement of the present order, something that might be possible with

the emergence of a truly revolutionary situation in the diagnosis of certain leftist political parties.[6] This last radical perspective is illustrated by some of the leaders and militants of the parties that in ideological and practical terms have asserted certain fundamental postulates of a highly dogmatic Marxism, especially as to three basic points: the nature of the historical moment, the role of organization, and the concept of power. They here exhibited great blindness and an absolute lack of any self-criticism during the internal fights that broke out in passing months for the control and leadership of the different neighborhood assemblies, at the next level in the Inter-City Assembly, and at the highest level in the Colombres Assembly.

The evolution of the assemblies studied can be characterized by the difficulty in resolving differences and rival views concerning the proper direction for political action, as well as the internal dynamic appropriate for the function of each of the assembly movements. Problem areas developed that became the center of tensions and, in the extreme, constituted insurmountable limits for even the bare maintenance of the level of participation and the social innovation so enthusiastically proclaimed at the beginning by those involved in this new form of politics.

In order to illustrate some of these difficulties, we offer a three-part discussion: in the first part, we develop two questions, one linked to the proper function of assemblies, and one to the changing level of assembly participation. In the second, we reflect more broadly on the tensions noticed about the identity and the political direction of the assemblies. Finally, we analyze some general aspects as well as the specifics of ties with groups outside the assembly movement.

Places and Identities: From the Need to "Secure" an Occupied Building to the Bother of Having a "Secure" Place

All of us are not interested in building anything; the place is always empty; there is never anyone. We need to recognize that this is a cycle that is over, and that the political parties are ruining the assembly. The independents allow us to be coopted by the political parties either due to their inexperience or due to being jerks. My concrete proposal is that the place be closed, that the cycle is over, that we cannot coexist, that we must accept defeat even if it is painful. Five of us put ourselves out, [but] no one ever comes to any activity. This space is not us. We are exhausting ourselves for something already dead.
—Independent activist from the Villa Crespo Assembly

This is not about whether the CGP (Centro de Gestión y de Participación [the municipality's Center for Management and Participation]) matters or not. But about having a place where we can think.
—Member of the Palermo Assembly

The seizure by members of the Villa Crespo Assembly of the building belonging to the Banco de la Provincia meant the abandonment of the public space found in the street, their most direct contact with the external world, to withdraw to an enclosed area where people could participate. The months after the appropriation of the building were marked by discussion about how over time to best secure the place they had seized. The concern for legality and over any eventual police effort to gain entry to the site produced arduous and extended discussion over the possibility of being stuck in the courts should such an event occur. An additional matter was the more general issue of the importance of the legality or illegality of the seizure in the context of the idea of a permanent struggle against all legal or institutional aspects of political and public matters.[7]

With time and the fading of the euphoria raised by the occupation, questions emerged concerning what to do to justify their stay in the occupied building. The organization of snacks, a weekly food kitchen, social and cultural activities (like help for schools, different craft workshops, film discussions, etc.) all functioned as group activities with varying degrees of effectiveness.

The issue of staying in the building overnight in the face of the likely possibility of being thrown out set off the most serious conflicts, leading to confrontations, accusations, denunciations, and even threats of expulsion. Despite the unity acclaimed as needed to secure the seizure, in terms of hard facts, only a handful of mostly young assembly members taking turns could be found to sleep there in the early days. With the arrival of "cartoneros" at the building and their inclusion in the snacks, their staying at night in the building served shortly afterwards as the subject for heated assembly discussions of incidents (thefts, messes left, etc.) involving them. Consequently, joint meetings were set up to consider the possibility of naming people responsible for the site and of creating rules for shared use, including prohibitions and punishments. But these measures were rapidly discarded in the face of the sharp rejection of any imposition of order in a space deemed "egalitarian and democratic."

The delayed implementation of any systematic plan of order was similar to the disagreement over the utility of the seizure of the building and the vagueness of the political goals being pursued there. Defeatist attitudes emerged concerning the possible closure of the site given the lack of any clear, convincing political argument justifying its continuation and denunciation of the "colonization" of the building by political parties. Nevertheless, faced with the choice between continuing at the site or returning to the street, a decision was made in favor of the first option despite some weekly meetings now being held outdoors at the assembly's original venue at the corner of Scalabrini Ortiz and Corrientes.

In contrast with Villa Crespo, the Palermo Assembly was much more vacillating and self-contradictory in respect to the question of having a site of their own. The topic was discussed at various weekly meetings, with members even deciding to participate in one of the Villa Crespo assemblies so as to ask advice on how to organize a takeover. Early on, two or three people were given the task of finding an unused building in the neighborhood that could serve as a place for the assembly. But finally, in accord with the caution that characterized the behavior of that assembly, its members voted to decide to accept a place provided at the neighborhood CGP (Centro de Gestión y Participación). Despite this decision, meeting at the CGP was a never-ending topic for the assembly that frequently became the focus of debate and conflict. Thus one group of members who had participated from the beginnings of the assembly decided to walk out of the site they considered part of the government or the state; if others continued attending the assembly, they insisted on denouncing the CGP, concerned about any loss of visibility of the assembly's site, desertion of members, and the claim that the street was the natural place for the assembly as an expression of mobilization, struggle, and political action.

But for another group of members, the street/CGP antithesis raised the false argument of thinking that politics could be done only in the street, there displaying the symbols that would identify the assembly. For such members, the space provided by the CGP provided an ideal place for reflection, a place where "we can hear ourselves" and develop the deliberation necessary to avoid marching uncritically behind whatever banners preceded successive mobilizations. They argued that politics should not be thought about in terms of places but in reference to concrete actions and activities that, in turn, had to appear based on reflection.

In sum, the debate over where the weekly assembly meeting should take place was not limited to the mere question of logistics. It helped to delineate a certain political vision concerning the relation with the state, the appropriation of public space, and ways of confronting institutional power. Here the street was conceived as a place for concrete and specifically defined activity; it was not just an arena where conflict became visible or one that served as the battle trench for struggle and mobilization, the decisive emplacement for uncompromising political struggle. One assembly member calmly stated, "The first response we have to give those who oppress us is [that they should] listen to us," synthesizing the difficulties of shifting from being interpreters of politics to becoming more personally politically involved.

Colombres, Full Autonomy, and the Definition of Political Goals

Discussing and making policy are important. The problem is when someone wants to make policy for everyone else. We all make policy when we state "I propose," and not "I propose for him." The political parties understood the assembly as an open shop window. But the assemblies have to defend and develop themselves because they are the genuine organizations that sprang from the "Argentinazo" [the events of December 19–20, 2001]. People must talk, act, and follow things up. How should we understand that they want to mess up the Cen-

tennial Park Assembly with their violence? We do not want any
organization to act behind the backs of another. It is easy to develop
a body in which someone proposes himself as a delegate. It is easy to
control such structures, and Argentina has lived through this over the
last one hundred and fifty years. We must turn things around with a
new style of democracy. We should avoid proclaiming ourselves anyone's delegates.

—Member of the Villa Crespo Assembly and of the MTR
[Movimiento Teresa Rodríguez] piquetero group

We said the other day that our goals needed to be clarified. To me this
seems rather secondary, merely a formality, whether we have that
discussion ourselves. But people run to us from everywhere in a
disorderly way to impose on us where we ought to be going. We do
have to debate political goals. It is difficult because we are all equal
among ourselves, quite unlike the political parties. We have to have a
discussion to know whom we are going to support.

—Member of the Palermo Assembly

The importance Colombres Street was acquiring as the highest venue for overall
political coordination of the assembly movement accentuated the tensions among
the political groups competing in the Villa Crespo Assembly (PO, MST, PC).
Colombres was proclaimed by MST and, to a lesser extent, by PC activists there
as a space for what they called "unity in diversity," a view opposed by the Partido
Obrero, the MTR, and some independent assembly militants. Such advocates of
Colombres as a space for all views proposed bringing their assembly's program
there, seeking points of consensus with other assemblies to be used in defining a
program for joint struggle. Those more critical of Villa Crespo's participation at
Colombres complained of the absence of democratic rules there and the creation
of a place for inter-party agreement that neither respected nor represented the
views of ordinary assembly members. Defining the assembly's political orientation
was proposed as a priority within a notion of group autonomy and sovereignty, so
as to later discuss in what manner members could participate in an egalitarian
setting in such places for inter-group coordination. With the recent strong decay
of the City-Wide Assembly process, people began to discuss the proposal of the
Cid Campeador Assembly to create a new place for independent unrestricted
coordination so as to strengthen cases of coordination in different city zones.

The political parties of the left encountered resistance in the Palermo Assembly. The limited impact of militant groups there helped make the focus on places
for coordination running from Colombres to the Palermo Inter-Zonal Assembly a
secondary goal seen to be of limited relevance to the members of this assembly.
The likely challenge to any such plan and the certain visceral rejection from some
participants of any proposal of party origin weakened the importance of any
central spot for general coordination as potential channels of sociability and as
enclaves for the articulation of a program or of a plan for joint action agreed to

by different social groups. The same attitude of distrust and an assumption of independence continued while participating in different demonstrations or mobilizations organized by other social organizations; assembly members were indignant over being seen as a mere appendage of the political parties. On various occasions, people voiced negative evaluations of such demonstrations—"the political exploitation of the assembly"—and people insisted on "giving priority to our autonomy." Even when assembly activists belonging to other social organizations like the Argentine Workers Central (Central de Trabajadores Argentinos or CTA) pushed the importance of discussing criteria for unity with allied groups, of abandoning political "purity," and of seeking to have a presence in all relevant places, most assembly members believed that political debate and reflection on group objectives and identity should prevail over the idea of favoring such proposals.

This cleavage went back to the traditional opposition of reflection to action, a view insistently rejected by certain intellectual arguments voiced within the assembly. Thus the long, polemical debate over basic structural factors like politics, economics, and ideology never produced any minimum program that, in general terms, expressed the political and ideological identity of the assembly as a social movement. The demobilizing nature of the assembly's fear of external ties from its beginning was superimposed on all this, resulting in only a few assembly members, in some cases only in an individual capacity, participating actively in demonstrations, marches, and pickets.

The Extremes of Disorder: Partisan Knowledge versus Expert Knowledge

I am in pain. I go from the assembly in pain. Today I am convinced that one cannot work with the parties. I want to be civic-minded. I don't want to be a McCarthyite. Day after day I believe you can't work with the parties. . . . I believe equally that there are many valuable activists (from my view, good people, "compañeros"). The independents of course, but also many kids from parties. And I believe that that is where much damage is done. I believe that politics can work ethically. I am not going to abandon the struggle. I don't even know from where I will go on fighting, but without any doubt I will continue. I expect to see them in the street.

—Resignation letter of an independent member
of the Villa Crespo Assembly

All the things that are happening to us have to be seen from some initial clash, the hesitation with respect to whether the assemblies were the germ of a new idea—a new and different form of government—or if the assemblies were a place for tolerance, an experimental place. So now we must participate urgently in every possible space. This is

something cultural and social. If we hurry with making commitments
in elections, it seems to me that we only want to see who would
replace the government through the choices made.
—Member of the Palermo Assembly

In general terms, it is good to remember that along with the political parties of the
left there were from the beginning intellectuals and professionals from the social
sciences who also became fully immersed in these new experiences, seeking from
their different perspectives to combine the double function of analyst and actor.
Nevertheless, also from the beginning, this double enterprise encountered a major
obstacle given that the assembly's basic dynamics were accompanied by a strong
demand that all be treated as equals: everyone was a "neighbor" where no particular sub-identity as party activist or professional could be used to claim a special
monopoly over knowledge. If such rejection appeared in the end to be radically
new, it was because it applied without qualification to all types of pre-existing
discourse.

The image of neighbor then became central, even if it appeared as a kind of
invocation of a rather broad group that nobody was very concerned with defining.
Despite this lack of specificity, this image of neighbor early on seemed highly
functional in establishing limits, especially on the repeated claims for such
particular identities. Later, the recognition of the different political activists and
professionals present in the neighborhood assemblies provided substance for a
new term, a kind of broader identifying label represented by the image of
"assembly member." Even later still, the assembly member became in one sense
that militant, now defined as quite different from a mere neighbor, who sought to
become involved in building new political projects through different neighborhood
activities.

The transition from "neighbor" to "assembly activist" now also expressed a
major turn that revealed the advance of special identities. This twist clearly carried
with it a changed situation reflecting the release of the sort of basic tension found
in the original dynamic of the assembly movement, with the open fight that the
left-wing parties initiated to dominate these new processes, as well as the less
explicit and supposedly less self-interested struggle unleashed by certain
unaffiliated leftist intellectuals. A competition of rival leaders was being staked
out to deal with this situation, illustrated not only by the visible action of the
leftist political parties, but also by the assertion of certain independent
intellectuals that they had a monopoly of expert knowledge, something that was
done in the name of building "new political projects." Such claims by these
intellectuals seemed to happen where, as with the Palermo Assembly, the leftist
political parties did not play any real role. On various occasions, plenary sessions
ended with lengthy harangues by professionals, amid others who had little
willingness to listen and a dialectic of frequent argumentative challenges. This all
took place despite the wish shown by many, especially younger, assembly

members to moderate the corrosive effect of a minimally cooperative style where sarcastic comments alternated with full professorial tone.

In sum, unlike other neighborhood assemblies that set out along the difficult path of autonomous action, the two cases studied here did not survive the impetuous attacks of the leftist political parties or the pressures of those claiming expert knowledge. The extreme fate of the assemblies of Villa Crespo and Palermo fully illustrates that kind of divisive tension reflecting the double impact of the militant practices of the traditional left affected on the one hand by its assimilation of party-based knowledge and on the other by its convergence with expert or professional knowledge. In consequence, an important opportunity to give these new spaces a truly novel democratic form was being lost, given the strength of this tension reflecting the negative impact of both types of knowledge, together with traditional political practices.[8]

In more general terms, the question of the different conceptions of politics had become the center of a basic tension whose emergence and apparent negative resolution contributed to set maximum limits for the movement: all this allows us to understand—despite the reoccurring demand for equal relations, the incessant speeches, the innumerable calls for direct democracy, and finally despite the real, concrete exercise of participatory democracy linked to neighborhood work and internal discussion—why the assemblies encountered such serious difficulties in making themselves a place for building consensus. At the end, this internal tension between different concepts of politics (and the de facto affirmation of a party-based hegemony from one side and a hegemony of expert knowledge from the other) led to a major impasse, one that made obvious the difficulty the assemblies had in turning themselves into a place for real political deliberation.

We wish to emphasize not only the negative role played by political party-based knowledge of which so much has been said but also the easily observable, not very happy connection between old political practices and so-called expert knowledge. If both played some part here, it is therefore worthwhile to stop to ask ourselves concerning such political practices what is the real nature of those positions considered novel in a type of politics that oscillated between what was represented by the image of "the bridge" and that of "the door." We ought to once more clarify that in those assemblies with a strong presence of the professional middle class and where the weight of leftist political parties was not determinant, expert knowledge did not always end up in part filling the vacuum left by political-party related knowledge. Other assemblies like those found in the Collegiales and the Palermo Viejo neighborhoods that had very high percentages of professionals and ex-party activists, as well as that from Cid Campeador where young people played a fundamental role, did finally manage to consolidate themselves as autonomous entities by controlling their internal tensions.

Social Interactions and Links with Others:
The Debate Between Charity and Self-Management

> The kids came alone any time to ask for food so we provided it. This became a habit for them and we ended up offering charity not solidarity, things separated by a thin line. The "cartonero" is not someone who is unemployed, he is someone who has a different way of thinking because he is used to producing some earnings. He doesn't have a timetable, there is no trade union that organizes them, there are no rules.
>
> —Member of the Villa Crespo Assembly

> The first experience with the "cartoneros" was one of mutual respect. They were docile and grateful.
>
> —Member of the Palermo Assembly

> The purpose and function of the soup kitchen was to rebuild the social fabric that broke down with the dictatorship.
>
> —Member of the Palermo Assembly

The assembly dynamic that developed exposed different competing views about political ties. These tensions and antagonisms were for some time, in effect, muted within a single broad policy axis containing the rival options of political autonomy and political subordination. It is necessary to focus on this crucial point for a moment.

Originally, the demand for autonomy expressed more than anything a general rejection of the political class and its institutional expressions. Sharing this negative view were both neighborhood independents who supported reform of the institutional system (the metaphor of the bridge) and those inclined to a more radical position but not identified with any party (the metaphor of the door). Nevertheless, even seen from a defensive perspective, assembly autonomy was emerging as a strong practical organizational principle, visible in the incessant effort to restrain the attempts at hegemony fervently pressed by militants of the left-wing parties, especially the different Trotskyite splinter groups.

On the one hand, this demand for autonomy provided a structural dimension to the movement to the extent that the assemblies had to confront other dilemmas: for example, in respect to the linkages to the state and, even more so, to the existent legal order, with the occupation of abandoned buildings. On the other hand, both the grave economic situation experienced by the country as well as the movement's internal political tensions reinforced the urgent need to carry out actions of solidarity with the less well-off sectors of society. Thus, looking inward, the image of social interconnection pointed out the great heterogeneity of the middle sectors represented in the assemblies; looking outward suggests the ties developed with other socially mobilized forces including piquetero groups, workers in occupied abandoned factories (the so-called "fábricas recuperadas") and, especially, the cartoneros.

Put simply, "looking outward" to the full range of possible ties, on one side could be found the piqueteros, organized social actors possessing consistency, projects, and their own ideological orientations. They were people with whom the assembly members had always maintained a rather ambivalent relation, given differences over the charity-like actions taken toward them. At the other extreme were the cartoneros, who with differing amounts of organization represented an embryonic social movement before whom the middle-class assembly members adopted what would appear to be a pedagogical attitude never far removed from being clearly pure charity.[9] Finally, "looking outward," it is appropriate to point out that there were a multitude of acts of social solidarity, not only the support to the piqueteros but that provided to the workers in the occupied factories. The paradigmatic case was the Brukman factory, which resisted three efforts to evict the workers during 2002. Each time, assembly activists were among the first in mobilizing to impede the ousting of the work force from the factory. The definitive eviction took place in April 2003, several days after an episode of strong repression.

Over time, the debates of a political nature over forms of democracy were replaced by acts of solidarity. Thus one type of action producing the highest membership mobilization (but one that was nevertheless still controversial) was that linked to food aid. Some experiences relating to linkages were especially symbolic, such as the campaign to vaccinate cartoneros, implemented by one of the most active assemblies in the northern zone of the Capital. Soup kitchens and the provision of snacks multiplied especially after the takeover of buildings that various assemblies in the Capital organized between June and September 2002. What to do was at the center of all assembly experiences.

In the case of Villa Crespo, the inauguration of both a snack service and a dining room attracted various cartoneros and poor neighborhood children to their site. The efforts of some militants redoubled to spread such activity thoughout the neighborhood and in the schools, as well as to solicit donations of food and medicine from neighborhood merchants. But a discussion of the charity-like appearance that was coloring the snacks and the dining room rapidly spilled over to various difficulties in sustaining such activity in terms of material and human resources. The act of providing food to eat led to an effort by political party groups to forge some political consciousness toward the cartoneros. Similarly, some more independent activists proposed to require from them a commitment and a responsible attitude in respect to their participation in assembly activities and their use of the site for sleeping. The short-lived stay of some cartoneros in the building in the views of some assembly members suggested disorder, lack of respect for the other "compañeros," and incidents of robbery of items from the site.

The failure to integrate reflected the reciprocal instrumental relation developed by both sectors. Seen as a failure, the experience with the cartoneros renewed the discourse in favor of the snacks as a political project aimed at connecting with the most impoverished parts of the neighborhood and giving them a model for emulation. Nevertheless, as the difficulties involved with the operation of the snacks increased, they became a factor in a furious dispute among different party groups. The object of working with the neighborhood unemployed became questioned, with some arguing that they had their own organizations and that the snacks were part of a strategy of one of the leftist parties to take over the building. This political debate that continued during several weekly meetings was transformed into a factor of denunciations, accusations, and personal grievances in which certain social representations negatively associated with the cartoneros were found that created pressure for the ending of the snacks.

In its turn, the Palermo Assembly found the organization of a weekly food kitchen a bonding activity where some neighborhood residents who had left the assembly plus new people began to participate, producing effects on an enlarged neighborhood membership. The food kitchen continued until the end of 2002 in one of the plazas in the neighborhood and attracted a group of cartoneros who frequented the zone. Despite some reticence, the majority of assembly members agreed on the need for this activity as an effort for greater impact in the neighborhood and for a link to other social sectors.

The propensity for developing charitable activity was a warning about the assembly's concerns. However, the traditional skepticism and defensiveness toward developments was silenced by the expectation and enthusiasm created when the food kitchen went into effect. With over 150 people continuously attending, an open organization was established to develop dialogue among the neighbors so that a commission seeking to integrate them all into the assembly would begin to function.

Therefore, in contrast with the Villa Crespo Assembly, where the activity of a dining room and snack service became the focus for strong confrontation and initial internal breakdown, an atmosphere of relative harmony and convergence of interest developed in Palermo. But the principal difficulty in the discussion about the food kitchen was how to think about such activity from a logic that would transcend mere charity. "How are we different from Cáritas [the Catholic charity]?" posed a disturbing question in a debate over political goals to be pursued.

In conclusion, the move to develop ties with vulnerable groups tended to activate a certain middle-class notion of playing the role of intermediary or person joining groups together, although it also brought to the center of the debate a discussion about charitable versus solidarity-building characteristics of action. In reality, an inward focus played as important a role as outward efforts in the resolution of the tensions and original ambivalence that passed through the movement. In this sense, the feelings of division and internal lack of cooperation of the individuals mobilized tended to reinforce an inclination toward isolation and self-focus that had been objected to equally in the repudiated "political class." At the end, this logic for action strengthened the disruptive character of the movement so that the kind of initial aspiration of universalistic character promoting the creation of a new kind of institutionality with the development of other forms of democracy could never conclusively be consolidated.

By the beginning of 2003, the basic space open to the piquetero movements and the progressive middle class after the June assassinations began to contract in a dizzying manner. Despite the discrediting of the traditional parties, a demand for "institutional normality" could be heard from those who a few months before had been part of the mobilizations demanding "let's throw them all out." This was at the time when a kind of saturation in respect to the street blockages and demonstrations began once again to reduce the degree of tolerance for social protest. In February 2003, a few months before the presidential elections, the government began a strong campaign against activist social groups that had as its purpose the clearance of the buildings taken over by the neighborhood assemblies and of the factories like Brukman Textiles occupied by their workers, and the jailing of known piquetero leaders in the interior of the country. As was pointed to and denounced by many social organizations, these repressive acts were meant to establish the idea that the elections would bring to an end a socio-political cycle as well as seek to erase the visible signs of self-organization and self-management from society.

The elections took place in an unusual climate of indifference. The fragmentation of the vote was such that, after a year and a half of mobilizations, the surveys carried out some weeks before saw the two right-wing neo-liberal candidates, Carlos Menem and Ricardo López Murphy, as the favorites in a runoff. Ultimately, faced with this depiction of the situation (suitably manipulated by the mass media), strategic voting by a progressive middle class tied to the always volatile political center-left took place, securing the second-place position in the first round for current President Néstor Kirchner, right behind Menem, who would soon withdraw.

The election results indicated a low percentage of absenteeism and of blank ballots. In addition, they suggested that even the supporters of those piquetero groups that had called for a blank or "ideological" vote had supported the two less conservative Peronist Party candidates, including the current president. Last, the leftist parties like the Trotskyites that ran candidates attained the worst results in their history. In sum, the presidential elections raised a major question about the efficacy of the intense mobilizations of 2002 in their questioning of political representation.

Rather than the persistence of Peronism in working-class parts of the population, the provincial elections that took place in 2003 seemed to corroborate the consolidation of a political scene presided over from now into the future by a kind of "everlasting Peronism," newly established due to the collapse of the other traditional parties. In any case, the facts once again emphasized the historical effectiveness of the political turns and ideological shifts of Peronism. Thus, via Kirchner, the political agenda seemed to introduce new themes and expectations, some of which had formed part of the demands of the numerous actors mobilized in 2002 (the purging of the Supreme Court and the cleansing of state institutions, among others) that had encountered an unfavorable reception in the previous administration.

Finally, going beyond the fact that the political reconstruction has been limited,[10] it seems worthwhile to ask what has remained at the end of such social excitement with all its high and low points from that undoubtedly extraordinary year 2002.

By Way of a Conclusion:
Hypotheses about a Still Uncertain Ending

> Autonomy is not a circle but an opening, an ontological opening and the possibility of passing beyond the circle of information, of knowledge, and of organization that characterizes self-made beings as submissive individuals. . . . Autonomy signifies the alteration of the system of knowledge and organization now existing; it signifies the constitution of a world with its own different laws.
> —Cornelius Castoriadis, *Los dominios del hombre*

Once we have noted the difficulties and limits that doubtlessly marked the assembly movement (and mobilizations in general), once we have accepted the change in political conditions, nothing would be easier—but nothing more forced—than arriving at negative or fatalistic conclusions about what really took place in 2002. In reality, going beyond the high expectations that the cycle of mobilization begun in December 2001 aroused in certain social sectors and in numerous foreign observers, we believe that the accumulated outcome is without doubt positive, and this despite all the difficulties indicated.

Certainly, the neighborhood assemblies never came close to sharing any single pattern of experience in common. Riddled by dissension and a series of ambivalent demands, the assemblies tended to expend a good part of their political energy in really destructive behavior. In many cases, the efforts to defend different views led merely to fragmentation and the multiplication of various shifting alliances, to the detriment of any genuine political expression. The result that many hoped for—that is, the rise of a new political process—in the end never took place. Consequently, the possibility of creating a new institutional form seemed weakened.

But the answers each assembly provided for these problems doubtlessly cannot all fit within a single model. What is certain is that in an important number of cases, the action taken and apparent resolution of these basic tensions contributed to indicate the very limits of the movement. Thus, by December 2002, the emergence of these dilemmas revealed a scenario very different from that of the first months. For example, after fierce struggle, the Villa Crespo Assembly was dominated by a group of left-wing party militants who, due to their isolation, were evicted at the end of 2003 from the building the assembly had occupied. In its case, the Palermo Assembly ended up dissolving itself, after encountering insuperable difficulties not just in its internal ideological disputes, but also given the impossibility of responding with any real political efficacy to member demands for creating a new institutional structure. At the end, only a few assemblies managed to maintain their autonomy, adopting a course of action similar to that of some parts of the MTD (Movimiento de Trabajadores Desocupados/Movement of Unemployed Workers) piqueteros, or shifting toward a new type of more socio-cultural movement (like the assemblies of Cid Campeador, Palermo Viejo, Colegiales, San Telmo, Florida Este, and Almagro, among others).

Despite such a result, plus the loss of members, the retreats, and the difficulties that really were the consequence of the assembly movement, no one ought to underestimate the accomplishments of this new experience showing the emergence of new political commitment toward social interaction. In reality, what the assemblies ended up confirming was the birth of a new ethos of militancy constructed on certain articulated principles including, among others, autonomy in respect to parties, unions, or the state; followed next by a strong counter-cultural vocation; and, finally, the move to create organizational structures that were flexible, anti-bureaucratic, and of local character.

But without doubt, the most important feature that emerged from the uneven assembly experience was the goal of autonomy. In the heat of discussions and practices that paradoxically reflected the same process of fragmentation and weakening of the assembly movement, the demand for autonomy was becoming clearer, becoming more detailed, eventually acquiring a clear mass, becoming in the end a type of variable indicating political configuration. Moreover, we would be able to claim that as an identifying variable, the demand for autonomy is found among a multiplicity of organizations of a social, political, and cultural nature that emerged here and elsewhere on the planet in the 1990s, organizations characterized by a style of construction that strongly contrasts with those found in the parties of the traditional left.[11] In sum, from a political point of view, the assemblies showed greater impact of certain concepts of the left whose key elements are found both in the affirmation of autonomy and in the development of flexible horizontal networks resistant to any case of decision-making from above.[12]

In this sense, it is necessary to remember that, in our country. autonomous organizations began to be created in the second half of the 1990s, in light of the effects produced by the neo-liberal model, as is the case of certain piquetero groups coming from the south of the Greater Buenos Aires area and of the first collectives of political art like the Street Art Group (Grupo de Arte Callejero/ GAC) and Etcétera that participated in the "escrache" protests of shouted insults aimed at corrupt officials carried out by the Hijos group. Something similar could be said about groups concerning militant cinema—like Insurgent Movies and the Alavio group—or of the Action Network, an alternative news agency created in Avellaneda that is today's ANRED. However, it was not until December 2001, when the country entered a period marked by intense social mobilization oriented toward direct action and self-organization "from below," that these groups grew more powerful, becoming visible in an increasing number of situations: collectives on art, photography, and anti-establishment information, and new piquetero groups of a more local character, among others. In other terms, the assembly process—and the mobilizations taking place in 2002 in general—produced the empowerment and the flowering of counter-cultural forces. The appropriate model for their social interaction and involvement was the neighborhood assemblies, but also some particular situations like the case of Brukman Textiles, which was the center of intense activism.

In conclusion, these counter-cultural collectives constituted one of the less known dimensions of the social movements present in Argentina today, ones that not only provide an account of what actually took place once the initial period of enthusiasm passed, but ones that alert us to the emergence of a political mind-set with its own special character; this is not really comparable to the experiences of mobilization and struggle that, even with their great heterogeneity, marked most of what was happening among the piquetero groups.

Notes

* Translated by Edward Epstein. An earlier version of this work was presented at the CEDES seminar, "Movimientos Sociales en la Argentina de Hoy," on December 5, 2002. It was written in collaboration with a research team consisting of Damián Corral, Mariana Barattini, and Marina García.

1. The assembly adopted the name of one of the young people killed in the days of December 19 and 20, 2001.
2. The question whether more autonomous commissions—with a greater role for "independent" activists—should participate or not and should respect the ideological perspective of the assemblies fits into this conflict over the proper shape and identity of that space.
3. The occupation of the Banco Provincia building had an effect on the neighborhood and on residents estranged from the assembly: in the first meeting after the takeover, some 80 people came together, over double the number of those participating in the assembly when it was held in the street.
4. An indicator of the charity-like character with which the quest for local neighborhood self-management was conceived was the philanthropic activity carried out by members of this commission in coordination with the assembly in Las Cañitas (an upper-middle-class neighborhood in the Capital): once a month they sought to collect disused clothes and shoes to give to needy children in both neighborhoods. Similarly, on Children's Day, they collected toys and food.
5. Georg Simmel, *El individuo y la libertad: Ensayos de crítica de la cultura* (Barcelona: Península, 1986).
6. In turn, both the image of "bridge" and that of "door" rested on important precedents in the piquetero movement, within an excessively varied range that to the present day includes center-left perspectives with clear elements of a social movement to completely anti-capitalist postures coming from autonomous groups and parties of the left. See Maristella Svampa and Sebastián Pereyra, *Entre la ruta y el barrio: La experiencia de las organzaciones piqueteras* (Buenos Aires: Biblos, 2003), chap. 4.
7. The fact that some names of assembly members are on record as responsible for the

takeover and that these names were never replaced by others was a matter of controversy among assembly members. Those so listed are presently under indictment in the courts. The occupied site was cleared out by the police in November 2003.

8. Note that the symbolic process and the disagreement in respect to social experience are not the same in the two cases. In its extreme form, then, the combination of the old practices of party militants with expert knowledge reflects a "dependent reversion" in which someone claims to have given up a specific symbolic model but where his practices continue being influenced by that model. Despite criticism of the forms on which the "old left" was built, and in spite of the illusion that the person has of abandoning that model, the question is in effect whether action continues to take place in this case under its imprint. The subject remains a prisoner of a model that he questions and of which, nevertheless, he is unable to completely divert himself. On the other hand, the situation of the party militant is different: his removal from the social experience with the replacement of that reality through a symbolic mechanism. On this theme, see Danilo Martuccelli and Maristella Svampa, *La plaza vacía: Las transformaciones del peronismo* (Buenos Aires: Losada, 1997).

9. On this theme, see Marina García, *Las asambleas barriales, esas delicadas creaturas: Tesis de grado* (Buenos Aires: Universidad Nacional General Sarmiento, 2002), an interesting work analyzing the relations of cartoneros and assembly members.

10. The Peronist political reformulation has clear internal and external limits. On the one hand, despite its positive social image, Kirchner's leadership hardly reorganizes within its ranks all the different internal Peronist factions; on the other hand, the different provincial elections of 2003 provide an account of a new growth of electoral abstention that in some cases exceeded 30% of those registered (*Página 12*, December 4, 2003).

11. In reality, the emergence of new forms of organization inclined toward autonomy is one of the most salient elements of contemporary social movements. In this sense, Argentina has not escaped from this worldwide tendency.

12. Although it is not possible to deal here with this theme, the question is not unimportant. By the facts of its nature, this perspective works against the possibility for true political expression considering the formation of a political being. For a different conceptualization in respect to political expression as a constituent element for a different identity, see Ernesto Laclau, *Nuevas reflexiones sobre la revolución de nuestro tiempo* (Buenos Aires: Nueva Visión, 1993).

7

Middle-Class Use of Barter Clubs:
A Real Alternative or Just Survival?*

Inés González Bombal and Mariana Luzzi

The Argentine model of social integration had very particular features that were definitely lost in the 1990s—social mobility, a certain degree of equality, and a strong middle class. The impact of such transformation was evident not only in the population's standard of living, but also in new forms of organization and social relations that these changes created. Among these, the rise in the middle of the decade of barter clubs (clubes de trueque) deserves particular attention. They were created in 1995 as places for the non-monetary exchange of goods and services, and their expansion was rapid and sustained throughout the next several years, reaching its greatest development toward the end of 2001 due to the national economic crisis.

Organized in regional and national networks from 1996 onward, the barter clubs were successful for various reasons: on the one hand, the clubs represented an intent to construct an "alternative market" where the principles of solidarity and mutual aid were to replace competition and the search for profit; on the other hand, in the context of economic recession and high unemployment, they offered an important sector of the population the possibility of acquiring certain goods and basic services without a cash expenditure.

In this chapter we discuss the phenomenon of the expanding networks of impoverished middle-class individuals that with the eruption of the 2001 crisis was expanded to include parts of the popular sector. This work touches on the potential and limits of an experience of a kind never seen before in Argentina in terms of the numbers of people involved and the causes of its present decay.

1. Barter Clubs as a New Form of Social Organization

Manuel[1] is over 60 years old. For years he worked as a translator, but without doubt what marked him throughout his life was his political activism. In telling about his past experiences, he mentions years of "social and political concern," years of "dreaming about social change," and, especially, the impact of his disappointment. It's been some time since Manuel has gotten together with his old activist companions to "think about what happened," where he discusses with them the changes of a world that did not evolve in the ways they expected and that today seems too hostile for the dreams that mobilized them twenty or thirty years earlier. In such meetings, they not only go over the past but also, once again, plan the future. It is a future that now is not thought about on a big scale, but on a small one, where the term "from below" takes on other meanings:

> There are lots of social organizations, NGOs, or new forms of production that appear everywhere—it's a very small thing—but there are many intent on seeking a new form of social organization, where it is not profit that matters, where people once again look at each other face to face, where one works so as to fulfill the needs of the other and that guy helps me with what he knows how to do. To once again take up ideals not through the Revolution or organizing to take power, but very small scale, creating a new culture, recovering from just over there what is around.

Manuel's friends, with time, have been finding different ways to channel their need to work "for a new culture"; some participate in university extension groups, others organize neighborhood workshops from their trade unions or propose sensitizing teenagers to ecological problems. Manuel, for his part, coordinates a barter club: "Everyone looked to his experience where mine was that of the barter club, a little place where we began to see a viewpoint that looked to us like something new, a civil society that organizes itself not within the larger world, but in small communities."[2]

Manuel's history as coordinator of one of the first barter clubs in the City of Buenos Aires is paradigmatic. This is so not only because it expresses the desire to construct an alternative system that inspired a good part of the pioneers in this experience, but also because it shows the strong linkages between the origin of Argentine barter clubs and their "neighbors" in the rest of the world.

In reality, organized barter is not a local invention. Distinct initiatives based on the idea of constructing a space for exchange as an alternative to the official economy were tried in the 1980s and 1990s, first in the Anglo-Saxon world (Canada, Australia, New Zealand, England, and the United States) and afterwards in France. In the first case, one was dealing with LETS (Local Exchange Trading Systems) and in France with SEL (Système d'Échange Local).[3] The first LETS arose in 1983 in Canada, and in little time the model was replicated in other countries. Its creator, Michael Linton, rapidly became an international leader; he was the first to envision the creation of a system of "communitarian" exchange maintained on the basis of a "local currency" as a solution to problems derived from lack of work and/or the meagerness of earnings. The first SEL, for its part, was born at the end of 1994 in the Ariège region in the French Pyrenees. The most famous of its originators was Alain Bertrand, a militant ecologist with abundant experience in development matters and years of work with the Third World. At the beginning of the 1990s, he was already familiar with the North American and English experiences and believed fervently in the results that they could have, even in a different context like France. The region where he lived offered a terrain propitious for experimentation: it had been populated in the 1970s by urban migrants who found the area quite attractive, enthused as they were by life in contact with nature and by projects for organic agriculture associated with ecological concerns and self-sustainable development. In both cases, a personal initiative quite influenced by an activist past and/or involved with the development of local-level organizations had characterized the beginning of the project.

The history of the birth of the Argentine barter clubs does not differ much from this account.[4] Assembled for the first time on May 1, 1995, in the garage of a family home in the locality of Bernal (in Buenos Aires Province), the group was led by three professionals (a chemist, a psychiatrist, and a librarian) with lengthy experience linked to local development and the creation of NGOs. The "barter club," as they called the new invention, was not their first project together. Previously, they had tried to develop a joint work in which two organizations created by them years before came together, the Program for Regional Self-Sufficiency (or Programa de Autosuficiencia Regional/PAR)[5] and the Professional Network (Red Profesional).[6] The barter club, however, would become an enterprise with another purpose and different members.

Contained in its "myth of origin" is the following story: some of the ecological projects developed by the PAR consisted in the promotion of domestic organic gardens worked by each family in its own home. The members of the NGO utilized this idea when one person grew vegetables on the roof of his house. In 1994, someone who later would be one of the founders of the barter clubs presented a woman neighbor with a very large chunk of a giant pumpkin harvested from the family garden. The woman, a widow whose only income was a small pension, during the year used the vegetable she received to make sweets that when sold gave her an income three times the value of her pension. The idea of the barter club was foreseen: "It was all a question of organizing a way to bring together the goods offered and sought by a large group of unemployed people, so as to do with them what we had done with the giant pumpkins!"[7]

Thus the basic principle of barter consists in each member of the barter club preparing items that later will be exchanged at a weekly group meeting, or market. What is offered can be anything: it includes goods produced by the members (prepared food, handicrafts, household goods, etc.) as much as services offered by them (the repair of electric items, carpentry, metalworking, painting, hairdressing, etc.). The idea is simple and attractive: "Barter today is what it always was—I have something that you need and you have something that I need . . . so we swap. And here there was no intermediary. We simply agreed among ourselves that I needed this and you needed that; this is how the business gets done. This is bartering."[8]

Obviously, the practice is not quite so simple. Barter, defined in its original terms as a "double coincidence of needs," takes place only in exceptional cases. More often, one is dealing with an exchange in which many people take part at the same time, something that the originators of the club called "multi-reciprocal barter." To express it in the language used above: I, A, have something that you, B, need; B has something that C needs; and A needs something that C has. What is offered by everyone meets the needs of everyone, but the exchanges do not require that the needs of "buyers" and "sellers" coincide every time.

The first difficulty that the group faced was therefore of a practical nature. If the "deals" do not take place between two people where each one has, in some sense, an account with credits and debits, how can a registry of each participant's transactions be made so each person can take theirs away with them? The first solution was rather basic: everyone possesses a notebook listing their purchases and sales, information that at the same time was passed on to the organizers of the group, who kept a central record. But the system was costly in time and effort. At the end of several weeks, the increase in the number of transactions made the task of keeping central records almost endless, making things more complex rather than simplified. The second solution, then, was more sophisticated: the organizers of the club placed at the disposition of the members a means of payment for "local-only" use. Everyone would have an equal number of units of such a means of payment that they would use to carry out swaps. Thus no one needed to remember to record every purchase or sale and the increase in the number of members or of transactions would not be an obstacle for the functioning of the group, but just the opposite. In this way, the "credit" emerged in 1996 as the barter club currency. With its creation, they sought to introduce an instrument to facilitate the organization of the clubs and to ease the operations of its members. As the founding group put it, "The symbolic elements employed by the barter clubs are an inseparable part of a service; they are only units of measurement rather than of value. If the Global Barter Network or GBN was a telephone system, the distinct swaps among the members would be equivalent to conversations among subscribers and the 'credits,' the cables and exchanges that make communications possible."[9]

The mechanism for the emission and distribution of credits was as follows: after a series of successive swaps (between two to four weeks on average), every new member received fifty credits in the form of an initial loan. These were to serve as a stimulus for their participation in the club and as help in the preparation of products or in providing services. They needed to be returned only if the member were to drop out. Beyond this initial installment, only the production of goods or the provision of services increased the quantity of money in possession of the members. There existed a constant relation between the "monetary volume" and the number of participants (each one received fifty credits once), a relation that could be modified if it was thought that the volume of transactions required a larger amount of credits in circulation.[10]

Two principles formed the base of the system. In the first place, every member of the club was linked to the group in the dual role of producer (supplier) and consumer (purchaser). Secondly, the basic function of the club consisted in creating a new space for exchange where all participants were considered equal.

The name "prosumer" given to all club members expressed the first of these principles. It was meant to summarize the basic dual function of individuals involved in barter. This term, present more in the organization's documents than in the discourse of its members, was not the invention of the group's founder, but was taken by him from the celebrated essay that Alvin Toffler published at the end of the 1970s, *The Third Wave*. According to that author, the final third of the twentieth century would witness the confusion of the distinction born in the industrial revolution of the roles of consumer and producer. In its place one would witness the development of a "prosumer ethic," so characteristic of *The Third Wave*, thanks to which individuals would be capable of again integrating both roles. Without explicitly discussing the model proposed by Toffler, from this general idea the promoters of the exchange club took one particular aspect, the positive consequences that it assumed about the individuals involved, their autonomy, versatility, diversity.[11]

In the particular case of the barter club, to be a prosumer implied being a consumer (that is, having access to the goods and/or services offered at the club) and also a producer (that is, being capable of preparing goods or providing services to be offered to the rest of the group).

The complement to the notion of "prosumer" was the idea of the reinvention of the market as an expression of the basic purpose of club activity. This is how the founding statement of principles for such activity expressed it in one of the club's programmatic documents:

> As "prosumers," we freely provide and simultaneously require goods and services, as much as producers as consumers, reinventing the market. A market that has space for reciprocity, solidarity, and distribution, that allows us to learn to productively utilize the energy of anger and indignation, that accepts what is new and risky as part of life itself, that invites us to cultivate the joy of sharing, the joy of quality not quantity, the joy of relating not possessing. In sum, we create a new space where one can live simply so that others can simply live. In this market, we all possess a type of capital that in my judgement is more important, human capital. This is the only thing that you can do against the affliction of poverty and basic need. This is a market without competition, that begins to advance as its members gain in satisfaction and quality of life.[12]

Thus the barter club emerges as a possible alternative to a specific problem—the ever greater difficulties of the population in gaining access to consumption. Faced then with the existence of "barriers to entry" in the market, the solution offered is to reinvent the market, to create a space for the circulation of goods where such difficulties would disappear or at least be reduced.

But for the barter clubs to make the reinvention of the market possible, it is necessary that those who are purchasers also be suppliers. Participation in a club implies both regaining one's capacity to consume, lost with the crisis, and recovering one's function as a producer, for which in many cases the official economy no longer provides space.

In this sense, the birth date of the barter club was hardly random. An unemployment rate that was less than 9% of the active population at the beginning of the decade exceeded 18% in 1995. These figures increased among low-income groups, reaching alarming levels in Greater Buenos Aires, where the barter club made its first appearance on May Day, the "Day of the Worker," 1995.

The barter clubs thus sought to demonstrate that an exchange network established among neighbors could contribute to alleviating many of the needs of families with economic difficulties. But it also sought to implant the idea that everyone possessed "exploitable" capabilities and skills, even if these were not recognized by the formal labor market.

In addition to its strictly economic goals, the barter club was a project for personal development. To be a prosumer was a job in itself to discover those abilities capable of being translated into the provision of goods or services. It supposed, using the idea found in the Declaration of Principles for barter clubs, that "our fulfillment as human beings does not need to be conditioned by money."[13]

Manuel counts himself among those prosumers who have adopted this search for other abilities:

> [There is] another idea that is fundamental: To rediscover the meaning of what one does. The goal of what one does is not necessarily gain but relates to what is enjoyable and serves others. Another idea here is that one does not have only a single profession. Everyone does what they know how to do; we invite those trained to prepare food, "please make food for the people here in need; make yourself known as someone skilled through food," we say. People have . . . take me, for example . . . I don't know . . . my work, in the last period was as a teacher, after being a translator. I'm asked to do some translation around here, but if not, I'll do some carpentry. Everyone does what they know how to do, almost like a family. . . . I might tell you about work and about production.

Like him, many others come to the barter clubs in the first years after their creation in search of a space where one can put into practice new forms of reciprocity and mutual aid. But among the ever more numerous prosumers, we find not only activists committed to an alternative project. Like Manuel himself, as he made clear to us on the occasion of our first meeting in 2000, "Those who come have two characteristics: some who really, definitely, have problems of no money and no job, and who are needy. There are others interested by the idea, probably without such dire need, but who come because the idea interests them a lot."

In effect, the enormous growth of the practice of barter experienced in Argentina between 1996 and the beginning of 2002 was due less to the expansion of a project of idealists than to the spread of a strategy that seemed effective in at least attenuating the consequences of the economic crisis.[14]

By 1996, one year after the launching of the first club, the number of members reached 1,000. This was the moment when the first network of clubs was created, transforming each club into a "node" and establishing means of coordination among the different existing groups.[15] In 1997, the number of members rose to 2,300; by 1999, it was 180,000. One year later, barter clubs attracted 320,000 in close to 400 nodes located in fifteen provinces and in the Federal Capital. In 2001, the number of nodes doubled and that of participants reached 500,000 in over twenty provinces. By the beginning of 2002, with the impact produced by the Argentine banking system crisis that added a notable decrease in the amount of money in circulation to the effects of the economic recession, people spoke of the existence of 4,500 active nodes and of a number of participants four times larger than that of the previous year.[16]

2. Barter Clubs as an Additional Way to Confront the Crisis

One of the persons who came to the barter club "through need" was Juana. In 1999, the business where she worked as a cleaning lady went broke, obliging her to seek other ways of adding to the income of her husband, the only employed member of their family. The salary he earned as a worker in a restaurant was insufficient to feed the five children still living at home, and getting a new job seemed impossible. It was due to a neighbor that Juana learned of the existence of barter clubs, located at that moment far from her home in another area of the Capital. "In those early times," Juana said "I could go forward, could dress my kids, dress myself, and take care of some things in my house, all thanks to the barter club." Every week, Juana prepared cupcakes, tarts, or fried cake that she "sold" at one of the nodes in exchange for credits. With these, in turn, she bought clothing or hired an electrician or carpenter whom she never would have been able to pay in pesos. Her participation in barter thus provided for a small investment in pesos (never more than five pesos per week) and access to goods and services that she could never have paid for with the only income on which her family could count.[17]

Hilda also sought a way of increasing her family's income through barter. Divorced, at 39 she lost her job in an office, losing with it medical coverage for herself and her family. From that moment, the only resources in her home (composed of herself and her three children aged 20, 15, and 13) were what came from the job she developed on her own as an herbalist and from the food money irregularly provided by her ex-husband. At the barter clubs, Hilda found above all a market for the herbs she grew with the help of her children. Thus, week after week, she obtained credits that permitted her to obtain food, clothing, and some books without the need to spend the few pesos that she found at home as a result of her sales that were not part of barter.

Neither Juana nor Hilda had participated in the past in associations or other types of organizations. As workers, they had never been affiliated with unions, never been members of cooperatives at their children's schools, nor had they ever felt tempted by membership in political groups or political parties. On the other hand, in reference to the barter clubs, they did not feel attracted to the "alternative project" the clubs represented to some. They did not define themselves as prosumers nor did they receive from their participation the sense of constructing a new form for personal realization unaffected by money or the profit motive.

Nevertheless, for them the positive aspects of barter were not exhausted by their ability to "squeeze out" the family budget. The clubs were also places with a different atmosphere, where one could "share things with other people, converse."

The valuing of this aspect of sociability in bartering appears recurrently in the accounts of the participants. For some, the "activists," this is really a central aspect of the experience. Here one is dealing with collectively building a space in which reciprocity and mutual aid prevail over the profit motive and competition. As Manuel emphasized, the barter club

> is not a shop or supermarket, even if in a shop where one goes one gets on well with the shopkeeper, because what interests him is that I pay him and what interests me is to find things more cheaply. This is a human relation, but a different relation where money does not matter. The barter club thus has a different look, what we would call a social appearance.

For others, sociability is not the motive for their participation in the clubs, but an appreciated by-product. Said differently, one does not go to the barter club to be with others, but to provide products and seek other products. However, from this practice are born relations with others in the same situation, and such relations continue to be cultivated.

Hilda and Juana came to bartering in 2000, at a time when this activity began to have large-scale exposure in the mass media. Barter clubs were not only found in the Federal Capital and Greater Buenos Aires but were also present in many cities in the interior of the country, where provincial or regional networks were created that grouped together the clubs of each zone. The barter clubs were distributed mostly in urban areas but also were created in some rural contexts. The majority of the oldest ones consisted of groups with high internal cohesion, where at least a great part of the members were characterized by a strong commitment to the ideological principles of such activity. But along with these came new clubs with a different profile: the rule now was not commitment to the idea of an alternative project, but the search for new strategies to deal with the economic crisis. In these cases, the barter club was "one issue more" along with many others: small occasional jobs, short-term services, self-employment, odd jobs of any kind. En route, some made a virtue of necessity, discovering in barter not only a way of gaining income, but also a space of particular sociability. For others, barter would be only a "business" or "one more job."[18]

3. The Explosion

To the extent that barter was spreading, such tendencies only became more marked. The media discussed the experience of barter clubs with increasing frequency, and throughout 2001, some 20,000 new members per month were registered in the country. But the big increase still had not taken place; it was the establishment of the so-called "corralito"[19] at the beginning of December 2001 that gave a final push to barter. From the moment in which difficulties in withdrawing money from bank accounts began, the number of people going to barter clubs exploded, reaching 5,000 new participants per day.[20]

It was not just the middle classes who saw the possibility of accessing their salaries strongly limited, but also workers in the informal sector traditionally paid in cash who were not able to collect for jobs done. The bank accounts were there, the dollar was still worth one peso, but "there was no money on the street." In this context, the barter club was seen by many as salvation: there was a place where even with no available cash one could buy things. It was not just that the number of nodes doubled and that of members tripled, but that new clubs arose overnight like mushrooms after a rain.

Now, even if this growth could be interpreted as a sign of success, it still signified a strong challenge to the organizers. The existing networks had already experienced difficulties in managing the large expansion of activity that occurred between 1999 and 2000. Serious internal problems in reference to the mechanisms for the emission of the credits produced successive splits within the Global Barter Network (Red Global del Trueque) and led to the creation of a new "grand network," the Solidarity Barter Network or SBN (Red del Trueque Solidario), representing many of the clubs of the City of Buenos Aires, plus some regional networks.[21] The deepening of the crisis nationally could only aggravate some of these problems.

One of the first consequences of the dizzying increase in the number of participants concerned "social money." The existing system of emission set out that the nodes would ask the corresponding network to print and hand over to the coordinator fifty credits for every new member. Labeled the "social frank" by the founding barter group, this mechanism centralized monetary emission in the networks and thus guaranteed the existence of a currency valid simultaneously in many nodes; that is, all those making up the same network throughout the country.[22] For the emission of credits to be maintained in relation with the quantity of active participants, a series of rules had to be followed: in the first place, the participants should not join more than one club (something that certainly seemed unnecessary since a member could participate in any node he wanted even without being a member there); second, participants who ceased participating should return to the club the fifty credits received upon joining; third, the clubs should respect the principle of fifty credits per participant and print only those credits strictly necessary.

As can be imagined, none of these conditions was easy to honor in a context as turbulent as that of late 2001/early 2002. The new members joined barter clubs and immediately began to participate in swaps without familiarizing themselves with the rules governing that activity or receiving any type of tutoring. The coordinators lacked time to organize the formerly obligatory training courses for new members, who themselves seemed too much in a hurry to allow this type of process. In some cases, the old course was replaced by a brief introductory talk given minutes before the opening of the club; in others, it was simply eliminated. Therefore many people joined all the nodes possible without even knowing that they were thus violating one of the basic barter club rules. Others, later on, did this consciously. In either case, the fraud was impossible to detect.

At the same time, the huge numbers contributed to the presence of illegal practices like the counterfeiting and sale of credits. From the beginning of 2002, cases of the sale of such "social money" in the environs of the barter fairs became increasingly more frequent, something that operated as a strong disincentive to production for the nodes. In short, it was much more convenient to buy credits illegally than to offer goods to obtain them.[23]

The second consequence of the crisis concerns the specific relation between the volume of supply and of demand in the nodes. Rapidly, the clubs filled up with participants—with empty hands. If factors endogenous to the system like the high availability of credits affected the fall of production for barter, so did external factors like the inflation unleashed beginning in January 2002 for popular consumer goods.[24] For those who prepared food, the area where the majority of "producers" for barter was found, the increase in the prices of ingredients meant the abandonment of production and its replacement with another type of item like used goods (generally clothes). The same happened with those who provided services that required materials unavailable through barter (spare parts, paint, construction material, etc.).

Thus the great transformation begun in December 2001 led, in the first place, to the impoverishment of the goods supplied in the nodes. It was not only that the volume of the goods and services provided did not increase at the same speed as the number of participants, but that the quality and variety of the products progressively diminished.

In the second place, the composition of the clubs also changed. If in the year 2000, one observed a process where barter became more heterogeneous in nature with the massive growth of the clubs, the tendency in 2002 seemed to be the reverse. Little by little, participants whose most basic needs were satisfied were abandoning the clubs, disappointed by a place no longer possessing "a different climate," and where the goods available had become as impoverished as the majority of its members. The only people who continued participating were those who through barter could "get by," for whom even the most limited swaps could make a difference.

4. Changes in the Barter Clubs

The panorama that the barter clubs presented in the year 2000 was, as we saw, obviously different from what was observed at the beginning of 2002. Beyond the differences existing between more centrally located clubs and those more on the periphery and the changing commitment to an "alternate project," the nodes could have been characterized by a type of behavior relatively common to all. Each club organized one or two fairs per week that the members anxiously awaited. "Barter day" was not like any other day: one had to prepare the products to offer, to take into account the requests received the previous week, to organize one's affairs so as to have the afternoon free. The swaps themselves never lasted more than two hours, but the meetings were greatly prolonged after the transactions were concluded. The great majority of the prosumers did not participate in more than the single node with which they were associated, where the practice had a weekly timetable about it. In respect to the goods offered, the variety reflected the heterogeneity of the participants: prepared meals, foods bought in bulk and resold in small amounts, products for cleaning, candles, flower arrangements, and general arts and crafts. The same happened with services, which ranged from hairdressing, electrical work, painting, metalworking, podiatry, and cosmetology to sessions of psychotherapy, Reiki, aromatherapy, and yoga classes.

This convergence of actors from different backgrounds with differing material and symbolic resources and not always similar goals was seen as one of the strong points of the barter clubs within a few years of their founding. If the participants came to the nodes to meet their needs in greater or lesser degree, these needs were far from being identical, but all were met for the first time through the same experience.

It was all a great novelty, especially for impoverished middle-class people. If at the beginning of the 1990s, sociology spoke of a new form of poverty experienced "behind closed doors,"[25] by the end of the same decade, approaches seemed to have changed. Barter clubs thus represented a first attempt by those groups to construct collective alternatives to impoverishment.

The question raised then was whether the convergence of the most impoverished parts of the former middle class with sectors of the "traditionally poor" could be considered a sign of integration from below.[26]

The proposal was not naïve, one not recognizing that such an encounter often was seen as constituting an unequal situation. Such diversity was not the same everywhere, being generally absent in the more peripheral nodes whose neighborhood social homogeneity was directly reflected in the barter clubs there. Furthermore, the goods circulating were evaluated differently: those first sought were the new and rare items (like shoes and top-quality clothing), while those seen as least desirable were used products (above all, clothes). Put another way, not everyone experienced this diversity under the same conditions.

The consequences of the crisis at the end of 2001 showed that the obstacles to the social integration suggested above were greater than what might have been. Manuel was the first to deplore it:

> In the previous stage, a good part of those who came knew each other, came repeatedly, conversed with each other. . . . But as it grew enormously, it unfortunately lost that appearance. One of the changes was about that then. And the quality of what was traded also [changed]. Despite everything, the people who came were people with needs, who brought things that before they had been able to trade, but now could not—for example, things of value. During the entire time the node existed, there was always lots of food. One quietly looked things over and could even find jewelry, perfume, every class of thing really . . . lots of new clothing really put together. [Now], in this avalanche, they don't come—to capture the real sense—they don't live it as they did previously. [There are] many very poor people who lack the minimum to invest, because I'll tell you now, one has to invest in the ingredients needed for something. The idea of barter is not the barter of used things but of what one produces.

As we said, the process that complements the avalanche of which Manuel spoke was the withdrawal from the club of its oldest members, those less pressed by need. In some cases, the estrangement was partial; the interaction continued but outside the nodes within small groups of prosumers who had first met in the clubs. Such a tendency was promoted by those who like Manuel considered that the central object of the barter club was to promote a "change of mentality":

> What we push is that parallel to or on the edges of the numerous nodes where group solidarity, the idea of the group as one of active members who know each other, has eroded some—it's not that it doesn't exist but it's lessened a lot—that, parallel with them or on their margin,

people form their own network with those who really make up a group, with those who share the same criteria, with those whom they can trust, who once again constitute a group with real meaning. It happens that many people who don't have a lot of need to go to the nodes do converse by phone, ask about things, meet. . . . What happens is that people tend to create their own groups; that's our tendency, but not in other places.

Whether or not one was now dealing with practices encouraged by the node leadership or by personal decisions, the impact of the withdrawal of these members was the same. The social heterogeneity of the barter clubs was reduced, and with it the diversity of goods and experiences that circulated there.

In great measure, it was those new to the clubs who had to deal with the crisis that broke out in 2002.[27] The reduction in the supply of goods and services in the clubs, the increase in prices of ingredients in the official economy, and the difficulties in obtaining by barter the products needed to produce food translated into a strong rise in prices within the system. Also of influence, as we saw, was the large supply of credits, due to their uncontrolled emission as well as the circulation of counterfeit ones. Faced with these problems, multiple strategies were tried. On the one hand, some coordinators established lists of maximum prices for basic goods so as to control the inflation unleashed in barter. At the same time, some clubs sought to adjust the volume of credits circulating, eliminating the validity of the currency in the hands of members and redistributing fifty credits to everyone, in one way "beginning all over again." This "new currency" was valid only within the node creating it; here club authorities sought not only to impose stricter control over this social currency, but also to create additional means of building member loyalty to the group. From the side of the participants, the principal strategy consisted in diversifying the means of payment. The first form such diversification took was to combine credits and pesos, a method often used by those who provide goods or services that required some investment in official money. In this way, the prices of products were set in two currencies. One portion of what was obtained was destined to cover the cost of the parts bought in pesos, the other was kept in credits. The second modification was to return to "direct barter"; that is, to transactions realized without money (either "social" or "official"). It was especially the producers of food who resorted to this. Conscious of the special nature of the goods they offered, they were unwilling to receive a completely devalued means of payment for them. The solution then was the exchange of one type of food for another.

Later on, the impact of such measures was profound. Not only did they imply the abandonment of one of the basic principles of the clubs (the absence of money in transactions), but they all tended to produce an increasing division within the nodes between those participants with resources (money and food) to continue actively in exchanges and those without to be limited to the slow and difficult circulation of secondhand goods.

If for barter clubs the creation of credit originally had supposed a decision to "do without the use of ordinary money in trading products and services with others, replacing the formal market that excluded them with a small-scale one emphasizing solidarity, where ordinary money was unnecessary because a replacement existed that could be adopted to the needs of each group,"[28] six years later this potential for adapting to the needs of participants was seen to be exhausted.

A consequence of the crisis of barter clubs was loss of confidence in the credit. In the first place, the centers issuing them ceased to provide institutional guarantees to support that currency: the over-emission, the lack of protection against counterfeiting, the dropping of the suggested equivalent value for the credit and the peso, and the tolerance of payment in pesos inside the clubs are examples of the abandonment of the rules that should have governed the printing and circulation of that currency. Second, the daily practices of the prosumers were evidence of the weakening of confidence in that money: the credit's instability as a mode of account (seen in the variation of prices), the reduction of the credit's purchasing power, and the introduction of the pesos or direct bartering as means of payment are examples of this process. Last, the constant recourse to modifying the bills (printing them with built-in security features, changes in design, the creation of special "club currency," etc.) as means of dealing with the problems of monetary circulation make manifest the difficulties that even affected the symbolic basis of the money.[29]

Finally, the crisis that broke out at the beginning of 2002 led by mid-year to a strong reduction in the number of participants and the closing of many of the clubs that six months before had seemed to be expanding. By October 2002, the media spoke of the disappearance of 40% of the clubs; two months later, it was claimed that only 3,000 of the 6,000 nodes in Greater Buenos Aires had survived the crisis, while in the Capital, only 80 were left.[30]

5. The Scope and Limits of a New Argentine Experience

The trajectory of the barter clubs presented up until here provides a multifaceted, complex account. It cannot be summarized as just the implementation of an idealistic project for an alternative economy, nor should it be limited to constituting only a survival strategy for families strongly hurt by the crisis. Both dimensions co-exist in the practice of bartering although, as we saw, over the years the second seemed to predominate over the first.

Presently, the clubs and the barter networks have not disappeared, but their economic and intermediary impact is infinitely less than what was known between 2000 and 2001. The greater part of the networks still active emphasize the creation of small groups, supported by the expressed commitment of their members, rather than the mega-fairs famous three years earlier. In respect to the barter currency, different means of control have been put into practice and the majority of the credits valid a year ago have been pulled from circulation or declared worthless. It seems risky at any rate to form conclusions about the state of these rearrangements. For the moment, the image present is that of the noisy collapse of an experience without precedent in the country.

Surely, one will have to wait some time to evaluate the marks that the barter clubs left on their participants, dealing now with those who enlisted fervently in the "alternative project" or with those who, at least for a time, found there an effective strategy for survival.

It would not be so risky to think that participation in the barter clubs might have been a form, if not of constructing social networks, at least of revitalizing pre-existent linkages.[31] At the same time, one could suggest that the experience of self-organization required for bartering could serve as a basis for future strategies designed by those involved, either from the impoverished middle classes or from popular sectors. But both hypotheses would require exploration of the paths of those actors after leaving the barter experience, something very difficult to do given their dispersion.

In whatever case, in every evaluation of the potential of the experience we ought to keep in mind the specific conditions that developed with barter between 1995 and 2003. In this sense, it is important to consider, on one side, the characteristics of the nodes for barter as organizations and, on the other, the manner in which the participants in the barter clubs came upon the experience and committed themselves to it.

In respect to their internal organization, the barter clubs possess a particular situation. If, on one hand, the nodes show evidence of a certain degree of formal structure distinguishing them from the non-commercial reciprocity networks traditionally described in the academic literature on Latin America,[32] on the other, they are not true organizations governed by norms on explicit functions and structured around formally sanctioned responsibilities. The role of coordinator that brings together all the organizational functions in the club (preparation of the meetings, contacts with the center providing the credits, mediation of conflicts among the members, etc.) is usually associated with strong personal leadership and generally is not performed with the active participation of the members in the administration of the node. Even more, despite the principles for administration understanding the coordinating role as one that ought to rotate among the differentmembers of the group,[33] it is only the most senior, typically those who took the initiative in founding the clubs, who are accustomed to performing these tasks.[34]

At the same time, from the perspective of the members, the club is less a place to which one belongs than a space through which one passes. One "goes" to the barter club as one usually goes to the market, to work, or to visit friends, without this gathering of people producing a strong mark of identification—as one would define oneself a prosumer. Distinct elements reinforce this "weakness" of the nodes as a source of identification for their members. On the one hand, the clubs do not usually possess their own permanent office; they organize their meetings in places belonging to schools, bars, church halls, soccer clubs, or neighborhood organizations. On the other, neither do the nodes maintain close ties with the institutions that provide them a place, but only form with them instrumental ties, limited to the granting of the space agreed to for holding the fairs and generally linked to the payment of rent.[35] Finally, the clubs themselves have, in a certain sense, an ephemeral character. Since the fairs are the only activity that the clubs organize (that which gives them a sense of themselves) and that provide the only time the members meet, one could say, in effect, that the nodes "exist" only through them.

In respect to the types of participation in the clubs, it is important to note that despite constituting a collectively constructed space for exchange, barter is seen by most of the members as an individual or family strategy and not a community project. Each participant decides on his or her own what to offer at the club and in the same way selects the necessary means to realize this. The same happens with decisions of strategy meant to sort out the difficulties imposed by the "crisis" situation for barter (the scarcity of offers, the rise in prices, etc.). The fundamentals that guide their decisions are not the price limits stated in the Declaration of Principles nor concern for the survival of the node, but personal interest and need. One of the clearest expressions of this individual perspective in what occurs in bartering is the absence of collective ventures within the clubs. Despite the repeated efforts of the founding group, concerned to design strategies for collective production capable of producing a "qualitative advance" in the generation of goods offered within the barter clubs, the participants rarely have supported this type of initiative. Not even in the cases where the ties with other prosumers preceded barter activities—members of the same family, neighbors, and friends who participate together—has cooperation in the production and commercialization of goods and services constituted a common practice.

The elements that we have just mentioned—the degree of formalization of the nodes as organizations, the importance of personal leadership in coordinating club activity, the scarce member participation in the internal management of the nodes, on one side, and the individual character of barter in the strategy of generating resources, on the other—have all been present, if varying in intensity, from the beginning of the clubs. As we have already indicated, the exponential and increasing growth of barter from 2001 only accentuated and aggravated certain tendencies. However, these should not be explained exclusively as the result of the massive incorporation of participants not committed to the "alternative project" and as consequent flooding of a weak organizational structure. Rather, they ought to be understood as the strains that accompanied the development of barter clubs in Argentina, that allow it to be defined and interpreted.

In this sense, every evaluation of the possible impacts of the barter experience, both at the level of the individuals involved and that of the communities belonging, ought to start with the consideration of these dimensions. It is in its limits and not only in its possibilities where one ought to seek the keys to interpreting a process that, perhaps as no other, managed to summarize the recent transformations of Argentine society.

Notes

* Translated by Edward Epstein.

1. The names of the persons quoted have been changed to protect their identity.

2. All the interview material cited throughout this chapter comes from two research projects carried out by the authors, the first between 1999 and 2000 and the second in 2002. In both we are dealing with semi-structured interviews with coordinators and members of different barter clubs in the City of Buenos Aires and in Greater Buenos Aires. Fabiana Leoni also participated in the fieldwork both times.

3. The information concerning the history of the first LETS and SEL has been taken from Smaïn Laacher, *Les SEL: Une utopie anticapitaliste en practique* (Paris: La Dispute, 2002).

4. We ought to nevertheless clarify that despite the Argentine barter clubs being created *after* similar experiences in the rest of the world, the founders of the local experience were not aware of this until some years later: "When they asked us the origin of our project, we had two clear answers: the first is that we began in a very particular way, because we were totally isolated in a corner of Buenos Aires Province and did not even have the possibility of looking for similar experiences, as we were then unaware of forms of contact with other realities like the present internet." See Horacio Covas, Carlos De Sanzo, and Heloisa Primavera, *Reinventando el mercado: La experiencia de la Red Global del Trueque en Argentina*, <http://www.trueque.org.ar/>, 3–4, 1998. (There also exists a Lilliput Edizioni version: <http://digilander.libero.it/paolocoluccia>, 2001.)

5. This NGO was created in 1989 with the goal of promoting the link between the urban and rural sectors through giving value to the environment and its economic, technological, and cultural resources for the production of organic food and the recycling of home wastes.

6. The Professional Network, created somewhat after the PAR, would be the third founding member of the barter club movement. It was a NGO whose principal object was to connect companies in search of advice with professionals who could work as consultants.

7. See Carlos De Sanzo, "Todo empezó con un zapailo a medianoche: La historia oficial," in Covas, De Sanzo, and Primavera, *Reinventando el mercado*, 16.

8. Cited by Inés González Bombal, "Sociabilidad en clases medias en descenso: Experiencia en el trueque," in *Sociedad y sociabilidad en la Argentina de los 90*, ed. Silvio Feldman (Buenos Aires: Biblos–Universidad Nacional de General Sarmiento, 2002), 100.

9. See Covas, De Sanzo, and Primavera, *Reinventando el mercado*, 13.

10. In respect to the "minting" of the money, that is, the printing of the bills, this was financed with the money that each new member paid as an initiation fee, usually between half a peso and two pesos.

11. The implanting of Toffler's proposal in the discourse of the promoters of barter is obvious if one takes into account the contrast this American author suggests between a "commercial ethic" and the new "prosumer ethic": "Instead of classifying people in

terms of what they possess as does the commercial ethic, . . . [the prosumer ethic] values what they do. Having a lot of money is still a factor of prestige. But other elements, fundamentally independence, the aptitude to adapt and survive in difficult conditions, and the capacity to do something with one's hands, whether it is installing a lock, preparing a large meal, making one's own clothes, or restoring an old set of drawers are also involved. Contrary to the 'production-oriented' or commercial ethic that glorifies the inputs of one person, the prosumer ethic requires various." See Alvin Toffler, *La Troisième Vague* (Paris: Éditions Denoël, 1980), 476.

12. See Horacio Covas in Covas, De Sanzo, and Primavera, *Reinventando el mercado*, 28.

13. This Declaration is composed of twelve principles that express the fundamental aspects of barter.

14. It is difficult to provide with precision an account of the evolution of the number of participants in barter clubs. The available information published in the press comes from the authorities of the barter networks, which are able to provide only approximate data in this respect. This is so because many participants are members of more than one club or network and therefore can be registered in more than one place at the same time, and also because participation in the activities of clubs usually includes the families as well as the members themselves. In respect to official statistics, the only data available come from a special section on "Job Quality" used by the Instituto Nacional de Estadísticas y Censos (INDEC) in the May 2002 number of its *Encuesta Permanente de Hogares* (EPH). According to this source, in May 2002, 87,800 people in the entire country worked providing goods or services for a barter club, with Greater Buenos Aires (55,800), Mendoza (17,900), Mar del Plata (3,600), and the City of Buenos Aires (3,300) the districts with the largest numbers of people so involved.

15. This first network was first named the Global Barter Network for Solidarity (Red Global de Trueque Solidario), later to be replaced by the Reciprocal Global Barter Network (Red Global de Trueque Multirecíproco). It was the first and best known of the country's networks. With the development of barter clubs over time, the network would become a true "network of networks," bringing together in it all the club groupings in each of the regions initially making it up. Furthermore, in 2001 there would be a split in this network. The existing differences inside the organization, especially those related to the emission and distribution of the currency for barter (the credits) would lead to the founding of the Barter Network for Solidarity (Red de Trueque Solidario), currently one of the networks with the largest public presence.

16. For data on the year 2000, see *Clarín*, Buenos Aires, January 22 and 28, 2001. For data on 2001, see Eduardo Ovalles, "Argentina es el país del mundo en el cual el fenómeno del trueque tiene mayor dimensión social," *Informe del Centro de Estudios Nueva Mayoría*, Buenos Aires, 2002, mimeo. For that on 2002, see the statements of Horacio Covas, founder of the Red Global del Trueque, in *Clarín*, Buenos Aires, February 14, 2002.

17. As an indicative sign, one can mention that according to data from the Encuesta Nacional de Gastos de los Hogares (ENGH-INDEC), the total monthly family income in 1997 for the three bottom quintiles of families was 275, 563, and 875 pesos, respectively. In the same period, the Basic Market Basket of Food for an adult was calculated as costing the equivalent of 67.36 pesos. See <http://www.indec.gov.ar/>.

18. For a more extensive presentation of the types of sociability encountered in barter clubs in this period, see González Bombal, "Sociabilidad en clases medias," 111ff.

19. The government measure imposing limits to the withdrawal from bank accounts (savings accounts and current accounts) known as the "corralito" caused a severe reduction in the pesos circulating during the month of December 2001.

20. See *Clarín*, Buenos Aires, December 9, 2001, and February 14, 2002. On this point, the conclusions of the research directed by Eduardo Ovalles of the Centro de Estudios Nueva Mayoría stand out, where Argentina is the country in the world in which bartering has the largest social impact. See Ovalles, "Argentina es el país del mundo."

21. The principal accusation that the SBN made against the GBN referred to the lack of control over monetary emission and the refusal of the GBN authorities to account for the quantity of credits issued. According to the SBN, the problem of the excess of credits from which barter suffered from 2001 was due much more to this uncontrolled emission than to the counterfeiting denounced by the GBN. One should remember here that at the moment of requesting one's initial fifty credits, each participant paid a sum (in general between half a peso and two pesos) destined to cover the costs of printing the bills. The accusations of lack of control of emission were usually accompanied by denunciations of the lack of transparency in the management of the organization's funds.

22. The credits issued by some networks were in practice also accepted by others so that most of the "bills" circulating were nationally valid. It is important to emphasize that, in this sense, the Argentine experience was different from that of its equivalents in the rest of the world, which were characterized by the existence of local means of payment valid only inside the small communities creating them.

23. By mid-2002, it was claimed that 30% of the credits circulating were fake, a figure that by October 2002 reached 90% of the money in some nodes. See statements by Patricia Colombres, a member of the Red Global del Trueque, to *La Voz del Interior*, Córdoba, on July 18, 2002: "Of the 100 million pesos worth of credits circulating in the country, at least 30 million were fake." For the data from the month of October, see the statements of members of the founding group of the RGT published in *Clarín*, Buenos Aires, October 17, 2002.

24. One should remember that between the months of January and May 2002, the rise in the Consumer Price Index was 25.9%, a figure that increased to 32.8% for the category of foods and beverages.

25. See the already classic work by Alberto Minujin and Gabriel Kessler, *La nueva pobreza en la Argentina* (Buenos Aires: Planeta, 1995).

26. For a more extensive development of this point, found within a research project that took place between 1999 and 2000, see González Bombal, "Sociabilidad en clases medias," 120ff.

27. Half of the participants we interviewed in 2002 in two clubs in the Capital and in one in Greater Buenos Aires became involved in barter during 2001. A third of the total joined after December, the same year.

28. See Heloisa Primavera, "En el principio fue el trueque,"<http://www.web iislam.com/00_3/artículos>, no date.

29. This evaluation of the loss of confidence in credits follows the argument proposed by Jerôme Blanc, "Monnaie, confiance de temps," in *La construction sociale de la confiance*, ed. Philippe Bernoux and Jean-Michel Servet (Paris: Montchrestien, 1997).

30. See *Clarín*, Buenos Aires, October 17, 2002, and *La Nación*, Buenos Aires, December 16, 2002.

31. This is in fact the hypothesis suggested by Fabiana Leoni for the case of the

nodes from the popular sector considered in her study. See Leoni, "Ilusión para muchos, alternativa para pocos: La práctica del trueque en los sectores populares," thesis for a bachelor's degree in social policy, Universidad Nacional de General Sarmiento, mimeo.

32. Of course the differences between barter nodes and non-commercial forms of reciprocity studied in Latin America by authors like Lomnitz do not exhaust the difference in the degree of formalization of each, but this is without doubt one of the elements to take into account. See Larissa Lomnitz, *Redes sociales, cultura y poder: Ensayos de antropologia latinoamericana* (México, D.F.: FLACSO and M.A. Porrúa, 1994).

33. See principle number 8 *in Declaración de Principios de la Red del Trueque.*

34. The organization of the barter nodes has also varied over time in this aspect. Despite the strong "personalist" imprint on the coordination of the clubs, at the beginning of this activity, the prosumers assumed a larger role in the administration of these groups. This was seen in the periodic membership assemblies that were set aside as the number of members massively increased.

35. There is no single criterion for setting the amount of such rent nor any standard price for it. The currency to be used in the agreements (pesos or credits or a combination of both) forms one of the conditions negotiated in each case by the interested parties.

Part IV

The Forces of Order During the Crisis

8

Crisis, Democracy, and the Military in Argentina*

Rut Diamint

Introduction

The crisis of December 2001, which began with the popular movement demanding the resignation of the minister of the economy, Domingo Cavallo, and which forced President Fernando de la Rúa to resign the next day, is suggestive that the military interventions to which we have become accustomed over sixty years have been banished from Argentine politics. Throughout a conflict between the elected authorities and the populace that revealed a profound questioning and general distrust toward political actors, the armed forces avoided participation in the process of negotiation that arose with the shift in government, did not voice an institutional position, were not present in the private meetings between candidates, and expressed no public preferences regarding the alternatives that were discussed among Peronist leaders. The state of siege and repression initiated by De la Rúa did not include the armed forces, even when the overflow of protestors, especially in Greater Buenos Aires and the Plaza de Mayo, suggested that the police could not restore order.

This is a healthy novelty for the Argentine political system, which in 1930 began a cycle of military coups (1930–1933, 1943–1948, 1955–1959, 1963, 1966–1973, 1976–1983) with an additional peculiarity: these military governments were fractured internally, reflecting at the same time repeated internal crises between a nationalistic army and a conservative one; between a nationalistic army and an economically liberal navy; between pro-industrialist and exporter factions. In summary, political instability was a characteristic not only of the elected governments, but also of the divided military governments.

There has been a favorable transformation in the behavior of the military. However, we are still far from having armed forces that respond systematically to the rules of democracy. The institutional framework created by the elected governments is not used to exercise democratic control over the military institutions, the governments persist without commanding the military through legal processes, and, as in other arenas of the political game, interest group power quotas are negotiated.

In this study, taking as a point of departure the fact that coups d'état are no longer a viable alternative in Argentine politics, we propose to reveal weaknesses in the democratic control of the armed forces that are apparent in two areas: the absence of a clear defense policy and confusion regarding the role assigned to the military.

Democratic progress cannot be minimized. Since 1983, with the return of democracy, a process is settling into place through which the armed forces cease to be a prominent and influential political player. It was the military itself that dented its power upon wholly failing in its political project, attempting to destroy leftist movements as well as Peronism. Its economic failure in promoting a new pattern of development as well as in stabilizing the ruling system was undeniable as well. And it failed its specific function in a conclusive way with the military and international defeat of the Falkland Islands War.

However, even when the Argentine military is no longer a powerful and autonomous political player, its institutional function is far from what it should be in a lawful state. In twenty years of democracy, the defense policy has not set directions and procedures for the function of the armed forces; personal relations prevailed and institutional spheres of special influence were maintained. In this study, we look at different stages of the relations between democratic governments and the armed forces up through the present time. We are interested in demonstrating that the relations between political power and the military were not institutionalized, avoiding the appropriate legal channels. In the context of institutional weakness that characterized successive administrations and that culminated in the crisis of 2001 and Argentina's defaulting on its national debt, the military institution was a player that obstructed the consolidation of Argentine democracy and affected the primacy of the law.

Conceptual Dilemma

The ministers of defense have not been agents for formulating a defense strategy and have not implemented doctrines for the deployment of the armed forces. As a result, today we have armed and security forces that reproduce the same models of behavior in place since their creation.

The debate on theories of civic-military relations has traditionally focused on topics of civil control over the armed forces, while relatively few have understood the deficiencies of defense policy and its effects on the consolidation of democracy. Samuel Huntington's traditional position establishes two types of civil control. Objective civil control considers that the professionalization of the armed forces keeps the military out of politics, thus avoiding a tutelary relationship and subordinating the armed forces to the state. The commitment to professionalism focuses on the officers in their professional capacity for the use of legitimate violence against external threats.[1] Subjective political control, on the other hand, is characterized by the personal dependent nature of the relationship of civil authority and the military, where political leaders seek to maximize their personal power by extending civilian control over the military.[2]

In states in which the armed forces seized power, the military also invested in improving its professional abilities and equipment. The only Latin American case in which the military government sent its officials back to the barracks was Chile, during the Pinochet dictatorship. S. E. Finer, questioning Huntington, recognized that its professional status is not the only condition that inhibits the military from intervening in politics. This condition is also achieved when the military assimilates the principle of the supremacy of civil power.[3]

Several authors specializing in the civil control of the armed forces in Latin America have added to these critiques. To summarize, these critiques coincide in pointing out that greater professionalism (objective control) does not imply less political involvement of the military.[4] J. Samuel Fitch stated that "in the Latin American context, higher levels of professionalism have resulted in more institutionalized military intervention in politics and high levels of military autonomy."[5]

Referring specifically to the Argentine case, the majority of authors consider that the transition from authoritarianism to democracy initiated in 1983 was able to establish democratic standards of civil control over the armed forces. These same authors, at the same time, point out flaws in civil control. For example, David Pion-Berlin affirms that a high level of civil autonomy for defining democratic policies exists and that while the necessary laws and structures were created, these are not effectively utilized.[6]

Wendy Hunter considers that the first democratic government of President Raúl Alfonsín marginalized the armed forces with the objective of subordinating them, while his successor, President Carlos Menem, completed the task, assigning them missions and giving them direction.[7] However, Hunter adds that during Alfonsín's government, the attempt to depoliticize the armed forces instead renewed their politicization and their challenge to the civil authorities and that although they were assigned professional tasks during Menem's administration, they maintained widespread autonomy in their own institutional matters.[8]

Other authors pointed to the switch in the orientation of military missions from internal to external goals as an indicator of civil control, especially for those forces that had concentrated their actions on the internal enemy.[9] In this case, the military acts professionally and therefore civil control is reinforced. These critical contributions presuppose that the governments that utilize their armed forces to support foreign policy are better able to formulate doctrines within the Defense Ministry for the use of force in ministerial environments.[10] But it is evident that Latin American governments still allow the military institutions to determine their own doctrine. Accepting that the peacekeeping missions had a positive effect on the democratization of the armed forces is still not sufficient proof for establishing the primacy of the civil authorities or the design of a system of defense based on democratic criteria.[11] It does not explain, for example, the instances where the military acts as defense policy advisors, determining for itself the kind of mission that it wishes to develop, nor does it justify the behavior of ministers who act only as the spokespersons of military interests.

Felipe Agüero coined the expression "civil supremacy," a situation typical of consolidated democracies that is produced when the democratically elected government manages to "carry out general policies without military intervention, define the goals and organization of national defense, formulate and carry out defense policies, and supervise the application of military policies."[12] This supremacy was not achieved in Argentina because of institutional errors in the formulation of defense policy, since Defense Ministry administrators under democratic rule dedicated themselves only to managing military affairs and not defining a public policy. If we use the concept of democratic control of the armed forces, we will understand better the critique of the Argentine process: "Democratic control of the armed forces is a reflection of the democratic quality of mentalities, norms, institutional structures and policy processes in a polity." It permits the establishment of "the proper relationships between government, state security institutions, and societal actors, such as the degree of inclusiveness in the formulation and implementation of policies; and especially, public expectations about the transparency and accountability of state security institutions and those entrusted to act in the public good."[13]

The notion of democratic control supersedes the concept of civilian control, since the latter can be accomplished under an authoritarian government, as occurred in Eastern Europe during the Cold War. Democratic control includes "constitutional arrangements and a legal framework in terms of powers, roles, and checks and balances, and mechanisms of accountability. It would be important to include in the analysis a critical evaluation of the congressional control and civilian supremacy in terms of effectiveness, transparency, and legitimacy."[14] However, "democratic control cannot be limited to legal and constitutional settlements but must be seen as a comprehensive transformation of political and military culture."[15]

Some of these aspects had already been incorporated by Alfred Stepan, who, in a comparative analysis of Brazil, considered that coexistence is possible between professionalism in the use of violence and military intervention in the civil and political spheres. Stepan argues that the absence of a strong and structured civil society made it possible for civilian politicians to appeal to the high military command to prop up or undermine civil governmental authority. In democracy, democratic civilian control is gauged by two measurements: on the one hand, military opposition to civilian policies and, on the other, military institutional prerogatives. The first dimension is evaluated by categories: the treatment of human rights abuses, decisions regarding the missions and structure of the armed forces, and the budget for the sector. Furthermore, Stepan highlights eleven prerogatives, including special legal status, special legal statutes, the capacity for the coordination of defense policies, relations with Congress, participation in intelligence, transparency in military enterprises, etc. The combination of both dimensions allows one to evaluate if there is a high or low degree of civil supremacy and if the armed forces have adapted themselves to the democratic process. As Caparini points out,

> History has shown that in practical terms, democracy is often not an either/or condition, but is composed of multiple variables and shifting perceptions of who is considered a legitimate citizen with attendant civic rights and obligations; what are the proper relationships between government, state security institutions, and societal actors, such as the degree of inclusiveness in the formulation and implementation of policies; and especially, public expectations about the transparency and accountability of state security institutions and those entrusted to act in the public good. A contemporary example is provided by various post-authoritarian Latin American societies, which are generally acknowledged to be consolidating democracies. Often, however, military withdrawal from politics was, and remains, contingent on the preservation of certain military prerogatives that are not concordant with prevailing Western views of what constitutes democratic control of the armed forces.[16]

We maintain, therefore, that civil control in Argentina underwent an important change, but that this progress was not complete due to the absence of an extensive and firm political guidance that would cover all fields of military activity: doctrine, displacement, missions, equipment, expenses, and personnel.[17] In any case, it is necessary to remember, as Richard H. Kohn affirmed, that civil control is a process, not a fact fixed in time, and civil supremacy is evidenced in the autonomy of political decisions regarding foreign policy, the economy, social themes, or military policy.[18] For this reason, it is difficult to pigeonhole the Argentine case, in which important advances were accompanied by substantial concessions.

The Reinstallation of Democracy and Military Disarmament

In a brief review of twenty years of democracy, we remember that President Raúl Alfonsín understood the necessity of institutionalizing the relations between the executive power and the armed forces as a basic resource of democratic reinforcement, establishing a chain of formal command and an organizational hierarchy that would overturn the deviations of earlier periods. In the words of the president, the military governments had led to "three un-integrated, independent armed forces, with attributions at times superior to those of the State itself and, on occasions, with notable rivalries between them."[19] The Radical government was not able to impose its own principles to reestablish democracy. The initial democratic impetus succumbed to special interest pressures, since, in spite of its declarations, it failed to impose the law, transparency, and responsibility in its public efforts.

President Raúl Alfonsín began his administration by bringing to trial the three military Juntas of the Process de Reorganization Nacional (Process of National Reorganization) that had seized power in 1976. He submitted to Congress a bill to revoke and declare null and void the amnesty that the military had bestowed on itself in September 1983, a month before the presidential elections.[20] The government also established a new structure of command, suppressing the ranks of commander-in-chief for the three armed forces and establishing a single superior rank, that of Jefes del Estado Mayor Conjunct (Head of the Joint Chiefs of Staff).

At the same time, reforms of the Code of Military Justice and the Code of Penal Procedures for civil justice were undertaken in order to permit appeals by civil courts of the judgments dictated in military tribunals.[21] This was a fundamental requirement for the elimination of the armed forces' prerogatives and for the establishment of a state of law. On the other hand, the military uprisings of 1987 and 1988 exemplified the failure of the Radical proposals. According to the declarations of Deputy Marcelo Stubrin, at the heart of the insurrections was a refusal that extended throughout the country to obey the order to arrest colleagues and/or to repress rebellious garrisons. All this buttressed the idea that the government lacked the capacity to impose its orders.[22]

An incompletely implemented plan included the dismantling of the oversized military-industrial complex that served no strategic purpose, the reduction of reserves, the resizing of the forces, and the relocation of the military regiments to conform to the necessities of external defense.

The failures of the Radical administration can be summed up in three points. First, the erroneous supposition that the armed forces would purge themselves, eliminating the supporters of the former regime.[23] While internal critiques of the Proceso government and of the Falkland Islands War did exist, the officers agreed that the fight against subversion was a mandate issued by the civil authorities that they had carried out legitimately.

In the second place, the government of President Alfonsín incorrectly evaluated the military opposition. While it did confront a divided armed forces, the latter were not resigned to losing their traditional spheres of influence: the three armed uprisings reflected a push for greater legitimacy through questioning the political authorities.

The third failure occurred in the administration of defense. The Ministry of Defense was not able to establish a public defense policy. The essential instrument, unanimously approved Defense Law No. 23,554, which eliminated all domestic functions of the armed forces and established that the military would act only in the external defense of the state in support of foreign policy, was approved, but the rules that would have made the law operational were never specified.

In terms of the typology presented by Stepan, military prerogatives were reduced in the legal field (limits on military court jurisdictions, especially for war crimes), in intelligence (cleaning house, changing agents, and Congressional supervision over activities in this area), in the prohibition of the military undertaking police activities (as determined by the Defense Law previously cited), in defining military promotions (the Senate determines these after consulting with human rights organizations), and in diminishing the business activities of the forces (privatization of the military industrial complex and closure of other military run firms). However, military opposition was high—as expressed through the three military uprisings—and the government did not set a defense policy over and above the task of wrestling control from the armed forces.

Negotiations and Menemista Power

President Carlos Menem assumed the presidency in 1989, six months before the end of Alfonsín's term, due to a new economic crisis. Menem's objective was to end the cycles of economic instability as part of a strategy to make Argentina a part of the international economic scene. Beginning with economic reform as a necessary precondition for political stability, he looked to placate military animosity, which had become an impediment for foreign investment and for the reformulation of external political alliances. The president applied a carrot-and-stick strategy, being aware that the ability to govern depended on his skill in not directly making an enemy of the traditional Argentine interest groups, the armed forces, the Church, and the labor unions, but dealing with them simultaneously, without granting them arenas of power that would limit his own capacity for action.

The president gradually introduced a different style: there would be no persecution of the military officers, but neither would he tolerate plots aimed at curtailing his presidential power. To this end, shortly after assuming the presidency, he conceded a general amnesty to the officers detained for the abuses committed during the military Proceso and to the soldiers arrested for the excesses committed during the assault on the barracks at La Tablada. With this pacification, Menem undertook a series of reforms that would diminish military power: reduction of personnel, budget, and military businesses. These policies were also the result of distrust provoked by the fourth "carapintada" insurrection directed by Colonel Mohamed Seineldín in December 1990, a day before George Bush's official visit to Argentina. It had little political support and was organized by small bodies of troops, mainly junior officers, who were unhappy with the military policies of the government. After the uprising of 1990, there was no further questioning of the political power, but neither were the relations between the government and the armed forces institutionalized.

The manner in which President Menem presented his political options, bordering on arbitrariness and displaying signs of despotism, was an incentive for the armed forces to regain their power,[24] transgressing the chain of command and the law. The minister of defense did not serve as the interlocutor for the armed forces as the upper echelons of the military pushed aside the normal channels of negotiation, preferring to seek to gain direct access to the president.

Restrictions were set through fiscal reform or the elimination of organizations controlled by the armed forces and the privatization and liquidation of military-run businesses, but the armed forces creatively held on to some resources outside of congressional control, establishing their own provisions policy.[25] To provide an idea of the changes occurring over time in relation to budget size, defense spending decreased from 4.86% of GNP in 1981 near the end of military rule to 2.31% in 1984 at the beginning of the Alfonsín administration, and to 1.88% by its end. With Menem's presidency, it dropped to 1.42% of the budget in 1992 and to 1.35% in 1999 under De la Rúa's administration.[26] Twenty-four businesses belonging to the military manufacturing conglomeration were privatized, among them Area Material Córdoba, the synthetic toluene and sulfuric acid–producing military plants, Petroquímica General Mosconi, the San Martín Military Plant, and Astilleros Domecq.

But at the same time, illegal transactions were carried out. Some funds came from the sale of arms, a case that caused scandal in both national and international public opinion. The sale of Argentine arms to Ecuador when the latter was at war with Peru in 1995 over the disputed region known as Altos de Cenepa unleashed a crisis with serious repercussions. At the same time that Argentina was selling arms to one of the rivals, it was, along with the United States, Brazil, and Chile, acting as a guarantor of the 1942 Treaty of Peace that was invoked in order to resolve the conflict between the two Andean countries.[27]

The most difficult matter in the relation between the military and society continued to be the treatment of the theme of human rights. The speeches in which General Balza admitted the army's institutional responsibility for acts of torture and repression provoked a spectacular about-face with respect to the traditional position of the armed forces. He said: "One only owes obedience to legitimate orders given by legitimate authorities . . . remember that these arms can only be employed when the constitutional power so directs."[28] The declarations of the head of the army were accepted by civil society and rejected markedly by retired officers.[29]

There were deep changes in the mentality of the officers that were reflected in the words spoken by General Balza at the end of his statement: "The Peace

Missions, Voluntary Military Service, the full and wide-scale incorporation of women, . . . the scheduled and rational administration of financial resources, and, essentially, the changes in the educational system, speak clearly to the depth and reach of the process of modernization successfully faced by the Army."[30] There were also significant changes in the relations between society and the military. But political subordination was not carried out on a foundation of legal-rational criteria, but informally, by means of special deals arranged with the powers that be.

The government made gains in dismantling the majority of military prerogatives and from the military point of view succeeded in calming the animosity within the ranks regarding the defense of human rights, upon granting a pardon to the military juntas. But Menem did not create institutional channels for setting defense policies by strengthening Congress or the Defense Ministry.

Negligence and Crisis

Near the end of Menem's administration, the military was confused. It had demonstrated its professional vocation, especially through its participation in peace missions. Its non-participation in politics and the acceptance of budgetary cuts had not translated into a recuperation of its military capacity that had been allowed to deteriorate relatively since the return to democracy. It was an active advocate of bettering relations with neighboring countries, abandoning historical rivalries, but could not participate in the overall decision-making process. Adding to this bewilderment was a new component related to its own social status: the military had become poor, marginalized by the reduction of salaries and the loss of institutional resources that it formerly controlled surreptitiously or with the acceptance of the civilian authorities. For this reason, the arrival of De la Rúa renewed its expectations that this deterioration would be reversed.

A lack of activity and directives characterized the new Radical Party administration. There were speeches but no acts, and this included military policy as well. For example, President De la Rúa, in *Revisión de la Defensa* (2001), a project that revised the White Book of Argentine Defense, asserted: "For this reason, the Defense Policy that we are working on is based on a profound Organizational Restructuring of the Sector and the structural transformation of its administrative and operative systems in order to achieve the maximum level of efficiency in the armed forces, with the present budgetary assignments."[31] No one believed in this restructuring of the defense sector.

In general, military officers practiced a policy of cooperation in their relations with the functionaries of this area, but achieved little institutionally during the De la Rúa administration. The team of ministerial advisors were more knowledgeable on defense matters than those who had preceded them, but several of them had previous contractual relations with the armed forces and thus did not act independently.

Expectations improved with the arrival of Horacio Jaunarena, who was defense minister under Alfonsín, but defense's share of the budget worsened. The head of the military, General Brinzoni, expressed his preoccupation, warning that "If the budget of 2001 were maintained, in 2002, the organizational capacity of the Army will be truly minimal."[32] One of the measures taken by the army, in order to lower operational and food costs and provisioning, was to give leave to 75% of the active soldiers of all units in rotation. The navy and air force extended winter leave from fifteen to thirty days to mitigate service costs.[33] The navy had to withdraw from its participation in the UNITAS maneuvers that, for the last forty-two years, were carried out under the coordination of the U.S. fleet, due to "the budgetary reduction imposed in order to achieve zero deficit."[34]

Added to this absence of leadership was the negative role of De la Rúa's party colleague, ex-President Alfonsín. In a return characterized by neo-nationalistic discourse and a call to his old party supporters, Alfonsín took the lead in calling for the inclusion of the military in a political project. This time it was through a plan to reinstate obligatory military service, a demand of some sectors of the armed forces, who saw in this mechanism a way to revive nationalistic sentiment in young Argentines. The chief of the army, Lieutenant General Ricardo Brinzoni, called it an "interesting project."[35]

Brinzoni demanded from President Fernando de la Rúa greater participation of the force he commanded in confronting the national economic crisis. In a harangue before the officers he said that "We are part of the power of the State and that is how we feel. We don't want to be mere spectators to the problems that afflict the country, which is why we are trying to be protagonists and collaborate in the State's response to such necessities."[36] Forming a chorus, the chief of the navy, Admiral Joaquín Stella, maintained that "the armed forces are not an actor in the political scene, but rather a state institution that deserves to be listened to and that has the right and the need to contribute whatever value it can."[37] It was a demand to be a legitimate part of the political decision-making process, but at least this time it did not want to replace the civilian government by means of a coup in order to resolve the economic crisis. Nothing was said about the role that the Defense Ministry should perform in the transmission of presidential decisions to its subordinates, the officers.

On the eve of the December crisis, it was ex-President Carlos Menem who suggested the inclusion of the armed forces in the Concertación Política (Political Accord), a desperate attempt at dialogue proposed by De la Rúa to save his administration. In a meeting with the head of the army, Lieutenant General Ricardo Brinzoni, Menem said: "It is fundamental that they participate," giving the army the possibility of entering into a conversation to which the official administration had not invited it.[38] General Brinzoni constituted himself as a go-between with the politicians and added that his force would not be disappointed with the possibility of forming part of a national agreement, "as a fundamental institution of the Nation."[39]

For the military, another means of gaining significance within the state was to play a relatively important role in matters of national security and foreign policy, contributing to better national planning. It shows an attitude for political interference that the military would justify due to the absence of any real civilian leadership. There was truth to this point of view. The defense ministers of the democratic transition had the primary objective of reducing military autonomy and power, but they failed as directors of the defense system. This vacuum was filled by the military, who added to their legitimate role of advisors that of decision-makers.

One officer expressed his displeasure with mistakes made by his political superiors in solving defense problems. He said: "Everything that has been said can be proved easily through a series of objective indicators such as the absence of National Defense in the plans and teaching programs of the University, which is where the future leaders of the nation are formed; the little importance attributed to the School of National Defense; the way in which the highest authorities of the area are designated."[40]

This lack of interest was characteristic of congressmen as well. General Balza expressed it when he was chief of the army. He said: "Esteemed officers, junior officers, and soldiers: I know the sadness that you feel when you listen to an ex-congressman of the nation say 'the army we have is worthless . . . it is totally inoperable and showed it in the Falkland Islands'; to hear another congressman brand the armed forces as 'out-of-date, obsolete, and inefficient,' or a third, attribute to the institution participation in a 'partnership for the illegal sale of arms.'"[41]

The area of greatest tension between Congress and the armed forces relates to Congress's constitutional role in approving military promotions. The issue of promotions refers to a central topic in the debate on the military: the trials on human rights abuses.

There are officers proposed for promotion who have been implicated in human rights violations during the past. According to international human rights organizations, De la Rúa's administration ignored its duties in regard to world-wide justice. For example, José Miguel Vivanco, director of Human Rights Watch's Americas Division, an organization that monitors the enforcement of the law in different countries, characterized the Argentine government as a member of the international community that is remiss in enforcing the trial verdicts regarding crimes committed during the last military regime.[42] The continued importance of this topic was reaffirmed when the federal court, reviewing the judicial processes, ruled that the End Point and Due Obedience laws are invalid and unconstitutional.[43] Defense lawyers for the military brought the case to the Supreme Court, which has yet to rule on the validity of the federal court verdict that would permit the prosecution of more than a thousand officers and policemen who participated in the illegal repression during the last military dictatorship.[44]

The political crisis of De la Rúa's administration also had the effect of increasing distrust in the democratic system. A retired colonel stated that "the political parties in Argentina have never fulfilled their roles completely; that is to say, the expectations that the system and society have towards them . . . thus they became primarily electoral machines for conquering power."[45]

Added to all these tensions was another matter exemplifying the absence of leadership in the Defense Ministry's formulation of policies: the participation of the military in tasks of internal security. In a document signed by the President of the Forum of Generals, an entity to which more than 250 retired officers belong, Brigade General Augusto J. B. Alemanzor (Ret.) labeled as "absurd" the intention to "impose the false concept of the separation of external and internal intelligence, as if the international enemy that we face [alluding to terrorism] respected borders or enclosures."[46] We must remember that the Defense Law prohibits the armed forces from carrying out tasks of internal order, a restriction insisted upon by the successor Law of Internal Security No. 24,059.

The challenge to the limits imposed by the Defense Law also drew support from the Radical Party ministers of defense. Ricardo López Murphy, De la Rúa's first minister, declared: "In this sense, it wouldn't make sense to formulate artificial barriers between the traditional roles of our armed forces (deterrence) and the roles denominated 'new (or reinvigorated),' given that the human and material capacities that allow us to respond satisfactorily to the traditional roles provide at the same time the foundation from which we can carry out in an adequate manner the 'new roles.'"[47]

Horacio Jaunarena, who replaced López Murphy when the latter became the minister of the economy, also promoted yet another plan for centralizing the security and defense forces.[48] The topic acquired relevance due to the terrorist attacks on the embassy of Israel (March 17, 1992) and the Jewish mutual aid society AMIA (September 18, 1994).[49] In this context, the then governor of the province of Buenos Aires and later president, Eduardo Duhalde, declared the necessity of preparing the armed forces for the fight against terrorism.[50] Subsequently, Jaunarena, on this occasion as defense minister for the Duhalde administration, proposed the unification of the Defense and Security Administrations.[51]

This initiative found new echoes among the officers following the September 11th attack on the United States. Jaunarena, with the support of the army, attempted to restructure the defense bureaucracy so as to regain power and resources through the unification of the security apparatus. "The distinction between security and defense is an obsolete category. At this point, dividing them into exclusive compartments is an anachronism," stated Jaunarena. The head of the army, General Brinzoni, added that "for ideological reasons and due to our history, possibly justified in the past, we have artificially made the distinction between external and internal threats. That's not how it is."[52] To clarify what was at stake, the actions of the defense minister undermined the legitimacy of the existing Defense Law by proposing that the military assume functions that were prohibited by the law—functions that had been secret but were now being advocated by the army command.[53]

The unrest that this debate generated reveals that, in Argentina, the democratic control of the armed forces is still an unfinished process. Many government officials and citizens of various political affiliations expressed the fear that the military would recover powers to spy on the civilian population. This public opposition to the position of the defense minister suffices to show that there still remain many unresolved issues having to do with civilian control of the armed forces. Furthermore, it is indicative that the debate over watering down the Defense Law did not occur in Congress, the only organization authorized to change the law, nor did it even appear as a plan organized by the Ministry of Defense. These were secretive discussions, which, although they were leaked to the press, clearly demonstrate the forms and methods that are utilized in Argentina to define state policy.

Final Comments

Soon after assuming the presidency in May of 2003, Néstor Kirchner trimmed the upper echelons of the military. Of the forty-four officers who were forcibly retired, only the ex-head of the army, General Brinzoni, publicly expressed his displeasure, consequently receiving a light fine. The decision of Kirchner's administration to annul the decree signed by ex-President Fernando de la Rúa—denying that judgments rendered against Argentine officers in a Spanish Court had exceeded its territorial jurisdiction, thereby allowing the military officers of the last dictatorship to be tried by the Spanish judicial system—did not unleash an institutional protest. That is proof of the overall subordination of the armed forces to civil authority. That much is true, there is subordination. But that does not imply that there will be no civil-military problems. Even in consolidated Western democracies there is constant tension in the civilian handling of many military matters.

The majority of authors who have studied the military problem agree that the transition to democracy in Argentina was successful. According to the criteria used by these specialists, the process of achieving civilian control over the armed forces has been completed as well. Nonetheless, a more detailed analysis reveals deficits in the relation between civilian command and military obedience. It is true that there is no chance for military coups, but that is an insufficient indicator of whether civilian supremacy in defense has been achieved. We utilize the concept of democratic control to point out failures in the process of consolidating the political regime: civilian democratic control *implies an effective reform* of the security sector and the establishment of mechanisms of governmental and societal accountability. Taking into consideration this definition, we conclude that twenty years of democracy and administrations of different political stances did not establish patterns for managing defense that would ensure the long-term development of a democratic society.

It's true that this situation is not worrisome in the same way as the repeated military uprisings of the past. But it is also necessary to remember that in December of 2001, fear of the intervention of the armed forces weighed heavily in the news and in the citizens' debates.[54] The armed forces are not presently formed of soldiers prepared to drive their tanks out into the streets in a coup d'état. Statements given by a general during the conflict in December of 2001 reinforce this idea: "The Army does not have rubber bullets, or shields, or sticks, or bullet-proof vests. If we put ourselves in front of a mob that attacks us with stones, what do we do, fire with our assault rifles? It would be a disproportionate response."[55] However, unfortunately, the military has not completely understood that it is not a decision-maker, that it does not determine its own mission, that it does not itself adjust its orders to its own interpretation of government rules.[56] But it is only fair to point out that the fault lies primarily with the civil authorities, who, although they no longer induce the military to revolt, knocking on the barracks doors, do not direct it with the supremacy conferred by constitutional provisions either. The lacuna created by the absence of direction is filled by the armed forces. The omission of the legislators and the abstention of the citizenry do not construct institutional practices in agreement with the norms of a state of law.

In summary, the monopoly of force inherent in the armed forces was never institutionalized through the correct channels and, as a result, produced tension between democracy and the ability to govern. A tacit agreement appears to have been reached in response to this tension: the military succeed in stipulating that in exchange for accepting civilian authority, those who govern and civil society would not intervene in military matters. Patrice McSherry, analyzing the Argentine process, mentions "custodial democracies that combine democratic forms with authoritarian enclaves. Argentina's case suggests that democratization is a constant struggle, with gains and losses."[57] The present administration of Néstor Kirchner appears to offer an opportune moment for translating democratic rules into bureaucratic procedures that could lead to the democratic administration of defense, sharing the tasks among a broad defense community. Of course, to struggle for a defense policy is not as dramatic or urgent as ending an authoritarian military coup. This seems to be the all too smug view of the majority of politicians and of many citizens. We can only hope that more serious thinking occurs before it is too late to rectify the current inadequate degree of democratic control of the Argentine military.

Notes

* Translated by Mark Anderson and David Pion-Berlin.

1. Samuel P. Huntington, "Reforming Civil-Military Relations," *Journal of Democracy* 6, no. 4 (1995): 9–10.
2. Samuel P. Huntington, *The Soldier and the State: The Theory and Politics of Civil-Military Relations* (Cambridge: Harvard University Press, 1957), 83.
3. S. E. Finer, *The Man on Horseback* (London: Penguin Books, 1976), 24.

4. See, for example, Augusto Varas, *La autonomía militar en América Latina* (Caracas: Nueva Sociedad, 1988); Felipe Agüero, "The Military and the Limits to Democratization in South America," in *Issues in Democratic Consolidation: The New South American Democracies in Comparative Perspective*, ed. Scott Mainwaring, Guillermo O'Donnell, and Samuel Valenzuela (Notre Dame: University of Notre Dame Press, 1992); Ernesto López and David Pion-Berlin, *Democracia y Cuestión Militar* (Buenos Aires: Universidad Nacional de Quilmes, 1996).

5. J. Samuel Fitch, *The Armed Forces and Democracy in Latin America* (Baltimore: Johns Hopkins University Press, 1998), 3.

6. See David Pion-Berlin, "Will Soldiers Follow? Economic Integration and Regional Security in the Southern Cone," *Journal of Inter-American Studies and World Affairs* 42 (Spring 2000): 43–69; and David Pion-Berlin, "Civil Military Circumvention: How Argentine State Institutions Compensate for a Weakened Chain of Command," in *Civil-Military Relations in Latin America: New Analytical Perspectives*, ed. David Pion-Berlin (Chapel Hill–London: University of North Carolina Press, 2001), 142.

7. Wendy Hunter, *State and Soldier in Latin America: Redefining the Military in Argentina, Brazil, and Chile* (Washington, D.C.: Working Paper Series, United States Institute of Peace, 1996), chap. 2.

8. Hunter, *State and Soldier*, chap. 2.

9. For example, David Pion-Berlin and Craig Arcenaux, "Decision-Makers or Decision-Takers? Military Missions and Civilian Control in Democratic South America," *Armed Forces & Society* 26, no. 3 (Spring 2000): 413–36.

10. Michael C. Desch, *Civilian Control of the Military* (Baltimore: Johns Hopkins University Press, 1999), 21; Pion-Berlin and Arcenaux, "Decision-Makers or Decision-Takers?" 416.

11. Rut Diamint, *Democracia y seguridad en América Latina* (Buenos Aires: Nuevohacer, GEL 2002), 98–103.

12. See Felipe Agüero, *Militares, civiles y democracia* (Madrid: Alianza Editorial, 1995), 126–49.

13. Marina Caparini, "Lessons Learned and Upcoming Research Issues in Democratic Control of Armed Forces and Security Sector Reform" (Geneva: Geneva Centre for the Democratic Control of Armed Forces [DCAF], *Working Paper Series*, no. 41, October 2002).

14. Hans Born, Marina Caparini, and Karl Haltiner, "Models of Democratic Control of the Armed Forces: A Multi-Country Study Comparing 'Good Practices' of Democratic Control" (Geneva: Geneva Centre for the Democratic Control of Armed Forces [DCAF], *Working Paper Series*, no. 47, July 2002).

15. Karl W. Haltiner, "Democratic Control of Armed Forces: Renaissance of an Old Issue?" (Geneva: Geneva Centre for the Democratic Control of Armed Forces [DCAF] *Working Paper Series*, no. 45, July 2002).

16. Caparini, "Lessons Learned," 12.

17. Haltiner, "Democratic Control."

18. Richard H. Kohn, "How Democracies Control the Military," *Journal of Democracy* 8, no. 4 (1997): 140–53.

19. Speech at the Dinner of Camaraderie of the armed forces, *Clarín*, July 6, 1985, 3.

20. It was the Decree-Law 22,924 of September 22, 1983, known as the Law of National Pacification, the last attempt of the armed forces to condition the future constitutional government.

21. Three levels of responsibility became apparent in the fight against subversion: (1) those in charge of planning and giving orders; (2) those who carried out orders given by their superiors; (3) those who carried out their orders in an excessive manner. These categorizations could not be implemented due to the dynamic between society and judicial power.

22. Rear Admiral, Libertad Navy Headquarters, April 18, 2002.

23. See Carlos Acuña and Catalina Smulovitz, "Militares en la transición argentina: Del gobierno a la subordinación constitucional," in Carlos H. Acuña, comp., *La nueva matriz política argentina* (Buenos Aires: Ediciones Nueva Visión, 1995).

24. Steven Levitsky, "The 'Normalization' of Argentine Politics," *Journal of Democracy* 11, no. 2 (2000): 56.

25. Elsa Llenderrozas, "La administración de la defensa después de los procesos de democratización: El caso de Argentina bajo el gobierno de Menem," in Héctor Luis Saint Pierre and Suzeley Kalil Mathías, *Entre votos y botas* (Campinas, Brazil: Universidad de Campinas, 2002).

26. Thomas Scheetz, "The Argentine Defense Budget: Its Context and a Methodology for Analysis," *Security and Defense Studies Review* 2, no. 6 (Summer 2002): 18.

27. "Una alta fuente judicial informó a *La Nación* que la situación del Ejército es muy comprometida en la causa por los envíos ilegales de cañones y municiones a Croacia," in *La Nación*, July 4, 1998; see also June 6 and 23, 1998. "La explosión de la Fábrica Militar de Rio Tercero habría sido intencional, con el objetivo de ocultar los envíos irregulares de armamento," in *La Nación*, November 3, 1997.

28. Speech given at the opening of the Colegio Militar de la Nación; in *La Prensa*, December 13, 1994. Furthermore, the new concept of "Due Obedience" outlined during the speech would be incorporated into the revised Code of Military Justice that the minister of defense, Domínguez, sent to the executive authority. In *La Nación*, April 6, 1998, 6.

29. The air force and the navy were more lukewarm and reticent in their statements on their role in the so-called "Dirty War."

30. "Mensaje del Jefe del Estado Mayor General del Ejército, November 1999," in *Memoria del Ejército Argentino, 1992–1999* (Buenos Aires: Ejército Argentino, 2000).

31. *Revisión de la Defensa* <http://www.mindef.gov.ar/secciones/revision/principal.htm>, 2001.

32. *La Nación,* November 18, 2001.

33. *Clarín,* August 3, 2001.

34. *La Nación,* October 11, 2001.

35. *La Nación,* August 22, 2001.

36. *La Nación,* November 21, 2001.

37. *Clarín*, December 12, 2001.

38. *La Nación,* December 12, 2001.

39. *Clarín,* December 12, 2001.

40. Humberto Lobaiza, "Las relaciones cívico-militares en la Argentina," *Revista de la Escuela Superior de Guerra* (July–September 1992): 111–12.

41. Message of the JEMGE (Jefe del Estado Major General del Ejército) on the anniversary of El Libertador, January 12, 1998, in *Argentina y la seguridad internacional*, ed. Rut Diamint (Santiago, Chile: FLACSO-Chile, Woodrow Wilson Center, 1998).

42. *Página 12*, December 13, 2001.

43. *La Nación*, November 10, 2001.

44. *La Nación*, November 10, 2001.

45. Lobaiza, "Las relaciones cívico-militares," 110.

46. *La Nación*, October 11, 2001.

47. *Revisión de la Defensa*, chapter "Fuerzas armadas para las nuevas necesidades."

48. *Clarín*, September 16, 2000.

49. "En este contexto, no parece conveniente que el estado se autolimite," in *La Nación*, December 17, 1996.

50. *Página 12*, September 23, 2001, and *Clarín*, September 26 and 27, 2001.

51. *Página 12*, June 11, 2002.

52. *Clarín*, June 1, 2002.

53. *Clarín*, January 6, 2002.

54. Horacio Verbitsky, "Para la olla," *Página 12*, December 23, 2001; Martín Granovsky, "El empate convoca fantasmas," *Página 12*, December 31, 2001; Guido Braslavsky, "Ley de Inteligencia: Una SIDE fuerte y militares sin injerencia interna," *Clarín*, December 15, 2001.

55. *La Nación*, December 21, 2001. On the other hand, *Clarín* reports that Minister Jaunarena had given directions for a "contingency plan," in a meeting of the high commanders, in order for the armed forces to give logistic support to security forces. *Clarín*, December 21, 2001.

56. The speech given by General Brinzoni in laying to rest the remains of de facto ex-President Leopoldo Galtieri, who was involved in several uprisings, is a clear indicator of the autonomy with which they take high-impact political decisions. See *Clarín*, January 13, 14, 20, and 22, 2003.

57. J. Patrice McSherry, "National Security and Social Crisis in Argentina," *Journal of Third World Studies* 17, no. 1 (Spring 2000): 21–43.

9

The Gendarmerie's Response to Social Protest in Argentina

Eric Stener Carlson

It's amazing the level of empathy [the gendarmes] have [with the protesters]. But it's more than empathy, I think, if the definition of empathy is the ability to put oneself in the shoes of the other guy. This is because the gendarmes *are* poor workers themselves. . . .

Introduction

I wrote the above entry in my field journal in late November 2001, while carrying out research in Argentina for my doctoral dissertation in political science at the University of California, Santa Barbara.[1] The gendarmes I am referring to are the men of the First Mobile Detachment of the Argentine National Gendarmerie (la Gendarmería Nacional Argentina in Spanish, also known as the GNA) based in the Campo de Mayo military complex in the province of Buenos Aires. They are part of an approximately 18,000-man-strong hybrid police-military force charged with a number of responsibilities, including customs control, anti-narcotics, counter-terrorism, and environmental protection throughout Argentina. The First Mobile Detachment (the Destacamento Móvil 1, or Móvil 1 for short) is one of five such detachments spread throughout Argentina, and their primary duty during the recent crisis has been to disperse illegal occupations by piqueteros of federal bridges and roads.

These piqueteros, or "picketers," constitute a broad amalgamation of economic, political, and social protesters whose main tactic involves setting up roadblocks—"cortes de ruta"—disrupting traffic and paralyzing commerce. A number of these illegal occupations are peaceful, although there is frequently a strong anarchical element in them that threatens and extorts motorists and destroys public and private property.

From November 28 to December 12, 2001, I carried out in-depth, semi-structured interviews with over thirty of the 417 gendarmes of the Móvil 1, and two years of further research and follow-up interviews with scholars and civilian-military experts in Argentina.[2] Just as I began my research, piquetero pressure that had been building for the last several years exploded, and waves of protests and looting broke out across the country.[3] Less than two weeks after I carried out my last interview at Campo de Mayo, a mass of protesters, angry at the state of the economy, staged what was virtually a civilian-led coup d'état outside the Casa Rosada in Buenos Aires, overthrowing President Fernando de la Rúa.

One of the most amazing aspects of these interviews—an amazement evident in my field journal—was that the gendarmes expressed deep empathy for social protesters. Many of the gendarmes told me they identified with the piqueteros' cause and felt an inner conflict in disbanding these protests. One of the reasons for this was that gendarmes viewed themselves as poor workers, as shaken by the same economic disasters as the protesters.

Moreover, gendarmes were not only expressing empathy for the protesters with words but also—apparently—with their actions. That is, according to their descriptions of counter-protest (contradisturbio or CONDIS) events in which they participated, the gendarmes used minimum, necessary, and proportional force against protesters in accordance with the internationally recognized concept of *jus in bello*, or "justice in war."[4] The three excerpts below are characteristic of how gendarmes described their treatment of protesters, reflecting this *jus in bello* approach:

> *From one Cabo (Corporal):* I can't shoot a protester with a pistol, because the protester is unarmed. If they're assaulting me with rocks, I'm not going to assault them with a projectile, shooting them with a bullet. . . . Because of that, we use gas and the rubber rounds (postade goma).

> *From a gendarme dog handler:* The canines are used more than anything . . . to not use gas. First you try it with the canines. . . . Well, if [the protesters] don't move back with the canines or they don't stop protesting. . . . After, gas is sprayed and, as a last resort, if the situation is very complicated, you have recourse to rubber bullets.

From a Primer Alferez (First Lieutenant) and water-cannon operator:
I know that at 15 meters, to give an example, if I shoot a burst of water at a tree, it's probable that I rip off the bark. That, translated to a person, if I hit him with a burst of water at a pressure of 1,900 liters per minute at 15 meters, it's very probable that I hurt him, that he breaks a rib. . . . The impact or the hit of the water makes him fall hard, and he can hurt himself, suffer a grave injury. So, you try as much as possible to aim at places that aren't lethal. . . . I try to make low shots, so the people leave the place. So that the people see that we [dissuade them] by way of the water.

As my foundational experience in Argentina had been investigating the almost inconceivable atrocities committed by soldiers during the "Dirty War" (1976–1982) in accordance with their perverse, Manichaean worldview,[5] neither the gendarmes' expressed empathy nor their self-reported restraint in using force against protesters seemed to "fit." Along the same lines, the view of gendarmes that began to emerge from my research, as the working poor in uniform, respectful of protesters' rights and reticent to use lethal force, clashed with the "popular" image often disseminated by the Argentine media, of gendarmes as fierce, unfeeling "Robocops," who enjoy violently "repressing" ("reprimir" in Spanish) the population and who are analogous in many ways to the dirty warriors.[6]

My goal in this current chapter is to challenge this "popular" perception of the Gendarmería Nacional. To do this, I shall first propose a factual, empirical basis for comparing gendarmes to dirty warriors, and then I shall present an affective, empathetic dimension of the gendarmes, both points virtually unexplored in the Argentine media. My intention is not to whitewash the few reports of gendarme abuse that do exist. (Indeed, I shall address them below.) Neither is it to vilify those protesters who make legitimate demands in non-violent ways. Rather, it is to signal what I believe is the exceptional—and welcome—difference between how men from the Móvil 1 interpret and respond to social protest today and how their counterparts in the police and military have done so in the past, particularly during the Dirty War. In other words, it is to indelibly mark what Dave Grossman describes as the "division in humanity between those [soldiers] who can feel and understand the pain and suffering of others, and those who cannot."[7]

Neither Empathy nor Respect:
The History of Argentine State Response to Dissent

If there exists such a thing as an empathy scale, on the extreme positive end there is the State Security Force officer who so identifies with the dissident, who sees the dissident's needs, fears, and feelings as his own, that he cannot bear to injure him or her. This person would be somewhat akin to a Janist who cannot kill any animal or person, a vegetarian who will not even farm because it would mean killing worms or insects. On the other end of the scale, there is the torturer, a person so void of empathy, so emotionally empty as a human being, that he can rape, mutilate, and kill easily. We may debate whether this extreme Janist would ever find himself in any state security force. What is certain, however, is that this other man, the one on the extreme negative end of the scale, has been well represented within the Argentine State Security Forces and has committed a number of atrocities over the past eighty years.

Over half a century before the last Argentine military coup in 1976, this sort of antipathetic stereotype was present during what historians refer to as "the tragic week" ("la semana trágica"), when metallurgical workers launched a massive strike on January 9, 1919. The army intervened, violently repressing the strike. They did not, however, stop vigilante mobs from carrying out revenge killings, focusing on Jews they blamed for masterminding the "Communist" plot.[8]

In this one event, we can see patterns of behavior that Argentine soldiers would often repeat throughout the century. The soldiers could not conceive that the workers, deeply affected by the depressed wartime economy, had legitimate claims. They could not identify with the workers, could not "put themselves in the shoes of the other guy," as I write so ineloquently in my field journal. The strikers had to be foreign (Jewish) and political (Communist) radicals, and, since they were so distanced and dehumanized, the soldiers and vigilantes felt they did not deserve to live.

After the military-approved killings in 1919, the armed forces continued to brutalize protesters. In 1922, soldiers in the far southern expanse of Patagonia carried out what one author calls "the most bloody repression of workers of the 20th century, except for the period of the Videla dictatorship," which inaugurated the Dirty War in 1976.[9] The now-infamous Lieutenant Colonel Varela's men ran protesting labor leaders through with sabers and shot to death perhaps as many as 1,500 rural workers. It is important to note the lack of emotional connection in these killings, and the presence of a deep-seated desire to humiliate and degrade. Varela's men did not confront these workers as equals at the picket line or on the battlefield. Rather, they captured them and forced them to dig their own graves and to strip naked before murdering them.[10]

From 1930 to 1976, the Argentine State Security Forces—both military and police—consistently showed little empathy for dissent, killing protesters and non-conformists and developing a range of torture techniques both inside and outside of democratic governments. For example, Juan Domingo Perón's forces combined torture with selective killing against "enemies of the workers," and the soldiers who overthrew him on September 11, 1955, employed the same repressive techniques against the "enemies of the Revolution." However, the greatest period of violations during modern Argentina undoubtedly took place from 1976 to 1982, when the armed forces launched its Dirty War against left-wing "subversion."

In the name of anti-communism, Argentine soldiers carried out a mass campaign of kidnapping and torture, mostly against civilian non-combatants. While I subscribe to the philosophy that in no case *whatsoever* is torture acceptable, the Dirty War torturers dwelt upon the truly irrational, sadistic nature of the act, with little thought to the "practical" (albeit still unacceptable) applications. As Frank Graziano writes, torture was not usually applied to extract information: "Torture rather endeavored to break down the victims physically and psychologically, keeping them alive so that they could be repeatedly and ceremoniously undone."[11]

Since the collapse of the dictatorship in 1983, the civilian police have filled the military vacuum, although many employ Dirty War tactics against criminals and protesters. In 1991, a joint report by two human rights organizations, the Washington D.C.–based America's Watch and the Buenos Aires–based Centro de Estudios Legales y Sociales (the Center for Legal and Social Studies, or CELS as it is known in Spanish), concluded that "the use of torture by the police is still widespread" and that "police killings continue which violate the standards of human rights and sometimes constitute summary executions."[12]

Although it is important to reach back to the early twentieth century to certify the lack of empathy within the Security Forces and their participation in a number of atrocities since la semana trágica, we need look no further into the past than December 20, 2001. It was on that day that police shot to death a number of unarmed protesters clamoring for President De la Rúa's resignation and beat others with horsewhips. The killings themselves were unnecessary and did not serve the very real need for crowd control that day. However, these whippings, while less lethal, symbolize the inherent degradation and objectification of the protesters, like the Patagonian workers who were forced to strip naked before being murdered eighty years before.

Bases for Comparing Gendarmes to Dirty Warriors: Legality and Restraint

A Legal Basis

The Dirty War was an illegal counter-insurgency campaign aimed at wiping out real and imagined terrorists and real and imagined guerrillas and subversive "thinkers" who sympathized with their military, political, or social goals. As General Jorge Videla, the first leader of the Argentine dictatorship in 1976, once said, "A terrorist is not just someone with a gun or a bomb but also someone who spreads ideas which are contrary to Western and Christian civilization."[13] As a result of this war against ideas, the military killed anywhere between 8,000 to

30,000 "subversives"[14] (although there were perhaps only 500 active guerrillas at the time of the 1976 coup), and they violated the constitution in doing so.[15]

In comparison, gendarme "contradisturbio" operations today aim at controlling and dispersing protesters for blocking traffic, not annihilating subversives for thinking. In pursuing these objectives, the gendarmes work under a very clearly defined legal framework. That is, when gendarmes from the Móvil 1 intervene in a protest event—and they can do so only at the request of a federal judge, a provincial governor, or the nation's president—they are upholding the freedoms of transit and commerce as guaranteed by Article 14 of the Argentine Constitution.[16] It is these constitutional rights that piqueteros violate when they build blockades of flaming tires on federal highways and bridges and threaten and extort motorists with metal pipes and billy clubs, crimes for which the Argentine national penal codes set fines and prison sentences.[17]

Furthermore, the National Gendarmerie Law (Ley de Gendarmería Nacional) number 19,349 provides gendarmes with a very clear mandate to protect these rights. Article 3, section i of the law states that one of the GNA's functions is "To intervene to repress (reprimir)[18] the disturbance of public order (la alteración del orden público) or, when this is subverted, or when its magnitude surpasses the possibilities of control of the police forces, or when it acquires the characteristics of guerrilla warfare, in any of its forms."[19] Article 5 of the same law defines the jurisdiction of the GNA, which includes section b, "tunnels and international bridges"; section c, "In whatever other place of the Nation's territory when it is disposed by the Executive Power with a view to maintaining order and public tranquility or to satisfy a national security interest"; and section d, "In whatever other place of the country at the requirement of the Federal Justice [System]."[20]

Critics of successive governments' use of gendarmes to disband social protests rightly point out that the *legality* of the gendarmes' intervention is one matter but that the *morality* of it is another. That is to say, many protesters in Argentina today are the victims of a series of poor economic decisions made by generations of self-serving, political strongmen. Desperately poor and disenfranchised, some protesters feel the only way they can force the government to do anything about their situation is to blockade roads. In one example, construction workers in the town of General Mosconi in the northern province of Salta in June 2001 called for an increase in their minimum wage from ninety cents of a peso an hour to two pesos and fifty cents (when one peso equaled one dollar). Given the economic and social context of the time, ninety cents hardly constituted a decent, living wage.[21] After the devaluation of the peso, the situation became even more desperate. By January 2003, approximately 21 out of 37 million Argentines were considered poor, in a country long admired for its strong middle class.[22]

Therefore, while sending in the gendarmes may be a strictly legal move on the part of the state to disarticulate these illegal protests, if it is not accompanied by a real and sustained effort to reactivate the economy, to generate decent jobs for those who want to work, and to create more transparent rules of the political game, then it is only half of the solution. That being said, however, that this admittedly short-term and incomplete response is legal and feeds directly from the Argentine Constitution is an enormous change from the rampant illegality of the Dirty War. The other enormous difference is that these interventions have not been marked by reports of massive blood-letting on the part of the gendarmes.

Few Records of Gendarme Violations

Certainly, there have been recent allegations of gendarmes committing abuses, including torture, and these should not be swept aside.[23] Most disturbingly, and as I discuss in greater detail below, a number of human rights organizations have blamed gendarmes for protester deaths.

Confirming or refuting these disparate allegations is complicated. Torture is often difficult to prove, even with a great deal of physical evidence, and this certainly is the case of the few acts of torture allegedly committed by gendarmes that have come to light. Therefore, in setting my parameters for comparing gendarmes to dirty warriors, I shall focus on alleged killings, because they would be the most tangible signals of gendarme abuse.

However, in pursuing this approach, there are still several limitations. To start with, there is no CONADEP (National Commission on the Disappearance of People) specifically and systematically investigating allegations of abuse against protesters, as there was for the abuse of political prisoners immediately after the fall of the dictatorship. To make matters more difficult, Argentine society is highly polarized along political lines, so it is a complicated process to sift between the versions of protest events presented by the apologists for repression—those who would overlook any gendarme violation of the law, as long as it preserved order—and the versions presented by the proponents of anarchism—those who want to disband, outright, the system of law and order in Argentina.

Against this difficult background, I have chosen to consult the most comprehensive (of the very few) Argentine databases I have come across containing information on alleged gendarme killings.[24] It is kept by a left-of-center, nongovernmental human rights organization called the Coordinadora Contra la Represión Policial e Institucional (the Coordinator Against Police and Institutional Repression or CORREPI) and contains allegations of deaths caused by Argentine Security Forces, including the gendarmes, since the return of democracy in 1983 until November 24, 2002.[25] With the information in this database, I believe we can construct the strongest possible case against the gendarmes.

CORREPI draws from several national newspapers (*La Nación, Clarín, Página 12, Crónica,* and *Diario Popular*), local newspapers, the Internet, and anarray of official and unofficial complaints from alleged victims' relatives.[26] The organization collects information on killings in which the perpetrators were members of Argentine Security Forces,[27] and in which "the victim did not, in any way, pose a danger to third parties or to the killer," including cases where Security Forces had "itchy trigger fingers" and faked clashes between themselves and their victims.[28] According to CORREPI, these guidelines reduce the pool of potential killings for analysis, and they believe a great many other unrecorded abuses exist. With these limitations in mind, the database provides information relating to twenty-four deaths attributed to gendarmes in the past nineteen years.[29]

Of those twenty-four deaths, CORREPI specifically mentions that thirteen of them resulted from gendarmes acting while on duty or during what we could broadly consider to be working hours.[30] For example, within these thirteen cases appears an incident in which a gendarme helped a married couple through a checkpoint and then raped the woman and murdered them both and stole their car.[31] Obviously, committing these crimes—for which, according to the database, this gendarme was convicted—was not part of his job, but one could argue that he acted, initially, in an "official" capacity by helping the couple through the checkpoint.

To be as inclusive as possible, we could add five more killings, in which CORREPI does not mention whether the gendarmes were on duty or not, thus making a total of eighteen.[32] The rest of the killings were allegedly committed by gendarmes and ex-gendarmes who were, apparently, off-duty, and they primarily killed family members or neighbors in domestic disputes.

Of the total of twenty-four alleged killings, however, the database suggests that only four of them took place during counter-disturbance operations. The killings of these men—Francisco Escobar and Mauro César Ojeda in the province of Corrientes on December 17, 1999, and José Oscar Barrios and Carlos Santillán in the province of Salta on June 16, 2001—are the strongest indication of abuse committed by the GNA mobile detachments.[33]

CORREPI's description of these events is, however, limited, so I have consulted CELS's recent, definitive report on social protests from 1996 to 2002 for further details.[34] Concerning the deaths of Escobar and Ojeda in Corrientes, CELS writes that the two men died in the context of a clash between gendarmes and civilians, some of them armed with paving stones and firearms.[35] CELS goes on to describe the complicated legal investigation of the event, including delays and changes of venue, and finally concludes that the "judicial investigation has not thrown much light on the legality of the state [read "gendarme"] action."[36]

Regarding the deaths of Barrios and Santillán in General Mosconi in the province of Salta in 2001, CELS's report also provides many useful details. However, as with the events in Corrientes, it is hardly conclusive. CELS reports that a local doctor observed that the bullet found in Santillán's head was "encamisada" (jacketed), suggesting, in agreement with the analysis by journalists, that it was shot from an "arma de guerra" (weapon of war), coming from the Gendarmería.[37] From my own investigations, I have found that ammunition produced in military factories is readily available at hunting supply stores in Argentina to civilians; therefore, the presence of a military-made encamisada bullet does not prove gendarme culpability. As for Barrios, CELS writes that, while he was wounded by a bullet in the hip, the cause of death "would have been a respiratory problem provoked by tear gas or by being crushed."[38]

Given the tumultuous environment of these "contradisturbio" events—the noise of the protesters' drums and chants, the sting of the gendarmes' tear gas, the charge of the gendarmes, and the shooting and rock throwing by the crowds—this information provides a wide margin for interpretation. In the case of Barrios, he could have been killed by gendarme use of tear gas, or he could have been crushed to death by the crowd. Moreover, CELS's report (describing, as it does, civilian use of firearms in Corrientes) lends credibility to gendarme allegations that these murders were committed by civilian snipers.

However, that we cannot find a literal, smoking gun does not automatically mean the gendarmes did not have a hand in these deaths. With the lengthy history of official cover-ups for human rights violations in Argentina and the inability (or unwillingness) of the courts to independently attribute blame, it is useful to approach these incidents with a healthy skepticism.

Therefore, erring on the side of prudence and in the absence of definitive proof, let us assume for a moment that gendarmes actually killed these four men. If this worst possible case were true, it would certainly be a black spot against the GNA, and it would still be a tragedy for the families of the victims. It would not, however, constitute a picture of systematic, excessive abuse.

This point deserves great clarity as well as caution. It is not to say that there is an "acceptable" number of state-sponsored killings during protest events every year. The only acceptable number would be zero. However, it is important to put these alleged killings into some sort of comparative perspective. While CORREPI suggests the *possibility* that gendarmes caused four protest-related deaths in the space of nineteen years, several sources hold Argentine police responsible for killing five protesters during one day alone, when crowds drove President De la Rúa out of office.[39]

Moreover, during those same nineteen years, CORREPI collected information on more than 1,293 deaths caused by all members of the Argentine State Security Forces combined.[40] Given this, we could, potentially, hold gendarmes responsible for approximately 1.9% (24 out of 1,293 killings) of the total reported deaths since the transition to democracy in 1983. Furthermore, when we compare the gendarmes' four alleged protest-related killings to the thousands of murders of labor union leaders, high school protesters, and pregnant mothers committed by the military during the late 1970s, we see that the actions of the gendarmes do not in any way approximate those of their Dirty War counterparts.

An Internal View of the Gendarmes: Empathy, Identification, Poverty

"One of the People"

I met my first Argentine gendarme in 1999 at Fort Benning, Georgia, where I was doing research on the human rights education program at the School of the

Americas. At the time, my knowledge of the gendarmes' history, their tasks, most especially their culture, was quite limited. In order to help me fill in the blanks, this officer, who was on an exchange program with the U.S. Army at the time, described himself and his colleagues as "one of the people" (uno del pueblo).

As an example of what he meant, he said that when gendarmes are assigned to remote border villages (where they help stranded tourists and interdict contraband, among other tasks) they normally sit down with the people and drink "mate" with them. For the reader unfamiliar with Argentine customs, this, of course, requires explanation. Mate is more than the traditional Argentine herbal tea. The ceremony of drinking it from a metal straw out of a gourd and passing it from person to person is the consummate symbol of Argentine camaraderie and community. By saying that gendarmes drink mate with villagers, this officer meant that gendarmes understand and accept poor Argentines, that they share their culture and concerns, that they identify with them.

Years later, when I was conducting interviews at Campo de Mayo for my doctoral dissertation, this phrase, "one of the people," emerged again and again. This was how one Cabo (Corporal) described the gendarmes to me. In fact, being one of the people is why—according to him—gendarmes respect human rights more than their counterparts in the military or police:

> The gendarme is from the people [pueblo]. . . . In the provinces, outside, you go to the provinces, let's say [the northern provinces of] Salta, Formosa, Chaco, or wherever, many times the gendarme has to be the school teacher, to help the indigenous people, to educate them. . . . They act as schoolteachers, they bring the doctor from the [Gendarmería], they act as nurses, they help. . . . Over there maybe [there is] a barbed wire fence [and] the owner of the land doesn't have people to repair it, and the gendarmes get off their horses and fix it. The gendarme is more . . . he has more community than the other [Security Forces].

I want to signal here the importance of this man's use of the word "community," because I tend to agree with the psychologist Alfred Adler's position that "the psychology of war . . . derives from an absence of community feeling," as "the enemy is the person toward whom one has no social feeling."[41] That the gendarmes look at many protesters as neighbors and not enemies is a point I shall take up later on.

If it is true that the gendarmes are one of the people, then the reverse is also true, that "the people" are gendarmes. That is to say, many of the gendarmes I interviewed come from the northeast provinces of Chaco, Corrientes, Formosa, and Misiones, a zone in which some of the most violent conflicts between gendarmes and protesters have taken place (the fierce street battles in the town of General Mosconi, in the province of Salta, particularly come to mind). As in the southern United States, where a military career has been admired historically, in the scattered, poor villages of northern Argentina, the gendarme's olive-green uniform is a symbol of prestige. Many a provincial boy dreams of becoming a gendarme, and those dreams are in good part what encouraged many of the men I interviewed to join the GNA.

Given their background, gendarmes frequently face off against protesters from their same province, sometimes from their same village. Perhaps that is why, when they talk of these confrontations, gendarmes tend to describe most protesters—these *community members*—in positive terms. Even for the gendarmes who come from big cities, there seems to be a common appreciation for these provincial protesters. They refer to them as noble workers, honest people going through difficult economic times. As one Sargento Primero (Staff Sergeant) told me, people from these provinces are "gente sufrida" ("suffering people") just as the gendarmes see themselves. They are "people who come from a blood-line that [says] you have to work."

Many gendarmes, themselves, use empathy as an explanation for their restraint, although they would not use that exact word. For example, a Segundo Comandante (Captain) explained to me:

> I try not to vent my anger (ensanarse)[42] on that person [who's protesting]. That is what we want . . . we convince the personnel, we convince them of it. Because, perhaps we're going to repress (reprimir) in [the province of] Formosa, and they are my people, who, what do I know, are protesting for something just. So . . . the only thing that I want is that they clear the highway, not that . . . they [my men] try to attack them [just] because I have more weapons than they do. . . . No, it's not like that. Everyone knows, everyone knows it. So, we give [our men] different examples: if one is from Corrientes, the ones from Corrientes feel touched, if he's from Formosa, the ones from Formosa feel touched, as the majority of us are from the interior [of the country].

Identification

This idea of close identification with the protesters is reflected in a photograph that appeared on the cover of the national daily newspaper *Clarín* on May 14, 2000. It is of a piquetero shaking hands with a gendarme, after the two groups had confronted each other in the town of General Mosconi in the province of Salta.

The image is striking, especially when we take into account that a violent confrontation had just occurred between gendarmes and piqueteros. The most interesting thing I find about this photograph, however, is the text that accompanied it in the newspaper article. The reporter writes that the encounter occurred soon after this piquetero, Juan Carlos González, had concluded negotiations with the government. His eyes red from the tear gas, González leaned over and said to one of the helmeted gendarmes standing next to him, "Excuse me, I want to say hello to you. Both of us are laburantes (laborers)."[43]

Several gendarmes I interviewed mentioned this photograph to me. One high-ranking gendarme in the university for GNA officers in Buenos Aires even had it framed and hung over his desk. For them, this photograph means community, solidarity. It means they are all laburantes. It means fair play and no hard feelings. Above all, it means that, after the day is over, the gendarmes can go back to their families like the rest of "the people," even though many angry protesters, snipers, and Molotov cocktail throwers do not feel the same.

Making Ends Meet: Sandwiches, Second Jobs, and Medical Bills

The gendarmes I interviewed tended to identify with these protesters, not only because many of them came from the same provinces, but also because they came from the same economic class.

At the time of my interviews, in November and December 2001, a recently admitted gendarme was making somewhere around 300 Argentine pesos per month. The Argentine economy was obviously heading for trouble, but the peso was still pegged to the dollar, so one peso equaled one dollar. In the six months following my interviews, the peso was devalued to approximately one-fourth of its past value. Like that of the rest of the working poor, the ability of gendarmes and their families to make ends meet was severely affected by the devaluation.

We can get a feeling for how difficult this situation is by taking something as basic as food prices into account. Gendarmes must pay for their own meals while on base. (On month-long missions in Salta, Corrientes, or Tierra del Fuego, with long hours under the sun and rain, their superiors do provide them with lunch, sometimes only a sandwich or a sausage.) When I was carrying out my investigation, the cheapest sandwiches available to the gendarmes in Campo de Mayo cost about one peso, which was a very good deal. What this meant was that the newly commissioned gendarme was paying about one-tenth of his salary per month just in lunches—that is, if he ate only this cheap sandwich and not a salad or a piece of fruit and did not buy a soft drink, which could make his lunches add

up to 20% or 30% of his salary. On top of this, the gendarmes, like all other civil servants, had recently been hit by a 13% pay reduction to cut government costs.

One Cabo (Corporal) with ten years with the Gendarmería describes the effect this had on him and on his family in the following way:

> This economy of ours, here . . . [is] each time worse. Yes, because now comes a famous 13% that lowered our salary, a barbarity. Yes, it was this year. And the salary here of a gendarme, more or less, is earning 400 pesos, 500 pesos. That is, in dollars, he's earning 400–500 dollars. . . . For example, I am earning more or less, 400 dollars

here per month, and with this I have to maintain my family, all of this, pay taxes for the house, all of this. . . . Yes, one always tries to look for work outside. In my case, my wife more or less saves me, who works outside too. It isn't a lot that she earns, but at least it makes it. My mother-in-law is a pensioner who at least gives [something]. Between the three of us, thus we manage.

Another Cabo with seven years of experience described how he and his family just barely made ends meet. As he explained, "I earn 500 pesos, and I have to travel, the rent is 250, and that leaves 250 pesos for me to live. And with my family, I have to distribute all of that." His wife was unable to work at the time, as she had just given birth a few months before the interview, and his inability to pay for health care weighed heavily on his mind. If a family member became sick, he was sure he would have to take out a loan to pay the medical bills. Up to that point, this had not happened to him. "But there are a lot of guys who are obliged to take out loan after loan to pay another loan, and there they go deeper in the hole, and when you realize it, you owe everyone, and your salary is nothing."

For this reason, several gendarmes moonlight at other jobs, mainly as remiseros (gypsy taxicab drivers) or security guards. Several of the gendarmes of the Móvil 1 have been murdered while working these second jobs. One particularly shocking death in the gendarmes' collective memory is that of a colleague who was recently killed while providing security for a kiosk. This event makes this Cabo wonder about a system that forces gendarmes to work outside: "Let's say, it really makes us feel bad to lose a partner like that, because he goes to work in another place, has five kids, leaves his wife with their kids. If one, I think, if one had a good salary, he wouldn't go to work outside. It would be enough just with the salary of the Gendarmería."

A Primer Alférez (First Lieutenant) feels the same way: "You pay for your lunch, you pay for part of your clothing, you pay the debts that you owe. . . . Here we all generally live like we're pawned." In conclusion, this officer suggests, "It would be so easy, so beautiful, if here they gave us a plate of food or a sandwich, a sausage sandwich and a soda, how well the Móvil would operate!"

The Poor Against the Poor

Certainly, this is not the portrait of the privileged warrior elite, set apart from the civilian world. The gendarmes do not live the way Argentine soldiers do, in private villages within the Campo de Mayo complex. Most gendarmes leave the base every night to live in their blue-collar neighborhoods, if they do not stay, locked-down in their bunkhouses when they are on call, ready to be deployed. They take the bus to work. Some travel several hours. Their uniforms have a used look to them. Their equipment is tarnished. They are, in fact, the uniformed, working poor. As the then head of the GNA, Comandante General Hugo Miranda, recognized on the anniversary of the creation of the Gendarmería in 2002, "We are, like any other citizen among the millions of Argentines, who now live below the poverty line."[44] One Cabo told me very much the same: "Let's say, economically, we're all in the same bag."

As in other investigations, I found that some of the most interesting information came after the tape recorder was switched off. During one interview, a gendarme asked me to turn off my tape recorder before he would answer the question of how he felt about having to confront people from his own village. With the tape turned off, he called it "The poor against the poor" (los pobres en contra de los pobres). A number of other gendarmes felt bold enough to use the same phrase on the record. One Sargento (Sergeant), for example, told me that, while some observers see the clash between gendarmes and protesters as "the good guys versus the bad," he sees it, instead, as "the poor against the poor. . . . Now I'm on this side, but I'm also thinking about the other people. Maybe it's right what they [the protesters] are asking for, and maybe it's a good thing for us as well."

When the gendarmes I interviewed said they were "of the people," it was not because they felt they were custodians of the people's mystic, spiritual needs, as many soldiers did during the Dirty War. What they meant was that they actually *were* part of the people, that they lived with them, drank mate with them, that they were sons of greengrocers and shoe salesmen and maids like the rest of the working class. And this self-identification is consonant with the absence of reports of gendarmes committing massive human rights violations.

Citizens, Not Enemies

In a number of atrocities around the world, soldiers engage in what Rieber and Kelly call "psychosocial kenosis," which is "an emotional catharsis and outpouring of oneself in an unusual way; one's least desirable traits and dispositions are projected onto another, transferred to the enemy. . . . One becomes more 'human' as the enemy becomes less so."[45] In the Dirty War, this was certainly the case. As I have written elsewhere, soldiers thought of themselves as holy warriors and thought of the "subversives" as demonic forces, the two engaging in the first battle of the actual, biblical Armageddon.[46]

We know from the sections above that the gendarmes see themselves as the working poor with a difficult job to do, not as Saint George versus the Communist dragon. Thus, self-beatification is one half of the kenosis that gendarmes are missing. The other half, that of "enemifying," demonizing protesters, they also lack. That is, the gendarmes I interviewed took pains to describe protesters, not as "enemigos" (enemies) but as "oponentes" (opponents) and "conciudadanos" (fellow-citizens). As one Cabo says,

> Bah, [according to] my manner of thinking, for me a protester is not

an enemy. Because he's protesting for a reason, for a right that they have. I can't treat a protester like an enemy, because I'm not going to go to liquidate (liquidar) the protester. The enemy, yes, but the protester no. . . . Yes, I repress (reprimir) them, I always try to repress in a situation . . . and that he has a place to escape to, never closing off an escape. You always have to close off the escape for an enemy, for a protester, no.

Finally, one young Alférez (Second Lieutenant) concludes,

Ours is not like the army. We don't see the person in front of us as the enemy. We don't work with enemies. We do not have to annihilate (aniquilar), we don't have to kill. We have to dissuade (disuadir). That's why we talk about "oponente": it is a person who has a different way of thinking and is disturbed (alterada).

There is quite a lot of information in the last quotation above, and it deserves some analysis. First, there is the distinction between "enemy" and "opponent" and responses gendarmes make according to those categories: kill versus dissuade. Then there is the matter of the protesters being "alterados."

"Alterado"—literally "altered" or "changed"—in this context means disturbed, upset, agitated, or irritated. Someone alterado, according to this Second Lieutenant, is someone "who is feeling bad, who is angry, who, in this moment, is doing something that perhaps, if he were calm, he wouldn't be doing." To this definition, a Corporal adds, "A 'disturbed citizen' (ciudadano alterado)? Yes, the protester is a person who is asking for something, and he gets alterado by being in a group. A nervousness takes hold of him that makes him angry, then he does what he does, he throws rocks and all those things. But that's very different from what an enemy is."

These gendarmes, then, consider a protester as a "citizen," a native son of Argentina. They also see him as caught up in transition from the way a citizen normally acts. This notion of mutability is extremely important. If the gendarme perceived, ahead of time, that all protesters were violent fanatics, that they were "like this and always like this," as the Argentine dirty warriors viewed civilians "infected" with communism, then all the intermediary steps, from displaying the dogs to spraying tear gas, would make little sense. By not essentializing his opponent, the gendarme can use force aimed at persuading him to desist from his illegal activities and not at destroying him. This is precisely because they believe the protester can be persuaded, can be turned around and brought back into the fold.

I suspect this attitude comes in part because, after the protest, after the tear gas has evaporated and the barricades have been removed, the gendarmes must coexist with the very people they were struggling against at the picket line, because they are neighbors, equals, community members. As one high-ranking gendarme at Campo de Mayo said to me, tellingly, "Amongst ourselves, we should not have enemies."

Empathy and Its Limits

While the presence of antipathy and human rights abuses has been well documented in a number of cases—this was quite clear in the Argentine Dirty War—there is no definitive proof that one directly causes the other. Turning this around, there is also no defined, causal link between empathy and respect for human rights. As for Adler, while I believe his idea of community richly informs this debate, I also agree with Rieber and Kelly that "The capacity for social feeling, as the Spartans knew, was no obstacle to war—or to having enemies."[47] That is, soldiers for thousands of years have shared cultural, class, and social affinities with those in the opposite trenches, but this has not stopped them from killing and torturing their counterparts.

At the same time, while the gendarmes' poverty and geographical origins and, thus, their empathy with protesters tell a compelling story about respect for human rights, we must remember that many Argentine police officers who daily kidnap, murder, and torture also come from the lower socio-economic strata, and they live in the same neighborhoods as their victims. Since mine is currently the only cultural study of the gendarmes' mobile detachments, we will need to carry out further research on them, and we will also need to study comparable police units, before we can say something more definitive about this link between empathy and restraint. For now, one can only suspect there are a number of intervening variables that lead to the gendarmes' (apparent) respect for protesters' human rights, such as obedience to authority, religion, gender roles, ethnicity, socialization, esprit de corps, and the like.

Assuming that empathy *does* exert a strong hold on the gendarmes, assuming it *does* encourage them to respect protesters' human rights, it certainly does not stop them from following orders to disband their protests and to use force in doing so. When I asked one mid-ranking gendarme how, given his men's deep identification with protesters, he kept them from "going native," from letting protesters loot and disrupt traffic, he responded, "It's the concept . . . 'I am Law and Order.' My nation starts in La Quiaca [northernmost Argentina] and ends in Ushuaia [southernmost Argentina]. I don't have provinces any more. I am a gendarme. I am a gendarme there and there."

When I asked one private why he did not drop his shield and join the protesters, if, as he said, he identified so very much with them, he replied it was because of "One's own pride that the country will go forward whatever happens and not put yourself on the other side with the protester, because you like the uniform, you love the uniform, you like your country." Another private certainly described himself as "a worker" to me, but he also described himself as a "funcionario" (civil servant). This is another facet of the gendarme identity. They are not merely poor workers but poor workers in uniform, a uniform that represents law and order and that compels them to serve the Argentine Constitution. This gendarme went on to say,

> One starts thinking about the protester's side, and realizes he's right. But . . . we follow orders, and our function is different. But there are many times that it hurts, it hurts because you see babies, old people totally malnourished [in the areas where protest arises], and, well . . . unfortunately we follow orders.

Moreover, it would be disingenuous to pretend the gendarmes empathize with *all* protesters they confront, that they feel it is "unfortunate" to follow orders. While gendarmes may look with understanding on hungry, hard-working provincial workers, most do not appreciate what they see as politically motivated "professional" protesters who are bused in by political machines from Buenos Aires.

One Cabo made a clear distinction within a group of protesters he confronted in Salta. On the one hand, there were people who were "reclaiming something just," "for a piece of bread," and, on the other, "there are people who go to make problems," people who filter into the first group "so that it's more . . . motivated." Expanding on this theme, he said:

> From my point of view, there were people that were from the town [in the province of Salta] and there were people that . . . were from the mountains. A lot of people infiltrated from the mountains. I think they came from somewhere else. I don't know if from the other side of the border or from some place, where a focus of protest was created, they filter in.

For these gendarmes, if a protester does not have a direct stake in the protest at hand, if he travels in from some far-off location, and, thus, he looks and speaks differently from the locals, then he is there for politics, and politics delegitimize his goals. Therefore, in contrast to the economic protester who "deserves" to be there, the political protester definitely does not. In this line, one Segundo Comandante (Captain) refers to the GNA's opponents in the town of General Mosconi as activists, who are sent here from Buenos Aires, whom the very same political parties pay. They can be . . . opportunists of the moment. They take advantage of the circumstance that there is an internal conflict and try to incorporate themselves into it to protest against the government. Then, they create chaos. You say, "What is this? There are peaceful protesters, but from their side, they're shooting at me."

What is interesting about these very negative descriptions of "political" protesters is that, even though the gendarmes express great dislike for them, they do not see them as the "enemy." They do not demonize them, they do not dehumanize them as their Dirty War counterparts once did. As one Primer Alférez made clear to me, protesters may "throw stones, shoot bullets," but there is no "enemigo" as long as "no armed army comes." That is, enemies for the gendarmes are classically conceived belligerents who wear uniforms and invade Argentina from another country. Protesters, whether gendarmes agree with them or not, whether they are motivated by economics or politics, are not enemies, and they deserve to have their human rights respected.

Conclusion

In the year 2000, a journalist writing for the Mothers of the Plaza de Mayo's electronic newsletter (once the Argentine human rights organization *sine qua non* but now radicalized under the leadership of the polemic Hebe de Bonafini) made a one-to-one comparison between the human rights abusers of Argentina's past and the gendarmes of the present. He wrote that, just as "[President] Yrigoyen sent troops at the command of Colonel Varela to annihilate the workers of the Patagonia Rebelde" in the 1920s, then President De la Rúa sent a gendarme commander with his men to "crush the people of Corrientes" in 1999.[48]

As I write above, it is indisputable that two men, Maura Ojeda and Francisco Escobar, died in that clash involving gendarmes in Corrientes in 1999. (It is also indisputable that José Oscar Barrios and Carlos Santillán died in Salta in 2001.) Moreover, although it was never proven, it is at least *possible* that the gendarmes sent to disband the protesters killed them. However, that is as much as we can say.

Neither in purpose, nor in scope, nor in number of fatalities are the events comparable. To equate the gendarmes (who *may* have killed four men in the space of nineteen years) to Varela's men in the 1920s (who killed, perhaps, over a thousand workers) or to the dictatorship's soldiers of the 1970s (who murdered at least 8,000 men, women, and children) is an exercise in hyperbole.

My interviews at Campo de Mayo and what little empirical evidence CORREPI's database provides paint a portrait of the gendarmes as the working poor in uniform, deeply empathetic with protesters, and highly respectful of what they consider their fellow-citizens' basic human rights. Along the hypothetical empathy scale, the gendarmes are certainly no Janists, but then again, neither are they dirty warriors, but, rather, somewhere in the middle: civil servants who use constitutionally authorized force to disband illegal protests. This is in opposition to the persistent and "popular" image of gendarmes as antipathetic state repressors.

Notes

1. This chapter draws directly from and is based on ideas expressed in the author's

dissertation, "Lawful Warriors: Respecting Human Rights while Policing Social Protest: A Cultural Study of the First Mobile Detachment of the Argentine National Gendarmerie," University of California, Santa Barbara, December 2003. Although at the time of publication the author was an official with the International Labour Organisation (ILO), the views and expressions appearing in this chapter are not intended to reflect in any way the position of the ILO and should not be construed as doing so. This chapter is the result of independent research, and, as such, the conclusions reached by the author are his and his alone. All translations from Spanish-language works and interviews are the author's unless otherwise noted.

2. My purposeful sample was composed of a range of officers and enlisted men.

3. Filippini, an Argentine human rights expert, writes, "In 1997, there were 104 road-block protests in Argentina, and the number of these protests grew as time drew onward. In 1998 no fewer than one thoroughfare was blocked each week, and in 1999 there was an average of a road-block protest every day and a half. By 2000 the number had increased to one per day, and the year 2001 averaged between four and five road-block protests each day." Leonardo Filippini, "The Popular Protest in Argentina," *Centro de Estudios Legales y Sociales Website,* December 2001, <http://www.cels.org.ar/-english/4_documents/documents _pdf/Popular_protest.pdf> (April 14. 2004), 5.

4. For a succinct discussion of *jus in bello,* see Ruth Linn, "Terrorism, Morality and Soldiers' Motivation to Fight: An Example from the Israeli Experience in Lebanon," *Terrorism* 11 (1988): 140.

5. See Eric Stener Carlson, *I Remember Julia: Voices of the Disappeared* (Philadelphia: Temple University Press, 1996).

6. In its description of the events of December 20, 2001, when police responded to protesters with violence but gendarmes did not, the Argentine news magazine *Noticias* wrote the following: "But, this time, the same gendarmes dressed like 'robocop' who repressed in [the northern provinces of] Corrientes and in Salta did not appear anywhere." Roberto Caballero and Juan Alonso, "El día que la Argentina lloró," *Noticias* (22 December 2001), 76.

7. Dave Grossman, *On Killing: The Psychological Cost of Learning to Kill in War and Society* (Boston: Little, Brown and Company, 1996), 183.

8. David Rock, *Argentina 1516-1987: From Spanish Colonization to Alfonsín* (Berkeley: University of California Press, 1987), 202.

9. Osvaldo Bayer, *La Patagonia rebelde,* edición definitiva (Buenos Aires: Planeta, 2002), 10.

10. Bayer, *Patagonia rebelde,* 8.

11. Frank Graziano, *Divine Violence: Spectacle, Psychosexuality, and Radical Christianity in the Argentine "Dirty War"* (Boulder: Westview Press, 1992), 38.

12. America's Watch and Centro de Estudios Legales y Sociales, *Police Violence in Argentina: Torture and Police Killings in Buenos Aires* (New York: America's Watch, December 1991), 1.

13. Appearing in Comisión Nacional sobre la Desaparición de Personas, *Nunca más,* 16th ed. (Buenos Aires: Editorial Universitaria de Buenos Aires, 1991), 342, as translated in Graziano, *Divine Violence,* 27.

14. Comisión Nacional sobre la Desaparición de Personas, *Nunca más,* 16. The National Commission on the Disappearance of People (the CONADEP, as it is known by its Spanish initials) sets the lowest official calculation of disappeared people at 8,960. The number of "disappeared" has been estimated as upwards of 30,000,

although the CONADEP number is much more directly verifiable and can be taken as a reliable, lower-margin estimate.

15. Emilio Mignone, late expert in human rights in Argentina and father of a "disappeared" daughter, contended that the number of actual left-wing guerrilla fighters active in March 1976 was around 400 to 500. Carlson, *I Remember Julia*, 11.

16. Article 14 reads: "All of the inhabitants of the Nation enjoy the following rights in agreement with the laws that regulate their exercise: to know; to work and to exercise all licit industry; to navigate and do commerce; to petition authorities; to enter, remain, travel and leave the Argentine territory; to publish their ideas in the press without previous censorship; to use and to dispose of their property; to associate with useful ends; to freely express their religion; to teach and to learn." Helio Juan Zarini, ed., *Constitución Argentina: Comentada y concordada*, 2nd ed. (Buenos Aires: Editorial Astrea: 1998), 51.

17. Specifically, article 194 of the Penal Code states: "He who, without creating a situation of common danger (peligro común), impedes (impedir), upsets (estorbar) or slows (entorpecer) the normal functioning of transports by land, water or air or the public services of communication, of the provision of water, of electricity or of energy sources, will be repressed (reprimir) with prison from three months to two years." Portal de Abogados website, <http://www.portaldeabogados.com.ar/codigos/codpenal05.htm> (April 14, 2004).

18. The word "reprimir" is difficult to translate, because of its multiple uses and connotations. The National Gendarmerie Law states that the gendarmes' legal duty is to "reprimir" illegal protests, and gendarmes use the same word to describe their activities. This means to "repress" or to "suppress," but it does not mean "being repressive" or violating human rights. It is, actually, a legal action. At the same time, critics of the Gendarmería accuse gendarmes of "repressing" protesters, in the sense of brutally beating them or otherwise abusing them. To make things even more complicated, gendarmes will also say that they intervened in a given protest, following the dictates of the law (which is to "repress"), but they did not "repress" the protesters.

19. Gendarmería Nacional Argentina website, "Ley de Gendarmería Nacional 19.349," <http://www.gendarme.com.ar/ley19349.html> (April 14, 2004).

20. Gendarmería Nacional Argentina website.

21. Centro de Estudios Legales y Sociales, "Hechos de protesta social en los que participó la gendarmería nacional." Note: CELS's representative, Gustavo Palmieri, gave this list to me at CELS's headquarters in Buenos Aires on March 4, 2002.

22. Data drawn from Ismael Bermúdez, "Ya son 21 millones los pobres en la Argentina," *Clarín* digital, January 5, 2003, <http://old.clarin.com/diario/2003/01/05/e01701.htm> (April 14, 2004).

23. For an example of one allegation that gendarmes strangled and beat a man in an attempt to solicit information, see Centro de Profesionales por los Derechos Humanos Argentina, "Listado de artículos," which reproduces a newspaper article from *Página 12* entitled "Denuncian por torturas a los gendarmes en General Mosconi," CEPRODH website, July 1, 2001, <http://www.ceprodh.org.ar/abogados.htm> (November 3, 2003).

24. For my doctoral dissertation, I also consulted a database managed by CELS, but it was not as complete or as detailed as the CORREPI database.

25. Coordinadora Contra la Represión Policial e Institucional, *Archivo de Casos: 1983–2002—Recopilación de muertes de personas a manos de las fuerzas de seguridad en Argentina*. Note: A version of this list appeared on the website <http://www.derechos.org/correpi/muertes.html> as of February 2, 2002, but it was

"frozen" with data ending in 1998, apparently by a decision made by the website host. The edition I am using for this chapter was sent to me by e-mail by a representative of the CORREPI on February 24, 2003.

26. E-mail communication with CORREPI member Gerardo Etcheverry, March 4, 2003.

27. I must underscore that CORREPI's database includes only allegations of torture that purportedly ended in the death of the victim. I have been informed by a CORREPI representative that their database is currently being updated.

28. This is a summary of information presented by La Coordinadora Contra la Represión Policial e Institucional, *Archivo de Casos: 1983–2002*, 1.

29. I have chosen to exclude four alleged killings contained in the CORREPI database. Two of these are the alleged disappearance of Nicasio Silva and the stabbing death of Inés Canteros (CORREPI case numbers 210 and 980) that took place in the province of Corrientes on September 29, 1998. According to the database, there were gendarmes originally implicated in the two deaths relating to property that was to be sold to the GNA, although it is unclear from CORREPI's presentation of the data who these gendarmes were and what their supposed role was. However, the database itself states that the case against the gendarmes was dismissed (sobreseído), while non-gendarmes were arrested and processed. The other two deaths are those of Maximiliano Kosteki and Darío Santillán (CORREPI case numbers 572 and 952) on June 26, 2002, in Avellaneda, Buenos Aires. According to the CORREPI database, Federal Police, Buenos Aires Police, Prefectura, and Gendarmería "repressed" various piquetero organizations that had taken over the Pueyrredon Bridge. During these events, these two men were killed and 150 people were wounded. However, as CORREPI also notes, two police officers have been charged (procesados) with the murders. From the newspaper reports I have read and from videotapes that were shown on Argentine television regarding the incident, the police are responsible for these deaths, and the Gendarmería have not been implicated. I believe excluding these four deaths from our consideration is rational, but for those readers who disagree, the total number of deaths attributed to the gendarmes by CORREPI would be twenty-eight instead of twenty-four.

30. They are CORREPI case numbers 1, 82, 95, 112, 186, 238, 340, 347, 517, 718, 951, 1020, and 1052.

31. These correspond to CORREPI case numbers 340 and 517.

32. CORREPI case numbers 548, 963, 684, 1146, and 1153.

33. The CORREPI case numbers are as follows: Escobar, 347; Ojeda, 718; Barrios, 112; Santillán, 951.

34. Centro de Estudios Legales y Sociales, *El Estado frente a la protesta social: 1996–2002* (Buenos Aires: Siglo XXI Editores Argentina, 2003).

35. Centro de Estudios Legales, 242.

36. Centro de Estudios Legales, 242.

37. Centro de Estudios Legales, 228.

38. Centro de Estudios Legales, 228–29.

39. Centro de Estudios Legales, 200. For a specific report of police firing into the crowd, see also Alberto Amato, "En la represión de diciembre hasta se usaron vehículos particulares," *Clarín* digital, August 5, 2002, <http://www.clarin.com/ diario/2002/08/05/p-01601.htm> (May 23, 2003).

40. The numbering in the CORREPI database is flawed. In a number of cases, I observed that lower numbers of cases follow higher numbers, and some different cases

are assigned the same case numbers. Therefore, it appears there are more than 1,293 separate killings listed in the database, but the highest "official" total—that is, numbered total—is 1,293.

41. This is Rieber and Kelly's interpretation of Adler from Robert W. Rieber and Robert J. Kelly, "Substance and Shadow: Images of the Enemy," in *The Psychology of War and Peace: The Image of the Enemy,* ed. Robert W. Rieber (New York: Plenum Press, 1991), 7–8. The authors offer this interpretation based on their reading of Alfred Adler, *The Neurotic Constitution* (New York: Moffat Yard and Company, 1917).

42. *Collins Spanish Dictionary* translates "ensanarse con," alternatively, as "to vent one's anger on," "to delight in tormenting," and "take a sadistic pleasure in the sufferings of." Colin Smith, *Collins Spanish-English English-Spanish Dictionary,* 3rd ed. (New York: HarperCollins, 1992), 296.

43. Photograph from front page of *Clarín* (May 14, 2000), 1; text referring to photograph from the same edition, "La crisis social: Desconcentración en la ruta 34," *Clarín* digital, May 14, 2000, <http://old.clarin.com/diario/2000/05/14/p-00401.htm> (April 19, 2004).

44. "La Gendarmería reclamó más presupuesto y apoyo," *La Nación Line*, July 31, 2002, <http://www.lanacion.com.ar/> (November 11, 2003). Note: Comandante General Miranda was removed from his post soon after making these comments, in part, one may suppose, for criticizing the government.

45. Rieber and Kelly, "Substance and Shadow," 16.

46. Eric Stener Carlson, "The Influence of French 'Revolutionary War' Ideology on the Use of Torture in Argentina's 'Dirty War,'" *Human Rights Review* 1.4 (July–September 2000).

47. Rieber and Kelly, "Substance and Shadow," 8.

48. Oscar Castelnovo, "Alianza para matar," Madres de la Plaza de Mayo website, January–February 2000, <http://www.madres.org/periodico/enefeb00/ elpais/alianza.htm> (January 23, 2004).

Part V

State and Foreign Responses

10

In the Name of the People:
The Possibilities and Limits of a Government
Relying on Public Opinion*

Isidoro Cheresky

The Primacy of Political Consent

Under President Néstor Kirchner, Argentina is in transition. Having abandoned the parameters that guided its economic activity in the 1990s, it is now in the process of redefining its institutional and political form. Although all these changes are interrelated, what is emphasized here is the modification of the political regime to produce a government whose actions depend on public opinion. It is important to note that this analysis is based on events that took place at the beginning of Kirchner's presidential term. Despite the changes that one presumes for the future, the close link between presidential leadership and opinion seems likely to persist, however much it varies in intensity.

For the present, the first steps taken by the new president challenge policies that were dominant not only in the 1990s but from the beginning of the process of democratization in 1983. The spectacular nature of decisions that confront the self-serving agreements and implicit pacts among the traditional parties has provided drama for these reforms.[1]

Do these reforms constitute a basic institutional "refoundation"? Since the debacle that produced the fall of the Alliance government, that term has been used and criticized due to its claims of a regeneration, changes that may be more likely to produce political instability than true reform. Nevertheless, it is correct to assert that we are presently at the dawn of a profound political renovation of institutions, even if there is still debate as to the extent of the changes, as to how much is new and how much continuity there is in what is happening, and as to the conditions needed to keep this beginning from being frustrated.[2]

The focus of this debate is in part the extent to which one perceives discontinuity in the party system and a broad abandonment by citizens of traditional political practices. An additional factor is the degree to which the institutional order emerging is one that removes the centers of corruption and the lack of protection of rights that have constituted vulnerable aspects of Argentine democracy.

For the present, the term "politics" has recovered its focus on the political consent associated with representation, after a long cycle in which the idea of politics as mere administration had spread, fully in keeping with the primacy of the unregulated market as a political model.[3]

The new president has thrown himself into the action of government, broadening the scope for state intervention and regulation, and emphasizing his own personal competence. He has given to political consent the sense of its being an act derived simultaneously from principles for action (or subjective convictions) and from efforts to link it to citizen representation. In so doing, he has pushed to the side special interest accords and negotiations with the traditional political forces including, to a certain point, those with the representatives of his own party and other allied forces. In this way, the weakness derived from his status as an "outsider" in his own party, one who rose to power through atypical elections, is transformed into a positive factor, providing momentum that allows him a considerable margin of political freedom. His utilization of political consent is based on his fairly unrestricted situation as president with greater possibilities to construct the political support that he needs—or that at least is the illusion behind a government like his based on public opinion.

After three months of his control of the presidency, one finds a government under way whose dizzying action transmits the sense of a pronounced change of direction and of a strong inclination to modify institutional bases and customs. The changes in the top leadership of the armed forces and the opening of the possibility of re-establishing judicial responsibility for the illegal repression and violence of the 1970s, the drive to pass judgment on the behavior of members of the Supreme Court, and that to audit the health fund for retirees (known as PAMI) have all been decisions that affect entrenched power as well as the interests and commitments of the traditional political leaders.

The manner in which the negotiation of the foreign debt and relations with international organs of credit and oversight were raised also suggests significant changes in direction that seem likely to endure. The president has established a politically astute relationship with the organs of financial regulation that serve our creditors by managing that the discussion on the refinancing of the debt introduces special concepts of development and the distinction between national and private interests. To the traditional notion (questioned today not only in terms of its justice but also in regard to the suitability of prioritizing the payment of the public debt as a means of regaining the confidence of investors who might serve as the engine for growth) is juxtaposed an alternative more centered on national development. Such development represents a serious effort at paying the debt while maintaining sufficient internal solvency to implement social relief policies and to push economic development with domestic resources. This latter notion supposes that investor confidence—that probably will in any case take time to be regained—can be based on a policy of responsibility and national dignity, one that with time can also be more credible to the world than the classic policy of submission to the supposed mandate of the markets.[4]

The political consent mentioned goes beyond that expected from a government that resulted from presidential elections that were initially marked by skepticism and citizen doubt. As demonstrated by high indices of approval and popularity on the order of 70% to 80% in its first months, the exceptional legitimacy acquired by the government does not seem to be derived from the completion of pre-electoral promises, but is due rather to the execution of unexpected although rapidly popular policies.[5] Perhaps one source of support for the president comes from the sense that his action deals with revisions and decisions in areas that had been considered intractable lest they put at risk price stability, public order, or the possibility of Argentina's successful insertion into the world. This affirmation of democracy seemed to go at hand (using an expression much in vogue even in academic circles) with an acceptance of an "ethic of accountability." Suddenly presidential decisions to seek citizen support and equality before the law with an almost naïve disregard for existing interests enjoy widespread support among those sympathetic with the government's ideological direction, as well as by many of those who are not so.

The claim as to the foundational nature of this period rests on such a consensus about political renovation and a shared republican spirit. For the moment, the variety of affected interests has not generated an equally broad spectrum of opposition, but rather has produced a sense of justice and has awakened the expectation for reforms that strengthen the state of law.

If one considers a context that favors those with exceptional presidential abilities, a parallel can be made with the conditions allowing Carlos Menem the liberty of action that he enjoyed in 1989 upon assuming office after the hyperinflationary shock. The debacle of 2001 for its part generated not only citizen discontent but a broad rejection of earlier experiences and political leaders. It offered conditions supportive of innovation similar to how hyperinflation facilitated Menem's change of policy direction in 1989. The debt default and the immediate consequences of the conversion of savings and debts from dollars into pesos brought the country to a very low point for economic activity and expectations, which in a certain sense provided the government with similar unusual margins of freedom in policy-making.

This reconstitution of political authority based on direct citizen support inaugurated a novel political style. Although it can be compared with traditional populist leadership (where one is alert to the institutional dangers that accompany it), what is certain in this case is that we are not dealing with a mobilized people, a plebiscitary source of power of a multitude meeting in the Plaza de Mayo and supported by a permanent organized apparatus in competition with or to the detriment of democratically organized political parties. Instead, we are talking of a citizenry repeatedly limited to acting in a public space as a surrogate for public opinion. But from the perspective of the functioning of political life and especially of ways for the recreation of legitimacy, changes have become evident.

In the 1980s, the cycle of democratic reconstruction presided over by Raúl Alfonsín was marked by the consolidation of citizen consent organized through two traditional political parties. At its head was presidential authority challenging the power of the interest groups, principally the military but also, to a lesser degree, the unions. The parties were themselves acting as democratic institutions, in part abandoning the historic claim of each as the only legitimate social movement, a situation that had restricted competition between and within the parties. But this late consolidation of the party system went a little against the increasing tendency in contemporary Western societies for the weakening of party identity and, in some cases, for the diminution of participation in public affairs. The inadequate performance of political leaders, especially in the 1990s, would accentuate the potential crisis of representation.[6]

In the 1990s, the presidential authority behind the turn to conservative modernization was personalist by nature, but with one inherited and one new organizational base. The presidential decision dragged Peronism into a changing world, inspired an alliance of the Peronist popular electorate with the world of the businesses reconstituted in the heat of that modernization, and neutralized popular social opposition. Here the Peronist origin of the president and of the leaders in power was decisive. Carlos Menem's authority had social and organizational support, but its durability depended on initial decisions that produced subsequent social and citizen alignments critical for its success.

The Alliance coalition between the Unión Cívica Radical (UCR) and FREPASO in the second half of the 1990s was created under new conditions for leadership popularity. If the Radicals revived amid the enthusiasm of a heterogeneous coalition that promised institutional cleanup and social reform, their majority of opinion tied to any serious organizational support became diluted by governmental incompetence that set the stage for the party's separation from such opinion and the collapse of the coalition.

The initial moments of Néstor Kirchner's administration have been characterized by the formation of a political authority that arose after the electoral process. The novice president could count on the beginnings of such authority provided by the overall respect for elections, something that should not be seen as contradicting the lack of citizen confidence in the political class alluded to earlier.[7] In other words, going beyond the particular circumstances of the electoral process, the president-elect was invested with legality, something that prevented any initial questioning of his authority. One plus that ought to be recognized is that immediately after the first round of voting, Néstor Kirchner became the certain winner in any runoff, favored due to a surge of negative opinion against his major opponent, ex-President Menem. If such a victory could not occur due to Menem's withdrawal from the election process, it impacted the post-electoral political scene. In contrast with the precarious condition of the previous Duhalde government, such formal legitimacy solidified only when government action was begun that managed to address inherited claims and frustrations. We are dealing with representation constructed from the top down, little mediated institutionally or supported by a direct tie between the person of the president and the citizenry. This authority linkage grew in the context of the weakness of institutions, something that explains the fact that the president's popularity generated majority support in Congress[8] and inhibited traditional Mafia-like special interest blackmail-like pressures.[9]

Presidential authority resting on the support of public opinion reestablished presidential capacity to the detriment of the other institutional powers. In the case of the members of the Supreme Court, the presidential call in a radio and televised message for the Chamber of Deputies to begin the impeachment of some Court justices and the denunciation of pressures to which he had been the object effectively inhibited the magistrates and spurred deputies to act differently from positions many of them had taken months earlier. The public appearances of the president have multiplied and his promise to reveal pressures or to denounce obstacles against his taking action has reoccurred. He has been a president who has had influence over the other powers due to the recency of his access to power and to his reformist zeal. This behavior may make sense if one sees it as characteristic of an exceptional situation: a president who accepts as his task a wish to create order from disorder and to weaken the institutional boundaries that shaped the situation that he encountered. This characterization of a presidential action that forged a kind of refoundation was favored by the public perception of institutional corruption and the strong criticism that became prominent with the debacle of the end of 2001. But it has raised questions as to the ultimate distribution of power in the regime and has stirred accusations or suspicion of presidential hegemonic ambitions coming as much from the right as from the left.

This freedom that the president has been enjoying cannot be considered just the traditional post-electoral "honeymoon" of a president-elect. In general, such freedom permits him to go beyond the usual limits in policy in the direction already anticipated; that is, a mandate that the supporters of the new power can be seen to enthuse over and the opponent as having reduced abilities to resist. Instead, the freedom of presidential action generated by the beginnings of the Kirchner order has a different nature since it derives from unexpected actions that gained consensus support not during the elections but only a posteriori. It can be considered that it constitutes a kind of post-electoral government support as a consequence of the mix of factors mentioned, among them the increased preference for Kirchner created between the first and second round of voting that, even in the absence of a runoff, played an important role in his subsequent support. In fact, many citizens consider that they voted for the president even when Menem's withdrawal clearly made this claim impossible.[10]

The unexpected and in a certain sense unusual way in which the resolution of the Argentine crisis can be understood requires a revision of the formulas for democratic consolidation that have been in vogue since the 1980s. For the present it points to personalism as a means of innovation in the face of the discrediting or sclerosis of traditional political organizations. Personalism aids the possibility of an adaptability that permits leaders to more freely construct proposals of a representative nature (unlike the traditional parties that are used to relying on a known tradition) but also supports an arbitrariness that allows a broad opportunity for individual decisions and personal styles to influence the direction of government. Néstor Kirchner certainly had a generic mandate to break with the 1990s, but the essence of such government discontinuity became known only once he was in power, receiving such support only after the elections. If the first measures that he adopted had been announced previously, they probably would not have created the necessary support. It is even possible that they would have aroused a coalition of "prudence and good sense" due to their being considered risky or unviable. We are thus entitled to ask if we are not facing a case of "delegatory democracy," since it is in such presidential discretion that hopes for reconstructing political representation are now placed.[11]

For its part, the presidential system of government has been criticized as an inheritance from the tradition of the caudillo that implied a concentration of power harmful to democratic consolidation; instead, its attenuation or even replacement by a parliamentary regime was considered a requisite for democratic progress in the region. But in the present circumstance, presidentialism appeared as an arrangement that heightens personal use of power and thereby makes political renovation possible. President Kirchner is presumed to be the advocate of a purifying deinstitutionalization: of the Supreme Court and the federal magistrates, of state offices with their entrenched sinecures, of the security forces and the prison system that seem to require outside intervention to reconstruct themselves, and finally in the party system itself, where tendencies for collective self-interest are at least partially restrained by presidential encouragement of extra-party alliances. But will that deinstitutionalization lead to a new institutional pattern or will it evolve in the direction of a plebiscitarian concentration of power? A new institutional arrangement supposes the stabilization of the relations between constitutionally divided powers, as well as granting a deliberative character to the citizens and their use of public space.

We are dealing not only with the conditions that ensure inherent political competition and pluralism in a democratic regime, but also with the viability of the reforms undertaken, the possibility that they have continuity over time.

The program of the Kirchner government has assumed an uneven form in decisive institutional arenas and, to a certain degree, in the economy as well. Such highly personal action has potentially estranged him from the Peronism that supported him in the presidential contest, but within whose ranks degrees of tension regarding presidential acts can be found. Such dissent probably will deprive him of the almost automatic support that he obtained from the ranks of Peronist and center-left deputies once the cycle of provincial elections has concluded in December 2003. In order that the specific decisions produce a new institutionality that includes new practices in officials and citizens, these have to be continued over time. That is to say that the decisions adopted up until now ought to be considered as beginnings, as starts that create a new course,[12] but that will solidify only to the extent that they acquire social support. One way is the uncertain possibility of continued support of opinion and the other the possibility of obtaining an increasing degree of cooperation from other national institutions.

The climate of a new beginning has generated citizen hopes and flexibility and even the propensity for a realignment of the institutional arena, but its future evolution is, nevertheless, problematic.

We know that, in general, support based on public opinion cannot have a lasting character. For this reason it makes sense to pause to consider the characteristics of the present presidential popularity. At the moment, the public opinion favorable to presidential power is not the correlate of a mobilized citizenry that would eventually be able to provide support for its eventual consolidation, but only that of a collective disposition whose external aspects correspond to an expected low degree of citizen activity: the state of opinion regularly shown in surveys, expressions of sympathy when the president is in public, and other virtual expressions of support such as tele- or cyber-voting.

The fluctuation in electoral preferences, the outbreak of street protests marked by banging on pots (cacerolazos) that marked the gap between those governing and those governed, and the omnipresence of public opinion that provides a virtual commentary on the principal themes of the public agenda are other signs of a citizenry that has evolved toward a growing autonomy and, therefore, toward being a decisive factor in public life. In the past this role was monopolized by political and social leaders who acted in the name of consolidated organizations; now the state of opinion has acquired a decisive weight in a society where individuals are not unconditionally but only partially linked to party organizations.

The public space in which opinion is displayed is characterized by the changing nature of the arena in which different actors intervene. The president has sought to use public opinion as support for his first dramatic decisions and as a resource with which to resist the pressure of the entrenched interests. In this way presidential decisions have succeeded in representing pre-existing demands and, more generally, frustrations. This plebiscitarian link has been decisive, but it is more fragile as it requires governing on the basis of already existing opinions or tendencies. With the role of individuals generally more passive, the alignment achieved in the political system in such cases has been characterized as constituting a poorly differentiated mass of citizens.

For the government to gain solid durable public support, it must promote deliberation of opinion. Such support can be achieved if the government formulates strategic plans where its decisions are explained in a way that allows them to be seen as part of its future program. While the impeachment of some members of the Supreme Court has been welcomed by a large majority of people and the new public procedure for replacing those members presented here has also been auspicious, what is unclear are the ideas the government has for the composition of this body and for the entire federal system of justice. If the government has begun a general reformulation that can be justified only as an exception, public argument and debate would be the appropriate means so that this undertaking is not seen as a completely personalistic act. The same can be said for the split between the government and the business lobby. The welcomed criticism of corrupt capitalism, monopolies, and tax evasion ought to be seen in a broader framework of intent about the kind of development and the legality and rights inherent in a stable future.

Using the public space as a forum for deliberation could lead to the formation of a social movement for sustaining the new direction.[13] But such action supposes the government opening itself to the debate of ideas, developing a plurality of actors and voices, and being prepared for corrections in its direction. A government that up until now seems to have selected a format that is oriented more to specific decisions than to a general program needs to recognize that to govern in this way is not only to utilize its electoral mandate—which is weak—but to proceed by modifying its action in terms of its ability to convince as well according to what it is learning from the same public deliberation. To govern by following public opinion, of course, carries with it the temptation for demagoguery as well as the danger of immobilism. In other words, in some cases, to decide on the basis of longer-term power can require one to go against opinion. It is ultimately in public debate where actions taken have to be justified, knowing that it is citizen judgment expressed as electoral decisions that finally will create support for continuity or change.

But institutional support for building power takes various forms. During the various elections of the second half of 2003 we will see if there is an adjustment or a transformation of the party system. At this moment, events confirm the weakness of the parties while Peronism generally maintains or even increases its institutional power, or at least the number of representatives of that label in electoral office. The fluctuation of the vote corresponds to circumstantial evaluation of the political candidates; it does not allow us to predict any basic reconstitution of the traditional political parties nor the possible consolidation of the new political forces that emerged in their first form in the presidential election. The party leaders with more or less solid political support networks according to the case seem to exercise influence but are not perceived to constitute a permanent structure for determining political competition.[14]

President Kirchner's reform project seems to require and at the same time to some extent to foment the decomposition of the traditional parties, especially of Peronism. Nevertheless, the future of such a strategy is doubtful because it would need to count on institutional support; that is, to probably require commitments from legislators and leaders of his party. Part of his efforts to build support has resulted in his involvement in the election campaigns of some of the principal districts. In those provinces where he has been able, he has favored candidates loyal to his project, to the detriment of party unity, favoring a strategy of seeking support from those of similar ideology across party lines (referred to as "transversalidad") with a view to increasing his power. This approach has had a certain degree of effectiveness given its support from the state apparatus.[15] But political support based on public consent coexists with other political approaches, so that the president's capacity to broaden his popularity in institutional power by intervening in other elections is limited.[16]

Peronism that seems to some analysts as the dominant party could be considered as a common political/cultural space lacking any political unity. Carlos Menem had been the de facto president of the Peronist Party, but his sworn enemies were the president, whose actions promoted the deinstitutionalization of the party, and an Eduardo Duhalde committed to maintain party unity only whenever control by Menem's adversaries could be ensured.

It seems certain that the process of political renovation will continue its present wavy path. To deepen the understanding of the transformation under way, it is useful to examine its immediate antecedents.

Presidential Elections with Political Fragmentation: An Unexpected President

The presidential elections of April 27, 2003, were influenced by the crisis of representation that broke out toward the end of the year 2001. Their date was decided irregularly to alleviate the situation of precarious legitimacy of then-serving President Eduardo Duhalde, thereby cutting half a year off his term.[17] The preparatory period was also marked by instability and manipulation. The call for open primaries for all political parties on the same day was set by law, but later was annulled, allowing each party to adopt its own procedures for candidate selection. In the Partido Partido Justicialisthe competition was dominated by the rivalry between ex-President Menem seeking re-election and Eduardo Duhalde. The latter succeeded in controlling the party congress, avoiding the choice of any official candidate, but authorizing the three obvious possibilities to compete as Peronists but without the party's official endorsement.[18]

The Radicals for their part carried out a primary the result of which was delayed for weeks in an endless dispute over the official counting and accusations of fraud that ultimately led to a court order to repeat the election in some provinces.

In this way, the more traditional parties reinforced the poor reputation in which they were held by public opinion and contributed to the pre-electoral climate of public skepticism. The series of changes of election dates and the selection process for the candidates were not the only irregularities. The advancement of the election date itself, the early stepping down of the serving president, and the subsequent extension of the term of the president-to-be all seemed to lack any real basis in law. Many of the most competitive candidates warned of possible fraud during the elections and in the vote count itself, a suspicion strengthened by the seeming equilibrium of support among the various competitors.

As will be seen from various points of view, the electoral situation was without precedent. What was most important was the considerable political fragmentation that for the first time would require the resort to a runoff (or ballotage) to determine the winner. The pre-electoral uncertainty related especially to the degree to which the elections approached and doubt as to their outcome cleared as the result of the campaign.

At this point it is necessary to remember and describe precisely the way in which the pre-electoral scene was dominated by the figure of Carlos Menem. Although he continued being the president of the PJ, his person seemed condemned to political ostracism by a public opinion—especially after the debacle at the end of 2001—that despite its ambivalence (which included nostalgia over the end of economic convertibility) saw him as largely responsible for the economic and institutional collapse. Throughout the year 2002, Carlos Menem returned to the center of the scene, succeeding in reevaluating the "golden nineties" (its first five years in the official myth) in the eyes of opinion. Later he appeared as the candidate with sufficient will to be the best guarantor of governability, even changing the nature of his political promises in a distributive direction that took account of the suffering of a very impoverished society.[19] If in the pre-electoral scene brilliant leadership did not clearly stand out, Carlos Menem managed to emerge with the passage of months from the back of the crowd to place himself at its head. To the extent that his popularity increased among the more working class Peronist electorate, important sectors of the business world saw in him the possibility of reestablishing a complete version of economic opening and deregulation and presumed to reestablish the confidence of the financial world on terms present in the 1990s.

His advance was gradual, with his nucleus of more committed voters grouped together in a situation of obvious volatility, but his progress seemed to have an impenetrable ceiling given that seven of every ten voters stated that in no case would they vote for him. Despite his progress in what pollsters call the "intention to vote," he continued being by far the political leader most disliked. Nevertheless, at the same time, almost half the voters thought Menem eventually would be the winner. One needs to mention the enormous impact of the image of a candidate who boasted of always having won and who seemed dominant. Didn't the fact that a good part of those who expressed hostility to him also saw him as the inevitable winner not reveal the possible fascination that his personality exercised and the eventuality that his camp of partisans would grow even more?

Thus, many political analysts judged his possibilities in terms of the margin he could establish with his closest rival in the first round.[20] The image of Menem was not only that of a winner but one of a decisive leader who had been able to impose his authority or, in other words, had been able to control scenes where he ended up triumphant. Here one notes the case of his swing from populist distributionary politics to conservative modernization upon assuming the presidency in 1989 or the Pact of Olivos that allowed him to seek and to obtain a first reelection.[21]

Table 10.1. Evolution in the Intention to Vote (%)

Candidates	June 2002	December 2002	Election Results April 27, 2003
Menem	7.2	13.8	24.45
Kirchner	4.4	8.1*	22.44
López Murphy	2.6	7.5	16.37
Rodríguez Saá	10.7	15.6	14.41

Source: Mora y Araujo - Ipsos.
* But by January 2003, Kirchner's intention to vote had risen to 16.6%.

From the moment in July 2002 when elections were called, the fluctuation in citizen preferences in surveys was continuous, although the scene would be dominated by low interest that persisted until a little before the elections when the possibility of system renovation seemed to gain support. The fragmentation among various candidates persisted, with the majority indifferent to traditional party ties or divided by party splits,[22] where no leaders emerged clearly dominant. But the relative position of the candidates varied over time.

Elisa Carrió, who had high indices of popularity after her break with Radicalism, headed the intention to vote at the time of calling elections. Her threat not to run if all elected office holders didn't agree to face the voters that she posed at various moments and an erratic election campaign led her support to decline but not as much as some studies of opinion predicted. Adolfo Rodríguez Saá, who at moments led in the polls, also slipped to the back of the pack. The other competitors who rose in the preferences were each in his own way symptomatic of a political system in the context of a crisis of representation.

Menem as was indicated emerged from a marginal position to become the Peronist candidate par excellence. His image as a strong leader counted in importance where order is a valued good and where the image of force being imposed can be a factor in social pacification. The idea that some voters would lean toward a winner simply to reinforce the dominant force may seem the result of rather elementary reasoning, but in the context of indecision about whom to vote for, this is likely to some extent. Among the most vulnerable groups, this image seems to have found a reply, and the hectoring of the candidate with his strident denunciation of poverty and insecurity appears to have reinforced it. As ex-president for almost half a decade, he benefited from a national appeal. Winning in twelve provinces, he was the candidate with the widest vote geographically in an election not very nationally uniform.

In respect to its candidate choice, Peronism presented a curious case illustrating its divisions. Menem consolidated himself as its popular leader since he was the candidate best known to the party faithful. His adversary President Eduardo Duhalde preferred not to get involved with the party's rank and file in terms of the selection of its presidential candidate, despite controlling the most powerful party machine—that of Buenos Aires Province. Confident of change, Duhalde believed that a Peronist candidate nominated by him would win with the support of independent voters.[23] Furthermore, as was seen, by giving legal character to a decision that deprived all the Peronist candidates of the internal struggle and the possibility to compete for the party label in a party primary, he gained an ample majority in the party congress where he also lined up delegates from the interior of the country. In fact, the party structure in many provinces divided, while in others, the Peronist leaders opted to avoid making a choice.

While the Peronist fight decisively marked the electoral process, can one see the presidential elections as limited to describing an internal struggle of Peronism?

As Menem installed himself on the public scene in the unexpected way indicated, President Duhalde (benefited throughout 2002 but especially in its second semester by a more favorable economic and international situation) tried to find an alternative candidate to his adversary, the ex-president. Like other searches,[24] this one did not correspond to any ideological criterion despite the fact that from the beginning of his time in office, Duhalde had defined himself in terms of a "change of the economic model" from speculation to production, consistent with his claimed link to historic Peronism. Given his moderate reputation as a Peronist, Carlos Reuteman, the governor of Santa Fe, seemed for a moment an apt fit; later, Juan Carlos de la Sota launched his candidacy with official support without ever finding much support from the public. These candidates, of orthodox preferences in the economic area and of conventional political position, did not fit the project for resounding political renovation that enthused Eduardo Duhalde three months prior to the elections. He gave his support to the traditionally headstrong governor of Santa Cruz Province, Néstor Kirchner.

The degree of political difference of the Peronist enemies Menem and

Duhalde was in fact subsumed by pragmatism as one and then the other changed his orientation seeking to maintain his relative power.

Using varied resources, Néstor Kirchner shaped his public presence so as to gain the voter support necessary to meet the electoral challenge. At the beginning, before the call for elections, he laboriously constructed a leadership of popularity using traditional resources, linking together dissident Peronist leaders with activists of a different origin seeking to build a progressive group that would support his candidacy. His Peronist identity was relative, since he saw that in Peronism there were contradictory ideological currents[25] while his goal was to construct a broad front made up of individuals of different origins.[26]

His project in the initial months of the campaign was really oriented to create a national organization for the next elections, those of 2007. Although he appeared as a Peronist pre-candidate, his predilection was not to build a party faction. If his candidacy had had to face a party primary, he probably would not have run, since the conditions that he proposed for such an eventuality were unacceptable to the other competitors.[27]

When Duhalde agreed to support him, making his decision public in January 2003, Kirchner as a candidate jumped in the polls, emerging as one of the favorites with support consistent with that needed to reach the runoff. In a scene where the vote was fragmented, his campaign targeted potential non-Menem voters and non-Peronists of the center-left, but its chances would depend on his capacity to differentiate his candidacy in the end. Its possibilities were the result of a selection process where he was chosen largely by default. Immediately after becoming the candidate of the Duhalde administration, his chances of success increased in the eyes of all; to the extent that they resulted from the support of the incumbent president, a mass of new resources could be added to the limited amount that Kirchner had had until then.

His campaign was mediocre, in part affected by the difficulty in adapting to his new position. Having been a critic of the administration, he now to a great extent became the candidate of continuity. By becoming Duhalde's anti-Menem player, he sharply felt the tension between, on the one hand, winning over a hesitant Peronist electorate and, on the other, convincing the independent middle sectors. His traditional style of campaigning oriented to meetings in small auditoriums, his initial plan to build support aimed at future elections, and his hesitancy up until a little before the elections to appear on the principal television programs all contributed to these problems. Kirchner really did not come over in the election campaign as a strong leader; additional measures were needed to strengthen his image. To build credibility with the urban middle sectors, he counted on Daniel Scioli as his running mate and especially on the announcement thatEconomics Minister Lavagna would continue in the government should Kirchner win. This last promise in particular provided a degree of certainty as to the candidate's intentions and added a modicum of popularity in a context in which that item was scarce.[28]

This clarification of Kirchner's unadorned message was necessary. He had produced a classic campaign protesting the unmet needs of the middle and popular sectors and designating monopoly capital as the enemy. But above all he tried to embody citizen frustration, promising to be an alternative to the "horrors of the past." The support of an economics minister who had represented a position somewhat less submissive to the IMF, but who on the other hand had re-established certain basic economic equilibria (even some resumption of growth) and who had proposed to re-establish economic ties with the world allowed the candidate to project a position that he liked to call more national and popular. In so doing, Kirchner could differentiate himself from other candidates who touched on the same theme, but who aroused fears of the populist policies resisted by the middle sectors.

Nevertheless, in the final stage of the campaign, the scene experienced significant changes. On the one hand, Menem's growth in support suggested a hard battle for the Peronist electorate to avoid giving the ex-President an important advantage in a runoff should he come out ahead in the first round. On the other hand, Ricardo López Murphy surprised everyone in the last two or three weeks by his dramatic rise in voter preference, leading some to speculate on the possibility that this candidate from the back of the pack might displace Kirchner from the second-place finish he sought. López Murphy had managed to transmit an image of authority and seriousness that made him the best representative of the urban discontent that had exploded a little more than a year earlier. The growth of his support among urban groups would allow him to obtain a considerable vote in the Federal Capital as well as in other urban areas.[29] Despite his deserved reputation as an orthodox economist who promised to continue the policies of the so-called Washington Consensus, he won support among those more open to the establishment of legal order and the fight against corruption. Identified as the non-Peronist candidate most likely to be in the runoff, he aroused the part of the electorate sensitized to that position. However, the reputation for inflexibility that he cultivated with the symbol of the bulldog, together with his disposition not to promise important public policies for dealing with social suffering, limited such a growth of popularity among moderate and progressive sectors of the electorate that otherwise regarded him sympathetically.

The fact is that toward the end of the campaign, an element of uncertainty and the perception—whether realistic or not—that Carlos Menem might regain power activated civic interest and expectations. In this context, a change in Kirchner's image as candidate emerged from a different source, from inside the Peronist machine in the province of Buenos Aires. Duhalde and his circle believed that, given the circumstances, the key to success was Kirchner gaining a minimum advantage of 5% over his opponent in the province, which would require carrying the Greater Buenos Aires region. For this they put pressure on a considerable number of hesitant mayors by building on the popularity of local leaders who appeared together with the presidential candidate in posters while activists were encouraged to solicit votes door to door.

Table 10.2. Vote Shift from Previous Presidential Election
(Column %)

	1999 Choice				
	PJ*	Alliance*	AR*	Blank	Spoiled
2003 Choice:					
Menem	42.8	9.1	17.7	14.5	10.1
Kirchner	34.1	25.2	11.3	24.4	33.3
López Murphy	4.5	20.7	45.2	12.2	21.2
Rodríguez Saá	11.9	9.5	4.8	8.4	9.1

Source: CEOP.
* PJ = Peronist Party; Alliance = Radicals and FREPASO; AR = Action for the Republic with Domingo Cavallo.

Unlike the typical presidential campaign dynamic, where influence flows from top to bottom, the strategy in this election made use of clientelist and particularist resources that doubtlessly influenced the results achieved by Kirchner.

Despite the instability of the last two weeks of the campaign, the vote results of the first round showed that no clear leader had emerged; there was little difference between the top two finishers, whose joint total was less than half (46.69%) of the valid vote cast. Until the final moment, there had been high electoral volatility that gave great weight to last-minute decisions,[30] as well as to the behavior of clientelist networks that, even if generally playing a marginal role, may have been decisive for Kirchner, the administration's candidate. The absence of any strong leader had its effect on the vote regionally where there was no national-level overall tendency. Rodríguez Saá and Kirchner had their zones of influence near the provinces where each had been governor. If Menem's vote was more nationally uniform, his epicenter of popularity was also his province of origin.

This pattern of fragmentation illustrates the semi-disappearance of the traditional axes of cleavage resulting in a pluralism based on personalities, many of which had experienced no major political responsibility in the past. The Radical Civic Union won an insignificant vote. In contrast, of course, one notes Peronism's collective growth with the multiplication of its candidates.

Table 10.3. Rate and Type of Electoral Participation (%)

Elections	2003 (Pres.)	2001 (Congress)	1999 (Pres.)
Voter Turnout	78.22	75.47	82.28
Valid Votes	97.28	76.02	95.49
Blank Votes	0.99	10.76	3.57
Spoiled Votes	1.73	13.23	0.94

With the results of the first round known, a new situation was created where the dominant characteristic exhibited in earlier months reemerged. The overwhelming rejection of Carlos Menem's candidacy foretold the triumph of a sweeping negative vote that would favor the other candidate making it to a runoff, Néstor Kirchner. The impotence in bargaining of the losing candidates who sought to intervene by influencing the vote of their supporters in the time between the two rounds illustrated as much the limits of personalist leadership as the force of the anti-Menem wave.[31]

The realization of the predicted outcome was frustrated when Carlos Menem gave up in the face of his certain loss, but not without previously trying to delegitimize the election outcome with charges of fraud that rebounded against him.

Kirchner thus gained the presidency through a process of fortuitous circumstances and as the bearer more of a negative vote than of a positive mandate. In this sense, Néstor Kirchner emerged as an unexpected president, the product of circumstances very different from those that used to characterize the selection of leaders in institutionalized democracies. Consequently, political analysts predicted that his legitimacy would be weak depending on the Peronist party apparatus, especially that in the province of Buenos Aires. Nevertheless, the crisis of representation seemed reduced given that if there were signs that the election loyalties were very special, what is certain is that voter participation was notable and positive even if the abstention rate was higher than in other presidential elections.

Conclusions

(1) The 2003 presidential elections and the subsequent course of political life confirm that significant changes are occurring, including the fragmentation of the political parties and possibly the marginalizing of some of these. Peronism persists as a political identity but instead of being seen as one party or even one political movement, it ought to be considered as a political space or tradition, a territory contested by rival and not very reconcilable political projects.

The fluctuation and volatility of the vote confirm citizen disaffection in respect to political identities, especially traditional ones, and the still-fragile linkages with personalist leadership.

This evolution of political life seems to suggest a true change and not just a crisis whose resolution would bring us back to a political system of the old type.

(2) The political dynamic seems to be characterized by "negativity," by the censure of an often personalist government act or project, and, in the case of the cacerolazo demonstrations, by the rejection of the politicians that seems to dominate the political arena. That feature causes one to doubt not only the survival of the traditional divisions (Peronism, Radicalism), but even others of more recent impact in national political life (left versus right), introducing an element of fluidity and uncertainty to politics.

(3) Popularity-based leadership has provided the bases for political support and the form of political competition. On this point, one must point out that such leadership is usually fragile and consequently does not always evolve into an established political force, although in all cases it at least promotes a minimum party structure.

Personalist leadership has shown a much greater capacity for adoption to political change and a greater aptitude to produce representative ties than traditional party organizations. But the fragility of this type of popularity and the absence of minimum organizational structures generates an instability that affects the whole of the institutional system.

A major unresolved question relates to the future relation to be established between leaders based on popularity and political parties.

(4) Under the conditions of fluidity noted, elections have become more than ever the principal democratic mechanism. As such, the legislation that regulates elections and that which defines representation, as well as the existence of public regulatory organs that limit manipulation, are basic requirements; they ought to be considered fundamental supports of the republican edifice.

(5) The citizens have contributed to the renovation of public life due to the weight of their eventual mobilization and especially due to their dominant autonomy. But the expectation of more active participation that might have arisen with the cacerolazo mass protests has been given the lie. Nor were they a significant reinforcement of civil society as the multiplication of neighborhood assemblies in their moment led one to expect. The present citizen is central in conditioning the acts of the politicians in a new way, but as a control over the course of public matters and as the expression of that through regular opinion polls.

(6) After the political cycle dominated by the idea of politics as mere administration reflecting rigid policies marked by economic determinism, the present government's approach to political consent opens new possible options for government and political actors. Although shifting between political decision-making and the restrictions derived from internal and international economic conditions is part of political analysis, it seems clear that the political studies of the past decade were strongly influenced by a presumption about the prerequisites for governability that considerably limited critical and independent analysis.

(7) Given the present crisis of party democracy, a personalist government based on public opinion like that of President Kirchner can obtain broad liberty of action in the short term. But its prospects can narrow if its popularity is not converted into formal institutional resources. In other words, the possibilities of a government relying exclusively on public opinion within a democratic regime ought to be set aside.

(8) The relation of a government with opinion and public space can include a range of possibilities where the consequences between one and another can be substantial for the political future. For the moment, the present government has turned to public opinion essentially in search of support, brandishing this tie as a final resource against special interest pressure. Another type of support would

derive from cultivating public debate through laying out the government's plans on its strategy and the public unfolding of its arguments. Seeking to persuade and exposing oneself to criticism can provide one with a public forum more likely to provide support for the government's program. But above all, such an idea can promote a public policy process that permits controls on government action as well as that of all political actors. From this perspective, to do so supposes improving decisions by submitting them to public examination, altering them in tune with deliberation, and implementing them when social conditions provide the means.

Notes

* Translated by Edward Epstein. This chapter was finished in September 2003.

1. One should not ignore the fact that earlier presidential administrations broke special interest arrangements. Alfonsín gained power denouncing a "military–trade union pact" and shook up the relation of the state with the military by promoting the trial of the military junta members responsible for political and humanitarian crimes. Menem, in his case, distanced himself from his pre-election promises, the tradition of his own party, and the union interests that brought him to power to promote a policy of conservative modernization. Once in power, he constructed an implicit coalition between the major beneficiaries of the new policy and the worst-off social sectors supporting Peronism.

2. See especially Marcos Novaro, *El derrumbe político en el ocaso de la convertibilidad* (Buenos Aires: Norma, 2002) and *Continuidades y discontinuidades en la crisis argentina* (Buenos Aires: FLACSO, mimeo, 2003).

3. Pierre Rosanvallon (2003) comments that the idea of the market from its initial formulation by Adam Smith has had the pretension of being a political model and not just an economic category. The idea of the market as a political formula claims that need and interest themselves regulate relations among men. "The basic consequence of this conception consists in the broad rejection of what is political." Rosanvallon, *Por una historia conceptual de lo político* (Buenos Aires: Fondo de Cultura Económica, 2003).

4. The ex–Vice President of the World Bank and Nobel Laureate in Economics Joseph Stiglitz was asked why the IMF had not adequately aided those countries that fell into default. The question related to the ideological position whereby undermining the sanctity of contracts in default would contribute to the weakening of capitalism. The author replied that risk of bankruptcy is an unwritten part of every contract and that its treatment in interstate relations ought to be seen as it is among individuals. In addition, he maintained that states are also obliged by a social contract that requires the provision of basic economic and social protection for their citizens. From this perspective, the IMF is an institution that has promoted policies that favor creditors, as opposed to what was its original purpose. The September 2003 agreement signed between the Argentine government and the IMF seemed to suggest a new stage in the relation of debtor countries with that organization. The conditions established there require the considerable effort of a 3% fiscal surplus over primary expenditures. Although other limits were left out by the international organization, Argentine recovery would take time. At any rate, the agreement provided the means for the re-establishment of dignity balanced with the requirements of a democratic society. This was illustrated by the unusual tone of the letter

sent by Horst Köhler, the IMF president, to the Argentine head of state: "I praise the announcement of the economic plan put together by President Kirchner. That plan is aimed at reestablishing economic growth and reducing poverty" (*La Nación*, September 11, 2003). It could be that the firm position of Argentina in the negotiation of the agreement had contributed to the change of direction in the international requirements for developing countries. Joseph Stiglitz, *El malestar en la globalización* (Buenos Aires: Taurus, 2002).

5. One can generally state that the government's course of action was unexpected. Kirchner's promises during the election campaign were general and could not refer essentially to the institutional aspects that are the first things that the government faced. Speculation prior to his assumption of the presidential office dealt with the weak original legitimacy derived from his low electoral support (for the most part borrowed) in the first round of the presidential elections—22.44% of the vote—that allowed Néstor Kirchner to reach second place and gave him the possibility of competing in the runoff. People then speculated about what political alliances would be able to strengthen his presidential capacity, especially about what would be his degree of dependence on the presumed power behind the throne, Eduardo Duhalde. From the first moment, Néstor Kirchner acted with a considerable degree of autonomy, publicly establishing a political style characterized by the full weight of his authority and seeking confrontation. But the most unexpected aspect of government action referred especially to the scope of what was politically possible as determined by the main actors and even more so by citizen expectations. Enthusiasm for the conservative modernization of the 1990s had diminished, providing room for unanticipated discontent and frustration; at the same time, however, the urban explosion and citizen hyperactivism visible for some months from the end of 2001 gave way to distrust and caution. The results of the mobilization for human rights continued to enjoy majority support, as did denunciations of corruption. But the extent of problems was such and the fall in living condition so large that the expectations of what any government could do beyond prudent negotiation with the world of credit were few. The dizzying action of the government took everyone in some sense by surprise. Its firmness in its dealings with the military, the unions, and the business world surprised both the leftist and rightist oppositions that were prepared to criticize the administration for the "pragmatic deals" often attributed to Peronist governments.

6. Bernard Manin, in *Los principios del gobierno representivo* (Madrid: Alianza, 1998), suggests that the disaffection with political parties and the increasing citizen autonomy, as well as the dissolution of socio-economic divisions that seemed the basis of political identity, have caused what he calls a metamorphosis of representation. With the end of party-dominated democracy, greater citizen autonomy in reference to party support would produce a different kind of representation. Now representation might be contingent, changing, more tied to the images of leaders gained from television and the other media with greater independence of party practices and even of political tradition. Certainly, even in the context of a democracy by opinion or by audience, one sees a genuine crisis of representation such as that noted in Argentina from the legislative elections of October 2001 with its "negative voting" that found its most eloquent expression in the "cacerolazo" demonstrations.

I use the term "crisis of representation" to refer to the crisis of party representation and the lack of confidence in their leadership that seems to persist, as I argue in this essay.

7. The negative vote in the legislative elections of October 2001 as much as the

urban protest of the cacerolazo have both had an element of respect for legality and even of a claim for political renovation through legal means; in no moment did one see any extra-institutional authoritarian leadership.

8. The so-called Talcahuano group of legislators loyal to the president does not exceed some twenty members. If Congress provided a majority vote for presidential initiatives, some of which at least partially undid earlier legislative votes, it was thanks to the realignment of the Peronist bloc in particular without doubt reflecting the force of presidential popularity. The most notable votes have been those that led to the impeachment of controversial members of the Supreme Court and the one that authorized the takeover of PAMI amid the protests of its users and the replacement of its directors and that which nullified the Due Obedience and End Point laws.

9. The Supreme Court saw itself restrained from seeking to cause problems for the presidential program in terms of undercutting the offensive to change its membership from the president. It desisted from issuing a holding ordering the dollarization of bank deposits, as had been threatened if impeachment against its members proceeded. Despite a so-called automatic majority hostile to the Kirchner government on these matters, it did not dare to act given conditions so unfavorable in public opinion.

10. A survey by Enrique Bollati and Associates carried out in Mendoza Province and published in *Diario Los Andes* of August 31 illustrates this imagined vote. In the presidential elections in that province, Adolfo Rodríguez Saá actually took first place with 36.68% of the vote, Carlos Menem third with 19.13%, and Néstor Kirchner only fourth with 9.71%. But of those interviewed in the survey, a plurality of 27.6% claimed that they had voted for Kirchner, a second place of 24.5% said that they voted for Rodríguez Saá, with Carlos Menem supposedly in fourth place with 8.4%. Of those surveyed, 76.9% had a positive image of the president's program and 58.6% said they would vote for him if elections occurred at the time they were interviewed.

11. See Guillermo O'Donnell's "delegatory democracy" in *Contrapuntos: Ensayos escogidos sobre autoritarismo y democracia* (Buenos Aires: Paidós, 1997), 287–304.

12. Hannah Arendt in *On Revolution* (The Viking Press, 1963) and *¿Qué es la política?* (Barcelona: Paidós, 1997).

13. Perhaps not as a social movement of effective mobilization in the public sphere as happened in the 1970s with the "new social movements," but as a movement of opinion with exponents, intellectuals, and some degree of group life.

14. The case of the two main districts, the province of Buenos Aires and the Federal Capital, illustrates these changes. In the Federal Capital, one sees a real decay of the political parties amid a varied pre-electoral scene with diverse elements of a coalitional nature. Aníbal Ibarra, the outgoing head of government seeking re-election, was at the local level trying to take advantage of the popularity of President Kirchner. With other national leaders, he was here seeking the vote of the center-left, on the presumption that the vote would be defined according to preferences previously expressed nationally. His principal challenger, Mauricio Macri, who comfortably led the majority of polls before the presidential elections created new alignments, emphasized a municipal program and criticism of Ibarra but at the same time organized a ticket that put together leaders and officials from both traditional parties. Both contenders sacrificed nominations for national deputies, giving in to the wishes of the different political factions that had formed, while of course retaining the local leadership and placing some of their own followers among the group of candidates for municipal council. Furthermore, Ibarra as much as Macri agreed to be part of the tickets of various groups for national or municipal legislative

positions. The candidacies of Patricia Bullrich and Luis Zamora corresponded to other patterns. The former sought to inherit the ideologically heterogeneous vote united in behalf of political renovation and public morality associated with the candidacy of Ricardo López Murphy. In respect to the former Trotskyist legislator, his goal was to represent a deliberative alternative in the legislature, something new in relation to the traditional heavy program of the mini-parties of the left. In the legislative elections of 2001, Zamora had received sociologically diverse, widespread sympathy because he was seen throughout the metropolitan region as representing the image of someone who was the opposite of the corrupt politician, an image broader than what was suggested by his ideology or even his policy proposals. In his moment, he was a kind of alternative version of the protest vote whose principal channel had been spoiled or blank ballots or abstention. But the political capital of sympathy of the Bullrich and Zamora groups had been eroded by the actions of the Kirchner government that for the moment provided responses to the majority of those demands. The president himself supported Ibarra's candidacy and placed some of his few original supporters from the Capital on Ibarra's ticket.

In the province of Buenos Aires, some of the characteristics of the presidential election were maintained since the main candidates for governor all competed as Peronists. The triumph of the official ticket for governor and legislators was overwhelming, given a variety of opposition tickets that split over half the vote cast, a sign of a high degree of political fragmentation. The losing tickets of a conservative Peronist origin identified with the crime issue and insensitive to the rule of law received a vote less than predicted, far less than that of the official ticket.

In both districts, a high percentage of absenteeism (and in the province of Buenos Aires, an important number of blank votes) suggested the reappearance of a significant body of voter disaffection.

15. The president's program had had only limited impact on a center-left divided and lacking in goals after the frustrating experience of FREPASO and the Alliance.

16. Presidential support for candidates had some influence but not comparable to his great popularity. In the same sense, his ability to place his loyalists on party tickets is also limited by the weight of the traditional machines as well as by the absence in many cases of such loyalists in a strict sense.

17. After the repression of a piquetero demonstration produced two deaths on June 26, 2002, the president decided to cut his term by almost seven months, promising to give up power on May 25. At first, the first round was called for March 30, 2003, but it was later postponed until April 27, allowing a runoff for May 18.

18. With the annulling of the law that required open primary elections on the same day for all parties that had more than one nominee, Peronism found itself with the dilemma of how to set a procedure for resolving its differences. Duhalde wanted an open primary, while Menem sought that only formal members could vote. The party was on the edge of a split and in effect the sides divided, including the legislative delegation. As a way of linking the high degree of divisiveness with the search for preserving the Peronist vote, they thought of using a version of the "ley de lemas" that would allow for the resolution of the dispute between the Peronist candidates in the general election where that Peronist with the most votes would be credited with the vote cast collectively for all of the party's nominees. Nevertheless, a procedure so openly different from what was established in the Constitution would produce objections, something seen as dangerous in the context of political and institutional crisis. Duhalde, who had a majority in the party congress, had the primaries set for February 2003 waived, as well as authorizing each of the different party candidates to run directly in the general election. This situation

with various Peronist candidates competing in the same election led some analysts to consider the total of the votes obtained by them all as the Peronist vote. But can one truthfully believe that such electoral resources would unite around whichever Peronist candidate, in case one was to compete in the runoff with a non-Peronist?

19. Parallel to the political change announced by Eduardo Duhalde in February 2003 when he decided on the nomination of Kirchner as the official government candidate, Carlos Menem embarked on a project to modify his image that continued though the end of the campaign. He renovated and rejuvenated his immediate staff and abandoned his promise for the return of currency convertibility, adopting a more heterodox economic image. This culminated with the introduction of Carlos Melconian as his principal economic advisor and with certain promises of fairer economic distribution that not all his Peronist competitors dared to make. But his change of image that included a vague self-criticism culminated with the promise to fight corruption, something that would be carried out in case of his victory through an investigation by Transparency International.

20. Menem's advisors considered that if he was ahead by five to seven points over the second-place finisher in the first round, this would make him appear as the unbeatable candidate and would ensure him victory in the runoff.

21. What is certain is that his effort to get whatever he wanted had reached an unsolvable limit when he sought to obtain a second reelection.

22. One view that puts the crisis of the party system into perspective tends to see Carlos Menem, Néstor Kirchner, and Adolfo Rodríguez Saá as equally Peronists and that Elisa Carrió and Ricardo López Murphy ought to be seen as parts of the Radical family.

23. A national CEOP (Centro de Estudios de la Opinión Pública) survey in November 2002 suggested that Carlos Menem would win a party primary if only registered members voted but would not maintain his lead if anyone could vote there, but that candidates linked to Eduardo Duhalde would have no chance:

	Members Only (%)	Open Primary (%)
Rodríguez Saá	32.3	31.3
Menem	41.7	29.4
Kirchner	10.2	20.4
De la Sota	12.6	12.6

24. After the resignation of Remes Lenicov as economics minister, Duhalde was attracted to various alternatives, including Guillermo Calvo, Carlos Melconian, and Alieto Guadagni, all of a decidedly different stripe from Roberto Lavagna, a heterodox economist advocating tough bargaining with the IMF.

25. Referring to the power vacuum created by the resignation of Fernando de la Rúa, Kirchner stated, "The only thing found in Peronism was a formal legal unity, because in it one found openly contradictory, mutually exclusive factions." Néstor Kirchner and Torcuato Di Tella, *Después del derrumbe* (Buenos Aires: Galerna, 2003).

26. Referring to his own prior experience as provincial governor, he argued, "In my government there [were] leaders from all over the political spectrum . . . we emphasize[d] the coalitional nature of Peronism, locating ourselves not in the party but in Santa Cruz," where this coalition was open "to the contributions of honest leaders of the center left and center right" (Kirchner and Di Tella, *Después del derrumbe*).

27. Kirchner argued, "Consequently, when I was asked if I would compete inside or outside of the Peronist Party structure, I told them that I would enter the party primary only if all Peronism agreed on a common program that the winner would defend. But Menem had a completely different position from ours!" (Kirchner and Di Tella, *Después del derrumbe*).

28. According to a poll by Artemio López at that moment, Roberto Lavagna re-

ceived a positive image from 24.4% of those surveyed, and 36% wanted him to continue in the government. Such popular support was seen as decisive at the time.

29. López Murphy won the city of Buenos Aires with 28.85% of the vote, an area where the candidate of ARI, Elisa Carrió, had beeen thought likely to win. As the candidate of the new party, Recrear, he came in second in Mendoza and Córdoba.

30. According to the Centro de Estudios de la Opinión Pública (CEOP), 30% of the voters made their choice at the last minute.

31. More recently, Luis Zamora's call to vote blank or to spoil one's ballot in the runoff of the elections for head of government of the City of Buenos Aires since the candidates remaining would just be "more of the same" was not followed. This was despite the presumption that the voters appealed to belong to an element more critical of political leaders and institutions.

11

The Argentine Political Crisis and Necessary Institutional Reform*

Juan Abal Medina[1]

Introduction

At the beginning of the 1980s, the countries of Latin America had to face the major challenge of reconstructing their former democracies in especially unfavorable economic circumstances. At that time, "democracy" seemed to be the magical solution to all the problems that burdened Latin American societies. An incessant debate took place among the studies of such transitions with the goal of discovering the best institutional alternatives for these new conditions. Interesting schemes were thus created, with elements imported from central countries that might at that moment serve to provide governability and democratic stability.

With the passage of time in Argentina, governments progressively saw their administrative capacity reduced, given an increasingly sharp and unmanageable economic crisis. Institutional political variables were soon replaced by what was needed for economic adjustment, shifting from the goal of deepening the quality of democracy to a new environment dominated by discussions that emphasized the need to reduce the size of an oversized state so as to balance fiscal accounts. Arguments about "political expenditure" dominated the center of debate, limiting possible modification of institutional design to what was related to cost factors, to the detriment of representivity.

Today, twenty years after the return of democracy, many of the problems of quality and efficiency of Argentine institutions posed in 1983 not only remain unresolved, but have worsened. Thus, one of the most notable features of our time is the solid consensus about the critical situation that our political institutions are going through. This broad consensus shared by social, political, and economic leaders as well as academic analysts derives from the crisis of late 2001/early 2002, the nadir of a long process in the declining popular legitimacy of Argentine democratic institutions affected by the notable size of the economic crisis.

If the public confidence obtained today by President Néstor Kirchner clearly has reduced the harmful effects of the crisis, it has not resolved them. Since his coming to power in May 2003, the new president has been implementing a body of measures tending to resolve various problems affecting society, measures that re-legitimized executive power but that, nevertheless, have not really improved the image of the political system as a whole. Thus, the public image of political parties and the legislature remains strongly negative and distrust of the courts and security forces continues, as does discontent with election procedures and their political consequences.

Perhaps more importantly, the same public optimism inspired by the policies of the new president requires that reform policies be rapidly implemented that would improve the nation's institutional design and durability, which, in turn, would institutionalize these gains over the long term, independent of the political wishes of those who momentarily hold government office.

We know that the crisis we are going through is not just institutional in nature, and it would be an unwise simplification to suggest that a single application of reforms would directly improve the quality of our democracy. Institutions provide an arena for action with rules of order that encourage or discourage one type of behavior over another but in no case constitute the only cause of such phenomena.

We have seen that defective institutional design can be overcome by the determination of political actors. But resolution of the reoccurring institutional crisis in the long term undoubtedly requires introducing modifications capable of consolidating such change over time. In this sense, no integral solution of the crisis is conceivable without important modifications in the institutions of representation and governance.

What Crisis?

The crisis that manifested itself with all its force in December 2001 includes a broad variety of phenomena. It was without doubt the final phase of the economic model generally associated with the Convertibility Law and so-called "neo-liberal" policies stressing the reduction of the role of the state in both size and economic functions.

The crisis was also the direct consequence of a social situation characterized by the growing impoverishment of various sectors of the population and the strong increase in income inequalities that worsened in the 1990s but had its origins in the mid-1970s, specifically during the last military dictatorship.

It is sufficient to take into account indicators illustrating the critical socio-economic situation we are describing. According to the latest PNUD Report on Human Development (2002), the percentage of the population lacking basic necessities increased to 23.8% in 2002; those beneath the poverty line doubled in the 1995–2002 period, to 53.3% of the population; and income inequality went steadily upward. At the same time, the Gross Domestic Product (in dollars) fell by 11% in 2002 (World Bank 2002), while income per capita during that time fell even more (PNUD 2002).

Another datum that allows us to flesh out this tragic account is the increase in open unemployment, from 6.1% in 1985 to 17.4% in 2001.[2] The situation is even worse if we take into consideration disparities between the different Argentine provinces. While 23.8% of the population on average lacked basic necessities in 2002, in the provinces of Chaco and Formosa that figure rose to almost 39%.

The crisis itself was the product of a long process of growing public disenchantment and weariness with how the political system functioned. After experiencing the political euphoria that the end of the military dictatorship in 1983 introduced, Argentines gradually lost confidence in all democratic political institutions. The process went through distinct phases, beginning with the alienation and disengagement of citizens from politics, then disaffection and annoyance, and finally anger and indignation.[3] Empirical signs of this process are shown by the fall in voter participation in one election after another (from 86.04% of eligible voters in 1983 to 78.22% in 2003), by the persistent decline in public confidence in political parties (from 20% in 1996 to 14% in 2002), in the legislature (from 27% in 1996 to 23% in 2002), in the judiciary (from 33% in 1996 to 25% in 2002), and obviously including the traumatic episode of the election of a new congress in 2001 (where blank and spoiled votes reached 21.1% and 27.1%, respectively, of the vote cast, and abstentionism rose to above average levels).[4] This situation reached its culmination with the spontaneous public protests of December 19 and 20, 2001, that precipitated the fall of President Fernando de la Rúa.

These facts reflect, in great measure, the inability of traditional representative institutions to meet the needs of society, leading social sectors to openly confront the state, moving away from the institutional channels that were seen to be totally unresponsive. It ought to be pointed out that up through about February 2002, an important part of the population preferred to express themselves directly through public protests such as cacerolazo demonstrators banging on pots and pans and street blockages by piqueteros and protestors rather than by participating in political parties (PNUD 2002).

The Political Crisis

Without trying to tackle the entirety of a political crisis as complex as the one Argentina has gone through, we can say that the negative views of citizens toward the overall functioning of the democratic political system revolve around three major interrelated concepts: the lack of political responsiveness, the self-centered nature of politicians, and corruption.

By lack of political responsiveness, we mean the public perception that the political system is incapable of improving the living conditions of the population. We refer here to a little-explored aspect of political party governance, that is, to the behavior of parties when they occupy formal positions in the state.[5] The public perception is that the various political parties that have governed have failed at even minimally satisfying the demands that got them elected. Here the failure of political organizations to convert societal demands and electoral programs into public policies remains publicly visible.[6] This interpretation is supported by any indicator one might select for the evaluation of government performance over these twenty years of democracy.[7]

Political self-centeredness refers to the public belief that the politicians concern themselves only with their own personal affairs, that is, those activities that offer greater power for themselves, while ignoring the issues that preoccupy the average citizen. Although the effect of this common perception by citizens is debatable (since here there is nothing to indicate that Argentine politicians are on this point very different from those elsewhere), what is certain is that this perception seems to reflect something similar to the lack of political responsiveness that we pointed to above, and the equally obvious existence of corrupt or clientelist practices that we will describe below. These political defects reached a degree that gravely harmed and put into question democratic legitimacy. In a like manner, the strongly negative image citizens have about the results of the inter-party deals or pacts struck during the 1990s generated a profound distrust of all political accords.

Finally, the matter of corruption is undoubtedly what has most profoundly de-legitimized Argentine politics. Social (and to a considerable extent judicial) awareness of the large number of shady deals of the past decade, added to the constant role as intermediaries of now-wealthy politicians, judges, and police, ended up convincing Argentines that the country's official leadership was dedicated to improving its members' lives at the expense of the future of the citizenry. According to the index of perceived corruption published by Transparency International, Argentina in 2003 was found in 92nd position out of the 133 countries so classified, and scored only a 2.5 (compared to Chile, for example, with a 7.4) on a scale where 10 corresponds to countries with the greatest transparency in government operations and 0 for the most corrupt countries.[8]

So, then, to what do we owe such perceptions? Traditionally, political science defined the processes of de-legitimation, popular disaffection, or distancing from politics as a crisis of representation, giving particular emphasis to a phenomenon present in the whole of the democratic world where representatives appear quite remote from their constituents.[9] For parties this fact has been explored basically in terms of its electoral dimension; that is, for the kind of relations that parties create with their voters.[10] This classic notion of a crisis of representation is only partially useful in explaining the problems that politics experiences generally in Latin America and specifically in Argentina.

The political crisis that Argentina has gone through is the result of the spontaneous impact of three factors that can be disaggregated analytically. First, the effects of the representational crisis existing at the world level; second, the crisis within particular nation states affecting Latin America quite intensely; and third, the crisis of the lack of political will that is especially evident in the Argentine case. Using a metaphor coined by Marcelo Cavarozzi, we can imagine the crisis we are living through as being like the collapse from top to bottom of a tall building, where upon falling the higher floors progressively affect the lower ones, increasing the velocity and dramatic aspects of the collapse.

First of all, we suffer, as do all existing democracies, from the effects of transformations in the forms of political representation. Whether through technological changes that have strongly affected forms of political communication, social changes that eroded the collective nature of groups in the post-industrial world (thereby producing a greater variety of demands), or through restrictions imposed by the process of financial globalization on the regulatory capacity of the nation state over the economy, what is certain is that parties throughout the democratic world are tending to become organizationally weaker, to adopt standardized ideological proposals, and, in the eyes of their electorates, to appear more removed from social demands.[11]

If much has been written on this phenomenon, parties continue today to occupy a central place in the democratic system[12] despite pessimistic forecasts of the 1970s and 1980s[13] on the future of party organizations. Nevertheless, it is also certain that when they assume governmental power, their freedom of maneuver has been reduced and, consequently, so has their possibility of convincingly offering collective incentives for their constituents.

Second, the crisis that states have gone through globally—as a consequence of the exhaustion of the social model centered around the Keynesian welfare state—has had a much more profound effect in the countries of Latin America than in the developed nations of the North Atlantic quadrant. The end of the postwar consensus that saw the state as the solution to the majority of social problems[14] created a much more pronounced vacuum in Latin American societies than occurred in the more developed nations due to the central role the state has always occupied in Latin America.[15]

If we summarize the state's role from its beginning as the political and ideological creator of the nation, progressing from its "task as substitute entrepreneur"[16] to its role in the "constitution of the working class"[17] or in its determination of appropriate levels of capital accumulation,[18] we can argue that the Latin American state has retained an absolute central position in the building of its society. For that reason, the impact of its crisis and the reduction of its room for action logically produced much more marked effects than in other cases influencing the make-up of those societies.[19]

Third, what we call the abdication of political will refers to the response of Argentine political elites in relation to the limits set by the other two factors previously mentioned. We can argue that faced with a reduction in the area for political action brought on by the global crisis in representation and the crisis of the Latin American state, the majority of Argentine politicians gave up fighting to expand this limit, accepting it, giving it an objective reality, rendering it non-debatable.

Within a few years of the democratic restoration, a political argument of what was thought plausible was emerging that ended up justifying what was seen as the impossibility of carrying out actions capable of transforming the reality by politically regulating markets. By way of defending their own inaction, the advocates for this position excoriated those who still suggested the possibility of political action, labeling them as "stuck in the past" or "ignorant about how the world is and functions."

In the best-case version, this abandonment of political action arose from erroneous but sincere beliefs in a unique neo-liberal model. But, in its turn, this also served marvelously for those who used this belief to avoid even minimally confronting the powers that be. This discourse of the possible as it related to governability encompassed both government action and a harmonious modus vivendi with established pressure groups, respecting their interests and thereby obtaining juicy personal advantages.[20]

This permanent search for agreement with the powerful cannot be restricted to just the great world powers (the International Monetary Fund or the United States, as naïvely argued in a certain rhetoric of our local left), but must rather be broadened to the entire social sphere, from the Buenos Aires provincial police to the businesses supplying goods to the state, including a world of mini-mafias embedded in Argentine society. In this way, the renunciation of political will ended up in a negative way becoming the job of those governing.

What we can call the collapse of the Argentine political system was the combination of these three processes, which led an indebted and bankrupt state to go on relinquishing more and more power, becoming increasingly weaker and incapable of regulating society. The traumatic end of the convertibility model at the beginning of 2002—and before that, its slow, agonizing decay during the last phase of the Menem administration and throughout the De la Rúa presidency—clearly make explicit the limits that the political system had imposed on itself.

The awareness of the exhaustion of the convertibility system, whether due to the inconsistency of fiscal policies or to the overvaluation of the currency, did not result in the political system urging an orderly exit from the model or in the adoption of reforms that would furnish some security against a worst-case scenario. Every time convertibility was discussed, the option chosen was the same: to increase the costs of dropping it.[21] Thus a scenario of ongoing escapism was followed that sought to avoid dealing with current difficulties by maximizing the future problems that abandonment of the model would bring.

The response the political actors gave to the recommendations to drop the model (recommendations generally made by foreign economic analysts) was always the same: it was politically impossible, given their inability to even think about confronting the problems that an orderly exit from convertibility would have entailed. In sum, the political system was seen as incapable of making any change in the exchange rate set at one to one with the dollar.

The Return of Political Will Following the Collapse

Finally, an incompetent political class left to the market the problem of how best to abandon convertibility and resigned itself to whatever the country might impose after the collapse of the peso. The provisional government of Eduardo Duhalde succeeded in halting the crisis by relying on a series of political, economic, and social measures. Although these measures did not resolve the dramatic situation inherited nor correct Argentina's deep-seated problems—leaving them for the next administration—they were sufficient to generate a sense of tranquility and the restoration of social order.

The new government assumed office in May 2003 in the midst of a political situation that appeared to foretell serious weakness. Néstor Kirchner was elected after a complicated process of moves and counter-moves in the Justicialist Party, managing to gain approval after getting a modest 22% of the votes in the first round, given the withdrawal from the race of Menem (who had gained the most first-round votes). In the same manner, the disorganized exit of Duhalde generated a chaotic national electoral timetable in which the new president had to assume power prematurely and face dozens of national and provincial elections even before the date of his constitutionally defined start on December 10.[22]

Surprising even the most optimistic diagnoses, Néstor Kirchner succeeded in a few months in reconstituting a good deal of the polity's legitimacy, obtaining important popular support that hovered around 70–80%, according to public opinion surveys. The most interesting aspect of this accomplishment is that it was accomplished without altering the negative conditions that had brought Argentina to its crisis, by means of reconstructing political will, the third factor that we identified in explaining the collapse of the national political system.

The problems coming from the global crisis of political representation as well as those from the crisis of the state obviously continue in force. That is to say, objective limits affecting political action continue being the same; what changed was the presidential willingness to act to confront such limits. In political science there is a vast literature that tackles the always complex relation between what are commonly called the "objective limits" (economic or institutional) on political action and the ability of actors to face them.[23] Generally, it is understood that the prevailing ideological variables constitute a kind of cognitive map that people have to deal with, guiding their perceptions of what is desirable and positive at a determined time and place. The perception of limits can lead to the setting of an unrealizable goal as much as to the underestimation of what falls strictly within the area of the achievable.

What we previously had defined as the abdication of political will could then be understood as an overestimation by principal actors of the limits that the national and international context places on the capacity for action of governments. President Kirchner's political behavior, mistakenly characterized as overly dominant, should be understood as constituting a break with the consensus of presumed political powerlessness that was formed during the last twenty years in our country. From the sadly remembered Easter proclamation where President Raúl Alfonsín publicly admitted the government's inability to prosecute those responsible for state terrorism to the Zero Deficit Law where Economic Minister Cavallo and President De la Rúa sought to assure international investors they were not thinking of emitting currency—obviously also including the Convertibility Law, the amnesties, and the privatizations—the principal policies implemented by the Argentine state implicitly or explicitly meant cuts in the state's own capacity for action.

With what is commonly known as the "K factor," President Kirchner has begun to build power by explicitly questioning the limits that Argentine politicians had imposed on themselves. His policy on human rights, his confrontation with privatized companies, and his position adopted toward the international financial organizations are all clear examples of the recovery of political will that has pleasantly surprised a society fed up with the 1990s discourse of impossibility. For them, the re-legitimation of politics is based on the most Argentine aspect of the crisis, the previous abdication of political will, and on current presidential action.

This recuperation of political will is a necessary but insufficient condition to reconstitute the polity's legitimacy. Its intrinsic potency requires it to continuously move ahead with institutional reforms that will give it long-term continuity. Some of those have already been implemented, such as the reform of the Supreme Court and the purging of the armed forces and the security services, but the opportunity that has been opened ought not to exclude reforms of other factors that continue to negatively affect the completion of Argentine democracy, such as the institutions for political representation and the state apparatus. Here it is necessary to re-emphasize that to translate these positive measures into long-term accomplishments, one must understand the need to implement institutional reforms that facilitate, implement, and re-create said changes throughout the political-institutional apparatus.

The Pending Institutional Agenda

Let us suppose that the government successfully continues on the course as out-lined, that the economy maintains its slow but persistent process of recovery, and that this leads to improvement in employment. And let us also suppose that, in its turn, the political will shown at the social-economic level continues with policies that reduce poverty and even the level of inequality. What are the political-institutional reforms needed to go with and to strengthen this course of action?

Some years ago Guillermo O'Donnell wrote that the crisis of the Latin American states has three dimensions—in reference to the state as a collection of bureaucracies capable of fulfilling their functions with reasonable efficiency, to the effectiveness of the law, and to the claim that state agencies normally base their decisions on some concept of the public good.[24] Similarly, in another work, the same political observer pointed out that "generalized particularism, delegative government, weak horizontal accountability, and consequently, the low level of transparency in representative processes and in the formulation of policies" are the most negative political characteristics of new, weakly institutionalized democracies.[25]

Applying these ideas to the current Argentine case, we can say that the insti-tutional agenda that ought to influence the country's reconstruction will have to orient itself in two directions: on one hand, toward the reform and reconstruction of the state and, on the other, toward the re-legitimation of the political regime.

When we point to the necessary reconstruction of the state, we do so in the wider sense indicated by O'Donnell. In the first place, the process of structural adjustment initiated in the 1990s not only sensibly reduced the scope of state functions, but at the same time seriously affected the state's capacities in strictly administrative aspects. This reduction refers not only to the federal state but also to the state organs in the provinces. For this reason, the state's rebuilding ought to occur on two levels simultaneously, as much in its various bureaucratic divi-sions as in the relations between these.

In reference to the bureaucracy, the list of tasks to carry out is extensive due to the need to reverse those policies that, on the one hand, undermined its admin-istrative capabilities (falling professional and wage standards, voluntary retire-ments, functional disorganization, lack of training, deterioration of physical infrastructure, etc.) and, on the other, reduced its capacity for social regulation given privatization, job task flexibilization, and decentralization that were not implemented through corresponding changes in formal regulations.

In regard to the state's administrative capabilities, a reform ought to be implemented that starts at the highest level of the administration, through the discussion of a macro-level plan that clearly delimits the competencies of each area and differentiates among levels of policy design, application, and control. Special emphasis is needed in the improvement of forms of oversight, avoiding duplications in function, and in introducing citizen input in some organizations.

Improvement is especially needed in administrative careers, giving priority to the training and professionalization of the upper and mid-level ranks. As I have pointed out elsewhere,[26] neo-liberal policies of economic adjustment cut a large portion of the courses intended to increase the skills of the different levels of the state bureaucratic structure. Consequently, the reorientation and planning of the education of the bureaucracy is one of the principal uncompleted tasks here. Similarly, the diversity of existing employment systems and the formation of parallel bureaucracies constructed ad hoc in each political administration with the hiring of contracted personnel both work against the possibility of relying upon a highly professionalized quality civil service.

There also are a broad series of actions needed to be carried out at the federal level of the Argentine state that run from the never-completed discussion of the fiscal structure to the construction of inter-jurisdictional areas for the coordination and the application of specific policies that would strengthen areas of local management while bringing order to the chaos resulting from the decentralization of the past decade. Another principal point to bear in mind is the implementation of an effective regionalization scheme for the country that would permit economies of scale to be created to implement determined public policies without resorting to efforts at adjustment that postulate the closure of "inefficient provinces." With respect to the federal question, one should point out that it is not possible to think of the state's administrative capacity in reference only to the national government; provincial and local cases are owed attention here as well.[27]

Unquestionably, a topic needing attention affecting state capacity in the broad sense is the immediate reform of existing regulatory legislation, a reform that ought to be accompanied by the redesign of agencies of control, making them genuinely independent of the interests of those providing public services and, at the same time, having real power to sanction them. In this sense, it is necessary to build truly autonomous agencies that are capable of exercising an effective control based on actual privatization contracts and one that will permit the resolution of user claims.

In terms of the state as guarantor of equality before the law, a series of policies ought to be developed that limit the particular areas of concern mentioned by O'Donnell.[28] The processes of reforming the judiciary should not concentrate solely at the federal level, but necessarily extend to the provincial courts. In the same sense, there ought to be a critical analysis of the role really played by institutions such as the Councils of the Judiciary that are the product of recent constitutional reforms. These bodies need to guarantee that the legal democratic system functions, here really meaning "no power escapes being subject to the legal authority of the other powers."[29]

In thinking about institutional reform of the current democracy, we ought to move beyond the discussion that begins and ends with the electoral system. On this point, perhaps it would be more critical to establish the goals or purpose of the reforms that ought to be put into practice. We believe that the central objective ought to be to increase the level of control citizens have over those governing them and their actions,[30] clearly understanding the connection of this point with the argument of previous paragraphs. No reform of the state is possible without greater levels of control by citizens.

Citizens' control over those governing them has taken two forms in contemporary institutional evolution: first, by electoral control—that is, the ability civilians have to choose their representatives through the vote,[31] which is tied to the functioning of the electoral system, the financing of political activity, and the size of the party system. Second, it refers to the control that citizens can directly exercise over governmental actions—the so-called mechanisms for citizen participation and control—that are related to processes that guarantee the transparency of political information.

The Argentine electoral system has been strongly questioned in regard to its most elementary functions: the way in which candidates are selected and its effectiveness in registering citizen preferences.[32] Similarly, one notes a clear majoritarian bias in the electoral rules—despite the D'Hondt formula being applied—and an important party skewing.[33] To this we ought to add the absence of real controls over party financing and the effects of territorial over-representation due to how Argentine federalism works.[34]

This weakness in electoral institutions is, in a rather fragmentary fashion, compensated for by mechanisms of citizen participation and accountability. Although these mechanisms exist in the letter of the national and provincial constitutions, in very few cases are they found to be effectively legally defined or applied.[35] Here, owing to the lack of basic consensus that would permit the prevailing laws to function, the right of citizens to access the new forms of semidirect democracy that were implemented in various districts after the constitutional reform process are obstructed.

Thus the most urgent tasks would include the discussion of an integral reform of the national electoral system that by increasing the proportionality of the vote would permit a greater awareness and hence accountability of representatives. Likewise, provincial electoral systems must be revised to end the system of double simultaneous voting (the so-called "Lema Law") as well as mechanisms that produce over-representation for winning parties. Also, the role of the Election Courts ought to be strengthened, perhaps by creating a specific authority, to the detriment of powers currently possessed by national and provincial executives. One interesting proposal would be to create a National Electoral Agency independent of existing bodies, as one can find in various countries. Finally, pointing only to the reforms we consider most urgent, an efficient accountability system for party financing ought to be created (especially for electoral campaigns) that would facilitate effective sanctions for non-compliance.

In light of the profound crisis that the political parties have gone through, it is also necessary to design policies that would lead to strengthening them as genuine instruments linking society and the state. In this respect, these policies ought to encourage the education and training of party staff, possibly by creating incentives and tying those to the public financing they receive. Similarly, and looking to limit the effect of clientelism, the reforms ought to create specific means of accountability over the internal candidate selection processes that are many times more corrupt and less transparent than official elections.

As far as mechanisms for citizen accountability and participation are concerned, initiatives ought to be generated to strengthen their implementation. Public auditing bodies, legislative initiatives, and mechanisms of citizen participation in the design of budgets and other similar measures can not only produce greater citizen control but also strengthen participatory practices that provide content and quality to the democracy. The use of these tools will make sense if accompanied by strong policies of informational transparency on the part of the three branches of government at the national, provincial, and municipal levels.

Finally, a proposal that can cut across the various points previously mentioned would be the establishment of a Democratic Quality Observatory as a non-state public organization capable of regularly evaluating the functioning of democratic institutions and at the same time generating proposals for action to improve and deepen those institutions.[36]

Conclusion

In summary, we can say that the phase begun in Argentina with the new Kirchner government permits us to be moderately optimistic. Although the large social and economic problems continue to exist along with the weaknesses and failures of the democratic state, the new president appears to have the political will to confront these problems.

The re-legitimation that politics has gained through Kirchner's decision to challenge the existing limits and to broaden the framework for action ought to be accompanied by institutional reforms that overcome the previous deficits and give these reforms long-term sustainability. That is, change in the content of policies ought to be likewise accompanied by a change in their institutional expression.

An institutional reform occurring along with the nation's rebuilding ought at the least to take on the reconstruction of the state and democratic political regime and provide instruments for the implementation, development, and legitimation of the public policies needed by the country. The objectives ought to be the strengthening of the state in all its dimensions, as well as of the mechanisms for direct and indirect popular accountability and participation, which together can create a citizenship of greater intensity and capable in the future of preventing a return to the situations experienced in the last decade.

Notes

* Translated by David Pion-Berlin.

1. This chapter was written in collaboration with Facundo Nejamkis (UBA-

CONICET), María Celeste Ratto (UBA-CONICET), and Matías Triguboff (UBA-CONICET).

2. CEPAL (2003), available at <http://www.cepal.org>.

3. This is demonstrated by various data. According to a PNUD study, 49% of the population does not care what type of political regime exists as long as it solves the nation's economic problems (Liliana De Riz and Juan Carlos Portantiero, *Aportes para el desarrollo humano de la Argentina* [Buenos Aires: PNUD Argentina, 2002]). In like manner, in February of 2002, some 74% of the population had little or no confidence in the president, 93% distrusted the Congress, and 94% distrusted the political parties, while a lukewarm 23% of the population had faith in democratic political institutions (Daniel Zovatto, J. Mark Payne, Fernando Carrillo Flórez, and Andrés Allamand Zavala, *La política importa: Democracia y desarrollo en América Latina* [Washington, D.C.: Banco Interamericano de Desarrollo, 2003]).

4. These statistics were calculated based on the definitive vote count provided by the National Directorate of the Interior Ministry.

5. Richard Katz and Peter Mair, "Changing Models of Party Organization and Party Democracy: The Emergence of the Cartel Party," *Party Politics* 1 (January 1995): 5–28.

6. Juan Abal Medina and Julieta Suárez Cao, "Postscriptum: Recorriendo los senderos partidarios latinoamericanos en la última década," in *El asedio a la política: Los partidos tras la década del neoliberalismo en Latinoamérica*, ed. Marcelo Cavarozzi and Juan Abal Medina (Rosario: Homo Sapiens, 2002), 433.

7. Among others we can mention increases in levels of poverty, unemployment, and inequality combined with the failure to stabilize macroeconomic variables in the long term.

8. Transparency International (2003), available at <http://www.transparency.org>.

9. H. J. Pulhe, "Still the Age of Match-allism? Volksparteien and Parteienstaat in Crisis and Re-equilibration," in *Political Parties: Old Concepts and New Challenges*, ed. Richard Gunther (Oxford: Oxford University Press, 2002).

10. Bernard Manin, Adam Przeworski, and Susan Stokes, *Democracy, Accountability and Representation* (Cambridge: Cambridge University Press, 1999), 232–34.

11. Russell Dalton and Martin Wattenberg, "Unthinkable Democracy: Political Change in Advanced Industrial Democracies," in *Parties without Partisans: Political Change in Advanced Industrial Democracies*, ed. Russell Dalton and Martin Wattenberg (Oxford: Oxford University Press, 2002).

12. José Ramón Montero and Richard Gunther, "Introduction: Reviewing and Reassessing Parties," in *Political Parties: Old Concepts and New Challenges*, ed. Richard Gunther, José Ramón Montero, and Juan J. Linz (Oxford: Oxford University Press, 2002).

13. As examples of this point of view, see Suzanne Berger, *Politics and Anti-Politics in Western Europe in the Seventies* (Cambridge: Daedalus, 1979); Claus Offe, *Contradictions of the Welfare State* (Cambridge: MIT Press, 1984); Kay Lawson and Peter Merkl,*When Parties Fail: Emerging Alternative Organizations* (Princeton: Princeton University Press, 1988).

14. Peter Evans, "El estado como problema y como solución," *Desarrollo Económico* 140 (1996), Buenos Aires; Gøsta Esping-Andersen, *Politics Against Markets* (Princeton: Princeton University Press, 1988).

15. Marcelo Cavarozzi, *El capitalismo político tardío y su crisis en América Latina* (Rosario: Homo Sapiens, 1996).

16. Evans, "El estado como problema," 535.

17. Dietrich Rueschemeyer, Evelyn Stephens, and John Stephens, *Capitalist Development and Democracy* (Chicago: University of Chicago Press, 1992), 183.

18. Albert Fishlow, "The Latin American State," *Journal of Economic Perspectives* 4, no. 3 (1990): 62.

19. Guillermo O'Donnell, *Contrapuntos: Ensayos escogidos sobre autoritarismo y democracia* (Buenos Aires: Paidós, 1997), 264–65.

20. If the construction of a discourse emphasizing the difficulties of challenging the status quo took place in the 1990s with the government of Carlos Menem, its high point was without doubt the administration of Radical Fernando de la Rúa, who was thrown out by the citizenry after two years in office. The latter desperately sought to avoid confronting anyone but ended up challenged by everyone.

21. Sebastián Galiani, Daniel Heymann, and Mariano Tommasi, "Expectativas frustradas: El ciclo de la convertibilidad," *Desarrollo Económico* 43, no. 169 (2003): 15–16, Buenos Aires.

22. Eduardo Duhalde had been elected by Congress on January 1, 2002, to complete De la Rúa's term; that is, to govern until December 10, 2003. Nevertheless, the magnitude of the social crisis led him to resign prematurely and set the date of his handover of the office for May 25, 2003. Thus the new president chosen in the April elections would assume office six months before schedule. In like manner, the enormous uncertainty that existed led the majority of provincial governors to seek elections separate from those for the national presidency. This produced a complex electoral calendar that would practically fill the entire 2003 year. To this, one needs to add that due to the particularity of Argentine election organization, not only were provincial elections spaced out over time, but national elections for the new congress in each province were broken up in almost every possible form. See Juan Abal Medina and Julieta Suárez Cao, "Análisis crítico del sistema electoral argentino: Evolución histórica y desempeño efectivo," *Revista de Ciencias Sociales* 14, Universidad Nacional de Quilmes.

23. Among others, Juan Abal Medina and Claudio Iglesias, "Acción estratégica y comportamiento colectivo: Una revisión," *Revista Argentina de Ciencia Política*, no. 1 (1997), Buenos Aires; Carlos Acuña, *La nueva matriz política argentina* (Buenos Aires: Nueva Visión, 1996); Jon Elster, *Ulises desatado: Estudios sobre racionalidad, precompromiso y restricciones* (Barcelona: Gedisa, 2003).

24. O'Donnell, *Contrapuntos,* 264.

25. O'Donnell, *Contrapuntos,* 327

26. Juan Abal Medina and Facundo Nejamkis, "Capacidades estatales: La construcción de capacidad administrativa y los cambios en el régimen de empleo público," *Revista SAAP* 1, no. 1 (2002), Buenos Aires.

27. On this point one would have to add the necessary reform of municipalities, taking into consideration their existing positive and negative experiences. As a consequenceof the economic difficulties and growing social demands, the municipal governments saw themselves obligated to assume greater economic and political leadership. In this manner, local development via strategic planning allows for a connection between public and private management, with greater reflection on the strengths and weaknesses of the local productive structure. Daniel García Delgado, *Hacia un nuevo modelo de gestión local: Municipio y sociedad civil en Argentina* (Buenos Aires: FLACSO-CBC-UCC, 1997), and "Ciudadanía, participación y desarrollo local," in *Alternativas frente a la globalización: Pensamiento social de la iglesia en el umbral del tercer milenio,* ed. Grupo de Pensamiento Social de la Iglesia (Buenos Aires: Editorial São Paulo, 1999); Daniel Arroyo, "Estado y sociedad civil en el proceso de descentralización," in *Municipios, democratización y derechos humanos* (Buenos Aires: CODESEDH, 2000), and "La gestión municipal en

Argentina: Entre la crisis social, la planificación y el desarrollo local," in *Desarrollo Municipal* (Lomas de Zamora: Instituto de Administración Municipal/Facultad de Ciencias Económicas, Universidad Nacional de Lomas de Zamora, 2001).

28. O'Donnell, *Contrapuntos,* 287–304.

29. Guillermo O'Donnell, "Teoría democrática y política comparada," *Desarrollo Económico* 39, no. 156 (2000): 556, Buenos Aires.

30. Although there is a substantial diversity in the main theoretical approaches regarding the significance of the concept of democracy (see David Collier and Steven Levitsky, "Democracy with Adjectives: Conceptional Innovation in Comparative Investigation," *World Politics* 49 [April 1997] and O'Donnell, "Teoría democrática"), it is possible to identify a clear area of agreement in the idea that any definition of democratic government ought to introduce controls on those governing by the governed (vertical accountability).

31. Juan Abal Medina and Ernesto Calvo,"Y Ud. ¿por quién dice que votó? Una agenda de investigación sobre los mecanismos electorales de control político," in *El federalismo electoral argentino: Sobrerepresentación, reforma política y gobierno dividido en la Argentina,* ed. Juan Abal Medina and Ernesto Calvo (Buenos Aires: EUDEBA, 2001), 248.

32. Abal Medina and Calvo, *El federalismo electoral argentino.*

33. In the election of national deputies, the combination of districts of different size into four large districts, Buenos Aires Province (35), the City of Buenos Aires (12 or 13), Santa Fe (9 or 10), and Córdoba (9)—and twenty other districts with small or medium weights—had the effect of causing a fragmentation of competition in the large districts, with effects on the majorities needed in the medium and small districts, strengthening the legislative representation of the traditional parties that tend to be stronger in districts with less urban population.

34. In sum, the prevailing electoral system reinforces the crisis of party representation by splitting their ranks and rewarding the smaller districts historically made up of safe seats. The overrepresentation of these districts, heightened even more by the equal representation of all provinces in the Senate, grants the governors the power to blackmail the president by becoming actors with veto power over various legislative policy proposals (George Tsebelis, *Veto Players: How Political Institutions Work* [Princeton: Princeton University Press, 2002]). When the national president loses his legitimacy, as happened in the last part of Carlos Menem's government, for almost the entirety of the De la Rúa administration, and during the first part of Duhalde's provisional government, the capacity for blackmail of provincial leaders increases, generating an increasing interchange of legislative political support by provincial delegations in return for budgetary concessions by the presidency. In this manner, it gives rise to a complicated game in which the leaders of the smaller provinces that are "poor" in terms of economic resources utilize their political "wealth" to obtain concrete benefits for their districts. They can even generate a kind of clientelism on a national scale for themselves, which has been presented in a positive light as a strengthening of federalism but that, in reality, hides a sort of neo-feudal transformation of Argentine politics where doubtful private negotiations prevail over publicly made agreements. The key to this process can be found in the territorial over-representation that we have mentioned, as well as the peculiar Argentine tax structure in which the taxes are largely collected by the national government, which afterwards shares them with the provincial administrations (Natalio Botana, "Prólogo," in Abal Medina and Calvo, *El federalismo electoral argentino*). In this way, there is an incentive for provincial

actors to be more disposed to obtain resources through this trading of legislative votes rather than through improvements in their own tax collecting capacities.

35. Catalina Smulovitz and Enrique Peruzzotti, "Social Accountability in Latin America," *Journal of Democracy* 11, no. 2 (2000): 147–58.

36. See here Guillermo O'Donnell, Jorge Vargas Cullell, and Jorge Osvaldo Iazzetta, eds., *Democracia, desarrollo humano y ciudadanía* (Rosario: Editorial Homo Sapiens, 2003).

Will Foreign Allies Help?
Argentina's Relations with Brazil and the United States*

Roberto Russell and Juan Gabriel Tokatlian

Introduction

Since the end of the nineteenth century, Argentina's relations with Brazil and the United States have occupied a place of increasing significance within the distinct schemata that guide the nation's foreign policy. In both cases, this place always constituted material for fierce debates. Brazil was considered an indispensable ally in enlarging the nation's autonomy and fortifying its capacity to negotiate internationally but was also the principal geopolitical rival that threatened the security and even the territorial integrity of Argentina. Likewise, the United States was perceived at one extreme as a dangerous imperialist engaged in permanent expansion and at the other as a central ally in order to ensure Argentina a successful linkage with the rest of the world. In the twentieth century, this debate more and more acquired a triangular character through a historical process marked at one and the same time by the decline of Argentine power and the relative increase in U.S. power on a global scale and that of Brazil in the South American orbit, respectively.[1]

On this point, the manner in which Argentina linked up with each of these two countries had a growing and essentially negative impact on relations with the other. Thus, the positive linkage with one of the vertices of the triangle resulted in confrontations, differences, estrangement, or suspicions with the other. To this day, Argentina has not succeeded in resolving this dilemma, and consequently has not articulated a simultaneous relation with Brazil and the United States that would serve its national interests.[2]

The debate about the place of Brazil and the United States in Argentina's foreign policy was accentuated through the exhaustion of each of the three arrangements that Argentina historically followed to guide its policy: (1) the special relation with Great Britain that extended from the end of the nineteenth century until the third decade of the twentieth century; (2) the global paradigm that began in the mid-1940s and concluded by the end of the Cold War; and (3) the strategy of pragmatic acquiescence that was initiated at the beginning of the 1990s and that, to varying degrees, guided the country's foreign policy until the premature end of the Alliance government in December 2001.

Following the crisis of December 2001, the last paradigm came under harsh questioning. The indifference and disdain displayed by the Bush government toward Argentina showed the falsehood of the paradigm's principal supposition: that yielding to the political and strategic interests of the United States—both globally and regionally—would ensure Argentina resolute support from Washington in circumstances of grave internal problems. At the same time, the crisis obliged Argentina to rethink its relations with Brazil that had gone through numerous fluctuations during the decade of the 1990s as much as had the strategic meaning of MERCOSUR (the Southern Common Market) for Argentina.

This chapter comprises four parts. In the first, we briefly review Argentina's ties with Brazil and the United States from the time its "special relation with Great Britain" was put into practice until the end of the Alfonsín government (July 8, 1989). Following that, we concern ourselves with the same theme during the Menem and De la Rúa governments (1989–2001), a period in which Argentina developed a strategy—unparalleled in Latin America—of submitting to the United States and basically reserving for Brazil a place as its economic partner. This position with respect to its two most important allies, in the official discourse of the era, became a source of friction and constant suspicion for Brazil. In the third section, we briefly examine the role Brazil and the United States played during the Argentine crisis of December 2001 and the period embraced by the Duhalde government (January 1, 2002, to May 25, 2003) as well as that government's behavior toward the two countries. Finally, we analyze Argentine relations with Brazil and the United States from the inception of the Kirchner government in order to conclude with some reflections about these relations in the near future.

The Place of Brazil and the United States in Argentina's Foreign Policy (1880–1989)

From 1880 until 1930, Argentina achieved a level of integration into the international system that it would never equal again. Beginning in 1860, but especially in the 1880s, the leading classes in the country constructed a foreign policy model that followed three principal orientations: "Europeanism," opposition to the United States, and isolation from the rest of Latin America.[3]

The tie with Europe, and particularly with Great Britain, was the key that permitted the country to successfully integrate itself in the world economy in the capacity of producer and exporter of raw materials and food. By contrast, the United States did not then offer any real possibility for exports to its market due to its protectionist barriers as much as to the low level of complementarity between the two economies. What's more, at the same moment that Argentina put into practice a foreign policy that would continue without variation until the 1930s, U.S. leaders, from the end of the Civil War, began to perceive Latin America as their hegemonic sphere of influence. This vision clashed headlong with the political aspirations of the Argentine elite to play a similar dominant role, at least in South America. The palpable economic fruits from relations with Europe gave growing sustenance to Argentine pretensions of regional leadership and at the same time produced a growing self-confidence that derived in many instances from a sentiment of cultural superiority toward the United States. The famous phrase uttered in Washington by the Argentine delegate to the First Panamerican Conference (1889–1890), Roque Sáenz Peña, "America should be for all of humanity," summarized better than anything else the foreign priorities for the country and at the same time the disposition of those within Argentine leadership circles toward the United States, a country that was perceived more as a source of threats than of opportunities.

For its part, Argentina's isolation from the rest of Latin America was a direct consequence of its weak commercial ties with the region and manifested in its systematic rejection of permanent linkages. This policy certainly included Brazil, a country that from its side adopted a similar position vis-à-vis Argentina. The low volume of economic interchange had its correlate in the field of culture and ideas, but not in foreign policy. Since the country's founding, the majority of Argentina's leaders perceived Brazil as a geopolitical rival—a vision that was nourished more from the fear of Brazilian territorial expansion and a power imbalance than from the territorial conflicts the two nations confronted during the years of consolidation of their respective nation states. From the end of the Triple Alliance War (1865–1870), the bilateral rivalry manifested itself in the search for allies among the Southern Cone countries in order to bring them into their own sphere of influence, and in the development of an arms race. Achieving regional supremacy and isolating the other were the principal foreign policy objectives of both countries toward the sub-region.[4]

By the beginning of the twentieth century, the predominant vision of Brazil as rival came into confrontation with cooperative visions that began to gather force at the end of World War II (convergence of interests, economic complementarities, the counterweight of U.S. power) but still within the framework of a pro-European policy that was acquiring an increasingly more defensive character in the face of the U.S. advance in Latin America.

The profound global, political, and economic transformations produced after the First World War challenged and increaingly reduced the viability of the model of a special relationship with Great Britain. From 1930 on, changes in the system of world trade made the efforts to maintain the old bilateral relations with London futile. In that era, Great Britain was no longer in a condition to provide to Argentina the capital, goods, and equipment that it needed to set in motion the new industrially oriented development programs. That role fundamentally fell to the United States. But at this time, conditions for constructing a vehicle that would operate as the functional equivalent to that created with Great Britain at the height of the export model were not present.

The demise of the model unleashed a wide debate about the alliances to be favored (with Europe, the United States, or, within limits, Latin America), the degree of opening of the economy to foreign trade, the development of the internal market, and the strategies of industrialization. While most Argentine leaders still believed that ties with Europe could recover their central role in foreign policy ("the return to normalcy," according to expressions of the era), other voices postulated establishing a tight relation with Washington as much for political as for economic reasons. Those adhering to this position also assigned to Latin America, and in particular to Brazil, a place of importance owing to the necessity of overcoming the narrowness of the internal market and of diversifying external markets.[5] Those taking a pro-Brazilian perspective expressed a more political view, one emphasizing their common national origins and similar under-development. For these authors, a rivalry with Brazil only played into the hands of those foreign and domestic interests seeking to divide the under-developed world.

In practice, the preoccupation with the sub-regional power balance and the competition for influence in neighboring countries continued to dominate the Argentine vision of Brazil. The attitude that both countries adopted after the beginning of World War II—an accentuation of Argentine neutrality and the consolidation of Brazil's alignment with the United States—gave rise to a new vision of Brazil within Argentina, colored by the logic of geopolitical rivalry, seen here as a key nation in future U.S. designs on the continent.[6]

From the end of the war, Argentine and world conditions were to give shape to a new foreign policy paradigm that definitively displaced that of the special relation with Great Britain to become the principal frame of reference for the nation's international actions until the beginning of the Menem government.[7] Its rough outline was drawn during the second half of the 1940s by Juan Domingo Perón, who, from the moment he took charge of the government, endeavored to find a modus vivendi with the United States that would satisfy Argentina's economic interests without renouncing his objectives of political sovereignty and economic independence. The scheme conceived by Perón comprised five basic elements: Argentina's cultural relevance to the West; the country's alignment with the United States in case of war with the Soviet Union; its non-alignment with the political and economic strategic interests of the United States—both global and regional—owing to authentic differences in interests and perspectives between the two countries as a consequence of their relatively unequal positions in the international system; the definition of a bilateral and regional agenda with clear prioritization of goals in which economic issues occupied first place even over questions of security; and, finally, opposition to U.S. intervention in the internal affairs of countries of the region.

These five points constituted the channel along which the parameters of Argentine foreign policy toward the United States flowed during the Cold War. Politically, this schema contained an autonomous component that did not ensure the Cold War loyalties that Washington hoped for from Latin America. Economically, it promoted heterodoxy that contrasted with the liberal and multilateral policies favored by the United States. With reason, it was perceived as a strategy oriented to reduce U.S. power and augment Argentina's and Latin America's negotiating capacity. The deepening of Argentina's economic dependence with respect to the United States since the end of the 1940s on occasion weakened this perspective of seeking national autonomy, but never led to its abandonment. Even those Argentine governments that were unequivocally determined to tighten ties with the United States tried to maintain their own decision-making space in the face of demands and pressures from Washington.[8]

In any event, Argentine diplomacy was less apt to confront the United States than it was in the era when the paradigm of special relations with Great Britain predominated, perhaps more from necessity than from conviction. Even more so, the greater economic rapprochement with the United States was generally represented as an instrumental means to achieve national development and, in practice, was balanced with policies toward Latin America, Western Europe, and the Socialist countries, as well as measures directed toward impeding U.S. hemispheric aspirations.

In the sub-region, Argentina failed to establish any lasting pattern of relations capable of overcoming old suspicions. The policies directed toward strengthening cooperation with Brazil by facing international issues and developmental problems with shared criteria were superseded by a focus on the politics of power that emphasized competition and the struggle for influence in the South American region. Thus, the Latin American cause supported by Perón never excited Brazilian governments, which viewed it not only with skepticism and mistrust but also as a threat to their special relation with the United States. Toward the end of the 1950s, shared visions about the regional and global realities made possible an unprecedented rapprochement between Argentina and Brazil that nevertheless remained divided by the internal situations of both countries.[9] From the second half of the 1960s on, Argentina's foreign policy agenda toward the region was dominated by a growing preoccupation over Brazil's ascension, reflected in its political and economic influence in South America. In this context, Argentina's relation with its neighbor was defined in terms of rivalry from two angles:

geopolitics, which emphasized the power imbalance between the two countries with an unconcealed envy of the Brazilian "miracle," and the theory of dependence, which pointed out the danger of "sub-imperialist Brazil" in the Rio de la Plata basin and Brazil's role as the "gendarme" of the United States in the sub-region resulting from its special alliance with Washington.

Then, after much policy inconsistency between the two countries, differences were significantly reduced with the signing of the Tripartite Accord on Corpus-Itaipú of October 19, 1979, between Argentina, Brazil, and Paraguay, which opened up interesting perspectives inviting progress in cooperation.[10] Soon thereafter, on May 17, 1980, Argentina and Brazil signed a cooperation agreement for the development and peaceful applications of nuclear energy. By that time, the neighboring country had already ceased being considered the most likely source of conflict in Argentine strategic military thought.[11]

During the Malvinas War, Brazil expressed its solidarity with Argentina although the former was not in favor of armed conflict. Argentina's defeat in this conflict permanently put an end to Argentine-Brazilian concerns about their security from each other. Soon after, the beginning of the democratization process in both countries helped to secure important agreements on integration and harmonization of foreign policy. During the Raul Alfonsín government (1983–1989) bilateral relations gradually evolved from competition to the construction of an alliance, conceived as a strategic plan to consolidate the democratic process in both countries, protect national sovereignty, spark Argentine development that would complement Brazil's, and gather the critical mass needed to increase international negotiating capacity. If in this first phase of Argentine democracy a more cooperative view of Brazil was encouraged by the Argentine government—abandoning the rhetoric of conflict—mutual jealousies did not completely disappear.

The Paradigm of Pragmatic Acquiescence: The Sharpening of Triangular Differences (1989–2001)

When Carlos Menem assumed the presidency of Argentina in July 1989, the international and internal context brought together two of the three conditions identified by Jakob Gustavsson needed to facilitate significant changes in foreign policy: a change in the fundamental structural conditions of the external environment (end of the Cold War and a new phase in economic globalization) and an internal crisis of great scope (hyperinflation).[12] The third condition—the presence of strategic political leadership—was increasingly shown by how Menem consolidated his internal political power, starting with the building of a new social coalition that yielded among other relevant things a dramatic revolution in Peronist ideology.

The existing foreign policy paradigm was considered not only dysfunctional for orienting Argentina's foreign policy in this new international and domestic environment, but also one of the principal causes of the nation's relative decline in the world. Replacing it, the Menem government proposed and then followed the premises of a new foreign policy paradigm that we call "pragmatic acquiescence."[13]

Brazil and the United States were defined as principal allies of Argentina, but each as having different roles. In the context of MERCOSUR, Brazil was considered a fundamental economic ally, while relations with the United States on the basis of a strategic accommodation with Washington constituted the principal axis for a new Argentine linkage with the world, on the basis of a strategic accommodation with Washington. This strategy was justified for two pragmatic reasons: the United States had just won the Cold War, and it had been the hegemonic power in much of Latin America since the end of the nineteenth century. Influenced by unconcealed nostalgia for its former prosperity and its special relation with Great Britain, the Argentine government calculated that a political and economic alliance with Washington would be key to ensuring the country's successful reinsertion into the world order. Besides—specifically in the South American context—acquiescence to Washington was perceived as the proper strategy for second-rate powers (that is, Argentina in South America) while the quest for a power balance naturally corresponded to first-rate powers of each region (Brazil in South America). Such explanations for Argentine acquiescence focusing on external variables (both the world and sub-regional context) need to be supplemented by a series of domestic factors: Argentina's vulnerability to external forces, its institutional fragility, its search for profits, and the Menem government's effort to preserve and strengthen internal political power.

Relations with Brazil were affected by images from the past of an earlier Argentina and an earlier Brazil where the latter had been a firm ally of the United States. Regarding the first, it appealed to the image of the prosperous Argentina at the close of the nineteenth century and first decades of the twentieth and to the national and international designs of the generation that built the country and successfully inserted it in the world. What was to be copied was a Brazil that had chosen to be the ally of the United States in the Second World War. That Brazil was seen in laudatory terms while the Brazil of the 1990s was perceived with worry. Its relative distancing from the United States and the search for greater external power and influence based on realpolitik were considered examples of policies that ought to be avoided as much for their anachronism as for their having significantly contributed to Argentina's decline.

Except for matters of style, the Alliance government (the Radicals, FREPASO, and other minority, center, and center-left parties) that assumed power on December 10, 1999, did not change the basic features of the foreign policy followed by Menem. At the beginning, the Fernando de la Rúa government appeared inclined to look more toward Brazil and to re-launching MERCOSUR. The predominant vision then was that ties to the neighboring country were proving to be equally essential, economically and politically. Nevertheless, very soon it became evident that relations with Brazil would not be substantially altered.

Argentina avoided committing itself to initiatives that could be seen as efforts to establish a balance of power with or opposition to the United States in the sub-region. Thus, on the occasion of the South American Presidential Summit convened in Brazil at the end of August 2000, the Argentine foreign affairs minister clearly stated that this meeting of the twelve countries should not be interpreted as an intent to create a South American bloc.[14] In fact, contradictions inherent in the ties with Brazil were only exacerbated. In the Argentine government, discrepancies between ministries and personnel at the highest levels led to greater diplomatic tension between Buenos Aires and Brasilia, making it clear that neither South American country had a clear, consistent vision of the other.

In sum, Argentine relations with Brazil and the United States were ones weighted in favor of Washington. Never were relations treated as a triangular relation with each tie of equal importance. If the progress made in economic relations with Brazil increased the interdependence between the two countries, there was no corresponding increase in foreign policy convergence, where the differences were notorious and growing. On this point, Argentine intentions toward Brazil and more specifically toward MERCOSUR were never clear for Brazilian diplomacy, which bore some of the responsibility for the lack of progress in relations. Consequently, any integration of the two countries remained caught between Argentine vacillation and Brazilian inflexibility.

The Crisis of December 2001 and the Duhalde Government

The crisis of December 2001—the most visible expressions of which were the premature demise of the vacillating Fernando de la Rúa government, the change of five presidents in twelve days, the numerous middle-class and popular-sector street mobilizations united under the slogan "que se vayan todos" (let's get rid of them all), and the joyful announcement of the cessation of debt repayment—generated a new debate about the course that Argentina ought to follow in matters of international relations. Brazil and the United States returned to occupy a central place in the country's foreign policy. Those advocating subservience to Washington continued to promote a negative vision of Brazil, which was presented as a country with an uncertain future and a foreign policy that could again drag Argentina down the wrong path. Given the gravity of the crisis and the extreme external vulnerability of the country, they insisted that subservience to the United States continued being the best strategy to get Argentina out of its hole at the cost of its relation with Brazil, whose role as a key economic partner was, however, worth maintaining. Challenging this position were those promoting making relations with Brazil the principal axis for foreign policy while simultaneously defending a selective rapprochement with Washington, freed from any kind of submissiveness. Eduardo Duhalde's transition government navigated with difficulty between these two alternatives, although it increasingly tilted in favor of the second.

Argentina's default had been anticipated in the world financial centers for some time, and for that reason it caused no kind of surprise when it finally occurred in December 2001. Nor was it surprising that De la Rúa abandoned power two years before the end of his constitutional term of office. In reality, the collapse of the Alliance government had begun after its defeat in the legislative elections of October 14, 2001, in which the Argentine population through the so-called "voto bronca" protest of October 2001 expressed its growing repudiation of the political class in general.

The return of Peronism to the presidency—with the ephemeral and populist Adolfo Rodríguez Saá as much as with his successor, Eduardo Duhalde—was received with mere formulaic comments by the Bush administration. In a letter sent to Rodríguez Saá, the United States President defined Argentina as "our neighbor, our valiant ally and friend," and announced that relations (between the two countries) would continue to be "excellent."[15] These words of support were followed by others less formal but precise: Bush himself and key members of his government repeatedly clarified that any kind of U.S. help would be extended through the International Monetary Fund and (in what would be his position on Argentina from the beginning) warned that to win Washington's support, the country would have to first put its fiscal and monetary policies in order and develop an economic program that would produce "sustained growth."[16]

After some initial hesitation, the Duhalde government rapidly concluded that signing an accord with the IMF was a necessary condition not only to reinstate Argentina in the world economy but also to begin to put the nation's economy in order.[17] Even more importantly, Duhalde tied the realization of this accord to his own survival. From this reading of it, two foreign policy priorities were set: achieving swift economic aid from the United States and support from the Bush administration in the arduous negotiations that were initiated with the multilateral credit organizations. To clear the road of obstacles, shortly after coming to power, Duhalde apologized to President Bush for the short-term measures that he had inherited or had been obliged to take and declared his loyal commitment to economic liberty.[18]

In those difficult and tumultuous days at the beginning of 2002, the Argentine government imagined that an agreement with the IMF would occur in the short term and that the G-7 countries with the United States at the helm would extend to Argentina a significant amount of foreign aid that would range between 15 and 18 billion dollars. Very soon, the facts demonstrated that these expectations were unreasonable. Not only did support from Washington not arrive but the Bush administration used Argentina as a "guinea pig" for its new policy toward emerging countries going through financial crises. As is known, that policy maintained that it made no sense to lend to countries whose debt structure was unsustainable nor to come to the rescue of those who made bad investments in high-risk economies in search of greater profits. For its misfortune, Argentina went from being the exemplar of the economic reforms promoted by the United States and the IMF for Latin America in the decade of the 1990s to becoming the test case of this new policy that in the end would be applied less stringently than elsewhere.[19] Washington's reasoning for its flexibility toward Argentina was that the costs in so doing for the United States would be low and that there would be no contagion effect in other emerging nations as had occurred with the financial crises of Mexico, Southeast Asia, Russia, and Brazil.

The U.S. Treasury echoed Bush's response toward Argentina, never better expressed than in the declarations of its then head, Paul O'Neill: "It is not fair to use the money of U.S. carpenters and plumbers to rescue banks and companies that have made bad investments in high risk countries in search of greater and quicker profits. If they were willing to run the risk they ought to assume the cost."[20] In a less blunt manner and with the subtleties unique to diplomacy, this position was completely embraced by the State Department. Thus, Argentine expectations that the United States would adopt a more political view of the crisis met the same fate as the dashed hopes in Buenos Aires that new funds would arrive in the first months of the year.

In the period immediately following the outbreak of the crisis, Argentina did not offer the international financial world and the G-7 governments—beginning with the Bush administration—the conditions required for an agreement with the IMF. In addition to a long history of non-compliance (since its entrance into the IMF, Argentina fulfilled only four of nineteen agreements that it signed with the organization), three factors at that juncture contributed to raising the already high level of external distrust with Argentina: the triumphant tone with which default was declared, the notorious incapacity of the Argentine political class—in the midst of the storm—to work in pursuit of greater governability, and finally the fear that the Peronist-Radical Alliance that had placed Duhalde in the presidency would turn toward statist and populist policies. To make things worse, the Argentine crisis burst forth only three months after the terrorist attacks in the United States on September 11, 2001. Soon after these occurrences, Paul O'Neill acknowledged in front of the Senate Banking Commission that "a week before, Argentina was on top of our to do list; now it is no longer in this position in the same manner as before."[21]

The country's destitution and its more than ten years of submission to the political and strategic interests of the United States did not move the Bush administration, which for several months coolly distanced itself and made no effort to help lift the diminished collective Argentine self-esteem. For example, and despite its status as a non-NATO ally, Argentina was not included in the list of Western Hemisphere nations with which, as conveyed by its new strategy of national security, the United States would endeavor to form "flexible coalitions" (the countries included were Brazil, Canada, Colombia, Chile, and Mexico).

Recently, however, at the end of 2002, the Bush administration along with other G-7 countries helped the IMF overcome its strong resistance to approving a temporary agreement with Argentina after a long year of hard negotiations.[22] The U.S. Treasury played a key role in the final phase of the negotiations to bring the positions of Argentina and the IMF closer together. Thus, for example, after the signing of a Letter of Intent, the Treasury Department in a communication to the Fund's directorate urged its members to deal with the accord in the "very near future."[23] This support of Argentina from the U.S. executive branch was personally acknowledged by Duhalde himself to U.S. Secretary of State Colin Powell, in a meeting they had on the occasion of the Davos Economic Forum in January 2003. After the meeting, the Argentine president declared that "The United States supported us with a collaboration I would define as very strong. They were in constant communication with our representative from the Ministry of Economics, the Central Bank, and with our Ambassador in Washington, to facilitate an understanding."[24]

Certainly, the United States' decisive support to hasten the closing of the deal with the IMF is not due to a change in position toward Argentina, but rather to practical reasons at that time. Among these, the following stand out: (1) it was better to come to an agreement than to default and, consequently, to return to more statist policies; (2) it would be advantageous to have the Duhalde government complete its term without financial embarrassment; (3) the accord would help to preserve macroeconomic stability during the transition to a new government; and finally (4) it would give some breathing room to the next government to confront the restructuring of the public debt.

Against the background of the extenuated and uncertain negotiations with the IMF, the Duhalde government endeavored not to contradict Washington on the political, diplomatic, and strategic matters that dominated the political bilateral agenda of that year. The clearest example of this was the continued Argentine support of the vote to condemn Cuba on human rights grounds in the annual session of the U.N. Human Rights Commission that took place in Geneva. When there was still hope in Buenos Aires for prompt economic aid from Washington, Argentina declared itself in favor of a vote of censure against Havana a month before the vote on the resolution that invited the Cuban government to make improvements in the realms of human, civil, and political rights. In Geneva, Argentina convened the group of twenty-three countries in favor of the condemnation that also included Costa Rica, Chile, Guatemala, Mexico, Peru, and Uruguay. In this manner, the Duhalde government maintained the policy of the previous governments of Carlos Menem and Fernando de la Rúa while ignoring the position of Congress that Argentina abstain from condemning Cuba.[25] The only Latin American country that voted against the resolution besides Cuba was Venezuela, while Brazil and Ecuador abstained.[26]

Argentina's position did not, as in other years, awaken major debates in the country. This is not only owing to the fact that the internal crisis relegated the theme to a secondary plane but also because the format of the condemnation adopted in 2002 was less harsh—it dealt with an invitation to the Fidel Castro government to introduce improvements in the realm of human rights. Besides, the resolution acknowledged "the efforts made by the Cuban Republic in the fulfillment of social rights for the population in spite of an adverse international environment."[27]

Buenos Aires and Washington also strongly concurred about the Colombian situation. In this case, the closeness of Argentina's position with that of the United States was a product not only of necessity, but also of genuine agreement between the two countries. More explicitly than any other South American government, the Duhalde government supported the new Colombian president, Alvaro Uribe, and his open strategy of "fighting against terrorism." He did so because he was persuaded that Colombian democracy was seriously at risk; because he feared a domino effect that via the political responses of the Colombian FARC guerrillas would affect an Argentina seriously torn apart by the crisis; because he was showing the United States that the country was seriously dedicated to combating terrorism (in the hope that the Bush administration would no longer insist on asking Argentina to send troops to Afghanistan and Iraq); and, finally, because it allowed Argentina to differentiate itself from Brasilia's strongly critical posture toward Washington and "Plan Colombia."[28]

Furthermore, Argentina was the only South American country to send its foreign minister to the meeting between President Uribe and his Central American counterparts (Costa Rica, El Salvador, Guatemala, Honduras, Nicaragua, and Panama) in Panama on February 11, 2003.[29] During this meeting—one solicited by Colombia owing to the increase in FARC's terrorist action after Uribe's assumption of power—the Argentine foreign minister categorically opposed the actions of the Colombian guerrillas and expressed the idea that "FARC would have to get the same treatment as Al Qaeda."[30] It is interesting to note that a few days after these declarations, and marking his differences with Argentina, Lula's principal foreign policy advisor, Marco Aurelio García, indicated that "Brazil would not make any evaluation of Colombian insurgents owing to the fact that, eventually, it would be seen as an impediment to [Brazil] being a mediator in a possible peace agreement."[31]

Once back in Buenos Aires, the Argentine foreign minister unsuccessfully urged a summit of the Rio Group's foreign ministers with the objective of adopting measures designed to control and immobilize financial resources and resources of other kinds that facilitated the regional expansion of "narco-terrorism." This frustrated intent constituted another clear example of the logic that guided Argentina's foreign policy toward Washington during the Duhalde presidency. The call for the summit was motivated by solidarity with Colombia but also because at that moment the U.S. Senate was deliberating on a bill to sanction countries that did not participate in the imminent war against Iraq, in which Argentina had already decided not to join.[32]

In the face of Washington's growing offensive against the Saddam Hussein regime, the Argentine government tried to find a compromise position that would satisfy internal public opinion—strongly opposed to military intervention—and that at the same time would not snub Washington's expectations and demands.

From an initial position that led to speculation about the possibility of sending peacekeeping troops to Afghanistan as well as Iraq (after the cessation of hostilities in the latter country), the government gradually moved to the position of not participating in war in any manner, whether or not the war would be initiated by a U.S. unilateral decision or within the framework of the Security Council. The Argentine government took various detours along this road, although it always maintained an ostensible willingness to distance itself from positions that could be interpreted by Washington as neutrality. In response to State Department inquiries regarding what kind of aid could be expected from Argentina in case a conflict were to begin, the Duhalde government offered to deploy an air force mobile hospital as well as military specialists in de-mining and chemical and biological arms. The Argentine government's offer constituted a kind of implicit validation of the war; although it was qualified as humanitarian aid, it was a contribution of military specialists in the context of a U.S. military operation and with the subsequent need to support that presence.[33] For his part, Foreign Affairs Minister Ruckauf always placed more emphasis on his criticism of the Baghdad regime and on the dangers that terrorism implied for international security than he did on the fact that the war was the result of a Security Council decision.

On balance, Washington considered Argentina's position positive for two principal reasons: its tacit recognition that the armed conflict was present everywhere and its low level of criticisms. Argentina did not adopt a firm posture against the war as did Brazil, which embraced the thesis advanced by France. And likewise, a few days before the beginning of the war, Argentina opposed a Brazilian diplomatic proposal to carry out a meeting of South American countries for the purpose of producing a common front against the conflict. The argument utilized by Argentina was that the global magnitude of the problem demanded the assembly of all of Latin America, and especially of Mexico.[34]

In the final phase of his government, and a little relieved by the first signs of recovery in the Argentine economy, Duhalde increased his opposition to the U.S. military intervention in Iraq, thinking more of the internal electoral process than of his country's relations with the United States. The same logic explains the change in the vote in the U.N. Human Rights Commission—from condemnation to abstention—on the question of human rights in Cuba, 2003.[35] At that moment, everything with an anti-Bush tone served the purpose of having his candidate, Néstor Kirchner, make it to the second round to defeat Menem in his bid for the presidency. The change of vote as well as the heightened level of criticism toward the U.S. war in Iraq were aspects of the strong differences between Kirchner and Menem, where (faithful to what his government had done in the 1990s), the latter was an advocate of joining the United States in Iraq and of continuing Argentina's condemnation of Cuba.

It is also certain that the vote to abstain took on something of the aspect of being revenge for Bush's coldness toward Duhalde. At the same time, it was a means of expressing Argentina's will to draw closer to Brazil and acknowledge

Brasilia's solidarity during the most dramatic moments of the crisis.[36] While Buenos Aires was criticized by Washington and various European capitals for its poor handling of the economy, the government of Fernando Henrique Cardoso argued that the International Monetary Fund should not be insensitive to the Argentine crisis and that Brazil continued to confide politically in its principal trade partner. Later, during the Argentine election campaign and with Lula now in power, Brazil was gaining the image of representing a type of development different from what was put into practice in the 1990s, representing a model for Argentina internationally where the two countries would be political partners in a joint enterprise. As president-elect, Lula traveled to Buenos Aires in December 2002 in his first foreign trip. A short time thereafter, and with Lula in the presidency, the two leaders had a meeting on January 14, 2003, in Brasilia in which they expressed their firm determination to deepen their bilateral strategic alliance, to extend it to new areas, and to transform it into the engine of South American integration. Also they recognized the importance of coordination between the two countries in international trade negotiations, especially with the European Union in terms of membership in the Free Trade Area of the Americas (FTAA).[37]

Upon concluding the meeting, Duhalde defined the friendship between the two countries as "inevitable" and "indispensable." The willingness of the new Brazilian government to strengthen MERCOSUR and relations with Argentina offered the latter important room for maneuver internationally within the limited number of foreign policy alternatives available. Nevertheless, the proclaimed desire of both governments to give a new impetus to bilateral relations and to MERCOSUR was a subject left pending, one that became one of the principal Argentine foreign policy challenges of the near future.

The Kirchner Government and Relations with the United States and Brazil

With the completion of Duhalde's mandate, Argentina now found itself in a situation suitable to revise its foreign policy, within obvious limits imposed by international and domestic circumstances. To the external environment marked by the U.S. military intervention in Iraq that violated international legality, one must add a domestic setting characterized by the exhaustion of the model of pragmatic acquiescence and the coming to power of a new president with a world vision and a leadership style that was at the time unknown to most Argentines.

This last aspect merits special attention. President Kirchner's two principal reference points are the frustrated experience of Peronism's return to power in the 1970s and the Peronist experiment of the 1990s under Menem's leadership, an experiment that he considered ghastly for the country.[38] For generational reasons, his first political experiences corresponded to the decade of the 1970s when his life was linked to the struggles that brought Perón back from exile, the Third Peronist

Government (1973–1976), the gradual eclipse of a nationalist Argentine business sector, the misadventures and atrocities of the last military government (1976–1983), and U.S. policy contradictions toward Argentina, which under President Ford viewed the 1976 coup favorably but soon thereafter under President Carter (1977) developed a position in defense of human rights. Kirchner's quest for the strict subordination of the military to civilian control, his strong support for human rights, his expectation that a more autonomous state would re-create more nationally oriented businessmen, and his willingness to set relations with the United States on a new course all derived from the logic of those 1970s experiences and his interpretation of them three decades later.

In turn, the socio-economic debacle of the late 1990s that ended with the crisis of 2001 brought new elements to the president's political surroundings. His disposition to combat corruption, his criticisms of the IMF's neo-liberal prescriptions, his inclination to deal harshly with certain domestic sectors (privatized firms) and foreign ones (holders of Argentina's defaulted bonds) and his willingness to strengthen ties with Latin America and move closer to Cuba was due, to considerable degree, to the logic of differentiating himself from Menem's legacy.

In regard to his leadership style—especially as it manifested itself in the international arena—there were two prevalent features during the first year of his government: the use of foreign policy for internal political ends and his personal handling of such policy. In the first case, Kirchner has utilized matters of international relations to strengthen his originally weak legitimacy and thereby widen his ability to govern. Thus, in good measure, the substance and style of his foreign policy ought to be seen in light of the priority he gave to domestic policy matters. The clearest example is his posture toward multilateral lending agencies and private creditors, one that combines a firmness of argument with a combative discourse reminiscent of the 1970s. At the same time, Kirchner was becoming notoriously outspoken on key foreign policy themes: the decision not to carry out joint military exercises with the United States owing to his opposition to granting immunity to U.S. military personnel; the new conditions specified in the agreement reached with the IMF in September 2001; the initial uncertainty of relations between Buenos Aires and Brasilia influenced strongly by personal conjectures and perceptions; the direct and ultimately ineffective veto of the former Alliance Economics Minister José Luis Machinea as head of ECLA (Economic Commission for Latin America); and finally the announcement that he would take personal charge of managing relations with the United States.

The president's cognitive map and management style—in the Argentine post-crisis context—acquire particular relevance for the analysis of Argentine relations with the United States and Brazil, in spite of the fact that they have not yet been translated into a definite foreign policy strategy. First of all, it is clear that there will be no return to a strategy of submission to Washington, but neither will there be a strategy of open confrontation. With less than two months in office, Kirchner traveled to the U.S. capital in July 2003 for a brief meeting at President Bush's request. Although it was treated as a protocol visit to get mutually acquainted, the question of Argentina's external debt dominated the conversations. The meeting reinforced the U.S. chief executive's interest in more explicitly supporting the negotiations between Argentina and the multilateral credit organizations;[39] not only had there been a change of government in Buenos Aires that needed external support, but Washington could no longer continue ignoring the socio-political turbulence that was shaking South America from north to south. To ignore Argentina, which had preserved its democracy in such difficult times, would have sent a terrible diplomatic signal to all of Latin America. For his part, the Argentine leader would not share the Bush administration's political orientation but was in no condition to begin his tenure without an agreement with the multilateral credit organizations; a default would have worsened both Argentina's international isolation and its domestic crisis. The first talks between Kirchner and Bush were marked by a joint pragmatism more than by any principled or ideological vision.

This pragmatism stamped the first year of bilateral relations. Despite the irritation of the Pentagon and the State Department over the cancellation of joint military exercises originally set for October 2003, Assistant Secretary of State Roger Noriega's January 2004 criticism of Argentina's decision to again abstain at the U.N. Human Rights Commission on the issue of Cuba, and the various differing positions of the two countries on other issues (on regional security, on trade negotiations within the Free Trade Area of the Americas as well as the Doha Round of the World Trade Organization, and the political situations in Bolivia and Venezuela), Argentina and the United States maintained their dialogue centering on financial matters.[40] The United States combined a mixture of support and pressure that was made plainly evident beginning in 2004. In effect, the Bush government played the role of moderator with those G-7 countries that took a hard-line stand against Argentina, to facilitate negotiations with the IMF at the time that it was exercising strong and growing pressures in defense of U.S. private bond holders.[41]

Argentine-Brazilian relations moved from being initially immobilized by a series of misunderstandings to a series of important advances that imparted new force to the relations. The first months of Kirchner's rule were characterized by assiduous references to Brazil's importance to Argentine foreign policy. Nevertheless, it quickly became apparent that whereas Brazil's foreign policy-makers were designing and executing an international policy with South America as its keystone, Argentina's policy-makers aspired to a more Latin American view. The different values assigned to one or the other geopolitical/economic unity—South America for Brazil and Latin America for Argentina—again expressed Argentine fears of an eventual Brazilian hegemony in South America.[42] The references to Brazil, on the other hand, were made in the context of the obvious stagnation of MERCOSUR: the repeated promises of its political "re-launching" could not obscure the fact that in terms of its economic significance, MERCOSUR showed manifest signs of exhaustion for lack of its institutional development. In brief,

Brazil was more a rhetorical ally than a highly important partner for achieving a common goal, in the first trimester of the Kirchner government.

In the second half of 2003, there were notorious fluctuations in relations between Buenos Aires and Brasilia. On the one hand, the Argentine government believed that Brazil—and Lula in particular—had maintained a disquieting silence about the deal Argentina reached with the IMF in September, which contemplated less onerous fiscal measures than those agreed to by Brazil with the Fund. On the other hand, and by contrast, it was during Lula's official state visit to Argentina in October that the two leaders sealed the so-called "Consensus of Buenos Aires" that called for, among other important items, the intensification of regional unity and integration, the rejection of the unilateral exercise of power in the international arena, and the specification of national policies favoring employment and production.[43]

Despite this agreement, different strategic perspectives again cropped up during the only joint interview agreed to by the two presidents on the occasion of that visit, when Lula pointed out:

> We are taking a decisive step toward consolidating and showing the world that there exist alternatives to dependence on the group of wealthy nations that often act as if we were inferior. Argentina and Brazil need relations with the U.S. and Europe, but we have much, much more to do among ourselves. Given the political and economic importance of both countries, we can set a good example, and motivate other countries to lean toward *South America* and look less overseas. . . . Thus, my foreign policy priority is South American integration and within that our relation with Argentina, given its importance.

Kirchner's response to the same question was,

> We firmly place our bets with the building of bilateral [relations], with the building of MERCOSUR, as not only an economic but a political bloc that is a model for a new point of departure in new times. That ought necessarily to be opened to the Andean countries, [and] we have to mount a very strong Latin American convergence that, together with relations with Mexico, will permit us to create a bloc with a strong voice that can negotiate seriously, to insert ourselves seriously in the world.[44]

At the beginning of 2004, Argentina's proximity to Brazil appeared to take on a more pragmatic and urgent meaning as a consequence of a complex combination of internal and external factors. Without doubt, the principal reason behind the bilateral rapprochement was the external debt's negative impact on the realization of reformist plans promoted by both governments. The Argentine government needed more external support—that it did not easily obtain from the G-7 countries—to legitimate a kind of "new treatment" model between the IMF and highly indebted countries and, at the same time, widen its margin for maneuver at a time when on the horizon it faced some tough negotiations with the IMF and private bondholders. Thus, the Kirchner government perceived that the Brazilian government's support for Argentina's critical positions with regard to the multilateral credit organizations was fundamental to endowing those criticisms with greater foreign legitimacy and credibility.

In Brazil, Lula failed to produce any economic growth during his first year in office (the Brazilian GDP contracted by 0.2% in 2003) nor concrete gains with his delicate internal social agenda. Besides, the Brazilian president was losing domestic support from business sectors as well as with the left-wing fringes and with the progressive groups that had put him in power, including part of his own political party (the Workers Party). He experienced a mountain of troubles with the explosion of corruption cases implicating close associates of his that resulted in a great loss of popularity and the political gains by the right-wing opposition. Lula could demonstrate his country's growing diplomatic stature in the political area and on themes that could develop only with time and consensus (for example, obtaining for Brazil a permanent seat on the security council of the U.N.), but he made little progress (when he wasn't moving backwards) in the economic and social fields.

The need to soften his adjustment policies so that he could invest in infrastructure and social action to avoid the risk of having another year without growth and even worse social indicators led him to tighten his ties with Kirchner's Argentina with the objective of recuperating part of his center-left discourse that he had buried during fifteen months of economically orthodox policy.[45] According to this appraisal, the converging necessities of both governments explain the practical and conceptual rapprochement expressed in the Joint Declaration on Cooperation for Growth with Equity signed by both presidents in Rio de Janeiro, on the 16th of March, 2004. In this document, and in an extremely moderate tone, Kirchner and Lula agreed among other notable aspects "to conduct negotiations with multilateral credit organizations assuring a fiscal surplus and other political economy measures that will not get in the way of growth and that will guarantee a sustainable debt, in such a way as to preserve infrastructure investment."[46]

For sure, a series of important external factors also helped to facilitate greater concurrence: the need to unify positions in the negotiations with the European Union and to build the Free Trade Area of the Americas; greater U.S. military deployment in Latin America through its Forward Operation Locations in El Salvador, Curacao, and Ecuador, accompanied by a growing pressure to involve militaries of the region in strictly police-related increase in political and military turbulence in the Andean region (the Venezuelan political-institutional crisis; the persistence of armed conflict in Colombia and its zonal impact; institutional instability in Bolivia, Ecuador, and Peru) that each time demanded more joint Argentine-Brazilian diplomatic action; and the reappearance of border frictions in

South America (Colombia-Venezuela, Chile-Bolivia) and their potentially destabilizing effect for the region in its entirety.

Up to this point, it is certain that from the Buenos Aires Consensus of October 16, 2003, through the Act of Copacabana of March 16, 2004, the two governments had taken encouraging steps.[47] In the financial area, Kirchner and Lula decided to increase and improve their coordination regarding the parameters they would follow to guide their relations with the IMF. There was no discussion of creating a debtor's club but rather solidifying some "conceptual umbrellas" for their respective negotiations with the IMF. In the area of trade negotiations, Brasilia and Buenos Aires had strengthened their commitment to act jointly in the Doha Round as well as with the European Union, and within the hemisphere as well. In the multilateral diplomatic environment, the two governments had reaffirmed their abstentions on the vote regarding the theme of Cuban human rights, within the U.N. Human Rights Commission. At the same time, within the framework of U.N. Security Council Resolution 1529, Brazil (with 1,100 soldiers) and Argentina (with 200 soldiers) committed themselves to deploy a stabilization force in Haiti, after the confusing resignation of President Jean-Bertrand Aristide. Finally, on the bilateral diplomatic front, Argentina established a diplomatic presence in Brazil's representation before the U.N. Security Council in 2004, and plans were in the works to create joint consulship within the Argentine and Brazilian consulates in Hamburg and Boston.

Conclusion

After the crisis of 2001, and for distinct but concurrent reasons, Buenos Aires, Brasilia, and Washington developed a sufficiently level-headed triangular relation that distanced itself from its traditional historic dynamic. As was pointed out in this chapter, the United States' gradual ascendance from hemispheric power (between the end of the nineteenth century and the beginning of the twentieth) to world superpower (at the end of World War II), and then to the only superpower (after the end of the Cold War), the low frequency of contacts between all three parties, the Argentine-U.S. competition until the first three decades of the twentieth century, and the persistent Argentine-Brazilian rivalry during a good part of the past century, made impossible a harmonious triangular relation. For their part, Buenos Aires and Brazil, in different historical circumstances, ostensibly opted for a policy of submission toward Washington (Brazil during the 1930s and the beginning of the 1970s, and Argentina during the 1990s), but never did they effectively converge in order to unite their positions vis-à-vis the United States. As supplemental players, Argentina and Brazil remained prisoners of their own disputes and of Washington's divide-and-conquer strategy instead of transforming their bilateral conduct and coordinating their respective policies toward the pivotal player, the United States. The most erratic of the three actors was

Argentina, changing its orientation toward the United States and Brazil much more than the latter two did with respect to Argentina.

In this new historic occasion, with the Argentine domestic situation so fragile, the disequilibrium among the three countries could have led to relations focusing on the two more powerful countries, with Washington and Brasilia demonstrating disinterest toward Buenos Aires or, worse still, Argentina being totally excluded. Nevertheless, a surprising mixture of pragmatism and prudence at the three corners of the triangle allowed for a concurrence of policies around what we could denominate a strategy of damage control. Although the Bush administration adopted a position of relative coolness toward Argentina at the beginning of the crisis, it always avoided letting bilateral political differences contaminate the process of economic negotiations between Argentina and multilateral lending organizations; instead, the United States ended up playing an important role so that Argentina could close the deal with the IMF, first with Duhalde and then with Kirchner. Brazil, from its own perspective and with the critical political-economic situation of all of its neighbors in mind, always tried to understand the political dimension to the Argentine crisis, and especially its consequences for democratic stability in the region. This reading of the situation explains why Brazil helped the G-7 members adopt a more flexible posture toward Argentina.

From this point forward, the principal challenge is for the actors to move from damage control to policies defined in positive terms that would make possible a more harmonious triangular relation. For that to occur, it is essential that all of the protagonists, and especially the United States, adopt broad changes in their thinking. The United States ought to understand and accept that a strengthened Argentine-Brazilian relation could be useful for its long-term security interests in South America. Brazil and Argentina could play a key role in helping to resolve numerous problems in the region (and especially the Andean region) and in ensuring that South America be a zone free of weapons of mass destruction and uncontaminated by international terrorism.

At the same time, Argentina and Brazil should not build their bilateral ties on the basis of opposition to the United States. Aside from being anachronistic, such a strategy would not only prevent the unity of the two nations, but would end up dividing them. The underlying common strategic interests of Argentine-Brazilian relations can be summarized in four fundamental points: the formation of a zone of peace, democratic consolidation, the creation of a common economic space, and the construction of a critical mass to strengthen the international negotiating capacity of the two countries. Presently, there exist powerful motor forces of a positive nature (democratization, integration, overcoming hypotheses of conflict, positive identification with the other, predominance of cooperative visions) as much as a negative nature (increase in the external sensitivity and external vulnerability of the two countries) that favor the development of a common strategic plan. Certainly this task will have to be fulfilled in a context in which the relative position of the two nations has changed significantly, to the detriment of Argentina. Nonetheless, instead of awakening prejudices about a new form of domination, this situation should be one of the principal motor forces to push Argentina to construct a relation of friendship with Brazil. As was shown in the European case, power asymmetries between countries do not impede the execution of a common strategic plan. Yes, it obliges the more powerful nations to restrain themselves and to give clear and persistent signs of a communal dedication. The experience of the 1990s and after the Argentine crisis of 2001 teaches us that conditions are still lacking for the two countries to definitively put their mutual suspicions and distrust behind them. That notwithstanding, the recent bilateral advances heretofore mentioned, although motivated more by practical reasons than by conviction, ought to be followed attentively, since they could lead to a qualitative change in Argentine-Brazilian relations exemplified by a new tone of friendship.

Among the Kirchner administration's principal pending tasks is to define a new and consistent foreign policy strategy that replaces the paradigm of pragmatic acquiescence. Post-crisis Argentina—internally weak and externally very vulnerable—needs to have friends and allies; it is highly improbable that such a critical scenario will resolve itself through isolation or confrontation. Independently of the specific foreign policy profile that is finally adopted, two things appear to be clear from this vantage point: that Kirchner will search for a new international connection in which there will be no room for either isolation or ideological confrontation with the major centers of power, and that he will try to establish good relations with Brazil and the United States, although each of a distinct nature. The first case is one of giving substance to the long-announced bilateral strategic alliance; the second case is one of constructing a positive and cordial tie that will be sustained in defense of specific interests. The ties with these two countries don't exhaust Argentina's wide universe of foreign connections but still constitute the principal basis for any successful foreign policy strategy.

Notes

* Translated by David Pion-Berlin.

1. Following Dittmer's definition according to which "a strategic triangle may be understood as a sort of transactional game among three players," the relation between Argentina, Brazil, and the United States has constituted a typical strategic triangle. In accord with the same author, "three different systemic patterns of exchange relationships are conceivable: the ménage à trois, consisting of symmetrical amities among all three players; the romantic triangle, consisting of amity between one pivot player and two wing players, but enmity between each of the latter; and the stable marriage, consisting of amity between two of the players and enmity between each and the third." Lowell

Dittmer, "The Strategic Triangle: An Elementary Game-Theoretical Analysis," *World Politics* 33, no. 4 (July 1981): 485–89.

2. For a more recent analysis of Argentine relations with the other two sides of the triangle, see Mónica Hirst and Roberto Russell, *El MERCOSUR y los cambios en el sistema político internacional* (Buenos Aires: Fundación OSDE, 2001); Deborah Norden and Roberto Russell, *The United States and Argentina: Changing Relations in a Changing World* (New York: Routledge, 2002); Roberto Russell and Juan Tokatlian, *El lugar de Brasil en la política* (Buenos Aires: Fondo de Cultura Económica, 2003).

3. Gustavo Ferrari, *Esquema de la política exterior Argentina* (Buenos Aires: EUDEBA, 1981); Juan Carlos Puig, "La política exterior Argentina y sus tendencias profundas," *Revista Argentina de Relaciones Internacionales* 1 (1975).

4. At the end of the nineteenth century, Brazil shifted the axis of its special relations from London to Washington. The United States constituted its principal market and at the same time its main supplier and financier. Secondarily, the search for a special relation with the United States was aimed at neutralizing Argentina's military power and threats to Brazil that could have led to a subregional coalition led by Argentina. This is how the policy was perceived in Buenos Aires. Even more, many leaders saw it as the first effort to divide influence in the hemisphere.

5. Federico Pinedo, *La Argentina en la vorágine* (Buenos Aires: Ediciones Mundo Forense, 1943), 112.

6. As explained by the editorship of a journal that would have much influence in configuring visions of Brazil, in the decade of the 1970s "it is understood by 'key country' that within a determined region it could serve pivotally in the policies of a great power, that which grants it priority in its aid programs and economic and military assistance, etc." See the Editors, "Argentine-Brazilian Relations," *Estrategia*, no. 5 (January–February 1970): 49.

7. We name this paradigm globalist because from the time it was put into place, Argentina procured a wide diversification of external ties and developed, as a medium-power country, an active role in international negotiations over political and economic themes of a global nature. This paradigm entails the following premises: non-alignment vis-à-vis the United States that never implied an equidistance between the blocs; urging Latin American integration, although from a gradualist perspective and grounded in the acknowledgment of the great variety of national economic situations; a high profile in international forums for peace, disarmament, and East-West distention; rejecting international regimes and organizations that sought to freeze the distribution of world power, particularly in relation to the development of sensible technologies; opposition to the establishment of supranational organizations that would curtail Argentine autonomy and development; execution of a development strategy oriented toward import substitution at a national and regional level as a principal route to overcome the vulnerabilities of the traditional primary export model; introduction of reforms to the international financial and economic system that contemplates the interests of developing countries; and diversification of the external commercial partnerships irrespective of ideology.

8. The policy shifts toward either a greater alignment or confrontation with Washington were ephemeral, given that they responded to internal as well as international circumstances of the moment and were promoted by groups, from the right to left ends of the political spectrum, that never achieved sufficient power to put in place alternative formulas.

9. The most important step that changed the direction of the bilateral relation from

one of competition for sub-regional influence to cooperation was the signing of the Uruguayan Accords of April 22, 1961, by Presidents Arturo Frondizi and Janio Quadros. The principal objective was to arrange for the two countries to engage in joint international actions, "a function of common South American conditions." See Juan A. Lanus, *De Chapultepec al Beagle: Política exterior de Argentina, 1945–1980* (Buenos Aires: Edición Emecé, 1984), 298.

10. The principal theme that divided the two countries in the 1960s and 1970s was the harnessing of energy from rivers and more specifically the dispute over the Itaipú hydraulic project that would soon be completed, which gave rise to a confrontation that transcended the bilateral plane.

11. It is important to note that Argentina's military deployment toward Chile realized by the end of 1978, as much as its deployment for the Malvinas War, ruled out the possibility that Brazil would take some type of hostile action against Argentina. See Rosendo Fraga, "Una visión política del Mercosur," in *Mercosur: Entre la realidad y la utopia*, ed. Jorge Campbell (Buenos Aires: GEL, 1999), 272.

12. Jakob Gustavsson, *The Politics of Foreign Policy Change: Explaining the Swedish Reorientation on EC Membership* (Lund: Tiden, 1998), 4.

13. Pragmatic acquiescence had the following premises: (1) subservience to the political and strategic interests of the United States, both globally and regionally; (2) the definition of national interests in economic terms; (3) active participation in the creation and strengthening of international regimes—especially in the area of security—in accord with the position of the industrialized, developed Western countries; (4) support for economic integration in the framework of regional openness; (5) executing a strategy of economic development structured along the lines of the so-called Washington Consensus; (6) confidence that market forces more than the state would ensure a new and successful international insertion for Argentina; and (7) acceptance of the basic rules of the international economic and financial order.

14. Adalberto Rodríguez Giavarini, "Hacia la integración latinomamericana," *La Nación*, August 30, 2000, 17.

15. "Bush promoted excellent relations." He sent a letter to Rodríguez Saá, *La Nación*, December 24, 2001, <http://www.lanacion.com.ar/01/12/24/dp_361815.asp>.

16. "El apoyo de los EE.UU. al gobierno de Rodríguez Saá," *Clarín*, December 28, 2001, <www.clarin.com/ultimo_momento/notas/2001-12-28/m-331784.htm>.

17. The multilateral credit organizations are Argentina's second largest creditors. With almost 28% of the public debt concentrated in these organizations, confronting the debt problem without first going through the IMF was unthinkable.

18. These ideas were expressed in a letter from Duhalde directed to President Bush on January 25, 2002, <http://www.merco-sur.net/opinion/Op=anteriores/opinion_2002/enero_2002>.

19. Then, after having supported important aid packages through the multilateral credit organizations, the U.S. government decided in December 2001 to turn against Argentina and not support the Fund's release of a disbursement previously agreed upon of 1.264 million dollars.

20. The arrival of Paul O'Neill, <http://nuevamayoria.com/ES/ANALISIS/martini/020806.html>.

21. Cited in María O'Donnell, "Las consecuencias económicas de los ataques," *La Nación*, September 21, 2001, <http://www.lanacion.com.ar/01/09/21/dx336913.asp>. Although Argentina lost relative importance for the United States after the terrorist

attacks, it was the same for the rest of Latin America, and it was very unlikely that it would have received some other treatment by the United States if the 9/11 events had not occurred. Before that day, the Bush administration was already prepared to apply exemplary measures toward Argentina for its reiterated non-compliance.

22. The accord, finally approved on January 25, 2003, lasted only eight months. During that same time, Argentina succeeded in postponing the payments it had to confront between January and August of that year for 11 billion dollars with the Fund and 4.4 billion with the Inter-American Development Bank and the World Bank.

23. One of the outstanding paragraphs of the communication said the following: "The implementation of an effective transition program could build and strengthen progress that the Argentine authorities are making to stabilize the economic and financial situation of the country." Cited in *La Nación*, January 17, 2003, <www.lanacion.com.ar/03/01/17/de_466871.asp>.

24. *La Nación*, January 26, 2003, <www.lanacion.com.ar/03/01/26/dp_469173.asp>.

25. See "La Cámara Baja se une con las reclamaciones del Senado," <www.lainsignia.org/2000/emero/be_156.htm>.

26. See the Human Rights Commission Resolution 2002/18, U.N. High Commissioner for Human Rights.

27. Human Rights Commission Resolution 2002/18.

28. One ought to note that in the 2002–2003 period, Buenos Aires did not declare itself against either Plan Colombia or Washington's later Andean initiative that de facto regionalized the "war against drugs."

29. The catalyst for this meeting was FARC's attack on the El Nogal nightclub (35 deaths, 165 wounded) in the center of Bogotá on February 7, 2003.

30. *El Espectador*, Colombia, February 16, 2003. Such was the recognition of Argentina's support for Colombia that President Uribe, who rarely attends inaugural ceremonies in the region—and for example was not at Lula's inauguration—attended the inauguration of Néstor Kirchner in good measure as retribution for the outgoing president Eduardo Duhalde.

31. *El Tiempo*, Colombia, February 19, 2003.

32. See Daniel Santoro, "Guerra a la logística de la droga Colombiana," *Clarín*, February 19, 2003.

33. See Joaquín Morales Solá, "Respaldo implícito Argentino a la ofensiva, ante un pedido de Estados Unidos," *La Nación*, February 6, 2003, <www.lanacion.com.ar>, and "La Argentina frente al nuevo orden mundial," *La Nación*, February 23, 2003, 27.

34. Interview with Carlos Ruckauf, "No inmiscuirse no es ser neutral," *La Nación*, March 23, 2003.

35. Again in 2003 the U.N. Human Rights Commission took up the Cuban case. On April 17, 2003, a resolution co-sponsored by Costa Rica, Nicaragua, Peru, and Uruguay requested that the Cuban government receive the personal representative of the U.N. High Commission for Human Rights to inspect the state of human rights on the island. The resolution passed with 24 votes in favor (along with the co-sponsors were Guatemala, Paraguay, Chile, and Mexico), 20 against (the only Latin American country to vote this way was Venezuela) and 9 abstentions (Brazil and Argentina were the two Latin American nations to abstain).

36. It can be pointed out here that one of the first measures taken by Duhalde after coming to power was to dispatch José de la Sota—former ambassador to Brazil and current governor of Córdoba—to Brazil to get that country to quickly accept the new Argentine

government without doubting its legitimacy and to support it in its negotiations with the multilateral credit organizations.

37. Joint Press Conference communication, "Encuentro de trabajo entre Presidentes Luiz Inácio da Silva y Eduardo Duhalde," *La Nación*, January 15, 2003.

38. In particular, see José Natanson, "Carlos Altamirano: Kirchner tiene una vision al estilo de los años 70," *Página 12*, February 17, 2004; and Juan Gabriel Tokatlian, "Kirchner frente al mundo," *La Nación*, February 6, 2004.

39. See Mara Laudonia, "George Bush invitó al Presidente Argentino a visi-tar la Casa Blanca," *El Cronista*, July 18, 2003; Ana Baron, "Un encuentro para reducir desconfianza," *Clarín 19*, July 2003; and Jorge Rosales, "La Agenda económica de Bush y Kirchner," *La Nación*, July 20, 2003.

40. See Daniel Gallo, "Peligra un ejercicio military con EEUU," *La Nación*, October 2, 2003; Matias Longoni, "Los más rebeldes de Cancún se dan cita en Buenos Aires," *Clarín*, October 10, 2003; José Rosales, "Criticó Noriega el auxilio de Kirchner a Cuba," *La Nación*, October 18, 2003; Daniel Santero, "EEUU criticó la relación con Cuba y hubo un entredicho diplomático," *Clarín*, January 7, 2004; Jorge Elias, "Misión conjunta a Bolivia," *La Nación*, October 17, 2003; and Julio Blanck, "Una zambullida de Kirchner en la política de la región." *Clarín*, January 16, 2004.

41. It is worth pointing out that 9.1% of the $87.05 million in defaulted Argentine bonds are in the hands of U.S. citizens—the fourth highest percentage after Argentina itself, Italy, and Switzerland.

42. The idea, for those who sustained it, of linking up with the whole of Latin America implied drawing closer to Mexico—a trusted ally of the United States—with the objective of counterbalancing Brazil's power and always leaving open the possibility of defection to get, for example, some kind of bilateral trade deal with the United States.

43. See Mónica Hirst, "Con Brazil, socios para crecer," *Clarín*, October 15, 2003; Joaquín Morales Solá, "Tras los disensos, Buenos Aires marcará la era de los consensos," *La Nación*, October 16, 2003; and Lucas Colonia, "Kirchner y Lula ratificaron su alianza," *La Nación*, October 18, 2003.

44. See Horacio Verbitsky, "Mucho más que dos," *Página 12*, October 19, 2003.

45. See Luis Esnal, "Brasil busca recuperar el discurso de centro-izqiuierda," *La Nación*, March 16, 2004, 8.

46. Joint Declaration on Cooperation for Growth with Equity, Rio de Janeiro, March 16, 2004, Ministry of Foreign Relations, International Trade and Culture.

47. See "Acta de Copacabana," Rio de Janeiro, Brazil, March 16, 2004, Mimeo.

Bibliography

Abal Medina, Juan. "Elementos teóricos para el análisis contemporáneo de los partidos políticos: Un reordenamiento del campo semántico." In *El asedio a la política: Los partidos tras la década del neoliberalismo en Latinoamérica,* edited by Marcelo Cavarozzi and Juan Abal Medina. Rosario: Homo Sapiens, 2002.

Abal Medina, Juan, and Ernesto Calvo. "Y Ud. ¿por quién dice que votó? Una agenda de investigación sobre los mecanismos electorales de control político." In *El federalismo electoral argentino: Sobrerepresentación, reforma política y gobierno dividido en la Argentina,* edited by Juan Abal Medina and Ernesto Calvo. Buenos Aires: EUDEBA, 2001.

Abal Medina, Juan, and Claudio Iglesias. "Acción estratégica y comportamiento colectivo: Una revisión." *Revista Argentina de Ciencia Política,* no. 1 (1997), Buenos Aires.

Abal Medina, Juan, and Facundo Nejamkis. "Capacidades estatales: La construcción de capacidad administrativa y los cambios en el régimen de empleo público." *Revista SAAP* 1, no. 1 (2002), Buenos Aires.

———. "El Estado." In *Introducción a la Ciencia Política* (nueva versión), edited by Julio Pinto. Buenos Aires: EUDEBA, 2003.

Abal Medina, Juan, and Julieta Suárez Cao. "Análisis crítico del sistema electoral argentino: Evolución histórica y desempeño efectivo." *Revista de Ciencias Sociales* 14 (2003), Universidad Nacional de Quilmes.

———. "Postscriptum: Recorriendo los senderos partidarios latinoamericanos en la última década." In *El asedio a la política: Los partidos tras la década del neoliberalismo en Latinoamérica,* edited by Marcelo Cavarozzi and Juan Abal Medina. Rosario: Homo Sapiens, 2002.

Acuña, Carlos. "Las causas político-institucionales de la actual crisis argentina." In *Nuevas cuestiones sociopolíticas en el escenario latinoamericano,* edited by C. Barbato. Montevideo: CEPAL-Trilce-INTAL, 2002.

———. *La nueva matriz política argentina.* Buenos Aires: Nueva Visión, 1996.

Acuña, Carlos, and Catalina Smulovitz. "Militares en la transición argentina: Del gobierno a la subordinación constitucional." In *La nueva matriz política argentina,* compiled by Carlos H. Acuña. Buenos Aires: Ediciones Nueva Visión, 1995.

Adler, Alfred. *The Neurotic Constitution.* New York: Moffat Yard and Company, 1917.

Agüero, Felipe. *Militares, civiles y democracia.* Madrid: Alianza Editorial, 1995.

———. "The Military and the Limits to Democratization in South America." In *Issues in Democratic Consolidation: The New South American Democracies in Comparative Perspective*, edited by Scott Mainwaring, Guillermo O'Donnell, and Samuel Valenzuela. Notre Dame: University of Notre Dame Press, 1992.

America's Watch and Centro de Estudios Legales y Sociales. *Police Violence in Argentina: Torture and Police Killings in Buenos Aires*. New York: America's Watch, December 1991.

Andersen, Martin Edwin. *La policía: Pasado, presente, y propuestas para el futuro*. Buenos Aires: Ed. Sudamericana, 2001.

Arendt, Hannah. *On Revolution*. The Viking Press, 1963.

———. *¿Qué es la política?* Barcelona: Paidós, 1997.

Arisó, Guillermo, and Gabriel Jácobo. *El golpe SA: La guerra de intereses que estalló en el 2001 y dejó al país en ruinas*. Buenos Aires: Norma, 2002.

Arroyo, Daniel. "Estado y sociedad civil en el proceso de descentralización." In *Municipios, democratización y derechos humanos*. Buenos Aires: CODESEDH, 2000.

———. "La gestión municipal en Argentina: Entre la crisis social, la planificación y el desarrollo local." In *Desarrollo Municipal*. Lomas de Zamora: Instituto de Administración Municipal/Facultad de Ciencias Económicas, Universidad Nacional de Lomas de Zamora, 2001.

Auyero, Javier. "Cultura política, destitución social y clientelismo político en Buenos Aires: Un estudio etnográfico." Pp. 181–208 in *Desde abajo: La transformación de las identidades sociales*, edited by Maristella Svampa. Buenos Aires: Universidad Nacional de General Sarmiento/Biblos, 2000.

———. *Favores por votos*. Buenos Aires: Editorial Losada, 1998.

———. "Introducción: Claves para pensar la marginación." In *Parias urbanos: Marginalidad en la ciudad a comienzo del milenio*, edited by Loic Wacquant. Buenos Aires: Manantial, 2001.

———. *La política de los pobres: Las prácticas clientelistas del peronismo*. Buenos Aires: Editorial Manantial, 2001.

———. *Poor People's Politics: Peronist Survival Networks and the Legacy of Evita*. Durham, N.C.: Duke University Press, 2001.

———. *La protesta: Retratos de la beligerancia popular en la Argentina democrática*. Buenos Aires: "Serie Extramuros," Universidad de Buenos Aires, Libros del Rojas, 2002.

Azpiazu, Daniel, Graciela Gutman, and Adolfo Vispo. *La desregulación de los mercados*. Buenos Aires: Norma, 1999.

Basualdo, Eduardo. *Concentración y centralización del capital en la Argentina durante la década del noventa*. Buenos Aires: Universidad Nacional de Quilmes, 2000.

———. *Sistema político y modelo de acumulación en la Argentina: Notas sobre el transformismo argentino durante la valorización financiera (1976–2001)*. Buenos Aires: Universidad Nacional de Quilmes, 2001.

Bayer, Osvaldo. *La Patagonia rebelde*, edición definitiva. Buenos Aires: Planeta, 2002.

Beccaria, Luis. *Empleo e integración social*. Buenos Aires: Fondo de Cultura Económica, 2001.

Berger, Suzanne. *Politics and Anti-Politics in Western Europe in the Seventies*. Cambridge: Daedalus, 1979.

Blanc, Jerôme. "Monnaie, confiance de temps." In *La construction sociale de la confiance*, edited by Philippe Bernoux and Jean-Michel Servet. Paris: Montchrestien, 1997.

Bluestone, Barry, and Bennett Harrison. *Growing Prosperity*. Boston: Houghton Mifflin, 2000.

Bonasso, Miguel. *El palacio y la calle: Crónicas de insurgentes y conspiradores*. Buenos Aires: Planeta, 2002.

Born, Hans, Marina Caparini, and Karl Haltiner. "Models of Democratic Control of the Armed Forces: A Multi-Country Study Comparing 'Good Practices' of Democratic Control." Geneva: Geneva Centre for the Democratic Control of Armed Forces (DCAF), *Working Paper Series*, no. 47 (July 2002).

Bosoer, Fabián, and Santiago Leiras. "Los fundamentos filosófico-políticos del decisionismo presidencial en la Argentina, 1989–1999." Pp. 41–90 in *Argentina entre dos siglos*, edited by Julio Pinto. Buenos Aires, EUDEBA, 2001.

Botana, Natalio. "Prólogo." In *El federalismo electoral argentino: Sobrerepresentación, reforma política y gobierno dividido en la Argentina*, edited by Juan Abal Medina and Ernesto Calvo. Buenos Aires: EUDEBA, 2001.

Cafiero, Mario, and Javier Llorens. *La Argentina robada*. Ediciones Macchi, 2002.

Calcagno, Alfredo F. "El régimen de convertibilidad y el systema bancario en la Argentina." *Revista de la Cepal*, no. 61 (April 1997), Santiago de Chile.

Calvo, Ernesto, and Juan Abal Medina. *El federalismo electoral argentino: Sobrerepresentación, reforma política y gobierno dividido en la Argentina*. Buenos Aires: EUDEBA, 2001.

Camarasa, Jorge. *Días de furia*. Buenos Aires: Ed. Sudamericana, 2002.

Caparini, Marina. "Lessons Learned and Upcoming Research Issues in Democratic Control of Armed Forces and Security Sector Reform." Geneva: Geneva Centre for the Democratic Control of Armed Forces (DCAF), *Working Paper Series*, no. 41 (October 2002).

Carlson, Eric Stener. "The Influence of French 'Revolutionary War' Ideology on the Use of Torture in Argentina's 'Dirty War.'" *Human Rights Review* 1.4 (July–September 2000).

———. *I Remember Julia: Voices of the Disappeared*. Philadelphia: Temple University Press, 1996.

Castel, Robert. *La metamorfosis de la questión social*. Buenos Aires: Paidó, 1995.

———. "¿Por qué la clase obrera perdió la partida?" In *Revista Actual Marx*, "Las nuevas relaciones de clase," vol. II, Argentine edition, 2000.

Castoriadis, Cornelius. *Los dominios del hombre: Las encrucijadas del laberinto*. Barcelona: Gedisa, 1998.

Cavarozzi, Marcelo. *Autoritarismo y democracia 1955–1996*. Buenos Aires: Ariel, 1997.

———. "Beyond Transitions to Democracy in Latin America." *Journal of Latin American Studies*, no. 24 (1992).

———. *El capitalismo político tardío y su crisis en América Latina*. Rosario: Homo Sapiens, 1996.

Cavarozzi, Marcelo, and E. Casullo. "Los partidos políticos en América Latina hoy: ¿Consolidación o crisis?" In *El asedio a la política: Los partidos tras la década del neoliberalismo en Latinoamérica*, edited by Marcelo Cavarozzi and Juan Abal Medina. Rosario: Homo Sapiens, 2002.

Centro de Estudios Legales y Sociales. *El Estado frente a la protesta social: 1996–2002*. Buenos Aires: Siglo XXI Editores Argentina, 2003.

Collier, David, and Steven Levitsky. "Democracy with Adjectives: Conceptual Innovation in Comparative Investigation." *World Politics* 49 (April 1997).

Collier, Ruth, and David Collier. *Shaping the Political Arena: Critical Junctures, the Labor Movement, and Regime Dynamics in Latin America.* Princeton: Princeton University Press, 1991.

Comisión Nacional sobre la Desaparición de Personas (National Commission on the Disappeared): *Nunca más: Informe de la Comisión Nacional sobre la Desaparición de Personas.* Buenos Aires: EUDEBA, 1984.

Covas, Horacio, Carlos De Sanzo, and Heloisa Primavera. *Reinventando el mercado: La experiencia de la Red Global del Trueque en Argentina.* <http://www.trueque.org.ar/>, 3–4, 1998.

Cross, Cecilia, and Juan Montes Cató. "Crisis de representación e identidades colectivas en los sectores populares: Acerca de la experiencia de organizaciones piqueteras." Pp. 85–100 in *La atmósfera incandesente: Escritos políticos sobre la Argentina movilizada,* edited by Osvaldo Battistini. Buenos Aires: Asociación Trabajo y Sociedad, 2002.

Crozier, Michel, Samuel Huntington, and Joji Watanuki. *The Crisis of Democracy.* New York: New York University Press, 1975.

Dalton, Russell, and Martin Wattenberg. "Unthinkable Democracy: Political Change in Advanced Industrial Democracies." In *Parties without Partisans: Political Change in Advanced Industrial Democracies,* edited by Russell Dalton and Martin Wattenberg. Oxford: Oxford University Press, 2002.

Damil, Mario. "El balance de pagos y la deuda externa bajo la convertibilidad." *Boletín Informativo Techint,* no. 303 (December 2000), Buenos Aires.

Delamata, Gabriela. "De los 'estallidos' provinciales a la generalización de las protestas en Argentina: Perspectiva y contexto en la significación de las nuevas protestas." Manuscript, Depto. de Ciencia Política, Universidad Nacional San Martín, 2002.

De Riz, Liliana, and Juan Carlos Portantiero. *Aportes para el desarrollo humano de la Argentina.* Buenos Aires: PNUD Argentina, 2002.

Desch, Michael C. *Civilian Control of the Military.* Baltimore: Johns Hopkins University Press, 1999.

Diamint, Rut. *Democracia y seguridad en América Latina.* Buenos Aires: Nuevohacer, GEL, 2002.

———, ed. Message of the JEMGE (Jefe del Estado Major General del Ejército) on the anniversary of El Libertador, January 12, 1998. In *Argentina y la seguridad internacional.* Santiago, Chile: FLACSO-Chile, Woodrow Wilson Center, 1998.

Dittmer, Lowell. "The Strategic Triangle: An Elementary Game-Theoretical Analysis." *World Politics* 33, no. 4 (July 1981): 485–89.

Dutil, Carlos, and Ricardo Ragendorfer. *La Bonaerense: Historia criminal de la policía de la Provincia de Buenos Aires.* Buenos Aires: Planeta, 1997.

Duverger, Maurice. *Los partidos políticos.* México, D.F.: Fondo de Cultura Económica, 1960.

Eisinger, Peter. "The Conditions of Protest Behavior in American Cities." *American Political Science Review* 67 (1973): 11–28.

Elster, Jon. *Ulises desatado: Estudios sobre racionalidad, precompromiso y restricciones.* Barcelona: Gedisa, 2003.

Epstein, Edward. "Explaining Worker Mobilization in Recent Argentina and Chile." Paper presented at international congress of the Latin American Studies Association, Washington, D.C., September 2001.

————. "Labor-State Conflict in the New Argentine Democracy: Parties, Union Factions, and Power Maximizing." Pp. 124–56 in *The New Argentine Democracy*, edited by Edward Epstein. Westport, Conn.: Praeger, 1992.

Esping-Andersen, Gøsta. *Politics Against Markets*. Princeton: Princeton University Press, 1988.

Estrategia Editors. "Argentine-Brazilian Relations." *Estrategia*, no. 5 (January–February 1970): 49.

Evans, Peter. "El estado como problema y como solución." *Desarrollo Económico* 140 (1996), Buenos Aires.

Feldman, Silvio, ed. *Sociedad y sociabilidad en la Argentina de los 90*. Buenos Aires: Biblos–Universidad Nacional de General Sarmiento, 2002.

Ferrari, Gustavo. *Esquema de la política exterior argentina*. Buenos Aires: EUDEBA, 1981.

Finer, S. E. *The Man on Horseback*. London: Penguin Books, 1976.

Fishlow, Albert. "The Latin American State." *Journal of Economic Perspectives* 4, no. 3 (1990).

Fitch, J. Samuel. *The Armed Forces and Democracy in Latin America*. Baltimore: Johns Hopkins University Press, 1998.

Fraga, Rosendo. "Una visión política del Mercosur." In *Mercosur: Entre la realidad y la utopia*, edited by Jorge Campbell. Buenos Aires: GEL, 1999.

Galiani, Sebastián, Daniel Heymann, and Mariano Tommasi. "Expectativas frustradas: El ciclo de la convertibilidad." *Desarrollo Económico* 43, no. 169 (2003): 15–16, Buenos Aires.

García, Marina. *Las asambleas barriales, esas delicadas creaturas: Tesis de grado*. Buenos Aires: Universidad Nacional General Sarmiento, 2002.

García Delgado, Daniel. "Ciudadanía, participación y desarrollo local." In *Alternativas frente a la globalización: Pensamiento social de la iglesia en el umbral del tercer milenio*, edited by Grupo de Pensamiento Social de la Iglesia. Buenos Aires: Editorial São Paulo, 1999.

————. *Hacia un nuevo modelo de gestión local: Municipio y sociedad civil en Argentina*. Buenos Aires: FLACSO-CBC-UCC, 1997.

Gargarella, Roberto. *La justicia frente al gobierno*. Buenos Aires: Ariel, 1996.

Giarracca, Norma, et al. *La protesta social en la Argentina: Transformaciones económicas y crisis social en el interior del país*. Buenos Aires: Alianza, 2001.

Godio, Julio. *La alianza*. Buenos Aires: Grijalbo, 1998.

González Bombal, Inés. "Sociabilidad en clases medias en descenso: Experiencia en el trueque." In *Sociedad y sociabilidad en la Argentina de los 90*, edited by Silvio Feldman. Buenos Aires: Biblos–Universidad Nacional de General Sarmiento, 2002.

Graziano, Frank. *Divine Violence: Spectacle, Psychosexuality, and Radical Christianity in the Argentine "Dirty War."* Boulder: Westview Press, 1992.

Graziano, Walter. *Las siete plagas de la economía argentina*. Buenos Aires: Norma, 2001.

Grossman, Dave. *On Killing: The Psychological Cost of Learning to Kill in War and Society*. Boston: Little, Brown and Company, 1996.

Gustavsson, Jakob. *The Politics of Foreign Policy Change: Explaining the Swedish Reorientation on EC Membership*. Lund: Tiden, 1998.

Haltiner, Karl W. "Democratic Control of Armed Forces: Renaissance of an Old Issue?" Geneva: Geneva Centre for the Democratic Control of Armed Forces (DCAF) *Working Paper Series*, no. 45 (July 2002).

Hirst, Mónica, and Roberto Russell. *El MERCOSUR y los cambios en el sistema político internacional*. Buenos Aires: Fundación OSDE, 2001.

Hopenhayn, Benjamin, Jorge Schvarzer, and Hernán Finkelstein. "El tipo de cambio en perspectiva histórica: Aportes para un debate." *Notas de Coyuntura*, no. 7 (October 2002), CESPA, Buenos Aires.

Hunter, Wendy. *State and Soldier in Latin America: Redefining the Military in Argentina, Brazil, and Chile*. Washington, D.C.: Working Paper Series, United States Institute of Peace, 1996.

Huntington, Samuel P. "Reforming Civil-Military Relations." *Journal of Democracy* 6, no. 4 (1995): 9–10.

———. *The Soldier and the State: The Theory and Politics of Civil-Military Relations*. Cambridge: Harvard University Press, 1975.

Katz, Richard, and Peter Mair. "Changing Models of Party Organization and Party Democracy: The Emergence of the Cartel Party." *Party Politics* 1 (January 1995): 5–28.

Kirchner, Néstor, and Torcuato Di Tella. *Después del derrumbe: Teoría y práctica política en la Argentina que viene*

Kohn, Richard H. "How Democracies Control the Military." *Journal of Democracy* 8, no. 4 (1997): 140–53.

Kosacoff, Bernardo, and Adrián Ramos. *Liberalización, estabilidad y desarrollo: El caso argentino*. Brasilia: FUNCEB, 2002.

Laacher, Smaïn. *Les SEL: Une utopie anticapitaliste en practique*. Paris: La Dispute, 2002.

Laclau, Ernesto. *Nuevas reflexiones sobre la revolución de nuestro tiempo*. Buenos Aires: Nueva Visión, 1993.

Lanus, Juan A. *De Chapultepec al Beagle: Política exterior de Argentina, 1945–1980*. Buenos Aires: Edición Emecé, 1984.

Latorraca, Martín, Hugo Montero, and Carlos Rodríguez. "Policía y corrupción policial." *Le Monde Diplomatique* (May 2003), Buenos Aires.

Lawson, Kay, and Peter Merkl. *When Parties Fail: Emerging Alternative Organizations*. Princeton: Princeton University Press, 1988.

Levitsky, Steven. "The 'Normalization' of Argentine Politics." *Journal of Democracy* 11, no. 2 (2000): 56.

———. *Transforming Labor-Based Parties in Latin America: Argentine Peronism in Comparative Perspective*. Cambridge: Cambridge University Press, 2003.

Linn, Ruth. "Terrorism, Morality and Soldiers' Motivation to Fight: An Example from the Israeli Experience in Lebanon." *Terrorism* 11 (1988): 140.

Llenderrozas, Elsa. "La administración de la defensa después de los procesos de democratización: El caso de Argentina bajo el gobierno de Menem." In *Entre votos y botas*, by Héctor Luis Saint Pierre and Suzeley Kalil Mathías. Campinas, Brazil: Universidad de Campinas, 2002.

Lobaiza, Humberto. "Las relaciones cívico-militares en la Argentina." *Revista de la Escuela Superior de Guerra* (July–September 1992): 111–12.

Lodola, Germán. "Social Protests under Industrial Restructuring: Argentina in the Nineties." Manuscript, Department of Political Science, University of Pittsburgh, 2002.

Lomnitz, Larissa. *Redes sociales, cultura y poder: Ensayos de antropología latinoamericana*. México, D.F.: FLACSO and M.A. Porrúa, 1994.

López, Ernesto, and David Pion-Berlin. *Democracia y Cuestión Militar*. Buenos Aires: Universidad Nacional de Quilmes, 1996.

Maier, Julio. "Breve historia institucional de la policía argentina." In *Justicia en la calle: Ensayos sobre la policía en América Latina*, edited by Peter Waldmann. Medellín: Biblioteca Jurídica Diké, 1996.

Maier, Julio, Martín Abregú, and Sofia Tiscornia. "El papel de la policía en la Argentina y su situación actual." In *Justicia en la calle: Ensayos sobre la policía en América Latina*, edited by Peter Waldmann. Medellín: Biblioteca Jurídica Diké, 1996.

Manent, Pierre. *Cours familier de philosophie politique*. Paris: Fayard, 2001.

Manin, Bernard. *Los principios del gobierno representivo*. Madrid: Alianza, 1998.

Manin, Bernard, Adam Przeworski, and Susan Stokes. *Democracy, Accountability and Representation*. Cambridge: Cambridge University Press, 1999.

Martuccelli, Danilo, and Maristella Svampa. *La plaza vacía: Las transformaciones del peronismo*. Buenos Aires: Losada, 1997.

McAdam, Doug, John McCarthy, and Mayer Zald, eds. *Comparative Perspectives on Social Movements: Political Opportunities, Mobilizing Structures, and Cultural Framings*. Cambridge: Cambridge University Press, 1996.

McAdam, Doug, Sidney Tarrow, and Charles Tilly. "Toward an Integrated Perspective on Social Movements and Revolutions." Pp. 142–73 in *Comparative Politics*, edited by Mark Lichbach and Alan Zuckerman. Cambridge: Cambridge University Press, 1997.

McGuire, James. "Distributive Conflict, Party Institutionalism, and Democracy." Pp. 262–86 in *Peronism Without Perón*, edited by James McGuire. Stanford: Stanford University Press, 1997.

McSherry, J. Patrice. "National Security and Social Crisis in Argentina." *Journal of Third World Studies* 17, no. 1 (Spring 2000): 21–43.

Merklen, Denis. "Inscription territoriale et action collective: Les occupations illégales de terres urbaines depuis les années 1980 en Argentine." Paris: Doctoral Thesis, Ecole des Hautes Etudes en Sciences Sociales, 2001.

Miguez, Daniel, and Alejandro Isla. "Conclusiones: El estado y la violencia urbana. Problemas de legitimidad y legalidad." In *Heridas urbanas: Violencia delictiva y transformaciones sociales en los noventa*, edited by Alejandro Isla and Daniel Miguez. Buenos Aires: Editorial de las Ciencias and FLACSO-Argentina, 2003.

Minujin, Alberto, and Gabriel Kessler. *La nueva pobreza en la Argentina*. Buenos Aires: Planeta, 1995.

Mocca, Edgardo. "Los partidos politicos: Entre el derrumbe y la oportunidad." In *¿Qué cambió en la política argentina?*, edited by Isidoro Cheresky and Jean-Michel Blanquer. Rosario: Homo Sapiens, 2004.

Montero, José Ramón, and Richard Gunther. "Introduction: Reviewing and Reassessing Parties." In *Political Parties: Old Concepts and New Challenges*, edited by Richard Gunther, José Ramón Montero, and Juan J. Linz. Oxford: Oxford University Press, 2002.

MTD (Movimiento de Trabajadores Desocupados en la C.T.D. "Aníbal Verón"). *Trabajo, dignidad y cambio social: Una experiencia de los movimientos de trabajadores desocupados en la Argentina* (May 2002).

MTD Solano (Movimiento de Trabajadores Desocupados de Solano). *Situaciones* 4 (December 2001).

MTSS (Ministerio de Trabajo y Seguridad Social). *Programa Trabajar III: Documento Base*. Buenos Aires: Secretaría de Empleo y Capacitación Laboral, 1998.

Norden, Deborah, and Roberto Russell. *The United States and Argentina: Changing Relations in a Changing World.* New York: Routledge, 2002.

North, Douglas. *Instituciones, cambio institucional y desempeño económico.* México, D.F.: Fondo de Cultura Económica, 1993.

Novaro, Marcos. *Continuidades y discontinuidades en la crisis argentina.* Buenos Aires: FLACSO, mimeo, 2003.

———. *El derrumbe político en el ocaso de la convertibilidad.* Buenos Aires: Norma, 2002.

———. "El presidencialismo argentino entre la reelección y la alternancia." In *Políticas e instituciones de las nuevas democracias latinoamericanas,* edited by Isidoro Cheresky and Inés Pousadela. Buenos Aires: Paidós, 2001.

Novaro, Marcos, and Vicente Palermo. *Los caminos de la centroizquierda: Dilemas y desafíos del Frepaso y de la Alianza.* Buenos Aires: Losada, 1998.

———. *El derrumbe político en el ocaso de la convertibilidad.* Buenos Aires: Norma, 2002.

Nun, José. *Democracia: ¿Gobierno del pueblo o gobierno de los políticos?* México, D.F.: Fondo de Cultura Económica, 2000.

———. "El enigma argentino." *Punto de Vista* 71 (December 2001): 1–5.

———. *Marginalidad y exclusión social.* México, D.F.: Fondo de Cultura Económica, 2001.

———. "Populismo, representación y menemismo." *Sociedad* 5 (October 1994): 91–122.

———. *La rebelión del coro.* Buenos Aires: Nueva Visión, 1989.

———. "Vaivenes de un régimen social de acumulación en decadencia." Pp. 83–116 in *Ensayos sobre la transición democrática en la Argentina,* by José Nun and Juan Carlos Portantiero. Buenos Aires: Puntosur, 1987.

———. "Variaciones sobre un tema de Hegel." In *La ética del compromiso,* by José Burucúa, et al. Buenos Aires: Altamira/Fundación OSDE, 2002.

Nun, José, and Juan Carlos Portantiero. *Ensayos sobre la transición democrática en la Argentina.* Buenos Aires: Puntosur, 1987.

Observatoire Géopolitique des Drogues. *The World Geopolitics of Drugs, 1998/1999.* Paris: Observatoire Géopolitique des Drogues, 2000.

O'Donnell, Guillermo. *Contrapuntos: Ensayos escogidos sobre autoritarismo y democracia.* Buenos Aires: Paidós, 1997.

———. "Teoría democrática y política comparada." *Desarrollo Económico* 39, no. 156 (2000), Buenos Aires.

O'Donnell, Guillermo, Jorge Vargas Cullell, and Jorge Osvaldo Iazzetta, eds. *Democracia, desarrollo humano y ciudadanía.* Rosario: Editorial Homo Sapiens, 2003.

Offe, Claus. *Contradictions of the Welfare State.* Cambridge: MIT Press, 1984.

Ollier, María Matilde. *Las coaliciones políticas en la Argentina: El caso de la Alianza.* Buenos Aires: Fondo de Cultura Económica, 2001.

Olson, Mancur. *Poder y prosperidad.* Buenos Aires: Siglo XXI, 2001.

Orlansky, Dora. "Políticas de descentralización y desintervención estatal." Paper presented at the XXI International Congress of the Latin American Studies Association, Chicago, 1998.

Ostiguy, Pierre. *Los capitanes de la industria.* Buenos Aires: Legasa, 1990.

Oviedo, Luis. *Una historia del movimiento piquetero: De las primeras coordinadoras a las asambleas nacionales.* Buenos Aires: Rumbos, 2001.

Palermo, Vicente, and Marcos Novaro. *Política y poder en el gobierno de Menem.* Buenos Aires: Norma, 1996.

Panebianco, Angelo. *Modelos de partido*. Madrid: Alianza Universidad, 1990.

Pinedo, Federico. *La Argentina en la vorágine*. Buenos Aires: Ediciones Mundo Forense, 1943.

Pion-Berlin, David. "Civil Military Circumvention: How Argentine State Institutions Compensate for a Weakened Chain of Command." In *Civil-Military Relations in Latin America: New Critical Perspectives*, edited by David Pion-Berlin. Chapel Hill–London: University of North Carolina Press, 2001.

———. "Will Soldiers Follow? Economic Integration and Regional Security in the Southern Cone." *Journal of Inter-American Studies and World Affairs* 42 (Spring 2000): 43–69.

Pion-Berlin, David, and Craig Arcenaux. "Decision-Makers or Decision-Takers? Military Missions and Civilian Control in Democratic South America." *Armed Forces & Society* 26, no. 3 (Spring 2000): 413–36.

Portantiero, Juan Carlos. "La transición entre la confrontación y el acuerdo." Pp. 281–82 in *Ensayos sobre la transición democrática en la Argentina*, edited by José Nun and Juan Carlos Portantiero. Buenos Aires: Puntosur, 1987.

Pousadela, Inés. "Los partidos políticos han muerto: ¡Larga vida a los partidos!" In *¿Qué cambió en la política argentina?*, edited by Isidoro Cheresky and Jean-Michel Blanquer. Rosario: Homo Sapiens, 2004.

Puex, Nathalie. "Las formas de la violencia en tiempos de crisis: Una villa miseria del Conurbano Bonaerense." In *Heridas urbanas: Violencia delictiva y transformaciones sociales en los noventa*, edited by Alejandro Isla and Daniel Miguez. Buenos Aires: Editorial de las Ciencias and FLACSO-Argentina, 2003.

Puig, Juan Carlos. "La política exterior Argentina y sus tendencias profundas." *Revista Argentina de Relaciones Internacionales* 1 (1975).

Pulhe, H. J. "Still the Age of Match-allism? Volksparteien and Parteienstaat in Crisis and Re-equilibration." In *Political Parties: Old Concepts and New Challenges*, edited by Richard Gunther. Oxford: Oxford University Press, 2002.

Reynoso, Diego. "La desigualdad del voto en Argentina." *Perfiles Latino-americanos*, no. 15 (1999), México, D.F.: 73–97.

———. "Sobre-representación distrital, permisividad electoral e inclusión partidaria." *Política y Gestión* 5 (2003), Buenos Aires.

Rieber, Robert W., and Robert J. Kelly. "Substance and Shadow: Images of the Enemy." In *The Psychology of War and Peace: The Image of the Enemy*, edited by Robert W. Rieber. New York: Plenum Press, 1991.

Rock, David. *Argentina 1516–1987: From Spanish Colonization to Alfonsín*. Berkeley: University of California Press, 1987.

Rojas Breu, Mariana. "El debate en torno a la dolarización: Ideas y propuestas." *Documento de Trabajo*, no. 2 (May 2002), CESPA, Buenos Aires.

Rosanvallon, Pierre. *Por una historia conceptual de lo político*. Buenos Aires: Fondo de Cultura Económica, 2003.

Rueschemeyer, Dietrich, Evelyn Stephens, and John Stephens. *Capitalist Development and Democracy*. Chicago: University of Chicago Press, 1992.

Russell, Roberto, and Juan Tokatlian. *El lugar de Brasil en la política*. Buenos Aires: Fondo de Cultura Económica, 2003.

Sain, Marcelo Fabián. *Seguridad, democracia, y reforma del sistema policial en la Argentina*. Buenos Aires: Fondo de Cultura Económica, 2002.

Scheetz, Thomas. "The Argentine Defense Budget: Its Context and a Methodology for Analysis." *Security and Defense Studies Review* 2, no. 6 (Summer 2002): 18.

Schuster, Federico, German Pérez, Sebastián Pereyra, et al. *La trama de la crisis: Modos y formas de protesta social a partir de los acontecimientos de Diciembre de 2001.* Buenos Aires: Informe de Coyuntura 3, Instituto de Investigaciones Gino Germani, Universidad de Buenos Aires, 2002.

Schvarzer, Jorge. *Convertibilidad y deuda externa.* Buenos Aires: Libros del Rojas, EUDEBA, 2002.

———. "Economía argentina: Situación y perspectives." *La Gaceta de Económicas* (June 24, 2001): 6.

———. "La estructura productiva argentina a mediados de la década del noventa: Tendencias visibles y un diagnóstico con interrogantes." *Documento de Trabajo,* no. 1 (July 1997), CREED, Buenos Aires.

———. "La fragilidad externa de la economía argentina." *La Gaceta de Económicas* (October 28, 2001), Buenos Aires.

———. *Implicación de un modelo económico: La experiencia argentina entre 1975 y 2000.* Buenos Aires: A-Z Editora, 1998.

———. "Indicadores industriales y diagnósticos de coyuntura en la Argentina: Precauciones de uso y elementos para un balance actualizado." *Documento de Trabajo,* no. 3 (December 1999), CREED, Buenos Aires.

———. *La política económica de Martínez de Hoz.* Buenos Aires: Hyspamerica, 1986.

Schvarzer, Jorge, and Hernán Finkelstein. "Bonos, cuasimonedas y política económica." *Notas de Coyuntura,* no. 8 (January 2003), CESPA, Buenos Aires.

Schvarzer, Jorge, and Ivan Heyn. "El comportamiento de las exportaciones argentinas en la década del noventa: Un balance de la convertibilidad." *Notas Técnicas,* no. 3 (November 2002), CESPA, Buenos Aires.

Schvarzer, Jorge, and Héctor Palomino. "Entre la informalidad y el desempleo: Una perspectiva de largo plazo sobre el mercado de trabajo en la Argentina." *Encrucijadas,* Revista de la Universidad de Buenos Aires, no. 4 (1996).

Schvarzer, Jorge, and Javier Papa. "El indicador sintético de servicios públicos y la marcha de la economía real (1993–2001)." *Notas Técnicas,* no. 1 (April 2002), CESPA, Buenos Aires.

Schvarzer, Jorge, and Mariana Rojas Breu. "Algunos rasgos básicos de la evolución económica argentina durante las dos últimas décadas vista en el contexto latinoamericano." *Notas Técnicas,* no. 2 (September 2002), CESPA, Buenos Aires.

Simmel, Georg. *El individuo y la libertad: Ensayos de crítica de la cultura.* Barcelona: Península, 1986.

Smulovitz, Catalina. "Judicialización y accountability social en Argentina." Paper presented at the XXII International Conference of the Latin American Studies Association, Washington, D.C., 2001.

Smulovitz, Catalina, and Enrique Peruzzotti. "Social Accountability in Latin America." *Journal of Democracy* 11, no. 2 (2000): 147–58.

Solá, Joaquín Morales. *Asalto a la illusión.* Buenos Aires: Planeta, 1990.

Sozzo, Máximo. "Usos de la violencia y construcción de la actividad policial en la Argentina." In *Violencias, delitos y justicias en la Argentina*, edited by Sandra Gayol and Gabriel Kessler. Buenos Aires: Manantial, 2002.

Stanley, Ruth. "Violencia policial en el Gran Buenos Aires: ¿Necesita el neoliberalismo una policía brava?" In *Violencia y regulación de conflictos en América Latina*, edited by Klaus Bodemer, Sabine Kurtenbach, and Klaus Meschkat. Buenos Aires: Nueva Visión/ ADLAF/HBS, 2001.

Stiglitz, Joseph. "Las dimensiones de las nuevas movilizaciones sociales." *El Rodaballo* VIII, no. 14 (July 2002), Buenos Aires.

———. *El malestar en la globalización*. Buenos Aires: Taurus, 2002.

Svampa, Maristella. "Las dimensiones de las nuevas movilizaciones sociales: Las asambleas barriales, segunda parte," in *Revista El Ojo Mocho* (2003), Buenos Aires.

Svampa, Maristella, and Sebastián Pereyra. *Entre la ruta y el barrio: La experiencia de las organizaciones piqueteras*. Buenos Aires: Biblos, 2003.

Tarrow, Sidney. *Power in Movement: Social Movements and Contentious Politics*. Cambridge: Cambridge University Press, 1998.

Thalmann, Rita. *La République de Weimar*. Paris: P.U.F., 1986.

Thurow, Lester. "Wages and the Service Sector." In *Restoring Broadly Shared Prosperity*, edited by Ray Marshall. Austin: University of Texas Press, 1997.

Toffler, Alvin. *La Troisième Vague*. Paris: Éditions Denoël, 1980.

Torre, Juan Carlos. "Los húerfanos de la política de partidos: Sobre los alcances y la naturaleza de la crisis de representación partidaria." *Desarrollo Económico* 42 (January–March 2003): 647–65.

Tsebelis, George. *Veto Players: How Political Institutions Work*. Princeton: Princeton University Press, 2002.

United Nations Office of Drug Control and Crime Prevention. *World Drug Report, 2000*. Oxford: Oxford University Press, 2000.

Vallespin, Alejandra. *La policía que supimos conseguir*. Buenos Aires: Planeta, 2002.

Varas, Augusto. *La autonomía militar en América Latina*. Caracas: Nueva Sociedad, 1988.

Verbitsky, Horacio. *La educación presidencial*. Buenos Aires: Puntosur, 1990.

———. *Robo para la corona: Los frutos prohibidos del árbol de la corrupción*. Buenos Aires: Planeta, 1996.

Villanueva, Ernesto, ed. *Empleo y globalización: La nueva cuestión social en la Argentina*. Buenos Aires: Universidad Nacional de Quilmes, 1997.

Waisman, Carlos. "Argentina." In *Democracy in Developing Countries: Latin America*, edited by Larry Diamond, Juan Linz, and Seymour Martin Lipset. Boulder, Colo.: Lynne Rienner, 1989.

Zarini, Helio Juan, ed. *Constitución Argentina: Comentada y concordada*. 2nd ed. Buenos Aires: Editorial Astrea, 1998.

Zibechi, Raúl. *Genealogía de la revuelta, Argentina: La sociedad en movimiento*. La Plata: Letra Libre, 2003.

Zovatto, Daniel, J. Mark Payne, Fernando Carrillo Flórez, and Andrés Allamand Zavala. *La política importa: Democracia y desarrollo en América Latina.* Washington, D.C.: Banco Interamericano de Desarrollo, 2003.

Index

About the Contributors

Juan ABAL MEDINA serves as subsecretary for coordination in the municipal government of Buenos Aires. He is a researcher at CONICET (the Argentine National Council on Scientific and Technical Research).

Eric Stener CARLSON is an official with the International Labour Organization office in Buenos Aires with an interest in human rights.

Isidoro CHERESKY is a professor of political science and sociology at the University of Buenos Aires, where he is a researcher with the Gino Germani Institute and at CONICET.

Damián CORRAL is a doctoral student in social sciences at the University of San Martín, where he holds a CONICET fellowship.

Rut DIAMINT is a professor of international politics and a researcher on civil-military relations at the Torcuato di Tella University as well as at CONICET; she is an advisor at the Argentine Ministry of Defense.

Edward EPSTEIN is a professor of political science at the University of Utah, where he researches social movements and organized labor in Argentina.

Inés GONZÁLEZ BOMBAL is a professor of sociology at the University of San Martín and a researcher at both the Center for Studies on the State and Society (CEDES) and at CONICET.

Mariana LUZZI is a doctoral student in sociology at the School for Advanced Studies in the Social Sciences at the University of Paris with a CONICET fellowship; she is on leave from teaching at the University of San Martín.

José NUN serves as secretary of culture in the Argentine national government; he is on leave as a researcher in political science at CONICET and as director of the Institute of Advanced Social Sciences (IDAES) of the University of San Martín.

David PION-BERLIN is a professor of political science at the University of California, Riverside, where he researches civil-military relations in Argentina.

Roberto RUSSELL is director of academic affairs at the Institute for Foreign Service of the Argentine national government and professor and director of the master's program in international relations at the Torcuato di Tella University.

Marcelo SAIN is interventor of the national Airport Security Police and is on leave as director of the Argentine government's Unit on Financial Information on money laundering; he is professor and researcher in sociology at the University of Quilmes.

Jorge SCHVARZER is director of the Research Center on the Argentine Situation and Perspectives (CESPA) at the University of Buenos Aires, where he is a professor of economics.

Maristella SVAMPA is a professor and researcher in political sociology at Sarmiento University and at CONICET; she is a visiting researcher at the Institute for Research on Development (IRD) of the University of Paris.

Juan Gabriel TOKATLIAN is director of political science and international relations at the University of San Andrés.